JANSENISM

EARLY MODERN CATHOLIC SOURCES

Volume 10

JANSENISM

AN INTERNATIONAL ANTHOLOGY

Edited by
Shaun Blanchard and Richard T. Yoder

THE CATHOLIC UNIVERSITY
OF AMERICA PRESS
Washington, D.C.

The paper used in this publication meets the minimum
requirements of American National Standards
for Information Science—Permanence of Paper for
Printed Library Materials, ANSI Z39.48-1992.

∞

Cataloging-in-Publication Data is available
from the Library of Congress

ISBN: 978-0-8132-3856-2
Paperback ISBN: 978-0-8132-3836-4
eISBN: 978-0-8132-3837-1

TABLE OF CONTENTS

ACKNOWLEDGMENTS

In a sense, all books are team efforts, but this is especially the case in a collection like ours. We would both like to thank all of the translators who contributed to this volume, men and women from five countries who did translation work in seven languages: Guido Stucco, Elissa Cutter, Philip Porter, Elizabeth Huddleston, Daniel Watkins, Jean-Pascal Gay, John Meinert, Luke Togni, Maxwell Pingeon, Marie Giraud, Keanu Heydari, Timothy Troutner, Andrea Smidt, Bradley Blankemeyer, Andreas Oberdorf, Kevin Blankinship, Mark Spinnenweber, and Glauco Schettini.

It has been a joy to work with such a talented and friendly team of colleagues over the last few years. John Martino has, as always, been a fantastic person to work with. We are grateful to many others at The Catholic University of America Press, especially Trevor Crowell, Brian Roach, the anonymous reviewers, and the copyeditors. We would also like to thank the series editors for their support of the project.

Richard Yoder's Acknowledgments

Undertaking this volume was something of a passion project, but it was not without its risks. When Shaun and I began, I was early in my doctoral program and looking to fill a summer when I would be away from the archives due to the Pandemic. As of the date of writing, I am in the process of finishing a dissertation on the history of the Jansenist *convulsionnaires*. Ultimately, I found that the two projects strengthened each other. Both this edited collection and my larger research have benefited from the financial support of the Cushwa Center for the Study of American Catholicism, the American Catholic Historical Association, the American Historical Association, and Penn State University's

College of the Liberal Arts, Department of History, and Consortium for Early Modern and Medieval Studies (CEMMS). I would like to thank all of them for their support. And I am grateful for so many scholars who have generously shared their time and expertise with me over the course of these concurrent projects: Nicolas Lyon-Caen, Valérie Guittienne-Mürger, Fabien Vandermarcq, Mita Choudhury, Eva Yampolsky, Rafael Mandressi, Serge Maury, Ralph Keen, Olivier Andurand, and colleagues at EMoDiR, ACHA, and the Sorores Project.

I would like to thank my academic mentors at Penn State, especially my supervisor, Ronnie Po-chia Hsia, and my other committee members: Amanda Scott, Greg Eghigian, Tracy Rutler, Marcy North, and C. Libby. I could not have gotten to the point of undertaking this endeavor without a number of other key mentors and allies along the way, especially Sarah Apetrei, Fr. Robin Ward, Mark Philpott, Kevin Hart, and Vigen Guroian. I am grateful as well to the many friends and colleagues who have encouraged me, and in some cases even helped contribute to this work—notably Kelly Kaelin, Frank Lacopo, Dom Benedict Andersen, Joshua Caminiti, Richard Mammana, and Fr. Carlos de la Torre. There are many more I could name, whether at Penn State, St. Stephen's House, the University of Oxford, or the University of Virginia. More broadly, I am grateful for the encouragement of many friends online, too numerous to name here, whose interest in and conversations about Jansenism helped spur us on in preparing this collection. I must however give special thanks to Alexandra Anokhina, the friend who, in our very first conversation so many years ago, challenged me to think empathetically about the Jansenists.

I am grateful to my coeditor, Shaun Blanchard, whose friendship, erudition, wit, wisdom, and hospitality made the preparation of this volume as much a pleasure as a duty; to Dr. Pat McCoy, Mrs. Suzanne Ragains, and Mrs. Jo-Ann McCauley, my first French teachers, who, I hope, would approve of my translations here; to Tara, Laura, Gatsby, Ramsey, Dudley, Poppy, and Finn, who watched me translate and edit late into the wee hours of the night during the early months of the Pandemic; and to my parents, Karen and Bob Yoder, whose unfailing love and support over the years taught me that I can do anything with a little faith and hard work. I dedicate this, my first book, to them.

Shaun Blanchard's Acknowledgments

My mind was first captivated by the story of Jansenism during my master's study at Oxford in 2009–10. I was based at Blackfriars Hall, where I routinely plied the infinitely patient (and knowledgeable) Fr. Richard Conrad OP with £6 bottles of St. John's port to answer as many of my theological and historical questions as possible. He introduced me to Baius, Molina, *de Auxiliis*, and the Jesuit-Jansenist conflict. I bought Leszek Kolakowski's *God Owes Us Nothing* at a used bookstore outside Christ Church and devoured it. Soon after, I discovered for myself the brilliance of Pascal and the women of Port-Royal.

During doctoral studies at Marquette—fittingly, a Jesuit university—my understanding of the richness and diversity of early modern Catholicism grew. Rather than meeting my growing interest in Italian Jansenism and the Synod of Pistoia with raised eyebrows, my *Doktorväter* Ulrich Lehner and Fr. Joseph Mueller, SJ, enthusiastically encouraged me to pursue these topics, which are far less known and less studied in the English-speaking world than are the classic French sources. Under the guidance of Lehner, I explored the turbulent early modern Catholic world in the second half of the eighteenth century. Through the generosity of the Smith Family Fellowship, I was able to examine original sources related to late Jansenism in many archives. I am especially grateful to the archivists at the Archivio Apostolico Vaticano and the Archivio del Dicasterio per la Dottrina della Fede in Rome, and the Archivio di Stato in Florence.

I also owe Dr. Lehner a debt of gratitude for introducing me to Rick Yoder some years ago. Rick and I hatched this ambitious plan for a Jansenism anthology somewhat spontaneously. We both shared a sense of frustration that the term "Jansenist" endures in discourse (especially intra-Catholic polemics) as a lazy slur, undergirded by mythology and usually unburdened by serious engagement, empathy, or consideration of original sources. We also knew from conversations with colleagues that there was a real need, both for research and for teaching, to have more ready access to selections of early modern texts in English. Rick's passion for the French sources and his great facility with that language combined with my knowledge of the "internationalization" of

Jansenism after 1750 made us ideal partners. I am so grateful to Rick for his vision, his tireless and painstaking research and translation work, and his kindness and friendship. The quality of his output is that of a seasoned expert in the field.

I would also like to thank the many colleagues and friends, in addition to many members of our translation team, with whom I have had productive exchanges about Jansenism: Rebecca Messbarger, Thomas O'Connor, Aris Della Fontana, Simon Icard, Christoph and Silvia Schmitt-Maass, Mona Garloff, Eva Batten, Jürgen Overhoff, Juliette Guilbaud, Paul Frost, Thomas Wallnig, Franz Fillafer, John McGreevy, Brad Gregory, Evergton Sales Souza, Sarah Blanchard, Bob Siegfried, and Bruv. I have had lengthy, helpful exchanges with Jeffrey Burson, and with two scholars who have recently passed away: Christopher Johns and Dale Van Kley. I am deeply grateful to Dale for the great amount of time he invested in me as an early career scholar.

I must also thank my long-suffering wife, Ann-Marie Blanchard, who has had to deal with a tremendous amount of chatter about obscure and long-dead Catholic rebels. I repaid her patience once with a holiday to Scipione de' Ricci's villa south of Florence, and I hereby promise her a second.

My own share of this work I dedicate to my parents, Dawn and John Blanchard, who taught me that being an *ami de la vérité* was the only needful thing.

JANSENISM

An Introduction to Jansenism

Shaun Blanchard and Richard T. Yoder

About ten miles southwest of Louis XIV's glittering palace at Versailles is a quiet ruin. A nineteenth-century chapel stands guard over the stones that once served as the foundation of a much grander medieval monastery. This was the cloister of Port-Royal des Champs, the Jerusalem of Jansenism. It was here that a community of nuns, hermits, students, and servants labored together for their salvation under the periodic blasts of the Sun King's persecution. Later Jansenists made pilgrimages to Port-Royal to restore their faith as a "righteous remnant," renewing the memory of the men and women who lived and died there.[1] Port-Royal's story, however, is not merely confined to Louis XIV's France. It is the symbolic heart of an international Catholicism deferred, a vision of the faith that offered an alternative to the ultramontanism that would triumph after the Age of Revolutions.[2]

The Jansenists are among the losers of church history. Officially condemned as heretics in multiple papal bulls, they are, with the exception of Blaise Pascal, mostly unread today. Their theological quarrels with the Jesuits usually seem trivial to the modern observer.

1. Catherine Maire, "Port-Royal: The Jansenist Schism," 301–52.

2. The term "ultramontane" as an ideological descriptor was well established in the eighteenth century. See Heribert Raab, "Zur Geschichte und Bedeutung des Schlagwortes 'Ultramontan.'"

Their persistence seems like arrogant obstinacy. Their Gallican ecclesiology has, at least officially, been a dead option within Catholicism since the First Vatican Council (1870).[3] While French historians have long recognized their significance, their place in Catholic memory is murkier.[4] When remembered at all, the Jansenists are depicted as the gloomiest of moralists, the most sanctimonious predestinarians, and the most perfidious of revolutionaries. Few moments in the history of the Catholic Church are more widely misrepresented; few defunct ecclesiastical factions are more promiscuously blamed for the ills of today.[5] They are the somber villains of the seventeenth and eighteenth centuries—eternally unsmiling nuns, more Calvinist than Catholic, who hate the Sacred Heart of Jesus for loving all mankind. Recently, Pope Francis himself attacked Port-Royal in a Christmas address to the Roman Curia.[6] Most of these visions are unfair caricatures detached from the primary sources. However, many of those primary sources have remained untranslated and, until recently, undigitized.

This anthology makes the Jansenist archive more accessible to Anglophone lay and scholarly readers. Other, similar works have focused exclusively either on French sources, on a narrower time span, or on specific authors.[7] In selecting and arranging the documents in

3. John O'Malley, *Vatican I*.

4. The scholarly literature on Jansenism is enormous. For a few recent overviews, see Dale Van Kley, *Religious Origins of the French Revolution*; Catherine Maire, *De la cause de Dieu*; Monique Cottret, *Jansénismes et lumières*; William Doyle, *Jansenism*; John J. Conley, *Adoration and Annihilation*; Nicolas Lyon-Caen, *La boîte à Perette*; Daniella Kostroun, *Feminism, Absolutism, and Jansenism*; Philippe Luez, *Port-Royal et le Jansénisme*; Cottret, *Histoire du Jansénisme*; Van Kley, *Reform Catholicism*; Olivier Andurand, *La grande affaire*.

5. For example, see two recent and opposing opinion pieces in the popular Catholic press, each accusing the other side of Jansenism—Michael Sean Winters, "The Four Cardinals and Their Five Doubts"; Jessica M. Murdoch, "The New Jansenism."

6. Christopher Lamb, "Church for the 'Pure' Is Heresy."

7. See the anthologies *Les Jansénistes*, ed. Nicolas Lyon-Caen, which has a temporal range comparable to ours but an exclusively French focus, and the chronologically tighter *Port-Royal*, ed. Laurence Plazenet; or the specialized editions of the women of Port-Royal, edited and translated by John J. Conley. See Jacqueline Pascal, *A Rule for Children*, and Angélique de Saint-Jean Arnauld d'Andilly, *Writings of Resistance*. Some other French-language studies that, due to their copious presentation of primary sources,

this anthology, we have instead attempted to cover the full range of the international Jansenist controversies across nearly two hundred years. Given how vast the archival deposit on Jansenism is, we knew that we would inevitably have to exclude some topics and voices that we might otherwise wish to include. However, we have chosen texts from both men and women, from many social classes, in a variety of genres, from both print and manuscript sources, in seven different languages, originating in eight different countries. We have tried, for the most part, to select works that have not been translated before, as well as texts that are particularly important or representative of Jansenist history. The result, we hope, is a broad picture of a complicated and pivotal segment of the history of global Catholicism.

Overall, we have followed a roughly chronological organization of these texts, broken into three broad sections: the first on the struggles of Port-Royal (c. 1630–79), the second on the controversies around *Unigenitus* (c. 1679–1760), and the last on the international, reformist Jansenism epitomized by the Synod of Pistoia (c. 1760–1810). Each selection includes a text-specific introduction, which we hope will help orient the reader. In making many of these choices, we were also confronted by the inevitable, perennial issue of terminology. In the first decades of controversy, when the embattled monastery of Port-Royal and its defenders had to justify their position, they denied any identity as "Jansenists." This was, to use Pierre Nicole's phrase, a "phantom heresy," a pejorative invented by the Jesuits to smear their critics as sectarians or pseudo-Calvinists. They were merely good Catholics, faithful "Disciples of Saint Augustine." Even some who had little direct interest in the disputes agreed. Cardinal Giovanni Bona (1609–74) went so far as to say that "Jansenists are Catholics who don't like the Jesuits."[8]

But there was some coherence to the ideas of those called "Jansenists," and it was not just a matter of anti-Jesuit sentiment.

---

function rather like anthologies include the foundational study by Charles-Augustin Sainte-Beuve, *Port-Royal*, as well as René Taveneaux, *Jansénisme et politique*, and Catherine-Laurence Maire, *Les Convulsionnaires de Saint-Médard*. The editions of Blaise Pascal's religious writings in English translation are innumerable.

8. Bona, quoted in Owen Chadwick, *The Popes and European Revolution*, 393.

Jansenism began as a tendency and ended as a tradition. That tendency was defined by several dispositions and commitments:

- An insistence on the efficacious and invincible operation of grace in the soul
- An assertion that love was the Christian life's absolute *sine qua non*
- Pessimism about the capacities of human nature, unaided by God's grace
- Sacramental and moral "rigorism," that is, strictness and severity
- A Christocentric emphasis on the particularity of God's revelation and election
- Skepticism about the scholastic method
- A Gallican or "conciliarist" ecclesiology that emphasized the leadership of bishops and ecumenical councils rather than the papacy
- Reverence for the Church Fathers in general and St. Augustine in particular
- A primitivist reformism that took austere Christian antiquity as its polestar
- A spiritual ideal based on monastic *mépris du monde* (contempt for the "world")
- A mounting insistence on the sacred rights of conscience alongside a growing suspicion of royal despotism (at least in France)
- A scriptural and liturgical piety averse to Baroque devotions, if not to miraculous relics; this piety included advocacy for personal reading of Scripture in the vernacular and, at times, a more participatory liturgy
- An unyielding mutual antipathy toward the Jesuits, matched by a reverence for the memory of Port-Royal

Such was the collection of attitudes that define "Jansenists" during most of the seventeenth and eighteenth centuries. Not all of these were unique to the Jansenists. However, it was the constellation of many or all these traits that made up "Jansenism" as an identifiable phenomenon in the intellectual, political, and religious life of early modern Europe. And Jansenism did change over time. Some of the foregoing features were more strongly pronounced in different authors, periods, or groups of Jansenists. Monique Cottret has pluralized Jansenism to "Jansenisms," a particularly useful intervention in helping historians approach the reception and reinvention of "Port-Royalist" ideas in the eighteenth century—including well beyond the French borders.[9] We agree with Cottret that there were "Jansenisms" rather than any one, discreet school of thought known as "Jansenism." Our selections reflect this diversity of Jansenist thought. However, for the sake of stylistic ease, we follow the typical scholarly convention of referring to "Jansenism" in the singular.

Ultimately, it is perhaps best to understand Jansenism as an alternative stream of Tridentine Reform. F. Ellen Weaver went so far as to call it "a Reformation that failed," since the controversies were, at base, a struggle over what constituted proper Catholic Reform. Along similar lines, R. Po-chia Hsia has pointed to Jansenism as a major "theological rift in Tridentine Catholicism."[10] The Council of Trent left certain questions unresolved: the nature of grace's operation in the soul, predestination, and the precise relationship of free will to both of these divine acts.[11] The Jansenists attempted to steer the Church back to what they regarded as her patristic roots on these questions, by which they meant St. Augustine and his major interpreters. Connected with this doctrinal issue was a set of questions about how best to reform both the Church and the individual believer. The saintly Archbishop of Milan, Carlo Borromeo (1538–84) was the episcopal ideal for these rigorists; and, all the way up to the French Revolution, they looked to hermits as models of lay piety.[12] But this otherworldly vision of the Christian life led the Jansenists to clash with the "Royal Religion" of France, centered

9. Cottret, *Jansénismes et lumières.*

10. F. Ellen Weaver, *The Inner History of a Reformation That Failed*; R. Po-chia Hsia, *The World of Catholic Renewal, 1540–1770*, 230. See also Domenico Masselli, introduction to Gelli, *Memorie di Scipione de' Ricci*, 11–14. Masselli makes this point about eighteenth-century Jansenism in its Italian, reformist key, but his point applies to the broader controversies as well.

11. Jean Delumeau, *Catholicism between Luther and Voltaire*, 100.

12. See for instance the enthusiasm of French Jansenists for the cause of Benoît-Joseph Labre: Bernard Plongeron, "Benoît-Joseph Labre au miroir de l'hagiographie janséniste." Robert Arnauld d'Andilly's translation of the selected lives of the Desert Fathers and Mothers, though not included in this volume, was nevertheless a seminal

on the sacred person of the monarch and sustained over the course of the seventeenth century as much by the "devout humanism" of Jesuit royal confessors as by the traumatic memory of the Wars of Religion.[13] The civil wars known as the Fronde did not improve the Jansenists' standing in the eyes of the monarch, for several of the most prominent Frondeurs were close to Port-Royal.[14] The amorous Sun King, already alienated from the Jansenists' moral rigorism, neither forgot nor forgave these connections.[15]

Soon after earning the ire of the most powerful King in Christendom, Jansenists also fell afoul of the papacy. What began in arguments over divine grace and penance morphed into an impasse within Catholicism regarding the essence of the Church itself and the nature and exercise of authority within it. Ultimately, Jansenism functioned as a counternarrative to "ultramontane" or papalist Catholicism, and a rebellion against it. This Jansenist counternarrative was not just condemned by popes in the seventeenth and eighteenth centuries. The First Vatican Council (1870), which defined papal infallibility, used Jansenist ecclesiology as a foil for its teaching on the jurisdictional

---

expression of this ideal. See Robert Arnauld d'Andilly, *Les Vies des saints Pères des deserts*.

13. The two classic studies of the "Royal Religion" remain Ernst Kantorowicz, *The King's Two Bodies*, and Marc Bloch, *The Royal Touch*. See also Barbara Diefendorf, *Beneath the Cross*, and Van Kley, *Religious Origins*, 16–58. On "devout humanism," see Henri Bremond, *Histoire littéraire du sentiment religieux en France*, vol. 1, and Van Kley, *Religious Origins*, 52–53.

14. The Fronde was a series of wars during the minority of Louis XIV fought by the royal government of Cardinal Mazarin and Anne of Austria, first against the *parlements*, and then against many of the most senior Princes of the Blood. Of the many Frondeur noblemen who were friendly with Port-Royal, none became as closely associated with its cause as Anne-Geneviève de Bourbon, Duchesse de Longueville (1619–79), who was one of the most prominent Frondeuse "Amazons." It was only after the death of this protector in 1679 that Louis XIV felt he could move against Port-Royal again. See Orest Ranum, *The Fronde*; Richard M. Golden, *The Godly Rebellion*; Howard G. Brown, *Mass Violence and the Self*, especially chapter 2; Kostroun, *Feminism*, 78–103, 196; David Parrot, *1652*, 209–10.

15. Daniella Kostroun has traced the impact of the Fronde on the broader Jansenist controversy, which was well underway by then. See Kostroun, *Feminism*, especially chapter 3.

supremacy of the pope. Even as late as the Second Vatican Council (1962–65), the memory of Jansenism was an antithesis against which to define orthodox Catholicism. That memory—though almost totally obscured by myth and polemic—endures today in parts of the Catholic world, where "Jansenist" is a slur for the morose nun, the scrupulous parishioner, or the priest who preaches hellfire and brimstone. This anthology allows English-language readers to get behind the pervasive myth of Jansenism. In examining the perspective of the "losers" in this story, we will not only better understand the past, we will also better understand the complex crucible from which modern, global Catholicism emerged.

Section One: The Disciples of Saint Augustine, c. 1630–1679

This anthology's first section focuses on the dramatic story of Port-Royal and includes some of the texts that would come to define Jansenist thought and identity. In its background is the "*De Auxiliis* controversy," a dispute between Molinist Jesuits and Thomist Dominicans over the doctrines of grace, free will, and predestination. These doctrines had always been discussed and debated by Catholic theologians. In the wake of the Protestant Reformations and the Council of Trent's negative response to Lutheran and Reformed theology, they took on a new urgency. For Catholics, however, it was not simply a battle between advocates of free will and strict predestinarians. All the combatants agreed that Christians were saved by God's gratuitous and eternal election. Molinists postulated that God decided to predestine for salvation those whom He knew would respond positively to the divine offer of salvation. The Thomists—and on this point they agreed with Jansenists and even Calvinists—argued that predestination took place "before" any foreseen merits. This dispute was connected to a somewhat more complicated question, namely, how grace operates in the soul of the "elect." The Molinists emphasized human cooperation in causing grace to work "efficaciously" in the soul. The Thomists disagreed, and instead argued that God's providence included human freedom, even though God, as sanctifier and first cause, ultimately and efficaciously achieved the work of grace.[16] Both sides were trying to avoid fatalism and uphold free will, while affirming the biblical truth that God's grace was a free gift that cannot be earned. After decades of sparring, Pope Paul V attempted to resolve the tempest with a truce, and in 1607 forbade any further publications on the disputed subjects. This ban was essentially a ceasefire declared by the papacy; nobody was condemned, and no position was crowned as *the* teaching of the Catholic Church. The contentious questions were left unanswered. Rome's attempt to force a peace by shutting down debate soon proved ineffective.[17]

"Jansenism" initially emerged in the wake of *De Auxiliis* from the connection of three Catholic Reformers. The first was Cornelius Jansen (1585–1638), the namesake of the movement. Jansen was a Dutch theologian of the University of Leuven. In 1636, he was appointed Bishop of Ypres in modern-day Belgium. Jansen earnestly believed that a return to the authority of the Church Fathers would combat the errors of Protestants, particularly Calvinists. In returning to Augustine, Jansen hoped to prove that the Catholic Church preserved the saint's teaching better than the Calvinists who invoked him to justify their "innovations."[18] His most famous and controversial work, the posthumous *Augustinus* (1640) presents a strongly predestinarian interpretation of the eponymous Doctor; we present an excerpt of it here, translated by Guido Stucco (Text 1).[19] Jansen describes efficacious, invincible grace as a kind of delight. In contrast to the earthly delight that holds the fallen human will captive, grace is a *delectatio victrix*—"victorious delight"—by which God infallibly frees the soul from sin and draws it to desire and choose the good, namely, love. Jansen's theology of grace

16. R. J. Matava, "A Sketch of the Controversy *de auxiliis*."

17. One example of an Augustinian treatise published years before Jansen's text is the Oratorian Guillaume Gibieuf's *De libertate Dei et creaturae* (Paris, 1630), commissioned by Cardinal Bérulle and admired by both Jansen and Saint-Cyran. See Anthony D. Wright, *The Divisions of French Catholicism, 1629–1645*, 121. For a short introduction to the *De Auxiliis* controversy in English, see Guido Stucco, introduction to *The Predestination of Humans and Angels*, by Jansen, 1–28.

18. Ralph Keen, "The Critique of Calvin in Jansenius's *Augustinus*"; Jean Orcibal, *Jansénius d'Ypres*.

19. See also Stucco's recent translation of another portion of the *Augustinus*: Jansen, *The Predestination*.

accompanied an antischolastic epistemological project. He insists that philosophy is radically distinct from theology, and casts little if any light on divine mysteries.[20]

In this respect, Jansen shows that he was not merely writing against the Calvinists. He also had another target in mind: the Jesuits. The Bishop of Ypres certainly regarded their theory of Molinism as a Semipelagian heresy, and the Jesuits were also still largely committed to Aristotelianism and the scholastic method.[21] Jansen was embroiled in the academic politics of the University of Leuven, and opposed Jesuit instruction there. A number of other intellectuals in the Low Countries collaborated with him in his anti-Jesuit efforts.[22] However, his most important ally was a Frenchman.

Jean-Ambroise Duvergier de Hauranne, the Abbé de Saint-Cyran (1581–1643), had befriended Jansen when they were both students at Leuven.[23] It was at Saint-Cyran's insistence that Jansen read through Augustine's works; Jansen would later claim to have read the *opera omnia* ten times, and the anti-Pelagian writings thirty times. The two shared the aspirations of the Catholic Reform, but believed that the Council of Trent had not gone far enough in restoring the pristine splendor of Christian antiquity.

Like Jansen, Saint-Cyran was not a stranger to ecclesiastical controversy. In the 1630s he published works under the name of "Petrus Aurelius," defending the divine rights of bishops against the Jesuits. This pseudonymous corpus won the plaudits of the Gallican episcopate and the Sorbonne, as well as the enmity of the French Society of Jesus.[24]

20. De Lubac, *Surnaturel*, 65–66.

21. For a discussion of the clash between Jesuit scholasticism and "positive theology," a biblical and historical method strongly associated with Leuven and, later, Jansenists more generally, see William J. Bouwsma, *The Waning of the Renaissance*, 236–37.

22. For more on Jansen and his circles in the Low Countries, see *Jansénius et le jansénisme dans les Pays-Bas*, ed. M. Schrama and J. van Bavel; Charles H. Parker, *Faith on the Margins*.

23. The standard works on Saint-Cyran remain Jean Orcibal, *Saint-Cyran et le Jansénisme*, and Orcibal, *La spiritualité de Saint-Cyran*.

24. Alison Forrestal, *Fathers, Pastors, and Kings*, 90–94, 106n85, 115, 121; Forrestal points out that, while technically censuring Petrus Aurelius, the French bishops actually ended up praising his contributions at great length, and even paid to reprint

But Saint-Cyran was better known as a prominent spiritual director among the Parisian *dévots*, a loose network of pious men and women committed to the renewal of Catholic life through devotion, charity, and mysticism.[25] His letters brim with practical advice on the spiritual life; his catechism, the *Théologie familière*, presents Catholicism through a subtle but clear Augustinian lens. We present selections from both in translation by Richard T. Yoder (Text 2).

Saint-Cyran also gave incipient "Jansenism" a new characteristic. His austerely rigorist vision of the moral life led him to emphasize that absolution in confession required perfect "contrition," that is, sorrow for sin based on love of God. As a result, it could be helpful for the soul to withdraw into solitude, away from Communion for a time, so as to cultivate love of God and true contrition. This "contritionism" contrasted strongly with the Jesuit position, which held that a soul could be forgiven on the basis of mere "attrition," or sorrow for sin based on a fear of punishment in hell. Saint-Cyran valorized a simple form of wordless prayer that he called "the prayer of the poor man," a recollection of the Divine Presence and a willingness to "[expose] one's wounds and needs to God the way the poor expose their miseries before the rich rather than worrying them with importunities and long discourses."[26] This, too, set him against the Jesuits' Baroque methods of Ignatian meditation. More broadly, Saint-Cyran taught an otherworldly spirituality, focused on the renewal of the inner life by means of solitude, penance, and ascetic avoidance of the "world" through "retreat." He looked to the Desert Fathers and the Carthusian monks as exemplars of this path.[27]

---

the work in 1641, during Saint-Cyran's imprisonment; Charles Clémencet, *Histoire littéraire de Port-Royal*, 1:251, 288–97. Thomas Palmer has noted the English reception of Saint-Cyran's Gallican writings. See Palmer, *Jansenism and England*, 16, 52–54, 98.

25. Barbara Diefendorf, *From Penitence to Charity*; Elizabeth Rapley, *The Dévotes*; Wright, *The Divisions of French Catholicism*, especially chapters 3 and 4; Joseph Bergin, *The Politics of Religion in Early Modern France*, especially chapter 4; Hsia, *The World of Catholic Renewal*, 217–20.

26. F. Ellen Weaver, *The Evolution of the Reform of Port-Royal*, 174. Without using this same language, John J. Conley has demonstrated the importance of this model of prayer in the thought of Jacqueline Pascal, and thus in the convent school of Port-Royal de Paris. See Conley, *The Other Pascals*, 46, 50.

27. Ted A. Campbell reads Jansenism as one example of "the religion of the heart"

This spiritual ideal notwithstanding, for several years, Saint-Cyran lived a fairly active life in close association with the *dévot* Cardinal Pierre de Bérulle (1575–1629), founder of the French Congregation of the Oratory, who, along with François de Sales (1567–1622), was the fountainhead of the so-called "French School of Spirituality."[28] The cardinal's deeply Augustinian theological sensibility, his suspicion of *raison d'état*, and his opposition to the influence of the Jesuits were all bequeathed to his *protégé*.[29] Saint-Cyran was also close personal friends with Vincent de Paul (1581–1660), another leading light of the *dévots*.[30] And in 1634, Saint-Cyran became the spiritual director of a fashionable convent then calling itself the Institut du Saint-Sacrement. The nun leading that short-lived foundation was soon to return to her original community, Port-Royal de Paris.

The Abbess of Port-Royal was the third and perhaps most formidable figure who shaped what would be known as "Jansenism." Jacqueline-Marie-Angélique Arnauld, better known as Mère Angélique (1591–1661), was highly regarded in *dévot* circles for her reforming zeal. Having received the office of abbess as a child when her family purchased the title, she eventually underwent a conversion, embraced her vocation, and dedicated herself to restoring Port-Royal to its original Cistercian rigor. She restored strict enclosure, forbade nuns to go to balls and masquerades, waived dowry requirements for poorer novices, reestablished the choral divine office, did away with private property,

---

that came to define affective Christianity across confessions in the early modern period; see Campbell, *The Religion of the Heart*, 27–29.

28. This term, coined by Henri Bremond, has had a long life, and not entirely without controversy. See Bremond, *Histoire littéraire du Sentiment religieux*, vol. 2; Yves Krumenacker, "Henri Bremond et l'École française de spiritualité," 115–38; Bernard McGinn, *The Persistence of Mysticism in Catholic Europe*, chapters 1–5.

29. Michael Moriarty, *Disguised Vices*, 170–71. Gazier is probably correct in conjecturing that, had Bérulle lived longer, he too would have been "encompassed with his friends Saint-Cyran and Jansenius in the affairs of Jansenism." See Augustin Gazier, *Histoire générale du mouvement janséniste*, 1:28. F. Ellen Weaver also notes that Bérulle's theology "could truly be called Theocentric since the divinity of Christ was stressed almost to loss of recognition of his humanity," a tendency sometimes glimpsed among the Jansenists. See Weaver, *The Evolution*, 95.

30. Alison Forrestal, *Vincent de Paul, the Lazarist Mission, and French Catholic Reform*, 246–66.

and instituted an austere aesthetic in ecclesiastical furnishings that took monastic poverty as its rule.[31] She also moved the nuns to Paris from their medieval motherhouse in the country, Port-Royal des Champs. In this urban setting, the nuns took in young female lodgers whom they educated in a convent school. In the 1630s, she attempted to found a new order in Paris, the Institut du Saint-Sacrement, but this experiment ultimately failed. However, it led her to establish perpetual adoration of the Blessed Sacrament at Port-Royal as one of the convent's major devotions.[32] Throughout these decades, Angélique's reputation grew. She met François de Sales, who for a time was her spiritual director.[33] Jeanne-Françoise de Chantal (1572–1641) became a close friend and confidante for the rock-ribbed Abbess. The public sermons of their chaplain, a disciple of Saint-Cyran named Antoine Singlin (1607–64), drew "a cultured public to Port-Royal."[34] Many other reform-minded Catholics wrote to her to seek her advice, especially on monastic reform. We present here one such letter, translated and introduced by Elissa Cutter, in which Mère Angélique advises a priest intent on reforming a convent (Text 3).

But she was not alone in this venture. Her family was, on the whole, committed to Angélique's program, and perhaps none more so than her sister, Jeanne-Catherine-Agnès Arnauld, known as Mère Agnès (1593–1672). In her *L'Esprit du Monastère de Port-Royal* (published in 1665, but composed earlier), Agnès outlines the communal ideals of the convent (Text 4). In this text, translated by Philip Porter, she emphasizes how grace initiates and sustains a monastic vocation. Prayer is absolutely essential, as is constant mortification of human pride—but not with a spirit of singularity, apart from the common life. She recommends the Divine Office and devotion to the Scriptures, a devotional sensibility shared by many Jansenists. There can be no doubt that these

31. Diefendorf, *From Penitence*, 55–56, 168; Conley, *Adoration*, 44–49; Weaver, *The Evolution.*

32. Elissa Cutter, "Monastic Reform in Seventeenth-Century France," 425–51; Kostroun, *Feminism*, especially chapters 1–2; Conley, *Adoration*, 43–112.

33. Louis Cognet, *La Mère Angélique et Saint François de Sales, 1618–1626.*

34. Conley, *Adoration*, 47–48, 121; Augustin Gazier, *Jeanne de Chantal et Angélique Arnauld.*

ideals express the very soul of Mère Angélique's reform, which Agnès sustained and extended over multiple terms serving as Abbess herself. In the *Esprit* and her other writings, Agnès attempted to show that Port-Royal was a model of Tridentine religious life.[35]

In summary, Jansen stood for a return to strict Augustinian doctrine. Saint-Cyran wanted to restore the rigors of ancient discipline in the sacramental and moral life. And Mère Angélique sought a return to the monastic purity of the Desert, St. Benedict, and St. Bernard of Clairvaux (though she was also a great admirer of Teresa of Avila, another female reformer). These projects were mutually supportive.

In 1637, their collaboration bore another fruit. Angélique's nephew, Antoine Le Maistre (1608–58), was one of the most promising young lawyers in Paris when he underwent a profound conversion. His aunt directed him to Saint-Cyran, who advised the young man to give up his place in the world and retire to a penitential life of prayer and solitude. Le Maistre settled on the swampy grounds of the nuns' mother-house, Port-Royal des Champs. Soon others followed. The men who moved to the abbey in the country became known as the *solitaires*, or "hermits," of Port-Royal.[36] Many of them left a place among the French elite to devote themselves to manual labor, teaching the boys at the "Petites Écoles de Port-Royal," or translating edifying texts.[37] Le Maistre's brother, the priest Louis-Isaac Le Maistre de Sacy (1613–84), led the *solitaires*' efforts to translate the entire Bible into French, which became the scripture of choice for subsequent generations of French Jansenists and their many sympathizers.[38] The brilliant younger brother of the Arnauld abbesses, Antoine Arnauld (1612–94), continued his copious theological and philosophical writings, and the moralist Pierre Nicole (1625–95) taught Greek. Together, they produced the *Logique, ou Art de Penser* (1662),

35. Conley, *Adoration*, 15, 113–27, 146–53; see also the various essays in a journal edition dedicated to Mère Agnès, *La Mère Agnès Arnauld (1593–1672)*, *Chroniques de Port-Royal* 43 (1994).

36. See the list of eighty-nine names compiled by Frédéric Delforge and Antony McKenna, "Appendice IV: Les solitaires de Port-Royal," in *Dictionnaire de Port-Royal*, ed. Lesaulnier and McKenna, 1057.

37. Alexander Sedgwick, *The Travails of Conscience*, 82–88.

38. For a wider discussion of Port-Royal's biblical translation efforts, see Els Agten, *The Catholic Church and the Dutch Bible*, 146–67.

better known as the *Logique de Port-Royal*, which quickly "supplanted Aristotle's *Organum* for the first time as the standard textbook of philosophical reasoning in European universities."[39] Robert Arnauld d'Andilly (1589–1674), a celebrated courtier and the eldest of the Arnauld siblings, spent much of his considerable fortune in improving the monastery's property, planting fruit trees, and translating the Fathers—notably, the *Confessions* of Saint Augustine.[40]

Of the many men who lived at Port-Royal des Champs for the four decades when there was an active community there, one stands out as perhaps the only great mystic. A physician named Jean Hamon (1618–87) joined the *solitaires* in 1650. He continued to practice medicine both at Port-Royal and in the surrounding villages. In the late 1660s, when the nuns of Port-Royal were imprisoned in their own monastery and forbidden access to friendly clergy, Hamon became a surrogate spiritual father to the community. He wrote at length on the spirituality of solitude, and composed several treatises on prayer, including the Desert Fathers' ideal of perpetual prayer. His prayers, such as those found in the *Entretiens d'une âme avec Dieu*, feature invocations of the "Holy Defenders of the Grace of Jesus Christ." These intercessions, translated by Yoder, served as models for the embattled Jansenist community (Text 7).[41]

That trouble began when, on 14 May, 1638, Cardinal Richelieu ordered the arrest of the Abbé de Saint-Cyran. Though he held Saint-Cyran in the Château de Vincennes for four years without charge or trial, historians have generally identified a few underlying motives for the Cardinal's actions. Richelieu knew that competent young men like Antoine Le Maistre were leaving careers of state service for a penitential life under Saint-Cyran's guidance. And while Richelieu was no great

39. Ethan Shagan, *The Birth of Modern Belief*, 212–18.

40. Conley, *Adoration*, 23; Saint-Beuve, *Port-Royal*, 2:291; Henri-Jean Martin notes the overwhelming influence of Augustine and Seneca on the literate French of the seventeenth century, a dual influence one can also observe in Jansenism. See Martin, *The French Book*, 58, 84.

41. Lilian Rea, *The Enthusiasts of Port-Royal*, 163–64, 264–65; Roberto Calasso, *The Ruins of Kasch*, 109–10; Mette Birkedal Bruun, "Prayer, Meditation, and Retreat," 667–87, here 669.

theologian, the one area on which he had expressed himself was the doctrine of confession. He was firmly within the "attritionist" camp. This was not a mere disagreement on principles; it had a bearing on foreign policy. As a counterweight to Habsburg Spain and the Holy Roman Empire, France had allied with the Protestant powers in the Thirty Years' War, much to the horrified disapproval of the *dévots*. A Jesuit confessor had already pressed King Louis XIII on this point. Richelieu was aware of Jansen's own scathing attack on French policy in his *Mars Gallicus* (1635), and he knew that Saint-Cyran was friendly with the professor.[42] The turning point came when an Oratorian priest set forth Saint-Cyran's contritionist position in a 1637 treatise. Louis XIII again felt the pangs of conscience; the *dévots* clamored for an end to the Protestant alliance. Richelieu thus imprisoned the foremost contritionist, a thorn in his side. For the rest of the cardinal's life, he kept Saint-Cyran behind bars.[43]

By the time that Saint-Cyran left prison, much had changed. Jansen had died of the plague in 1638, with the *Augustinus* coming out posthumously to immediate controversy. Saint-Cyran himself was a greatly weakened if not broken man. Thus, when the Jesuit Pierre de Sesmaisons attacked Saint-Cyran's view of the sacraments, the Abbé asked a much younger theologian to respond. He chose wisely. Antoine Arnauld was the *wunderkind* of the Arnauld family, a doctor of the Sorbonne as well as a *solitaire* of Port-Royal. He would go on to become the most prolific and influential Jansenist theologian of the seventeenth century. But first, he threw himself into the defense of Saint-Cyran. The result was the massive *De la fréquente communion* (1643), excerpted and translated here by Yoder (Text 5).

Arnauld levies patristic and Tridentine authorities against his Jesuit opponent, taking pains to point out the antiquity of the rigorous disciplines he sought to vindicate. These include a limited withdrawal from receiving Communion in order to cultivate true contrition, the

42. Philip IV (King of Spain from 1621 to 1665) named Jansen the Bishop of Ypres in part to thank him for attacking French policy in *Mars Gallicus*. See Émile Appolis, *Les jansénistes espagnols*, 10.

43. Jean-Vincent Blanchard, *Éminence*, chapter 8; Van Kley, *Religious Origins*, 66; Moriarty, *Disguised Vices*, 170–72; Lucien Goldmann, *The Hidden God*, chapter 6.

deferment of absolution until the completion of penance, the use of public penance for obstinate public sinners, and a period of preparation for Communion which would efface any attachment to venial sin. These disciplines, Arnauld argues, are essential to preserve the purity of the sacrament and the health of the soul. The book received wide acclaim among the French episcopate, though it was not without controversy. Beyond the opposition of the Jesuits, it also earned the ire of Vincent de Paul, who had once counted Saint-Cyran as a close friend.[44] In some sense, *De la fréquente communion* inaugurated a definite fissure within the community of French *dévots*, hitherto largely united in the face of Protestants, cultured skeptics, and prelates of state like Cardinal Richelieu. The doctrinal division introduced by the *Augustinus* in 1640 was aggravated by irreconcilable differences over sacramental discipline, epitomized in Arnauld's tome.

Yet the tensions might not have been permanent had Rome not intervened as it did. This was not a quick reaction, though the *Augustinus* received an original papal censure in 1642 for violating the "truce" imposed after the *De Auxiliis* controversy.[45] In 1649, the Sorbonne condemned seven propositions ostensibly extracted from the *Augustinus*, and forwarded them to Rome in the hope of winning a universal condemnation. In 1653, Pope Innocent X issued the bull *Cum Occasione*, which condemned as heretical five of the seven propositions allegedly taken from the *Augustinus*. These propositions are:

1. Some of God's commandments cannot be observed by just men with the strength they have in the present state, even if they wish and strive to observe them; nor do they have the grace that would make their observance possible.
2. In the state of fallen nature interior grace is never resisted.
3. In order to merit or demerit in a state of fallen nature, it is not necessary for man to have freedom from necessity, but freedom from coercion suffices.
4. The Semipelagians admitted the necessity of prevenient interior grace for every act, even for the beginning of faith; and their heresy

44. Forrestal, *Vincent de Paul*, 246–66.

45. Eric DeMeuse, "The World Is Content with Words," 259n50.

consisted in this, that they held this grace to be such that the human will could either resist it or submit to it.

5. It is Semipelagian to say that Christ died or shed his blood for all men without exception.[46]

However, the pithy bull did not cite specific passages in Jansen's text, leading some to question whether the statements accurately reflected his theology—or were even taken from the text.[47] Pope Alexander VII later went on to declare, in the 1656 bull *Ad sanctam*, that the propositions were found in the *Augustinus* and condemned precisely in the sense that Jansen meant them—though once again, without citations.[48]

Many claimed that the propositions could be understood in both a heretical (Calvinist) sense and an orthodox (Augustinian) sense. According to these writers, Jansen's intent was only to follow Augustine. Antoine Arnauld argued that, in receiving such papal judgments, one must distinguish between fact (*fait*) and right (*droit*). According to this logic, the pope possessed the power to bind the faithful on matters of right—that is, faith and morals—and in this respect, the Church as a whole possessed the gift of infallibility. However, neither the pope nor anyone in the Church was infallible in matters of fact, nor did they have the right to bind the faithful in such matters. The most that they could demand in these empirical questions was a "respectful silence" on the dispute. Arnauld and those Jansenists who accepted this *fait/droit* distinction could argue that they fully acquiesced to the condemnation of the Five Propositions. However, they did not cede the point that these propositions were found in Jansen, nor that Jansen propagated heresy. Arnauld defended these principles in his *Seconde lettre à un duc et pair* (1656), written after the Duc de Liancourt was denied Communion for

46. See Heinrich Denzinger, ed., *Compendium of Creeds, Definitions, and Declarations on Matters of Faith and Morals*, as revised by Peter Hünermann (hereafter cited as Denzinger-Hünermann), 2001–7.

47. For example, in a 1654 treatise, Arnauld and Nicole asserted that only the first could be found in Jansen's work, and even then, it was modified and ripped from context. The others, they alleged, were fabrications easily contradicted by the plain meaning of Jansen's text. See Antoine Arnauld and Pierre Nicole, *Réponse au P. Annat, Provincial des Jésuites.*

48. Conley, *Adoration*, 11. See Denzinger-Hünermann 2010–12.

his allegedly "Jansenist" ideas. In the *Seconde lettre*, Arnauld makes two controversial claims. First, he argues that *Cum Occasione* had erred in the matter of *fait* by condemning propositions not contained in the *Augustinus*, and second, that at the moment of his denial of Christ, St. Peter could not have acted obediently, since he lacked the grace to do so.[49] The Sorbonne reacted harshly to these arguments. In 1656, Arnauld's colleagues revoked his doctorate, expelling him from the faculty of theology.[50]

This calamitous turn of events provoked another Jansenist to take up his pen. The mathematician and scientist Blaise Pascal (1623–62) had moved in Port-Royalist circles since 1646, when he made the acquaintance of two disciples of Saint-Cyran.[51] In 1652, his sister Jacqueline entered Port-Royal de Paris.[52] Yet it was not until 23 November, 1654, that Pascal experienced a definitive conversion, which he memorialized in a short, poetic fragment that he would carry on his person for the rest of his life (Text 6).[53] His encounter with the "God of Abraham, God of Isaac, God of Jacob" brought him ever closer to Port-Royal and its scriptural, otherworldly spirituality. And in 1656, he began anonymously publishing a series of letters defending Arnauld, Port-Royal, and the Jansenist doctrine of grace. These *Lettres Provinciales* (1656–57), however, are better known for their scathing attacks on the Jesuits, and especially Jesuit casuistry.[54] With biting humor and copious citations,

49. This soteriological point had barely concealed ecclesiological implications, as when Arnauld writes of St. Peter, "that all men must see in the fall of the Church's chief [*chef de l'Église*], deprived of the helps of grace, that they can do nothing without grace." He then proceeds to argue that the papal condemnations of Jansen's doctrine contradicted the clear teaching of earlier popes. See Antoine Arnauld, *Seconde lettre de M. Arnauld . . . à un Duc et Pair de France*, 218–26, here 220.

50. Conley, *Adoration*, 11–12.

51. There is a mountainous literature on Pascal. Recent publications of note include Michael Moriarty, *Pascal: Reasoning and Belief*, as well as Paul Griffiths, *Why Read Pascal?*

52. John J. Conley, "Jacqueline Pascal (1625–1661)," *Internet Encyclopedia of Philosophy*.

53. The popularity and relative accessibility of Pascal in English have led us to allocate him less space in this anthology than might be expected.

54. Casuistry was a form of reasoning used by moral theologians to determine the ethical value of an act, frequently in the form of confessors' manuals, and often

Pascal effectively, if often unfairly, decries the Jesuits as inveterate laxists in the confessional and self-interested subversives within the Church at large.[55] Published to wide acclaim, the *Lettres* endure as a monument of early modern anti-Jesuit thought and an important example of French epistolary polemic.

During the composition of the *Lettres*, events took an unexpected turn. On 24 March, 1656, Pascal's ten-year-old niece, Marguérite Périer, a boarder at Port-Royal, was cured of an allegedly incurable lachrymal fistula when a relic of the crown of thorns was applied to her sore. For many Jansenists, the "Miracle of the Holy Thorn" became a divine vindication of their cause. The event inspired Pascal to begin writing an apologetic work on miracles and Christian belief. It was left unfinished at the time of his death, but the nuns of Port-Royal later published this fragmentary treatise as the *Pensées* (1669/1670).[56]

Neither the *Lettres Provinciales* nor the Miracle of the Holy Thorn were enough to save Port-Royal. Things went from bad to worse when Louis XIV assumed personal government in 1661. The Sun King pushed the Assembly of Clergy to mandate that clergy, vowed religious, and teachers all sign a "formulary"[57] condemning Jansen. To put pressure on the nuns, royal authorities dismissed their confessors, closed the

---

using unusual cases of conscience to illustrate general principles. Casuistry was not exclusively a Jesuit enterprise, but many prominent casuists, especially of the school known as "probabilism," were Jesuits. Probabilists held that one could safely follow any moral judgment that conformed to a "probable opinion," that is, an opinion held by a theologian, even in contradiction to the Fathers and Doctors of the Church. Jansenists, who execrated probabilists as laxists, generally preferred to follow tutiorism, the moral doctrine that, instead, says that one must follow the most certain or most probable opinion. See Julia Fleming, *Defending Probabilism*, 4–7; James Franklin, *The Science of Conjecture*, 64–101.

55. In the Jesuits' defense, Hsia writes, "The accusation of Jesuit casuistry missed the essential point: cases of conscience arose precisely out of the difficulties of applying strict Tridentine standards to measure the behavior of the Catholic multitude. Jesuit laxity was no more than adaptation to popular religiosity." See Hsia, *The World of Catholic Renewal*, 223. For a detailed study of the French controversy over casuistry, see Jean-Pascal Gay, *Morales en conflit*.

56. Henri Gouhier, *Blaise Pascal: Commentaires*, 131–49; Conley, *The Other Pascals*, 126–27.

57. An official statement requiring formal assent by a signature; in this case, the

convent school, and expelled all postulants, forbidding Port-Royal to take any further vocations. And, in August of that year, Mère Angélique died.[58]

The Formulary Controversy posed an enormous crisis of conscience for the nuns of Port-Royal and their sympathizers. They would have to choose between their duty of obedience to canonical and political superiors, and loyalty to the Truth—which for them meant both the Augustinian doctrines of grace and the good name of a bishop many regarded as holy. The nuns attempted to cut this Gordian Knot by signing the formulary along with a note qualifying their assent with Arnauld's fact/right distinction.[59] This attempted compromise was lost upon Louis XIV, for whom Port-Royal was rapidly becoming little more than a hive of dissidents. The authorities annulled the nuns' signatures. In 1664, Archbishop Hardouin de Péréfixe of Paris (1606–71) personally visited the convent in an attempt to extract new, unqualified signatures. He was not expecting to find highly intelligent, theologically sophisticated women who outwitted his every argument. Upon leaving one of these interviews in fury, the exasperated archbishop famously complained that the nuns were "pure as angels, but proud as devils."[60] Shortly thereafter, Péréfixe arrived at the monastery with armed guards. He deprived the women of Port-Royal of the sacraments, installed Visitandine nuns as their new superiors alongside hostile confessors, and exiled twelve of the most adamant *nonsigneuses* (non-signers) to imprisonment in various convents around the city.[61] Among these mil-

so-called "Formulary of Alexander VII," named for the pope who promulgated it in the bull *Regiminis apostolici* (1665). See Denzinger-Hünermann, 2020.

58. Conley, *Adoration*, 13.

59. Conley, *Adoration*, 13–14.

60. Daniella Kostroun provides a masterful feminist reading of these scenes in Kostroun, *Feminism*, 148–62, 164–68; see also Rea, *The Enthusiasts*, 255. The much-repeated accusation has come down in various forms, but the import and the attribution always remain the same. As Weaver notes, "In context, [this phrase] is part of a quite devastating account of the loss of control of the Archbishop of Paris, Hardouin de Péréfixe, before the calm refusal of the nuns to betray their trust in their leaders by signing." See Weaver, *The Evolution*, 106n3.

61. Ruth Clark, *Strangers and Sojourners at Port Royal*, 22; Conley, *Adoration*, 126; Kostroun, *Feminism*, 164–68.

itant nuns was the daughter of Robert Arnauld d'Andilly, Angélique de Saint-Jean (1624–84). Perhaps the greatest intellectual among the women of Port-Royal, Angélique de Saint-Jean was also fiercely cognizant of her privileged status as both a vowed religious and a daughter of a *conseiller d'état*. Péréfixe sent her to the Annonciade convent, where she lived as a prisoner for two years. Her *Relation de captivité*, published in 1711 and translated here by Elizabeth Huddleston, bitingly recounts the story of her time in custody (Text 8). It is one of the major texts memorializing the persecution of Jansenists.[62]

In 1666, the *nonsigneuses* were separated from the minority who had signed the formulary by being exiled to their medieval motherhouse, Port-Royal des Champs. Louis XIV awarded the vast majority of the convent's wealth to the obedient *signeuses*, including the Paris property. He installed military guards at the country monastery. Péréfixe kept the nuns under interdict, refusing them the sacraments as well as access to friendly clergy.[63] The state also put pressure upon the *solitaires*. The biblical translator Le Maistre de Sacy was imprisoned in the Bastille from 1666 to 1668.[64] Others dispersed to various refuges; Arnauld and Nicole went into hiding.[65] It was perhaps in this context that Nicole composed his "Règles pour les tems d'épreuve et de persécution," translated here by Daniel J. Watkins, featuring eighteen meditative "rules" on how to endure persecution for the Truth (Text 9).

Eventually, however, sympathetic bishops intervened. They helped broker a peace between Port-Royal, Louis XIV, and Pope Clement IX, who in 1669 accepted a qualified signature of the formulary with "respectful silence" on the question of *fait*. This resolution came with a canonical separation between the two Port-Royals, even as Rome cleared the nuns of all wrongdoing. The *solitaires* could regroup at Port-Royal des Champs, where they fixed their polemical aim on safer, Protestant targets. They reopened their schools in the country. The nuns were

62. For a larger translation of the *Relation* than we provide here, as well as other texts by Angélique de Saint-Jean, see Arnauld d'Andilly, *Writings of Resistance*; also Conley, *Adoration*, 175–236.

63. Conley, *Adoration*, 14–15.

64. Agten, *Catholic Church and the Dutch Bible*, 155; Rea, *The Enthusiasts*, 270.

65. Rea, *The Enthusiasts*, 269.

permitted to accept novices again.[66] As a community, Port-Royal entered a brilliant phase that Sainte-Beuve has aptly called its "beautiful autumn."[67] It was not to last.

Section Two: The Storm of *Unigenitus*, c. 1679–1760

This anthology's second section includes texts that span the eighty or so years after the end of the Formulary Controversy. These decades include several distinct phases, each marked by a major turning point. The first of these phases, the decades leading up to the papal bull *Vineam Domini Sabaoth* (1705), is generally known as the "Peace of the Church," or the "Peace of Clement IX." This era saw the emergence of theologies and strategies that would come to define Jansenism in the eighteenth century. In spite of its name, it also saw ongoing controversies that would lead to further conflict between the embattled Jansenist minority and their opponents.

And in 1679, the Peace of the Church was profoundly shaken by the authorities. Louis XIV moved against Port-Royal des Champs, then under the abbacy of Mère Angélique de Saint-Jean. Louis sent the Archbishop of Paris to visit the monastery, where he ordered the *solitaires* to disperse, closed the schools, and forbade the nuns from taking any more postulants. These onerous conditions were never lifted, condemning the convent to a long, slow death.[68] Many of the *solitaires* went into political exile. For instance, Antoine Arnauld fled to Belgium, and he eventually died in Liège in 1694.[69]

The monastery's final suppression by Louis XIV came in 1709. When the French crown once again required signatures condemning Jansenism, the nuns refused. This was the last straw for Louis in his decades-long combat with the nuns.[70] On October 29, the lieutenant of

66. Kostroun, *Feminism*, 182–205; Conley, *Adoration*, 15–16.

67. Sainte-Beuve, quoted in Conley, *Adoration*, 16.

68. Conley, *Adoration*, 16–17.

69. Bruno Neveu, *Sébastien Joseph du Cambout du Pontchâteau (1634–1690) et ses missions à Rome*, 75–239; Rea, *The Enthusiasts*, 291–93.

70. "Port-Royal," 314.

police arrived at Port-Royal with two hundred soldiers. He assembled the elderly nuns who still remained at the convent and read them the king's orders. Given only three hours to prepare, they were to be immediately scattered, living out their last days as prisoners in unfriendly religious communities across the kingdom.[71] Over the course of the next two years, the Sun King ordered the buildings razed and the bodies of the nuns and *solitaires* disinterred from the convent cemetery. The violence against Port-Royal left the wider Jansenist community shaken. The suppression helped transform Port-Royal's ruins into a center of pilgrimage, the very fate Louis sought to avoid.[72] But this transformation likely would never have happened at all without a bombshell which followed in 1713, perhaps the most serious theological dispute arising within Catholicism since the Reformation.[73]

Despite the "peace," theological conflict between Augustinians and Molinists still raged during the period from 1670 to 1700. The mission field was one stage of this fight. Jansenists were not alone in targeting Jesuit missionaries, whose strategies of presenting the Gospel in culturally accommodating ways became particularly controversial in China.[74] In erudite polemical works like the *Morale pratique des Jésuites*, translated here by Yoder (Text 10), and even in popular songs and poems like those translated by Jean-Pascal Gay (Text 11), the *messieurs de Port-Royal* accused Jesuit missionaries of a litany of crimes. Their sins included permitting idolatry, hiding the scandal of the crucifixion, depriving the Chinese of the Sacred Scriptures, frustrating the work of other missionaries, and lording it over the Chinese like Mandarins. These accusations, it must be said, were in many cases unfair and ill-informed. However, they extended the earlier Pascalian critique of Jesuit laxism to a new, international scale.

By the end of the century, however, head-on confrontation between

71. Kostroun, *Feminism*, 236–39.

72. Maire, "Port-Royal," 314; Conley, *The Other Pascals*, 130–31.

73. Maire, "Port-Royal," 314.

74. D. E. Mungello, ed., *The Chinese Rites Controversy*; Luke Clossey, *Salvation and Globalization in the Early Jesuit Missions*; R. Po-chia Hsia, *A Jesuit in the Forbidden City*; Ines G. Županov and Pierre Antoine Fabre, eds., *The Rites Controversies in the Early Modern World*; Claudia von Collani, "The Jesuit Rites Controversy."

Jansenists and anti-Jansenists was back out in the open. In general, extremists on both sides, and the grudges they bore, caused the "peace" to break down.[75] Conflict accelerated when an imprudent "Case of conscience" (*Cas de conscience*) submitted to the Theology Faculty of Paris for debate in 1701 reignited the thorny parsing of anti-Jansenist bulls. Around the same time, an ex-Oratorian priest named Pasquier Quesnel (1634–1719) living in exile in Brussels had his papers seized. To the alarm of King Louis XIV, Quesnel's correspondence showed the endurance and even spread of Jansenist networks, active not only in France but in Rome.[76] Enraged, the French King petitioned the pope for yet another condemnation of Jansenism, which came in Clement XI's *Vineam Domini Sabaoth* (1705). This bull exploded what remained of the "peace" by explicitly condemning the refuge that Jansenists had taken in respectful or "obediential" silence toward papal censures.[77] Truces and tacit understandings had failed. The inner sanctum of scrupulous Jansenist consciences was no longer a ceasefire zone.

But *Vineam Domini* was not enough. Hardcore anti-Jansenists were not satisfied, and King Louis XIV demanded total religious conformity in his kingdom. The French king and his allies pressured Clement XI to deliver a final, sweeping, and thunderous condemnation of Jansenism, understood not just as a set of errors on divine grace but as an alternative system of the Christian life, touching everything from penitential practice to participation in the liturgy. In stark contrast to the dense theological tome of Jansen, the target for this anti-Jansenist syllabus of errors was a popular biblical commentary. The author was Pasquier Quesnel, who was by now the clear successor of Antoine Arnauld.

With his *Réflexions morales sur le nouveau testament*, Quesnel continued the Jansenist preoccupation with biblical literacy and intense individual piety. These *Moral Reflections* were an accessible explanation of the New Testament, complete with the vernacular text of Scripture. We present here a selection from Quesnel's commentary on Jesus's Last Supper discourse in the Gospel of John, translated by

75. Jacques Gres-Gayer, "The *Unigenitus* of Clement XI," 261–62.

76. Lucien Ceyssens, "Les papiers de Quesnel saisis à Bruxelles"; É. Jacques, "Les petits foyers du Jansénisme à Bruxelles," 161–97.

77. Denzinger-Hünermann, 2309.

John Meinert (Text 12). Exegeting John 15:1–11, Quesnel presents the Jansenist-Augustinian commitment to God's efficacious grace to a popular audience. Quesnel's commentary on John 15:5 provided fodder for the second condemned proposition in Pope Clement XI's response, the Apostolic Constitution *Unigenitus* of 8 September 1713.[78]

Unigenitus condemned 101 propositions extracted verbatim from Quesnel's book—there would be no "fact" and "right" distinction to hide behind. Nevertheless, the Bull was not without its own destabilizing ambiguities. For one thing, the 101 statements of Quesnel were censured *in globo*, as a whole. That is, specific theological "notes" of censure—which ascended from "scandalous" and "offensive to pious ears" all the way to the gravity of "blasphemous" and "heretical"—were not attached to specific propositions from Quesnel's book, but rather listed all together at the end of the document.[79] Additionally, supporters of *Unigenitus* had to explain the embarrassing fact that a few of the condemned propositions seemed to be fairly straightforward summaries of ideas found in patristic sources (chiefly in Augustine), or, even worse, verbatim quotations from the Church Fathers themselves.[80]

Jansenists felt cornered, since in their view the bull condemned the true Catholic doctrine regarding divine grace, an understanding based not only on St. Augustine and his followers but on Scripture itself. They believed that the papacy had also contradicted itself, since popes in late antiquity had "received" Augustine's teaching and confirmed the decrees of synods and provincial councils[81] that, for all intents and purposes, taught the same things as Quesnel. Those who received *Unigenitus* tended to argue that what was condemned in Quesnel was not Augustine's thought, at least not properly understood. But some anti-Jansenists were bolder. They put their finger on a crucial

78. Denzinger-Hünermann, 2402 (*Unigenitus*, article 2): "The grace of Jesus Christ, which is the efficacious principle of every kind of good, is necessary for every good work; without it, not only is nothing done, but nothing can be done."

79. Denzinger-Hünermann, 2502.

80. The work of Lucien Ceyssens is fundamental for the study of *Unigenitus*; see especially Ceyssens and Joseph Tans, *Autour de l'Unigenitus*. Also see Gres-Gayer, "*Unigenitus*."

81. E.g., the Second Synod of Orange (529), confirmed by Pope Boniface II. See Denzinger-Hünermann, 370–400.

methodological difference: they argued that the Church's *current* teaching authority (in this case, Pope Clement XI) had the right to determine what was and was not Catholic tradition, and that while Augustine was a revered Doctor, he was not infallible. The pope, however, was—at least when making solemn doctrinal judgments as universal pastor.

Some non-Jansenists were alarmed by *Unigenitus* as well. The Dominican Jacques-Hyacinthe Serry (1659–1738), in addition to humorously lambasting the ambiguity inherent to an *in globo* condemnation, actually argued that only one of the 101 propositions taken from Quesnel's book deserved unambiguous rejection.[82] There was also concern, and not just from Jansenist partisans, that Clement XI had lost a hold on the traditional papal duty to peacefully arbitrate between the theological "schools." Recently, for example, Rome had self-consciously pursued a mediating role in the debates between Molinists and Thomists, and between rigorists and laxists. There were even murmurs that the pope had allowed an ultramontane and Molinist party to unduly steer him and the resulting document. Anti-Jansenist zealots, like the Jesuit Cardinal Carlo Agostino Fabroni (1651–1727) and King Louis's confessor, Michel Le Tellier (1643–1719), also a Jesuit, do seem to have successfully pushed Pope Clement a good bit further in *Unigenitus* than he initially wanted to go.[83] Later pontiffs had to clean up this damage: the Dominican, and therefore Thomist, Benedict XIII (pope from 1724 to 1730) and the Augustinian-leaning Benedict XIV (1740–58) bent over backward to make clear that *Unigenitus* should not be interpreted as a triumph of Molinism over Thomism or Augustinianism.[84]

The Roman committee judging Quesnel's book, chaired by Clement XI, did not limit itself to censuring extreme Augustinian views of grace. In statements that shocked and embarrassed many Catholics—and seemed to confirm the worst suspicions of Protestants—*Unigenitus* censured Quesnel for his positions on universal Bible reading in the vernacular and the participation of lay people in the liturgy. A flood of anti-*Unigenitus* literature appeared: at least two hundred books and pamphlets in 1714 alone, and hundreds more by 1730.[85] As an example

82. Émile Appolis, *Le 'tiers parti,'* 103.

83. Gres-Gayer, "*Unigenitus*," 279–80.

84. Appolis, *Les jansenistes espagnols*, 14–17, 192–93.

85. Van Kley, *Religious Origins*, 74.

from this first wave of popular literature, we present a striking defense of the right of women to read the Bible and to "join their voice to the voice of the whole Church," rights which appeared to be reprobated by *Unigenitus* articles 83 and 86. Translated by Elizabeth Huddleston, the *Lettre d'une dame de Paris au pape sur la constitution*, published under the pseudonym Ursule de la Grange, is one of the finest examples in the popular genre of anti-*Unigenitus* literature and a fascinating comment on the struggle of women at this stage in the history of Catholicism (Text 13).

While there was some possible wiggle room in the interpretation of *Unigenitus*'s condemnations, the censures of Bible-reading and liturgical participation are examples of how anti-Jansenism overreached, drawing contentious issues into the orbit of debate that could have remained separate, or at least distinct, from the original matters at hand. Nowhere was such overreach more apparent than in the realm of ecclesiology. Many Catholics who were not Jansenists chafed at the implications of this stark assertion of papal authority, and not just in France.[86] The French ecclesiological tradition of Gallicanism denied papal infallibility, looking instead to the conciliarist tradition which saw the ecumenical council as the final arbiter of the church's faith. Gallicanism exalted the temporal authority of the king and the ecclesiastical authority of the bishops over that of Rome. These principles, which went back centuries, were codified at an assembly of French clergy in 1682, held at the height of a quarrel between King Louis XIV and Pope Innocent XI. Led by Jacques-Bénigne Bossuet (1627–1704), one of the most venerable preachers and writers in the history of French Catholicism, the clergy formally declared four articles that summarized the Gallican ecclesiological and political system. These "four Gallican articles" became a shorthand for an ecclesiological counternarrative to

86. For example, the reception of *Unigenitus* in the Holy Roman Empire was a more troublesome and complicated affair than has traditionally been acknowledged. See Juliette Guilbaud, "Die Rezeption der Constitutio *Unigenitus* (1713) im Alten Reich." Catholics living under Protestant rule in Britain and Ireland also had to deal with these issues: see James F. McMillan, "Jansenists and Anti-Jansenists in Eighteenth Century Scotland"; Thomas O'Connor, *Irish Jansenists, 1600–70*; Eamon Duffy, "'A Rubb-Up for Old Soares': Jesuits, Jansenists, and the English Secular Clergy, 1705–1715."

papalism or ultramontanism. As *Unigenitus* and the events surrounding it made clear, Rome had always seen the articles of 1682 as far more of a threat than the five propositions on grace supposedly extracted from a Leuven professor's tome.[87] The nearly century-long story of the fraught reception and rejection of *Unigenitus* makes clear that the real dispute was over papal authority, not divine grace.[88]

In calling down the hammer of papal authority in this manner, Louis XIV was trying to have his cake and eat it too. This is not without some irony, since it was Louis's clash with a previous pope that had prompted the codification of the Gallican Articles in 1682 (in a further layer of irony, that pope, Innocent XI, was accused of crypto-Jansenism). The clear message from Pope Clement XI's Rome, however, was that the bishops were to accept and defend *Unigenitus* as a solemn and irreformable dogmatic judgment of the Successor of Peter; they were not to deliberate over whether the pope's teaching in fact reflected the faith of their local churches, as in the Gallican-conciliarist model. Additionally, Clement XI repeatedly refused to clarify the meaning of the bull, offending many Gallicans whom he might otherwise have won over. Thus, the rejection of *Unigenitus* became about much more than Quesnel's book. Such rejection, for many, was "an appeal to an ideal conception of authority in the church."[89] With different nuances, the work of French historians Luciens Ceyssens, Bruno Neveu, and Jacques Gres-Gayer has shown that *Unigenitus* provided "a way for Rome to resolve another and more crucial question, that of papal authority, against Gallican principles, in favor of the personal power of the Roman pontiff."[90] *Unigenitus* furthered the alignment between Jansenism and Gallicanism-conciliarism, turning a struggle over a book that was representative of a small, mostly French sect, into a much broader "struggle between two conceptions of Western Catholicism."[91]

87. See Gres-Gayer, "*Unigenitus*," 264; Orcibal, "Jansenius et Rome," 27.

88. Lucien Ceyssens called papal infallibility "the great dogma under dispute." Quoted in Gres-Gayer, "*Unigenitus*," 263. Gres-Gayer concurs in this judgment.

89. Gres-Gayer, "*Unigenitus*," 282.

90. Gres-Gayer, "*Unigenitus*," 272.

91. Gres-Gayer, "*Unigenitus*," 282. See also Louis Cognet, "Le jansénisme, drame gallican."

This ecclesiological crisis came to a head when four French bishops entered the Sorbonne in Paris on March 5, 1717, and formally appealed *Unigenitus* to a future ecumenical council. We present this Appeal (Text 14), translated by Guido Stucco. As these "Appellant" bishops made clear, the opponents of *Unigenitus* had numerous grievances, beyond the doctrines of grace. Worst of all, the bull symbolized Roman contempt for the liberties of the Gallican Church and the denigration of the God-given rights of bishops. It evidenced a creeping understanding of the pope as an infallible monarch who ruled over the bishops, rather than as the central guardian of a tradition protected by all the local churches. The four Appellants were soon joined by 97 of the 110 doctors of the Theology Faculty of Paris, and by priests and bishops all over France, with the crucial addition of the Cardinal-Archbishop of Paris, Louis-Antoine de Noailles (1651–1729). Overall, three to five percent of eligible French clergy formally joined the appeal, though sympathy for the Appellants was much higher. And in some critical areas like Paris, appeal was the norm—three-fourths of the 450 *curés* (parish priests) in the capital were Appellants.[92]

Such open and widespread dissent from *Unigenitus* would probably have been impossible if Louis XIV had not died in 1715. The regency government under the Duc d'Orléans was, at first, an amenable environment for opponents of the pope's bull. But the Appellants were slowly choked out. For example, more than a hundred doctors were expelled from the Paris Faculty of Theology between 1721 and 1730.[93] Cardinal Noailles held out for years, but ultimately submitted to *Unigenitus* just before his death in 1729. The four original Appellant bishops were severely censured by another bull of Clement XI, *Pastoralis Officii* (1718). For the time being, however, they were not deprived of jurisdiction over their dioceses. The efforts of Cardinal André-Hercule de Fleury (1653–1743), the staunchly anti-Jansenist first minister of the new king, Louis XV, turned the tide against the Appellants. Fleury led a harsh campaign of repression, jailing priests and exiling *parlementaires* who

92. McManners, *Church and Society in Eighteenth-Century France*, 370–97; Van Kley, *Religious Origins*, 86; Cottret, *Histoire*, 156. On the French bishops and *Unigenitus*, see Andurand, *La grande affaire*.

93. Jacques Gres-Gayer, *Théologie et pouvoir en Sorbonne*, 70.

refused to accept *Unigenitus*. The fate of the Appellants was sealed in 1730, when *Unigenitus* became a law of the state. Opposition to it thus formally became a political crime. The successor of Louis XIV had definitively aligned the immense powers of church and state against Jansenism, and, rather paradoxically for the defender of Gallican Liberties, on the side of papal authority.[94]

As fervent believers in the providence of God and diligent readers of the Bible, it is not surprising that Jansenists developed a distinctive mode of scriptural interpretation to fit their increasingly desperate situation: figurism. For figurists, people and events from the Old and New Testaments were symbolically interpreted as "figures" of present struggles. These figural applications helped the embattled Jansenist community recast their defeats as preludes to triumph, following the example of biblical heroes who were ultimately vindicated by God. Popularized by a circle connected to the Oratorian seminary of Saint-Magloire in Paris, Jansenists used figurism to give meaning to their suffering at the hands of the French state, and cope with the even more painful reality that the "Truth" had been betrayed by the majority of French bishops and even the pope himself. The genius of figurism was its prophetic potential; not only was God going to make crooked lines straight, as the Almighty had done in Scripture, but the persecution that Jansenists were suffering was actually confirmation that they were following God's will. Through figurist exegesis of Scripture, a Jansenist, as a member of the faithful "remnant," could mystically align his or her own suffering and anxiety with the apostolic community and with Israel of the Old Testament.[95]

Jacques-Joseph Duguet (1649–1733), author of the fundamental *Règles pour l'intelligence des Saintes-Écritures* (1716), is considered the father of figurism. Duguet first popularized the idea that the mass conversion of Jews to (Jansenist) Catholicism after widespread Gentile apostasy would serve as a divine vindication of their cause; this

94. Louis Cognet, "Jansenism in Eighteenth-Century France"; McManners, *Church and Society*; Van Kley, *Religious Origins*; Cottret, *Histoire*; Andurand, *La grande affaire*.

95. On figurism, see Maire, *De la cause*, 86–234; Maire, "Les jansénistes et le millénarisme"; Ephraim Radner, *Spirit and Nature*, 195–276; Van Kley, *Reform Catholicism*, 92–93; Lyon-Caen, *La boîte à Perrette*.

apocalyptic prediction, relying chiefly upon an interpretation of the Epistle to the Romans, became an important trope in some Jansenist circles. We include selections from a work by one of Duguet's most prolific disciples, the Oratorian Jean-Baptiste Le Sesne des Ménilles d'Étemare (1682–1770). The Abbé d'Étemare's *Explications de quelques prophéties touchant la conversion future des juifs* (1724), translated by Luke Togni (Text 15), provides scriptural grounding for the Jansenist hope that God would turn tragedy into triumph. What seemed on the surface like the failure of the church's infallibility, and God's failure to protect the orthodox from persecution and contempt, was actually foretold all along by Paul and the prophets: d'Étemare's exegesis reveals "the truly wonderful harmony" between the biblical sources and present sufferings.

Other figurist texts were more directly confrontational. For example, the Abbé Jacques Gudvert (d. 1737) wrote a wild screed titled *Jesus-Christ sous l'anatheme et sous l'excommunication* (1727), excerpts from which are also translated by Luke Togni (Text 16). Some desperate Jansenists identified their own sense of intense grief and alienation with the suffering and rejection of Jesus Christ. Was not Jesus himself, they asked, solemnly condemned by the religious and civil authorities of his own day? Gudvert's figural lens cast Quesnel in particular as a Christ-figure, which left the ignominious role of the chief priests, scribes, and Pharisees to the Roman Curia, the Jesuits, and the French authorities.[96] Predictably, Gudvert's full frontal assault on the pope and every bishop who accepted *Unigenitus* quickly landed his work on the Index of Forbidden Books, and French authorities had it publicly burned.

Figurists gave *Unigenitus* itself pride of place as the "abomination of desolation" set up in the holy place (a reference to Jesus' prophecy in Matthew 24:15 and Luke 21:20; cf. Daniel 12:11). Present-day Jansenists were thus living through the "mystery of iniquity" (2 Thessalonians 2:7), in which God allowed fundamental truths of the Catholic faith not only to be obscured, but actually to be condemned—and by the very shepherds of the church who were supposed to protect them. The forces of

96. Marina Caffiero, "La verità crocifissa."

Antichrist, then, were not Turks or Protestants, but Jesuits and other traitors within the fold who deceived the Catholic people and their pastors.

While these texts are vital monuments to the figurist tradition, an oral component of preaching, exhorting, and "witnessing to the Truth" is at least as important to the story of figurism as any text.

Two further developments from this period came to mark eighteenth-century Jansenism. The first was ecclesiological, but, as ever, had political undertones. In the wake of *Unigenitus*, French Jansenists reached back to an ecclesiological tradition called Richerism, named for a seventeenth-century syndic of the Sorbonne, Edmond Richer (1559–1631). Works such as Nicolas Le Gros's two-volume *Du renversement des libertés de l'église gallicane* (1716) adapted and expanded upon elements of Richer's thought.[97] Drawing on Richer and other conciliarist authors, Le Gros argued that parish priests were the successors of the seventy-two disciples commissioned by Jesus (Luke 10). While not equal in authority to bishops, who were successors of the twelve apostles, Jesus had intended priests to exercise *de iure divino* (God-given) authority alongside their bishop. Crucially, this included acting as "judges of the faith," a title that more conservative Gallicans, to say nothing of ultramontanes, reserved to bishops alone.[98]

The spread of Richerism among the lower clergy was certainly strategic. It provided a framework for Jansenist *curés*, their lay supporters, and sympathetic *parlementaires* to resist the "domination" of bad bishops. But the turn to Richerism was a principled strategy, insofar as it was an organic extension of the kind of primitivism that made Gallicanism such a natural ecclesiological fit for Jansenists. Accusations that Jansenists were advocating ecclesial democracy or a Protestantized "presbyterianism" quickly followed. But Richerism, in its origins and in its eighteenth-century permutations, was really just a radicalized Gallicanism, extending the same kind of synodal and "constitutional" thinking to the parish priests that was already extended to the bishops.[99]

97. Van Kley, *Religious Origins*, 77–82.

98. On Richer, see Philippe Denis, *Edmond Richer*. On eighteenth-century Jansenist Richerism, see Edmond Préclin, *Les jansénistes du XVIII*[e] *siècle*.

99. Francis Oakley, *The Conciliarist Tradition*; B. Robert Kreiser, *Miracles,*

The second development was political and ecclesiastical. In something of a contrast to the Jansenist resistance to royal absolutism in France, Jansenists in this period made important intellectual contributions to the development of regalism and "enlightened despotism" in other Catholic lands. These trends gathered steam and reached their zenith in the second half of the century. In addition to his role in shaping figurism, Jacques-Joseph Duguet authored one of the most important eighteenth-century works of political theology, the *Institution d'un Prince*. We include excerpts discussing the thorny question of the proper boundaries of temporal and spiritual authority, translated by Luke Togni (Text 19). Begun in 1711, this handbook of instruction was not published until 1739. The *Institution* quickly became an important resource for the enlightened Catholic prince. The popularity of Duguet's text across Europe, even in non-Catholic contexts, evidences the growing appeal of Jansenist and philo-Jansenist authors.[100] Since Jansenism did not have the same politically subversive connotations outside of France, reforming prelates, statesmen, and sovereigns often found Jansenist accounts of church history, theology, and politics useful in their campaigns against the Jesuits, the mendicant orders, and papal interference in their territories.

A new chapter in the controversy over *Unigenitus* opened in 1727, at the death of a young deacon named François de Pâris.[101] Recognized for his piety, austerity, and charity toward the many poor in his Parisian parish of Saint-Médard, the Deacon Pâris was hailed as a saint. Reports of miraculous cures began at his funeral and continued for years after his interment in Saint-Médard's cemetery. Cardinal Noailles investigated these claims and, upon the strength of the evidence, declared Pâris

Convulsions, and Ecclesiastical Politics, 9, 24–25; Dale Van Kley, "Civic Humanism in Clerical Garb."

100. Caroline Chopelin Blanc, "L'*Institution d'un Prince* de Duguet."

101. There is an enormous literature on the *convulsionnaires*, but what follows is chiefly dependent upon Gazier, *Histoire générale*, vol. 2; Kreiser, *Miracles*; Maire, *Les Convulsionnaires*; Daniel Vidal, *Miracles et convulsions jansénistes au XVIIIe siècle*; Maire, *De la cause*, 237–365; Lyon-Caen, *La boîte à Perette*, 309–42; Charly Coleman, *The Virtues of Abandon*, 105–15; Marie Sophie Giraud, "Convulsionary Miracles and Women in Print Culture in France, 1737–1747"; Anne C. Vila, "Shaking Up the Enlightenment," 9–37.

a "Blessed," that is, a heroically virtuous Catholic on the road to formal canonization as a saint.

However, Pâris was also a committed Appellant and a Jansenist who revered the memory of Port-Royal. After Cardinal Noailles died in 1729, his successor, Archbishop Vintimille du Luc, turned against the nascent cult of François de Pâris. In 1731, he rejected some of the most famous miracles out of hand—notably the healing of a working-class woman named Anne Lefranc, whose account is translated here by Maxwell Pingeon (Text 17). Vintimille also forbade further veneration of the popular "saint."

It was around this time that the Deacon's persistent devotees started to shake and cry out at his tomb. These involuntary movements, which soon came to characterize the healing miracles, earned them the name of *convulsionnaires*. At first, Jansenists made much of these phenomena, pointing to the miracles as proof that God was on their side. Cardinal Fleury saw the potential danger of these erratic, politically dissident devotions. In January 1732, the French police closed the cemetery of Saint-Médard. This led to a famous bit of graffiti: "De par le Roi, défense à Dieu/de faire miracle en ce lieu," meaning, "By order of the King, God is forbidden/from performing miracles in this place."

However, the cult did not go away. It merely scattered and hid, with loosely associated cells of *convulsionnaire* "Brothers" and "Sisters" meeting in private to pray, venerate Jansenist relics, convulse, and prophesy. In the face of imprisonment and ostracism, a new and startling development emerged: the *grand secours*, or "great help." *Convulsionnaires* (usually women) would cry out from pain in some part of their body. They would shout for help, *secours*, and then other devotees (usually male) would comply with an act of targeted violence. For instance, if a *convulsionnaire* had pain in her chest, her *secouriste* might take up a hammer and start beating her breast, or perhaps stab her with a knife or poker. If her pain was in her legs, she might direct her *secouriste* to drag her around the room, perhaps for hours at a time. Terrible meals of bile, dust, or feces were not unknown in these settings. And occasionally, *convulsionnaires* were even crucified. These episodes recast figurist theology in a theatrical key.[102] The fact that the *convulsionnaires*

102. Maire, *De la cause*, 237–365; Radner, *Spirit and Nature*, 195–364.

demanded this treatment, that they usually claimed to be unharmed or even improved by it, and that they often endured it while prophesying at length—all of these aspects, the *convulsionnaires* insisted, figuratively testified to the persistence of Catholic "Truth" (i.e., Jansenism), manifesting the presence of the divine.

Or, perhaps, the diabolical. Many conservative Jansenists sided with their opponents and condemned the convulsions. Some said the *convulsionnaires* were hysterical women, sexual deviants, or simple frauds. Others discerned demonic possession. And still others asserted that there was a mixture of all these phenomena alongside genuine miracles. To answer these objections, the *secouriste* magistrate Louis-Basile Carré de Montgeron (1686–1754) became a *convulsionnaire* apologist. In the three volumes of his *La Vérité des miracles*, Montgeron embraced and justified the most extreme elements of *convulsionnaire* worship. He presented numerous cases of *convulsionnaire* miracles, such as the narrative translated here by Marie Giraud (Text 18). In spite of Montgeron's efforts, however, the *convulsionnaire* cause continued to dwindle throughout the eighteenth century, mostly laughed off by skeptics and reviled by the "orthodox," including most other Jansenists.

The cult of François de Pâris was one way that the cause of the appeal became a popular movement. Another was the emergence, in 1728, of a roughly biweekly newspaper known as the *Nouvelles ecclésiastiques*. The *Nouvelles* spent its seventy-five years of publication putting the Jansenist case before the public eye. The newspaper kept up a constant complaint about the treatment of Jansenists, Jesuit perfidy, and the bishops whose "despotism" fell heavy on the shoulders of "the Friends of the Truth." It did so anonymously, under the threat of police action; the *Nouvelles* was never legal, and it survived due to a complicated system of clandestine reportage, editing, illustration, printing, and distribution which prevented any one member of the network from knowing much else about it.[103] The editors faced their situation with a sense of humor that Catherine Maire has called "suprême coquetterie," as when they mockingly published a chart of their own secret model

103. Monique Cottret, "*Les Nouvelles ecclésiastiques* et l'histoire religieuse du XVIIIe siècle"; Richard T. Yoder, "From the Dove to the Eagle."

of organization, or when they managed to sneak a copy into the police chief's own carriage.[104]

Besides its theological position, one thing that made the newspaper stand out was that the editors were more than willing to engage with ordinary people of virtually any class. As Arlette Farge notes, the *Nouvelles* was "the only newspaper to give much space to popular speech . . . and it based its strategy on the idea that the people were one of the best and most active justifications of Jansenist endeavors."[105] Like Montgeron writing on behalf of the *convulsionnaires*, the *Nouvelles* made an impassioned "appeal to the people" in parallel to the bishops' "appeal to the Council."[106]

The *Nouvelles* deployed this strategy to great effect during the Refusal of Sacraments Controversy. The zealots of the anti-Jansenist camp, led by Christophe de Beaumont (Archbishop of Paris from 1746 to 1781), began denying last rites to suspected Jansenists. Beaumont went so far as to require that suspected individuals show a *billet de confession* (confession certificate) from a pro-*Unigenitus* confessor in order to receive the deathbed sacrament. The French public widely reviled this disruption of pastoral practice, touching the most intimate moments of life, as needlessly cruel and invasive.[107]

The *Nouvelles ecclésiastiques* wasted no opportunity to report on these events. We produce here one such account (Text 20), translated by Keanu Heydari. The weekly paper of 7 August 1749 recounted the struggle between Jansenist and anti-Jansenist clergy at one of the locations of the Hôpital général de Paris, an institution that served both charitable and carceral functions. The *Nouvelles* reported on the good education and pastoral care that the "choirboys" (mostly orphans) were receiving at their residence, and the efforts of anti-Jansenist clergy to disrupt this. In the spirit of opposition to *Unigenitus*, the *Nouvelles* here testifies to the voice of "Truth" being revealed to the "little ones," while it is hidden from their worldly persecutors. This was in continuity with

104. Maire, *De la cause*, 226; Brian Strayer, *Suffering Saints*, 171.

105. Arlette Farge, *Subversive Words*, 36; Maire, *De la cause*, 225–28.

106. Cottret, *Jansénismes et lumières*, 270–301, but especially 291–96.

107. Mita Choudhury, *Convents and Nuns*, 33–69, esp. 56–67; Dale Van Kley, *The Damiens Affair*; Van Kley, *Religious Origins*; Cottret, *Histoire du Jansénisme*, 179–87.

the Jansenist strategy of presenting the defenders of "the Truth" as a righteous minority found at every level of society—male or female, young or old, rich or poor.

The *parlements* of France, especially that of Paris, had become something of a bulwark for Jansenist men ambitious for public careers, as such men were normally barred from priestly ordination. Our first of two texts from the remarkably productive career of the lawyer and member of the Paris *parlement,* Louis-Adrien Le Paige (1712–1802), provides a further window into the Refusal of Sacraments Controversy. In a 1756 pamphlet, translated here by Timothy Troutner, Le Paige evinces the kind of aggressive legal counterattacks that Jansenist *parlementaires* used to defend their community from persecution (Text 21). Le Paige's dissection of a pastoral letter of Archbishop Beaumont on both civil and ecclesiastical grounds is a classic from the pen of one of the most important French Jansenists of the eighteenth century.

The conflict over sacrament refusal marks a time of transition in the history of Jansenism. The "judicial Jansenism" of the *parlements* concerned political and ecclesiastical matters more than theology *per se.*[108] But theological convictions and political ideals were often mutually reinforcing. For example, the ideal of an ancient, pristine ecclesiology held to by Jansenists and many Gallicans paralleled Le Paige's political claim that the *parlements* of France were in fact the successors of the ancient Merovingian Royal Court and the General Assemblies of the Franks. The *parlements* thus co-ruled the realm with the king by right, and were not merely the executors of royal will—just as bishops co-ruled the Church with the pope, and assemblies of bishops were true judges of the Catholic faith and did not merely rubber-stamp papal doctrinal decisions.[109] For Le Paige and his followers, the antidote to episcopal, papal, or royal tyranny could be found in a (highly idealized) past of constitutionalism, conciliar in the case of the Church and parliamentary in the case of the state.[110]

The Refusal of Sacraments crisis ended with yet another alignment between royal and papal policy, but this time in the Jansenists' favor.

108. On "judicial Jansenism," see Van Kley, *Religious Origins*, 108–14, *inter alia.*
109. Van Kley, *Religious Origins*, 254–55.
110. Maire, *De la cause*, 378–95; Van Kley, "Civic Humanism in Clerical Garb."

King Louis XV, exasperated by renewed Jansenist-related conflagrations in his kingdom, imposed silence on the issue, an outcome which played into the hands of Jansenists. From Rome, the irenic, "enlightened" Pope Benedict XIV intervened decisively with the bull *Ex omnibus* (1756). Like all popes, Benedict XIV stood by *Unigenitus*. Nevertheless, *Ex omnibus* was a practical victory for the Jansenist cause. It effectively ended crusades like Archbishop Beaumont's by making the bar for sacramental denial too high to clear on any large scale. While Benedict XIV was no Jansenist, his Augustinian sympathies were clear.[111]

By the 1750s, the age of Appellant bishops was over. When the Appellant Charles de Caylus died in 1754 after fifty years as bishop of the diocese of Auxerre, the leadership of the French Jansenist community had already passed almost completely to *parlementaires* and scattered networks of lower clergy and laity. Though the "Friends of the Truth" had suffered repeated setbacks in France, Jansenism was becoming more international by the death of Benedict XIV in 1758. Ominously—at least for the papacy and the Society of Jesus—this international Jansenism included in its ranks energetic reforming bishops and powerful regalist statesmen. They were to increasingly earn the favor and protection of Catholic sovereigns.

Section Three: The Jansenist International, c. 1760–1810

The anthology's third section features texts spanning the 1760s until the early nineteenth century, which tell the story of the "Jansenist International."[112] Reflecting this internationalization, we present texts translated from Spanish, Portuguese, Latin, Italian, German, French, and even Arabic.[113] Jansenism, or perhaps, more accurately,

111. Mario Rosa, *Riformatori e ribelli*, 49–85; Gaetano Greco, *Benedetto XIV*, 150–53.

112. For this recently coined term, see Dale Van Kley, "Jansenism and the International Suppression of the Jesuits"; Douglas Palmer, "The Republic of Grace." The term "late Jansenism" denotes figures in the final half or third of the eighteenth century. Italian scholars regularly write of *tardogiansenismo* and German-speakers of *Spätjansenismus*.

113. An additional text, the *Acts and Decrees* of the Utrecht synod of 1763, was produced by Catholics in the Netherlands but published in French.

"Jansenisms," gained new ground from Lebanon to Latin America in this period. French conflicts and French texts, however, remained fundamental. The "century of *Unigenitus*" culminated with the Revolution of 1789 and all the achievements and tragedies that followed it.[114]

In France, the alliance between the court of King Louis XV (r. 1715–74) and a new generation of bishops caught "the Friends of the Truth" between the hammer of royal power and the anvil of the ecclesiastical establishment. Since the crown controlled episcopal appointments, there would be no second generation of Appellant bishops to rally around. While in some ways severely weakened, French Jansenism refused to die a slow death. It instead transformed, looking beyond the Alps and the Pyrenees for new *amis de la verité*. Such an expanding focus is observable in the pages of the *Nouvelles ecclésiastiques*, which began to report more and more on the wider Catholic world: Italians who revered Port-Royal, anti-ultramontane English Catholics, Spanish and Portuguese enemies of the Jesuits, Germans and Austrians who preferred strict Augustinianism to Molinism and "lax" casuistry.[115] Hopeful signs abounded.

In fact, by the 1750s Rome itself had become something of a hotbed, not so much for Jansenists in the original French sense, but for what Italian scholarship calls *filogiansenisti* ("philo-Jansenists").[116] These sympathizers with the Jansenist cause venerated Port-Royal, tended to oppose the Jesuits, wanted lay people to have easier access to the Bible and the liturgy, and employed critical historical scholarship in the service of societal and religious reform.[117] Philo-Jansenists were emboldened by the publication of defenses of strict Augustinianism by the Italian theologians Gianlorenzo Berti OSA (1696–1766) and Fulgenzio Bellelli OSA (1677–1742), as well as by Benedict XIV's defense of Cardinal Enrico Noris (1631–1704), whose writings against

114. The title of the third part of Cottret's *Histoire du Jansénisme* (pp. 151–235) is "La Siècle de l'*Unigenitus*." See also Van Kley, *Damiens Affair*, 99.

115. See, *inter alia*, Charles H. O'Brien, "Jansenists and Josephinism"; David Hudson, "The *Nouvelles ecclésiastiques*, Jansenism, and Conciliarism"; Pietro Stella, *Il giansenismo in Italia*, 1:284–89.

116. The essential overview of Jansenism in Italy is Mario Rosa, *Il giansenismo nell'Italia del Settecento*. The definitive study is Stella's three-volume *Il giansenismo in Italia*.

117. Enrico Dammig, *Il movimento Giansenista a Roma*.

"Pelagianism" were posthumously censured by the Spanish Inquisition as Jansenist.[118]

In Rome, a circle of intellectuals called the *Archetto*, who met in the Palazzo Corsini, were evidence of a fusion between philo-Jansenism and the kind of "enlightened Catholicism" associated with Lodovico Muratori (1672–1750) and Benedict XIV. At *Archetto* gatherings, philo-Jansenist Tuscan scholars Giovanni Bottari (1689–1775) and Pier Francesco Foggini (1713–83) led critical discussions of the Church Fathers and of liturgical and ecclesiastical history. They enjoyed the patronage of scholarly, enlightened prelates, including powerful cardinals like Corsini, Passionei, Marefoschi, and Gonzaga. The *Archetto* and other philo-Jansenist networks were increasingly potent facilitators of anti-Jesuit action, which ultimately culminated in the suppression of the Society in 1773.[119]

The prominence of philo-Jansenists in the heart of papal Rome was indicative of the signs of the times. The "Friends of the Truth" now spanned much of Europe. In addition to a coherent program of assault on the Jesuit Order and ultramontanism, the Jansenist International also took up a closely related cause: that of the "persecuted" Church of Utrecht.

In 1724, the Cathedral canons of the Archdiocese of Utrecht insisted their right to elect an archbishop did not default to the papacy when the Netherlands became a Protestant state. The pope excommunicated them and all who adhered to their cause. While Jansenism as such was not the triggering issue for the schism, the kinds of ecclesiological divisions that *Unigenitus* inflamed were just underneath the surface. Additionally, since Catholics enjoyed relative toleration in the Netherlands, Dutch cities such as Amsterdam and Utrecht had long functioned as havens for French Jansenist exiles, including Quesnel.[120]

The Utrecht Catholics became a *cause célèbre* around the Catholic world. The ecclesiological implications of the schism and the established

118. Stella, *Il giansenismo in Italia*, vols. 1 and 2.

119. Dammig, *Il movimento Giansenista a Roma*; Hanns Gross, *Rome in the Age of Enlightenment*, 270–85; Raffaele Belvederi, "Il giansenismo negli anni di Benedetto XIV"; Dale Van Kley, "Setting the Scene."

120. Angela Berlis and Dirk Schoon, "Jansenism across the Border."

connection with Francophone Jansenism meant that "the cause of Utrecht" was a *shibboleth* for philo-Jansenist and anti-ultramontane Catholics around Europe. Taking advantage of this situation, the Utrecht clergy held a Provincial Council in 1763. The *Acts and Decrees* of their small synod, published in French, formed an ambitious theological and ecclesiological manifesto. Selections from this synod, translated by Shaun Blanchard (Text 22), show the Utrecht clergy's strategy of capitalizing on the popularity of anti-Jesuitism, in this case jumping on the bandwagon of outrage against a popular novelistic adaptation of the Bible by the Jesuit Isaac-Joseph Berruyer (1681–1758). Claiming to offer a middle way between Jesuit ultramontanism on one hand and Protestantizing errors on the other, the Utrecht synod was an assertion of a systematic Augustinian Catholic orthodoxy. Hundreds of "letters of communion," supportive statements from clergy around Europe recognizing the purity of the Church of Utrecht's faith and ecclesial communion with it, showed how widespread sympathy was. Additionally, such actions were clear assertions that the papal excommunications were unjust and even invalid.[121]

The *doyen* of the Jansenist International was the Abbé Augustin-Jean-Charles Clément (1717–1804). Through tireless letter-writing and extensive travel, Clément became the chief propagandist for the cause of Utrecht and of "the Truth" of Jansenism. Clément found, to his delight, that he had fervent allies even in ultramontane heartlands like Spain and Rome.[122] One of these allies, Joseph Climent i Avinent (1706–81), the Bishop of Barcelona, is a good example of the spread and appeal of philo-Jansenism during the third quarter of the eighteenth century.[123] While Spanish Jansenism *per se* did not "appear in broad daylight" until the 1780s, some Spaniards openly allied with Jansenists and championed many of their causes as the Bourbon Reforms under

121. On Utrecht see Bastiaan Abraham van Kleef, "Das Utrechter Provinzialkonzil vom Jahre 1763"; Samuel J. Miller, "Portugal and Utrecht"; Pietro Stella, "Il dissidio con la Chiesa di Utrecht"; Jan Visser, "The Old Catholic Churches of the Union of Utrecht"; Dale Van Kley, "Catholic Conciliar Reform in an Age of Anti-Catholic Revolution"; Daniel Watkins, *Berruyer's Bible*; Charles Parker, *Faith on the Margins*, 36; Peter-Ben Smit, *Old Catholic Theology*.

122. See Augustin-Jean-Charles Clément's *Journal de correspondances et voyages*.

123. Andrea J. Smidt, "Josep Climent i Avinent."

King Carlos III (r. 1759–88) picked up speed.[124] Bishop Climent formed a close friendship with the Abbé Clément, who saw such promise in the Catalan prelate that he visited him personally in his diocese. Bishop Climent's famous pastoral letter of 26 March 1769 (Text 24), translated by Andrea J. Smidt, defended the Church of Utrecht and was praised by the *Nouvelles ecclésiastiques*. Climent's circle in Spain included one of the few prominent late Jansenist female voices, María Francisca de Sales Portocarrero, the Countess de Montijo (1754–1808). The Countess translated Jansenist and Gallican texts from the French, including a book by the famous historian Claude Fleury (1640–1723) that was the primary subject of Climent's 1769 pastoral. She later became a formidable figure in Spanish Jansenist circles.[125]

Some philo-Jansenists, like Bishop Climent, were uncomfortable with elements of the regalism ascendant in many Catholic lands. Most, however, were happy to ride the waves of anti-ultramontanism and anti-Jesuitism that had become so fashionable in the courts of Catholic rulers. After the death of the conciliatory Benedict XIV in 1758 and election of the intransigent Clement XIII, philo-Jansenists lost what little hope they had left in the papacy as a reforming force. Partly as a consequence of this alienation from Rome, reformers generally saw the best chance for real change in fiercely episcopalist local bishops who operated under the protection of powerful sovereigns.

For their part, Catholic princes were quite happy to take the counsel of those claiming that the pope had no right to interfere in their domains, that the mendicant orders were too often superstitious and wasteful, and that princes answered to none but God in all things that were not "spiritual" (interpreted very strictly), including matters related to the vast property and funds held by the Church. From the German-speaking lands, an auxiliary bishop of Trier named Johann

124. On Spain and Jansenism see Appolis, *Les jansénistes espagnols* (cited phrase on page 8); Joël Saugnieux, *Le Jansénisme Espagnol du XVIII*^{e} *Siècle*; Saugnieux, *Les jansénistes et le renouveau de la prédication dans l'espagne*; Andrea J. Smidt, "*Luces por la fe*"; Charles C. Noel, "Clerics and Crown in Bourbon Spain, 1700–1808"; Maria Giovanna Tomsich, *El Jansenismo en España*; Joaquin Pugivert and Joan Bada, eds., *Bisbes, Illustració, i Jansenisme a la Catalunya del S.XVIII.*

125. See Appolis, *Les jansénistes espagnols*, 85–89; 105–14; 143–53.

Nikolaus von Hontheim (1701–90), writing under the pseudonym "Febronius," published an anti-ultramontane manifesto beloved by Jansenists called *On the State of the Church and the Legitimate Power of the Roman Pontiff* (1763).[126] In Portugal, the Oratorian priest António Pereira de Figueiredo (1725–97) penned a number of works which provided historical and theological support for the regalist regime of King José I (r. 1750–77) and his Machiavellian first minister, the Marquis de Pombal (1699–1782).

It would be a mistake to see late Jansenism as simply a matter of politics and ecclesiology. For example, Pereira was concerned with the education and spiritual nourishment of the people of the Portuguese Empire, leading him to translate the entire Bible into the vernacular (1778–90). The explanatory notes that Pereira provided reveal that an Augustinian or even Jansenist theology of divine grace was central for him. Translated by Bradley Blankemeyer, we provide Pereira's commentary on Paul's Letter to the Romans, chapter five (Text 25), some of which is borrowed directly from Port-Royalist authors.[127]

Sovereigns and their regalist ministers tapped into a century of Jansenist animosity and polemic in their campaigns to destroy the Jesuit Order, a process which began with Portugal in 1759 and was completed by a weakened papacy in 1773. The Jansenists, of course, could not have been happier to help in this enterprise; their ruthlessness was born from long-seething desires for revenge after *Unigenitus* and the destruction of Port-Royal.[128] But anti-Jesuitism was just one prong in the reformist agenda that took shape when the interests of philo-Jansenists, regalists, and some veterans of the earlier, more

126. See *Justini Febronii jurisconsulti de statu Ecclesiae . . .* (Frankfurt, 1763); Ulrich Lehner, *On the Road to Vatican II*, 143–70.

127. On Pereira and Portuguese Jansenism see Evergton Sales Souza, *Jansénisme et réforme de l'Église dans l'Empire portugais*; Sales Souza, "L'incontournable jansénisme"; Cândido dos Santos, *Jansenismo e antijansenismo em Portugal*; dos Santos, *Padre António Pereira de Figueiredo*; dos Santos, "Os jansenistas franceses e os estudos eclesiásticos na época de Pombal"; dos Santos, "António Pereira de Figueiredo, Pombal e a Aufklärung"; Samuel Miller, *Portugal and Rome*.

128. On Jansenism and the suppression of the Jesuits see Van Kley, *Reform Catholicism*; Jeffrey Burson and Jonathan Wright, eds., *The Jesuit Suppression in Global Context*; Van Kley, *The Jansenists and the Expulsion of the Jesuits from France*.

moderate Catholic Enlightenment all coalesced in the latter half of the eighteenth century. The resulting phenomenon, which many scholars call "Reform Catholicism," issued the most striking challenge to the papacy and its supporters since the Protestant Reformation. Riding this momentum, the 1780s saw the high-water mark of the Jansenist offensive, the closest that the "Friends of the Truth" came to achieving lasting institutionalized success.

With the Jesuits defeated and the papacy on its heels, Jansenists had reasons to be optimistic, and not just about the situation in Spain and Portugal. With roots in mid-century Muratorian circles, networks of philo-Jansenist clergy and statesmen had also arisen up and down the Italian peninsula and throughout the Holy Roman Empire. When Maria Theresa died in 1780, her son Joseph II (1741–90) began a decade of sole rule of the Habsburg lands. The energetic and confident Emperor intensified the process of "Josephinism," a program of state centralization and societal reform emanating from the Habsburg capital of Vienna. A major plank of Josephinism's modernizing agenda was a centralized state church animated by anti-Baroque, philo-Jansenist, and anti-ultramontane ideals. While Josephinism in Austria and Reform Catholicism in German-speaking lands were not simply coterminous with Jansenism, these phenomena enjoyed a mutually reinforcing relationship.[129]

A good test case for the cross-pollination between Jansenism and Josephinism is religious toleration. This vexing question came to the fore in a multireligious Empire with a history of violent confessional strife. The Emperor's *Toleranzpatente* of 1781–82—granting liberal measures of toleration to Orthodox, Protestant, and Jewish subjects in his territories—was a momentous program of legislation. The theological and political underpinnings of Imperial policies of toleration were influenced by Jansenists, and Joseph's actions in turn emboldened them, not only in Habsburg territories but around Europe. Needless to

129. Peter Hersche, *Der Spätjansenismus in Österreich*; Harm Klueting, "The Catholic Enlightenment in Austria or the Habsburg Lands"; Michael Printy, "Catholic Enlightenment and Reform Catholicism in the Holy Roman Empire"; Derek Beales, *Joseph II*; Elisabeth Kovács, *Ultramontanismus und Staatskirchentum*; Hans Hollerweger, *Die Reform des Gottesdienstes*.

say, Catholic conservatives were deeply worried, including the pope, who saw religious toleration, especially when conceived of as a positive good, as merely a step on the path to indifference and unbelief.[130]

While most of the best known philo-Jansenists in the German-speaking world were either bishops or academics,[131] perhaps the most prolific figure was an Austrian parish priest, Marx Anton Wittola (1736–97). Through his correspondence with Gabriel Dupac de Bellegarde (1717–89), another tireless advocate on behalf of Utrecht, Wittola became a key player in the Jansenist International. He was a contributor to the *Nouvelles ecclésiastiques* and reprinted some of their material in two periodicals under his editorship. The first was the *Wiener Kirchenzeitung* (1784–89),[132] a weekly paper aimed at the public, which was followed by the *Neueste Beiträge zur Religionslehre und Kirchengeschichte* (1790–92). The latter, published six times a year, was geared toward clergy and aimed at fostering "a Christian Enlightenment."[133] While Wittola's own writings were influential, he was most important as a translator and transmitter of key French and Italian Jansenist texts to the German-speaking world.[134] We include selections from the first of Wittola's four defenses of religious toleration in the 1780s (Text 26), translated by Andreas Oberdorf. Passionately arguing for the toleration of Protestants as a positive political and social good as well as a theological demand of the Christian gospel, Wittola illustrates the congruence between late Jansenism and Josephinism on an issue central to Enlightenment discourse.

130. Charles H. O'Brien, *Ideas of Religious Toleration at the Time of Joseph II.*

131. Peter Hersche, "Jansenistische Sympathien in der deutschen Reichskirche"; Hersche, *Der aufgeklärte Reformkatholizismus in Österreich*; Hersche, "Erzbischof Hieronymus Colloredo und der Jansenismus in Salzburg"; W. R. Ward, "Late Jansenism and the Hapsburgs."

132. Juliette Guilbaud, "Die Wiener Kirchenzeitung im Spiegel der *Nouvelles ecclésiastiques* (1784–1789)." For this and other important recent studies of German-speaking Jansenism see Christoph Schmitt-Maaß, ed., *Der Jansenismus im deutschsprachigen Raum, 1670–1789*. Harm Klueting reviews the German-language scholarship in "Der bekannte Unbekannte," 11–40.

133. See the introduction to the first issue of Wittola's *Neueste Beiträge* (April 30, 1790); O'Brien, *Ideas of Religious Toleration*, 56.

134. Manfred Brandl, *Marx Anton Wittola*; O'Brien, *Ideas of Religious Toleration*; Hersche, *Der Spätjansenismus in Österreich.*

Owing to a similar convergence of theological and political concerns, late Jansenism was flourishing across the Alps, from the Piedmont down to the Kingdom of Naples. Habsburg Lombardy and Tuscany produced particularly important figures. These include Pietro Tamburini (1737–1827), a theologian at the University of Pavia, and Scipione de' Ricci (1741–1810), the ecclesiastical right hand of Peter Leopold, Habsburg Grand Duke of Tuscany. As a young man, Ricci had sat at the feet of the *Archetto* philo-Jansenists in Rome. He had none of the moderation of his teachers. From a noble Florentine family, Ricci was, rather awkwardly, the great-nephew of the last Jesuit Superior General (Lorenzo Ricci), but Scipione loathed the Jesuits as bitterly as any French figurist. Upon his consecration as bishop of the combined Tuscan diocese of Pistoia-Prato, Ricci embarked on an aggressive reform campaign. It appalled ultramontanists and alienated many moderates, but delighted the Jansenist International, who eagerly watched this incubator for regalist-protected Jansenism in the heart of Italy.[135]

Ricci's Synod of Pistoia in September 1786 proved to be the high-water mark of late Jansenism. On the surface, the synod was unexceptional: it was a ten-day diocesan gathering of about 250 clergy in a relatively unimportant Italian city. However, Ricci and his circle of advisors, which included Tamburini, were men of international standing. Additionally, Ricci had much more support among parish priests (the *parochi*) than their detractors ever gave them credit for. The Richerism that had functioned defensively in the French context, as a form of resistance to episcopal "tyranny," was gaining ground in Italy as a positive program of collaboration between (philo-)Jansenist bishops and priests under the protection of anti-ultramontane states. For a brief window of time, a new generation of Italian *parochi* were being trained in Jansenist theology and devotional and liturgical practice, if only in a handful of dioceses.[136]

We include here selections from two decrees of this remarkable and

135. Pietro Stella, *Il giansenismo in Italia*, vol. 3; Stella, "Pietro Tamburini nel quadro del giansenismo italiano"; Bruna Bocchini Camaiani and Marcello Verga, eds., *Lettere di Scipione de' Ricci a Pietro Leopoldo*.

136. Pietro Stella, ed., *Atti e decreti del concilio diocesano di Pistoia dell'anno 1786*, 2 vols.

recklessly provocative synod (Text 27), translated by Shaun Blanchard. These decrees, concerning liturgical and devotional life, sought to concretely instantiate reformist impulses that went back to the origins of the Jansenist tradition and in some cases beyond.[137] The Roman reprisal in the 1794 bull *Auctorem fidei* correctly saw the synod as, fundamentally, an ecclesiological challenge: the eight censures of "heresy" in the pope's bull all targeted ecclesiological propositions. However, the Synod of Pistoia is best known today as a failed attempt to instantiate practices that only widely came to fruition in the wake of the Second Vatican Council (1962–65), including vernacular worship.

The Synod of Pistoia was intended as a dress rehearsal for an anti-ultramontane, synodal, and Jansenist reform of the entire Catholic Church. Friend and foe interpreted it as such, including the increasingly alarmed and bewildered Pius VI (pope from 1775 to 1799). It was a startling challenge to papal authority and popular Catholicism on the eve of the French Revolution. But there was to be some reprieve for the papacy before the storm of the next decade. Though Ricci and his allies were actively promoted and protected by the Grand Duke, about three-fourths of the Tuscan bishops made it clear during an episcopal convocation in Florence in 1787 they would not follow the Pistoian agenda. This decisive meeting, combined with riots in Pistoia and Prato, led to Ricci's resignation and exile. Jansenists could be tolerated if they stuck to abstruse theological debates, but when they threatened local customs and legends, or interfered with devotion to cherished images of the Virgin Mary, they could be met with literal violence. Tuscan rioters colorfully demonstrated this when, fueled by Ricci's ransacked wine cellar, they made bonfires out of the bishop's books and then ripped his episcopal throne out of the cathedral, burning it in the piazza.[138]

The Synod of Pistoia proved to be "the last great manifestation of the Jansenist movement in Europe."[139] The *Acts and Decrees* of the synod, translated into multiple languages, spread quickly throughout the

137. Enrico Bini, "*Mysteria mystice*"; Shaun Blanchard, *The Synod of Pistoia and Vatican II*; Keith F. Pecklers, "The Jansenist Critique," 325–38.

138. Carlo Fantappiè, *Riforme ecclesiastiche e resistenze sociali*; Alessandro Aiardi, ed. *Scipione de' Ricci e la realtà pistoiese*.

139. Peter Hersche, "Die Auswirkungen der Synode von Pistoia," 275.

Catholic world and sparked spirited denunciations and impassioned defenses, as well as curiosity from Protestants.[140] Similar efforts at radical synodal reform were attempted by prelates like Friedrich Karl Joseph von Erthal (1774–1802), Archbishop-Elector of Mainz, and Ricci's friend Giovanni Andrea Serrào (1731–99), bishop of Potenza in the Kingdom of Naples. Both attempts were thwarted, but not by the papacy. The chaos unleashed by the French Revolution quickly swept through the Rhineland, engulfing Mainz, and Serrào was lynched by a counterrevolutionary mob led by Cardinal Fabrizio Ruffo.[141]

Despite the resounding defeat of the Pistoian reforms in Italy, the ideals of the synod found echoes as far afield as Lebanon. Under the leadership of the Archbishop of Aleppo Germanos Adam (1738–1809), Melkite Catholics held a synod in Qarqafé in 1806. Adam had studied in Rome and visited Jansenists in Italy, including Ricci. This enterprising Eastern prelate tried to craft a Melkite Catholicism that combined their native anti-ultramontanism with Jansenist ideals. We include a selection from the acts of Qarqafé, translated from the Arabic by Kevin Blankinship and Mark Spinnenweber, in which a minimalist Jansenist reading on indulgences was promulgated (Text 28).

The final major condemnation of Jansenism came with Pius VI's bull *Auctorem fidei* in 1794, almost eight full years since the Synod of Pistoia convened. The Roman authorities, initially hesitant to condemn a synod championed by a Habsburg prince (who had become Holy Roman Emperor in 1790, but died in 1792), felt they had no choice but to act. Their reasons, however, had more to do with France and Spain than Italy or Austria. By 1794, France was, quite literally, a political and ecclesiastical battlefield, and the pope and his allies believed the theological and political errors of the Jansenists were a major cause of the calamities currently afflicting the "eldest daughter" of the Church. Spain, it was feared, might be next. The philo-Jansenist statesman Gaspar Melchor de Jovellanos (1744–1811) was bragging that the

140. Stella, ed., *Atti e decreti*, 2:111–46; 658–62. Stella, ed., *Il Giansenismo in Italia II/I: La bolla 'Auctorem Fidei.'* For "echoes" of the synod in multiple national contexts, see the many essays in Claudio Lamioni, ed., *Il sinodo di Pistoia del 1786*.

141. See Hersche's discussion in "Die Auswirkungen," 287–94; Blanchard, *Synod of Pistoia*, 216, 230–34; Domenico Forges Davanzati, *Giovanni Andrea Serrao*.

students in Salamanca were "Port-Royalists of the Pistoian variety" and the *Mercurio histórico y politico*, a Madrid periodical, had reported positively on the synod, printing large excerpts from its decrees.[142] The evidence suggests that the rumor of an imminent translation of the Synod of Pistoia into Castilian Spanish convinced the pope to accept the risks of confrontation. In *Auctorem fidei*, Pius VI issued a thunderous and comprehensive condemnation of Jansenism that reasserted traditional ultramontane prerogatives.

But the challenge of the Synod of Pistoia paled in comparison with the ecclesiastical and political chaos unleashed in France beginning in 1789. The relationship between Jansenism and the French Revolution is an intriguing, if complex one. There was, of course, no single Jansenist position on the proceedings of the National Assembly, the Civil Constitution of the Clergy, or the fate of the monarchy, though all Jansenists were appalled at the campaigns of dechristianization and the chimerical Cult of the Supreme Being. The ultramontane allegation that Jansenists were part of a cabal with *philosophes*, Freemasons, and Protestants to bring down throne and altar in France was a groundless conspiracy theory.[143] And yet, one can trace a line from French Jansenist protest against ecclesial "despotism" in the wake of *Unigenitus*, through parliamentary appeals to the original French "constitution" contra royal "despotism" in mid-century, up to the hyper-Gallican rhetoric of the early revolution.[144] Though perhaps only 30 of the 1200 members of the National Assembly were Jansenists in any meaningful sense of the word, it has been persuasively argued that, from a *longue durée* perspective, the Jansenist crisis as a whole helped to lay the groundwork for the Revolution.[145] In the words of Dale Van Kley,

142. Antonio Mestre, "La repercusión del sínodo di Pistoya en España"; Smidt, "*Luces por la fe*," 441–42; Blanchard, *Synod of Pistoia*, 235–37.

143. On the conspiratorial interpretation of the Revolution by ultramontane Catholics, see Glauco Schettini, "The Catholic Counter-Revolution."

144. Choudhury, *Convents and Nuns*, 33–69; Ambrogio Caiani, "The Cesena Popes, Pius VI and Pius VII."

145. Van Kley, *Religious Origins*; Henry Légier-Desgranges, *Du jansénisme à la Révolution*. Tracing a *longue durée* connection is not, in itself, new. See, for example, Préclin, *Les jansénistes du XVIIIe siècle* (1929); Jacques Parguez, *La bulle Unigenitus et le jansénisme politique* (1936).

though not "causing" the events of 1789–1790, Jansenism "conditioned" key elements of it.[146]

For a leading French Jansenist whose career illuminates this claim better than anyone, we return to Louis-Adrien Le Paige. Now nearing eighty and losing his sight, Le Paige's tireless production of pamphlets and treatises united the Jansenist preoccupations of the early decades of the century with the "judicial Jansenism" of the *parlements* that marked later decades. A gnarled veteran in the fight against *Unigenitus*, a proponent of figurism and a lifelong *convulsionnaire*, Le Paige's loyalty to "the Truth" was inseparable from his political agenda. The career and thought of this *éminence grise* of French judicial Jansenism helps us trace a line from the appeal of *Unigenitus* to the Civil Constitution of the Clergy (Text 29).

The rejection of the Civil Constitution by about half of the clergy of France, who became non-juring "refractories" set against "constitutional" priests, presaged and helped lead to the violent divisions that rent the French nation and were in some cases exported to the rest of Europe. Unsurprisingly, the refractory clergy had support in Pope Pius VI, who after some hesitation condemned the Civil Constitution in two briefs in the spring of 1791, excommunicating those who accepted it.[147]

By no means all Jansenists, French or otherwise, supported the Civil Constitution and the extremes to which it subjected church to state.[148] Some of its most ardent opponents came from the rarefied ranks of the ever-more-apocalyptic *convulsionnaires*. Unlike their confrère Le Paige, authors like the Dominican friar Bernard Lambert (1738–1813) and the southern priest François Jacquemont (1757–1835) mixed millenarian complaints with an attack upon the new order.[149] They were inspired by

146. Catherine Maire has criticized Van Kley's thesis. See Maire, "Aux sources politiques et religieuses de la Révolution française." For the language of not "causing" but "conditioning," see Van Kley's response to reviews of his *Reform Catholicism* on the online forum *H-France Review*, vol. 19, no. 233 (November 2019).

147. Gérard Pelletier, *Rome et la Révolution française*.

148. Bernard Plongeron, "Nacimiento de una cristiandad republicana (1789–1801); Plongeron, "Unità tridentina e diversità francese"; Maurice Vaussard, "Les jansénistes italiens et la Constitution civile du clergé"; Yann Fauchois, "Les jansénistes et la constitution civile du clergé."

149. Bernard Lambert, *Avis aux fidèles*; Lambert, *Avertissement aux fidèles*; François Jacquemont, *Instruction sur la vérité*; Jacquemont, *Avis aux fidèles*.

the common convulsionary belief that the Prophet Elijah would soon appear and initiate the end of the world, converting the Jews to the faithful remnant of those who held to the *œuvre des convulsions.* And they watched for the coming of his dark twin, the Antichrist.

In this respect, as in so many, these later *convulsionnaires* were guided by the prophecies of charismatic women. When the convulsionary royalist Claude Desfours de la Genetière (1757–1819) published a collection of prophecies meant to connect the Revolution to the End Times, he drew extensively upon the writings of Angélique Babet (d. 1786). A married woman who had been a prominent player in the *séances* of the 1730s and 1740s, Angélique was drawn into a national network of *convulsionnaires* initiated by the former Oratorian Michel Pinel (1708–75). Returning to the *oeuvre* after a long hiatus in 1772, her visions of Christ, the Divine Wisdom, Mère Angélique Arnauld, François de Pâris, biblical Patriarchs, and other figures soon earned her a high perch in the Pineliste hierarchy. After Pinel died in 1775, Babet became the undisputed spiritual leader of the sect. Through her correspondence, she cultivated numerous disciples across the country, especially in and around Lyon (among them no fewer than six Dominican priests). We present here Richard T. Yoder's translation of one of her visions of the Papal Antichrist, read by Desfours as an anticipation of the Revolution's deceptive, demonic power (Text 30).[150]

Nevertheless, the fact that a number of high-profile Jansenists like Ricci and Clément did defend the Civil Constitution, and on both theological and political grounds, forever solidified the place of Jansenism in the counterrevolutionary and ultramontane "chain of errors" narrative that ran from Protestantism to Jansenism to the *philosophes* to the Revolution, thus terminating in secularization and violent De-Christianization. It would be inaccurate to call the Civil Constitution a "Jansenist" document. Nevertheless, it was a piece of

150. There is a growing and substantial literature on later *convulsionnaire* groups, including the Pinelistes and their successors. See Daniel Vidal, *La Morte-Raison*; Jean-Pierre Chantin, *Les Amis de l'Œuvre de la Vérité*; Yves Krumenacker, *Du Jansénisme à la secte*; Guy Janssen, *La Petite Église en trente questions*; Véronique Alemany, *La dernière Solitaire de Port-Royal*; Serge Maury, *Une secte janséniste convulsionnaire sous la Révolution française*; Rupert M. A. F. Allen, "The Last Sentinels of Gallicanism"; Jean-Pierre Chantin, *La Famille*.

legislation imbued with a Gallicanism that was so radicalized by the twists and turns of the "century of *Unigenitus*" that it cannot be understood apart from the history of French Jansenism.

The Jansenist International, so aggressive and confident in the 1780s, suffered near total shipwreck in the 1790s. At the same time, the papacy was in a desperately weak position. It attempted to assert itself with *Auctorem fidei*, but numerous Catholic governments simply refused to publish the bull in their domains. Things got so bad for the papacy that some speculated that Pius VI, who died in a French jail in 1799, would have no successor. And yet, the window of opportunity that "the Friends of the Truth" had so eagerly seized upon was suddenly closed. The chance for institutionalized philo-Jansenist reform was, ironically, a casualty of the very Revolution for which French Jansenists had helped prepare the way. The Successor of Peter, on the other hand, suddenly found himself once again allied with the great Catholic sovereigns, who now looked on papal Rome as a necessary bulwark against revolutionary chaos rather than as an obstacle to their agendas of reform and modernization.

The Constitutional Church of France, led by prominent *amis de la verité* like Clément and Henri Grégoire (1750–1831), now both bishops, attempted to continue the path of radical synodal reform. Identifying their communion as "the Gallican Church," these excommunicated clergy harkened back to Pistoia and Utrecht in two "national councils" held in 1797 and 1801.[151] Ironically, the anti-ultramontanism that had so endeared radical reformers to princes now became their undoing. Napoleon, a sovereign far more despotic in his treatment of the Church than Joseph II or Peter Leopold ever was, correctly saw that a cooperative pope could lend much more legitimacy to his imperial ambitions than a divisive group of Constitutional bishops.

While Jansenism was far from dead at the dawn of the nineteenth century, it had lost the vital energy of an international reform movement. It would never recover. In the new era of restoration and romanticism, the See of Peter underwent a stunning reversal of fortune. By 1814,

151. Stewart Stehlin, "The French Constitutional Church and Christian Renewal, 1795–1801."

Pope Pius VII was even in a position to resurrect the Jesuits, the oldest and bitterest enemies of "the Truth."

The "Friends of the Truth" were used to idealizing and commemorating the past. As early as 1767, Abbé Jean-Antoine Gazaignes had published a *Manuel des pèlerins de Port-Royal*, which included a Mass and Office for the relics of Port-Royal. We include this liturgy (Text 23) in the original Latin and in an English translation by Richard Yoder. Some prominent nineteenth-century Catholic intellectuals, like the Abbé Grégoire, cultivated nostalgic commemoration of Port-Royal. A selection from his *Les ruines de Port-Royal* (1809), translated by Glauco Schettini, completes our selection of texts (Text 31).

The concordat of 1801 between Pope Pius VII and Napoleon marks the beginning of one of the greatest reversals in all of Catholic history. Eighteenth-century popes had been repeatedly ignored or bullied by the Catholic sovereigns, forced into the humiliating suppression of the Jesuits, then hounded into captivity by the anti-clerical revolutionary armies of the French. Under intense pressure from Napoleon to help repair the breach between Catholics and the French state, Pius VII forced all the bishops (Constitutional and refractory) to resign their Sees in the 1801 brief *Tam multa*. Pius then reappointed some bishops from each batch in order to restore one unified diocesan structure to France, which for all intents and purposes ended the schism. With this stroke of the apostolic pen, Pius VII asserted a level of ecclesiastical control that would have been unfathomable before the Revolution. Indeed, such a bald exercise of papal power would have been difficult to fathom even two years before, when Pius VI was dying in a French jail. In hindsight, however, we can say that Pius VII inaugurated nineteenth-century ultramontanism with a bang, simultaneously signing the delayed death warrant not only of Gallicanism, but of its fellow-traveler, Jansenism.[152]

152. See Ambrogio Caiani, "The Concile National of 1811."

Conclusion: The Death of Jansenism and the Survival of Anti-Jansenism

Our anthology concludes in the early nineteenth century. By the time Grégoire published *Les ruines de Port-Royal*, it was clear that Jansenists had definitively squandered the auspicious circumstances for institutional reform that the late eighteenth century presented. Jansenists would never again see such windows of opportunity. This is easy to see from our vantage point, surveying the rise and indeed triumph of ultramontane and Romantic Catholicism in the nineteenth century.[153] But the story does not end in 1809, with Ricci languishing in exile and Grégoire wistfully eulogizing Port-Royal. The story of Jansenism continues throughout the entire nineteenth century and even into the twentieth. There are two major reasons for this. The first is that Jansenism, despite its failures, had birthed fertile spiritual and intellectual traditions. Reformist Catholics continued to draw on these traditions long after Jansenism ceased to have any institutional power. The second and much more decisive reason is that "Jansenism," real or imagined, became a key antithesis against which the Roman Magisterium defined Catholic orthodoxy.

Jansenist influence on the thought of Catholic clergy and intellectuals was especially apparent at the intersection of politics and ecclesiology. True to the French roots of resistance to royal absolutism and papal despotism, Jansenist thought presented a fertile tradition for nineteenth-century Catholic republicans, liberals, and anti-ultramontane regalists to draw on.[154] Some Catholic clergy and politicians in Spain, Portugal, and Latin America tapped into a Jansenist and Gallican heritage in their attempts to shape a new ecclesial and political *status quo*.[155] In addition to a genuinely theological survival of

153. Carol E. Harrison, *Romantic Catholics*. See also Caroline Ford, *Divided Houses*.

154. Franz Fillafer, 'Il crepuscolo del giansenismo"; Monique Cottret, "Aux origines du républicanisme janséniste"; Dale Van Kley, "From the Catholic Enlightenment to the *Risorgimento*"; Van Kley, "Religion and the Age of 'Patriot' Reform"; Valérie Guittienne-Mürger, *Jansénisme et libéralisme*.

155. Pamela Voekel, *For God and Liberty*; Alberto de la Hera, "El movimento conciliar regalistica en America"; Juan Marichal, "From Pistoia to Cádiz"; Evergton

Jansenism in parts of Italy,[156] there were clear connections between the Jansenist tradition, political liberals, and the unification movement that eventually swept the entire peninsula (*Risorgimento*).[157] Indeed, Count Cavour's slogan "a free church in a free state" was of Jansenist provenance.[158] Some Catholics in the Rhineland and Austria continued to call for church reform in a manner unmistakably marked by the legacy of late Jansenism. These tendencies, however, were often difficult to distinguish from the broader survival of Josephinist and Febronian currents.[159] In France, where the deepest roots lay, the Jansenist legacy also endured as a literary and spiritual tradition even into the twentieth century.[160]

Probably the most important factor in the nineteenth-century survival of Jansenism, however scattered and emaciated it may have been, was that some Catholics seeking a counternarrative to the rising tide of ultramontane orthodoxy inevitably found they had affinities with at least parts of the Jansenist tradition. This fact also largely explains the perduring Roman investment in the rhetoric of anti-Jansenism throughout the nineteenth century and into the twentieth.

From the very beginning, Jansenism was a key link in a "chain of

---

Sales Souza, "Jansénisme et réforme de l'Eglise dans l'Amérique portugaise au xviiie siècle"; David A. Brading, "El jansenismo español y la caída de la monarquía católico en México"; Samuel J. Miller, "Dom Frei Joaquim de Santa Clara (1740–1818) and later Portuguese Jansenism."

156. Stella, *Il Giansenismo in Italia*, vol. 3, esp. 121–75.

157. Carlo Fantappiè, "L'eredità del giansenismo e le radici del 'cattolicesimo liberale' in Italia"; Maurice Vaussard, *Jansénisme et Gallicanisme aux origines religieuses du Risorgimento*; Angelo de Gubernatis, *Eustachio Degola, il clero costituzionale e la conversione della famiglia Manzoni*; Ettore Rota, "Il giansenismo in Lombardia e i prodromi del Risorgimento italiano"; Francesco Ruffini, *I giansenisti piemontesi e la conversione della madre di Cavour*.

158. Francesco Margiotto Broglio, "L'origine giansenista della formula cavouriana 'libera chiesa in libero stato.'"

159. Blanchard, *Synod of Pistoia*, 263. On Josephinism in the nineteenth century see Franz Fillafer, "Habsburg Liberalisms and the Enlightenment Past, 1790–1848." On the survival of Febronianism see Sylvio De Franceschi, "Le spectre turinois d'un renouveau du gallicanisme et du fébronianisme."

160. Alemany, *La dernière Solitaire de Port-Royal*; Bremond, *Histoire littéraire du sentiment religieux en France*; Clark, *Strangers and Sojourners*.

errors" that counterrevolutionary Catholics used to narrate a history leading up to and culminating in the disaster of the French Revolution. This narrative usually began with Luther and Protestantism, who shattered the spiritual and political unity of Christian Europe. Next, the Jansenists acted as a fifth column within Catholicism, undermining the papacy, stabbing the Jesuits in the back, and finally selling out to power-hungry sovereigns who encroached on the rights of the Church. Enlightenment philosophy was the next link in the chain, which culminated in the violence and chaos of the Reign of Terror and dechristianization.[161]

The old "paladins of anti-Jansenism," many of them ex-Jesuits with very personal skin in the game, pushed this narrative of church history.[162] They were not just interested in bemoaning or apportioning blame for the past. Enterprising counterrevolutionary Catholics, like Mauro Cappellari (1765–1846), were hard at work constructing a future for Catholicism that was firmly ultramontane and anti-Jansenist. When Cappellari was elected Pope Gregory XVI in 1832, he was able to advance this agenda from the Chair of Peter.[163]

Even though the Synod of Pistoia (1786) was a distant memory, the Bull *Auctorem fidei* proved an incredibly useful and multifaceted weapon in the nineteenth-century struggle for ultramontane hegemony.[164] It was in fact the mid-1850s, half a century after its promulgation, that marked "the apogee of the diffusion of the bull."[165] More comprehensive even than *Unigenitus*, *Auctorem fidei* condemned an entire program of Jansenist reform—from liturgical and devotional

161. Schettini, "The Catholic Counter-Revolution"; Darrin M. McMahon, *Enemies of the Enlightenment*; Alessandro Guerra, *"Contro lo spirito del secolo": Giovanni Marchetti e la biblioteca della Controrivoluzione*.

162. Stella, *Atti e decreti*, 2:180.

163. Giuseppe Alberigo, *Lo sviluppo della dottrina sui poteri nella Chiesa universale*; Yves Congar, "L'ecclésiologie, de la Révolution française au Concile du Vatican"; Sylvio De Franceschi, "Les problématiques ecclésiologiques françaises au prisme des lectures italiennes."

164. For an excellent *longue durée* treatment see Jean-Baptiste Amadieu and Simon Icard, eds., *Du jansénisme au modernisme*.

165. Rémy Hême de Lacotte, "De la polémique anti-gallicane à l'affirmation d'un catholicisme intransigeant," 199.

proscriptions to marriage law to even moderate conciliarist ecclesiology.[166] Thus *Auctorem fidei* functioned as a "doctrinal Swiss army knife" in the hands of the papacy.[167] Nineteenth-century popes evoked the specter of Jansenism to condemn insufficiently ultramontane Eastern Catholics, Germans who called for the abolition of mandatory clerical celibacy, cooperation with Bible societies, so-called "Americanist" desires to amend church discipline, and opposition to the Sacred Heart devotion.[168] Seven of the eighty propositions censured in Pius IX's *Syllabus of Errors* (1864) depend upon that pope's 1851 condemnation of the Peruvian politician Francisco González Vigil as a Jansenist.[169]

The term "Jansenist," always an insult flung too indiscriminately, came to function as an even more inexact slur in the nineteenth century. For example, the efforts of Bishop Félix Torres Amat (1772–1849) to translate the entire Bible into Spanish earned him opposition from the Inquisition and accusations of Jansenism.[170] In England, figures as impeccably orthodox as John Lingard (1771–1851) were slandered as Jansenists for their critical historical research and opposition to papal and Marian maximalism.[171]

As the nineteenth century wore on, Catholic clergy more and more deeply imbibed an ultramontane worldview, with anti-Jansenism as a constituent ingredient. It was taught by orthodox historians like Réné-François Rohrbacher (1789–1856) and theologians like Giovanni Perrone (1794–1876). Perrone's student Heinrich Denzinger (1819–83) helped diffuse this ultramontane narrative through his doctrinal sourcebook. By the First Vatican Council (1869–70), even moderate adherents of conciliarism were doctrinally suspect. Ultramontanes like Cardinal Antonio Saverio De Luca (1805–83) found the Gallican minority guilty by association: he aligned them with "the Jansenist

166. Stella, *Il Giansenismo in Italia II/I: La Bolla* Auctorem fidei; Phillippe Boutry, "Autour d'un bicentenaire."

167. Blanchard, *Synod of Pistoia*, 264.

168. Blanchard, *Synod of Pistoia*, 261–70.

169. See Denzinger-Hünermann, 2915, 2921, 2923, 2930, 2951, 2954, and 2968; all cite the Apostolic Letter *Multiplices Inter* of 1851 (not to be confused with Pius IX's more famous *Inter Multiplices* of 1853, abolishing the Gallican liturgies).

170. Appolis, *Le 'tiers parti'*, 555–70.

171. Shaun Blanchard, "John Lingard's Dislike of Newman."

school" in "violat[ing] the ordinary and immediate power of the Roman Pontiff."[172] A group of fourteen bishops, led by Cardinal Giuseppe Trevisanato of Venice, even wanted the council to avoid an image as orthodox and indeed biblical as the Mystical Body of Christ, since it was associated with Jansenist ecclesiology.[173] The framers of the Dogmatic Constitution *Pastor aeternus*, which defined the pope's infallibility and jurisdictional supremacy, specifically targeted the work of Pietro Tamburini, chief theologian of the Synod of Pistoia.[174] Further highlighting the link between papal infallibility and anti-Jansenism, some held up *Unigenitus* and *Auctorem fidei* as good templates for how the dogma could concretely function.[175]

Had any Jansenists been living when Pope Pius X christened Modernism "the synthesis of all heresies" in the 1907 encyclical *Pascendi Dominici Gregis* (§39), they might have been relieved to see their torch pass to a new catch-all term for heterodoxy. Jansenism is only evoked once in *Pascendi*. In article 24, Pius X stated that "the principles from which [Modernist] doctrines spring" regarding church and state were "solemnly condemned" in *Auctorem fidei*. This single evocation is, however, a revealing one. The enduring crime of Jansenism—what made it a forerunner of the "synthesis of all heresies"—was ecclesiological error. The reason for the Roman Magisterium's constant references to Jansenism, even more than a century after the "Friends of the Truth" lost the ability to muster institutional power of any kind, was the symbolic power of a Catholic counternarrative to ultramontanism.

At the popular level, the legacy of Jansenism endured for different reasons. "Jansenism" became a synonym for rigorism, joylessness, and severity in religion. A powerful and persistent myth arose in the English-speaking world; one version of the story had Irish priests embracing Jansenism during their seminary studies in France and Leuven (foreign education being necessitated by anti-Catholic penal laws). The Irish then spread this spiritual disease back to the home

172. *Mansi* 49:573–55, at 574.

173. *Mansi* 51:760–62. See the comments of Yves Congar in "L'ecclésiologie, de la Révolution française," 108 and n99.

174. Shaun Blanchard, "Settling Old Scores."

175. Blanchard, *Synod of Pistoia*, 267–68.

country. "Irish Jansenism" was in turn exported to Québec, Australia, and the United States. Anyone who has spent enough time in Irish or American parishes has heard versions of this myth. Curiously, Jansenism is here linked with pre-Vatican II Catholicism, even though priests throughout the English-speaking world (and beyond) were educated in uniformly anti-Jansenist seminary environments. Jansenist works littered the Index of Prohibited Books before the Council, while the ecclesiology of Bellarmine and the explicitly anti-Jansenist moral theology of Liguori was in favor.[176] Indeed, Pietro Stella's exhaustive research has found that not a single manual of moral theology, dogmatics, canon law, or liturgy published between 1850 and 1950 failed to reference *Auctorem fidei*.[177] The Irish Catholicism epitomized by the indomitable Cardinal Paul Cullen (1803–78), whatever else it was, had the most sterling ultramontane and anti-Jansenist credentials.[178] This myth of "Irish Jansenism" has shown no signs of abating, and has merged, awkwardly and heterogeneously, with a kind of black legend regarding pre-Vatican II Catholicism.

As the Liturgical Movement gathered steam in the twentieth century, at times with papal encouragement, it was inevitable that the memory of failed Jansenist reforms would be revived. In Pius XII's landmark encyclical *Mediator Dei* (1947), he contrasted organic liturgical renewal with the "exaggerated and senseless antiquarianism" that he attributed to Jansenists like the Pistoians. While negative papal evocations of Jansenism were commonplace, it was not often that popes worried that their own reform agenda could be in any way confused with or mistaken for Jansenism. The liturgical reforms that were eventually instantiated at and after the Second Vatican Council (1962–65) were indeed remarkably similar to reforms that Jansenists had long clamored for: increased use of the vernacular, an audible canon, only one altar in each church, an emphasis on the (baptismal) priesthood of all believers, a Christocentric pruning of devotional life, etc.

The first drafts of numerous Vatican II documents cited *Auctorem*

176. On Liguori and Jansenism, see Frederick M. Jones, *Alphonsus de Liguori*, 266–69, 280–82, 291–95.

177. Stella, *Il Giansenismo in Italia II/I: La bolla*, v.

178. O'Malley, *Vatican I*, 202–3.

fidei to establish a number of doctrinal points. These drafts were all produced before the majority bloc, led by reformist *ressourcement* theologians like Yves Congar and Joseph Ratzinger, seized the momentum of the Council. After that, evocations of Jansenism were generally made by the Council "minority," who were fighting a rear-guard action. The most important of these evocations concerned ecclesiology, and particularly the highly contested doctrine of "collegiality," that is, the co-rule of the universal church by bishops with and under the pope. The Vatican II majority generally saw collegiality as a return to a more biblical concept of church government, supported by patristic texts and practice. The minority feared collegiality was really a conciliarist Trojan Horse. In a tense episode, Luigi Carli, the Bishop of Segni, strongly implied that the council fathers pushing for collegiality were in violation of the Bull *Auctorem fidei*. A number of fathers of the majority pushed back, arguing that their understanding of the *de iure* rights and duties of bishops was not anti-papal.

Rather ironically for an ecumenical council held in Rome and presided over by the papacy, Vatican II instantiated a number of reforms that Jansenists had called for centuries before. These include an emphasis on reading and listening to the word of God (*Dei Verbum*), a renewed theology of the laity and the episcopate in *Lumen gentium*, and a commitment to civil religious liberty while affirming the uniqueness of Christian revelation. Mainstream postconciliar liturgical reform bears remarkable similarity to the liturgical principles promoted by Jansenists from Port-Royal to Pistoia, a fact that Traditionalist opponents of Vatican II have been eager to point out.[179]

Nor was the memory of Jansenists limited to the ecclesiastical. Particularly in France, they have left a multifaceted cultural legacy. Starting with the monumental study undertaken by the literary critic Charles Augustin Sainte-Beuve (1804–69), Port-Royal has cast its austere light upon French letters.[180] A Pascalian influence is particularly notable among some of the luminaries of the French Catholic revival of the early twentieth century, such as François Mauriac (1885–1970),

179. See Blanchard, *Synod of Pistoia*.

180. Sainte-Beuve, *Port-Royal*.

Julien Green (1900–98), and Simone Weil (1909–43).[181] Henri de Montherlant captured the drama of the Formulary Controversy in his 1954 stage play *Port-Royal*. Lissa McCullough goes so far as to claim that the climate of French intellectual life in this period was characterized by "a pervasive residual Jansenism."[182]

The Jansenists also found a surprising modern reception among decadents and surrealists. The Catholic novelist Joris-Karl Huysmans (1848–1947) discusses the *convulsionnaires* in his novel of modern Satanism, *Là-bas* (1891).[183] Likewise, André Breton (1896–1966) was fascinated by the *convulsionnaires*, visited their haunts, collected historical materials relating to their practices, and mentioned them in his long poem "Pleine Marge."[184] In Luis Buñuel's (1900–83) satirical film *La Voie lactée* (1969), nuns wearing the habits of Port-Royal process into a chapel, where, like the *convulsionnaires*, they proceed to crucify one of their sisters. Outside, two men in eighteenth-century garb start to duel. One is a Jansenist nobleman, and the other a Jesuit priest. As they fight, they argue about grace and free will. But Buñuel's satire suggests the ultimate futility of their theological squabble; they walk off together, seemingly at peace.[185]

In reality, however, there was no truce. The Jansenists lost the battle. There is value in examining the losers of history, and in hearing their side of the story, especially since the Jansenists became particularly influential losers. But the question remains—why, ultimately, did they lose? After all, there were powerful people in Port-Royal's circle. There was never any shortage of sophisticated apologetic literature setting forth the case of strict Augustinianism. And up to the Revolution, Jansenists in the legal profession did what they could to protect themselves under the aegis of constitutionalism. But it is not enough to say that Port-Royal alienated king, cardinal, and pope, nor can we be satisfied with the simple fact that the Jansenists, their allies, and their

181. Jean-François Durand, ed., *Pascal-Mauriac*; Éric Pépino, *Julien Green au miroir du Grand Siècle*; Lissa McCullough, *The Religious Philosophy of Simone Weil*, 218–20.

182. McCullough, *The Religious Philosophy*, 220.

183. Joris-Karl Huysmans, *Là-bas*, 402–3.

184. Tessel M. Baudin, *Surrealism and the Occult*, 164; Maury, *Une secte janséniste*, 14.

185. *La Voie lactée*, directed by Luis Buñuel, 50:05–59:42.

later sympathizers were often poor political strategists. That much is all true, and the Jansenist tendency to wait for God to intervene and right the "disorders" of the Church (taken *ab absurdum* in the case of the *convulsionnaires*) was a palpable handicap for their cause.

Outside of France, Jansenist elites often struggled to appeal to ordinary people, and sometimes earned their hostility. While Jansenist bishops like Ricci in Tuscany and Serrào in Naples could boast of a network of cultured admirers around Europe, diocesan flocks generally saw such bishops as at best out-of-touch and at worst actively threatening the faith of their fathers. Ricci could print whatever books he wanted, but when his attempts to "purify" Tuscan devotion threatened the relic of the Virgin Mary's belt—the prized possession of the city of Prato—the people's patience was at an end. While Ricci escaped with his life from the torches and pitchforks of the mob, Serrào was not so lucky, butchered in his bed for his religious and political (pro-French) sins.[186] Even sovereigns could impose reform only to a certain point when the people in the pews remained unconvinced or disgruntled. While all of this late eighteenth-century unrest was causally complex, anti-Jansenist resentment was one ingredient in the rebellion against Joseph II in the Austrian Netherlands and the rioting in the Electorate of Mainz.[187] Idealistic Jansenist evangelizers fared no better. The charismatic Genoese priest Eustachio Degola (1761–1826) could captivate a learned audience, but his team of "patriotic" missionaries armed with Degola's new catechism gained few converts as they travelled around Liguria preaching republicanism and Jansenist reform. Counterrevolutionary mobs rioted there too, eagerly egged on by ultramontane clergy.[188]

But beyond politics, perhaps the deeper spiritual reason for the Jansenists' defeat is that their vision of the Christian life made success impossible. For the vast majority of people, it was unlivable. A bit like the Spiritual Franciscans, Jansenists stood for some of the most

186. Davanzati, *Giovanni Andrea Serrao*.

187. T. C. W. Blanning, *Reform and Revolution in Mainz*.

188. Caissiano da Langasco, "Un esperimento di politica giansenista?"; Van Kley, "Religion and the Age of 'Patriot' Reform," 281–82. On Degola see also Grazia Grasso, "La plus forte réaction italienne à la bulle *Auctorem Fidei*."

radical, otherworldly, and inconvenient bits of the Gospel. When they read in St. James's epistle that "Whosoever therefore will be a friend of this world, becometh an enemy of God" (James 4:4), they listened. And when a Jansenist said, with St. Paul, that "the world is crucified to me, and I to the world" (Galatians 6:14), she meant every word. For the disciple of Port-Royal, you really *do* have to remove yourself from entanglements with the "world" in order to find safe passage to heaven. If that means leaving a promising career to do penance in the country, so be it. If that means keeping yourself from an advantageous marriage, so be it. If that means enduring imprisonment to preserve your conscience, so be it. Anything less is a terrible gamble. Let the Jesuits give false comfort to those who, like the rich man in the parable, "feast sumptuously every day" (Luke 16:19–31); Port-Royal chose the part of Lazarus, dying at the gate. That was simply the price of the Gospel.

Nor was this merely a question of outward loss and divestment. For the Jansenist, you really *do* have to love God "with thy whole heart, and with thy whole soul, and with thy whole mind" (Matthew 22:37). Love of God is not optional. It cannot be watered down. Anything other than this sincere and totalizing charity was unworthy of the Christian life. Any servile superstition, or any cowardice before the unrighteous, was little better than an infantilizing idol erected in love's place. Any apparent virtue without love was nothing more than the soul's whitewashed tomb. And that supernatural charity could not be obtained without God's grace moving efficaciously, secretly, and irresistibly in the souls of His chosen few. The collection of these rarefied, reformist tendencies, shaped by decades of persecution and commemoration, eventually became the transnational tradition of Jansenist Catholicism.

Put another way, Jansenism was an elite movement *by design.*[189] Anyone could be part of that elite—in fact, the poor and the lowly were more likely to be among God's favored remnant than the rich and learned. Hence Jansenism's socially egalitarian tendency, which grew more pronounced over the course of the centuries. Perhaps if Saint-Cyran's followers had moderated the severity of his message, they

189. Leszek Kołakowski has made a similar argument. See Kołakowski, *God Owes Us Nothing.*

might have begun a French Catholic version of Methodism.[190] But that did not happen. It was instead the Jesuits who taught a Christianity within the grasp of all, a humanistic, emotional, and accommodating vision of faith that was already spreading Catholicism across five continents.

Making no compromise with the weakness of human nature, condemning the world for hating God, convinced of the powerful purity of the Gospel, the "Disciples of Saint Augustine" accepted their fate as a small ark in a great sea of the damned. Theirs was a very hidden God, and they have followed him into silence and obscurity. It is our hope that this anthology will help more people discover their forgotten voices.

190. Indeed, John Wesley was a tremendous admirer of Quesnel, in spite of his Arminian theology. He was horrified by "that diabolical Bull *Unigenitus*, which destroys the very foundations of Christianity" (Wesley, quoted in Clark, *Strangers and Sojourners*, 257).

Section One
The Disciples of Saint Augustine, c. 1630–1679

1. Cornelius Jansen on Theology and Philosophy

Cornelius Jansen

Translated by Guido Stucco[1]

Cornelius Otto Jansen (1585–1638), also known as Jansenius, Bishop of Ypres, never had any intention of lending his name to a movement that would define the internal struggles of Catholicism for the next hundred and fifty years. Gaunt and erudite, ever the professor at heart after years on the University of Leuven's Faculty of Divinity, Jansen saw himself above all as a Catholic reformer. He and his good friend the Abbé de Saint-Cyran (1581–1643) shared a desire to restore the Church to her primitive purity. Jansen sought to do this by vindicating the soteriology of Saint Augustine, snatching it away from both the Protestants who had, he believed, usurped the Doctor of Grace's authority to justify their errors, as well as the Jesuits, who had abandoned it entirely in favor of a more optimistic Molinism. In pursuing the research for this grand project, he allegedly read the whole of Saint Augustine's *oeuvre* ten times, and the anti-Pelagian works thirty times.

When he died in 1638, Jansen left behind the manuscript that would

1. Cornelius Jansen, *Augustinus seu doctrina S. Augustini de humanae naturae sanitate, ægritudine, medicinâ adversus Pelagianos & Massilienses*, vol. 2 (Leuven: Jacobus Zeger, 1640), columns 1–70. The following five chapters are a selection from Jansen's *Liber proemialis* (consisting of thirty chapters) in the second volume of his monumental *Augustinus* (consisting of three volumes).

define his legacy. Published in 1640 as *Augustinus*, it sparked an immediate firestorm, especially in France. After years of polemics between Jansen's supporters and his critics—above all, the Jesuits, who coined the pejorative term "Jansenism" to evoke the heresy of Calvinism—five hyper-Augustinian propositions allegedly extracted from Jansen's book were condemned by Pope Innocent X in the 1653 Bull *Cum Occasione*. Yet this did not quell the controversy; if anything, it only poured fuel on the flames. Some of Jansen's sympathizers, such as Antoine Arnauld (1612–94), suggested that while the Pope had the power to teach on questions of right doctrine (*droit*), he did not have the authority to bind the conscience on questions of fact (*fait*). This distinction raised the question of whether Jansen actually taught the five propositions, or if he did, if he meant them in a heretical sense. Yet some Jansenists, such as Jacqueline Pascal (1625–61), one of the intellectual nuns of Port-Royal, simply refused to condemn a book they had not read by a bishop they regarded as holy. This affair, known as the "Formulary Controversy" after Alexander VII's formula of assent to the condemnation, proved to be only the opening stage of what would become a much greater tempest in early modern Catholicism.

This selection from the *Augustinus* lays out several themes that would become foundational to Jansenist thought: the importance of St. Augustine's doctrines of grace, criticism of pagan philosophy and pagan virtue, and a theological epistemology that centers on the operation of divine love in the heart. For Jansen, there is a stark difference between the knowledge obtained by philosophy, which belongs to sinful human nature, and the insights of supernatural charity, which is only ever granted by grace to the faithful, and which comes from divine revelation. A deep pessimism about the capacity of unaided human reason undergirds an almost mystical view of theology itself.[2]

Richard T. Yoder

2. The editors and translator would like to thank Frank Lacopo for his help in reviewing this translation.

Augustinus, Volume II.

Prefatory book concerning the use of reason and authority in theological matters. In this book the limitations of human reason in theological matters are investigated and the authority of St. Augustine in expounding the mystery of predestination and grace is made known.

Chapter I

The truth of the grace of Christ must be held dear by all Christians as their life and salvation.

Among the wonders of divine wisdom that the great, most beautiful, and most admirable theater of this world has taught us, is the fact that such wisdom has endowed all kinds of living beings with various types of instincts and temperaments; some of them are very mild and others most fierce; some of them are ready to pounce on their prey, while others are very vigorous in their self-preservation. Regardless of their differences, all animals have this inner instinct to defend themselves in any way they can, at least with their voice or wailing, every time their lives or well-being are in danger: they do so by running on rough ground and through fire; or by using their claws, beaks, or paws or even by resorting to overwhelming strength. Thus, a small dog is not intimidated by a lion, and deer or rabbits are not mindful of their lives when facing the danger posed by furious dogs. Therefore, if such small, worthless creatures move and fight with such great impetus that no external force, by rushing in from the outside, can break this bond with which they are tightly bound to their mortal limbs, then what solicitude, impetus, tension of mind and soul, moaning, wailing, and shedding of tears should real Christians display whenever their lives are in danger! I am not talking about the wretched and mortal biological life they share with other living beings in this filthy prison we call Life: I am referring to that life through which they are freed from all types of suffering of this world and from death itself, in order to be able to finally attain a new happy existence in a most blessed eternity! This type of life is known by all those who are familiar with the Catholic doctrine, which teaches us in a very useful way that just as the body's life consists in the soul, in the same way the "soul's life" is God himself, and that this God, in order to make us partakers of this life of His forevermore, through the grace of the New Testament (a grace that has the name of Jesus, or the Savior) has come in to this world and was put to death on a cross for the sake of sinners. Speaking from the perspective of this faith, the apostle Paul forcefully proclaimed about himself: "By the grace of God, I am what I am";[3] and about others: "By grace you are saved through faith";[4] and about everybody: "But the grace of God, life everlasting, in Christ Jesus our Lord."[5] Unfortunately, there are times when this life risks being taken away from the faith of believers, a faith through which they attain salvation in this world. It was for the sake of this life that our Lord Jesus Christ, through his great grace "of God is made unto us wisdom, and justice, and sanctification, and redemption,"[6] and through which grace he lives now in our hearts and is destined to live in eternal beatitude. Therefore, when this life through which they are saved in this world is taken away from the faith of believers, what is more congruous to the natural disposition of all things and to the laws of God's holy love than the fact that anything that Christian piety has offered to redeemed people in the form of participation of the soul and its powers in this gratuitous life now acts in unison as if it was threatened by an incumbent death, just as danger itself awakens people from their slumber and strengthens them in their weakness?

For quite some time certain people have tried in various ways to destroy this life and to deprive Christians of it. I am talking about those who have attempted to replace their Redeemer with a ghost, or a mere man, or a confused mixture of man and God, through whose work human nature allegedly would be able to attain salvation, which was lost with death, and redemption, which was lost with ensuing damnation. However, no one has ever conspired in a more nefarious way to their

3. 1 Cor 15:10. Translator's Note: All biblical quotations in this translation are from the Douay-Rheims 1899 American Edition (DRA). Scripture citations appear in the margins of the original document.

4. Eph 2:8.

5. Rom 6:23.

6. 1 Cor 1:30.

own detriment than those who have attributed to lost and damned human beings so much power as to believe in the strength of their free will as if it was God himself, or think human beings are able to renounce evil and do good without God intending this or bringing it about through his grace. These people have endeavored to uproot from the faith and hearts of Christians the very cause why the Son of God descended from heaven, and to even abrogate Jesus' title of Savior, and thus to cut off from their roots the last threads of divine grace through which we live now and will live forever in the afterlife. Having thus disposed of the necessity or the truth of the heavenly help by means of those supposedly great powers of human nature that are thought to be sufficient for people to regulate their behavior and to operate what is good (without God intervening to enable and will any of this), we may as well conclude that Jesus surely died for nothing; that He is called "Savior" for no particular reason, and that He offered us His help and grace in vain; and that, once the foundation of the Christian faith is thus removed, He came to save sinners in this world or give life to the "dead" for no apparent reason. In conclusion: there is no real reason due to which we need to be submitted to His name or take pride in the need to be Christians. It is the Pelagians, or at least all those who once upon a time and even now have developed such teachings, who, as they exaggerate in upholding the powers of human freedom, either consciously promote feelings that are opposed to the Christian faith, or for lack of prudence are driven to them. These people, "by defending or rather by extolling free will in order to promote sacrilegious pride, leave no room for God's grace, in virtue of which we are Christians."[7] And further on, "They uphold these evil views by which they endeavor to subvert the foundations of the Christian faith."[8] The Fathers of the Council of Milevis used a similar expression when they said that "they strive to completely destroy everything that makes

7. Translator's Note: Augustine, *Letters* 175, 2. Translation of quotations from Augustine, unless otherwise noted, are my own. This letter, written by the Fathers present at the Council of Carthage (416 AD), informed Pope Innocent of the errors of Pelagius and Caelestius, exhorting him to condemn them. I used the critical edition of Augustine's letters at https://www.augustinus.it/latino/lettere/index2.htm.

8. Translator's Note: Augustine, *Letters* 175, 6.

us Christians."[9] Augustine himself added: "They strive to subvert the foundations of the entire Christian faith."[10] In fact, our faith is called "Christian" after Jesus Christ. If indeed the need for grace is abolished, through which Jesus became Christ for our sake, and if He is not necessary for human beings, He came in vain; in vain, too, people become Christians, according to Augustine's view about the authors of such doctrines: "They claim that human nature is free in order not to seek the Liberator; they claim that it is already saved in order to regard the Savior as superfluous."[11] Augustine says that in this case people can be called Christians "only in a nominal sense." Truly, the more these views are frightening and the more dangerously they aim at the life that is in Christ and divine grace as well, the more faithfully and courageously all true Christians must fight in defense of the truth of this saving and vivifying grace. We must indeed do so in order not to be satisfied at the mere mention of Jesus' name and, by extolling the natural powers of human nature, end up tacitly allowing the elimination of the need of saving grace (and more specifically, of Jesus our Savior) and tolerate the presence of dangers to our eternal life with less solicitude than we display when we fight against wild beasts in order to protect our transient and ephemeral material possessions.

Chapter II

The reason for writing about this labyrinth of questions that are raised concerning grace.

I have mentioned these things so that no one may marvel or blame me for reaching the conclusion that after such protracted and fierce disputes conducted by so many people concerning the medicinal grace

9. Translator's Note: Augustine, *Letters* 176, 3. This letter was written by the Fathers present at the Council of Milevis (416 AD), informing Pope Innocent of the errors of Pelagius and Caelestius, but unlike the recommendation of the Fathers present at Carthage, they asked the Pope to exhort these two heretics to be reconciled to the faith.

10. Translator's Note: Augustine, *Letters* 178, 2. Augustine wrote this letter to his fellow bishop Hilary to inform him of the decisions of the two African councils.

11. Translator's Note: Augustine, *Letters* 177, 1. In this letter, Aurelius, Augustine, and other bishops warned Pope Innocent about the hypocritical way Pelagius upheld grace at the Synod of Diospolis (415).

of our Savior, we still need to fuss about or to add something more on this issue. Without a doubt, there are two reasons that have led me to engage in this work: truth and love for people. In virtue of being a Christian and having been introduced to the mysteries of Jesus the Savior, I acknowledge in my own faith and in the prayers of the Church the value and necessity of salvific grace, and carry it inscribed in my heart. Because of that, in the midst of so many views that are opposed to each other in an absolute manner, I came to the conclusion that nothing should be dearer to me than being able to penetrate even with my intellect, if that was indeed possible, the purest truth of the One in whom we live by faith. Having begun this process with God's illumination, I resolved to make it manifest even with my soul, writings, and own voice. I did this so that, being casually carried away by views not congruous enough with our faith, I may not undermine that life which I seem to profess in my faith, by perceiving it in an erroneous manner or by departing from it. Everyone can see how fruitful their work has been for the Christian community, in the case of those who were able to understand this with God's help; those who were not able to, can see how justifiable their efforts have been in regard to the life of grace, the foundation of humility, the beginning of salvation, the truth of Christian life, the essence of the name of Christ Jesus, and the true glory of the Crucified One who atoned for our sins.

That unresolvable controversy between very learned men who are constantly debating each other did not dissuade me from investigating with all sincerity the purity of divine grace: on the contrary, this grace offered me an even more intense stimulus thanks to the author of said grace, as I hope is the case. Therefore, I began to realize how much importance this controversy really had, as it squared off against each other with such great animosity all the theological schools of the Christian world, and even eliciting the attention of the Church's tribunal.[12] Moreover, I came to realize what a great benefit the discovery

12. Translator's Note: Jansen is probably referring to the *Congregatio de auxiliis*, established in 1597 by Pope Clement VIII, which for eight years heard arguments set forth by Dominicans and Jesuits concerning grace, free will, and predestination. The Congregation was dismissed in 1606 by Pope Paul V, who refused to adjudicate on the controversy.

of that truth was, since the light that it shed scattered the darkness of so many controversies and soothed with the peace stemming from a much-wished-for reconciliation the minds of people who had become distracted by more burdensome studies.

However, there was something that caused me to be restless and perplexed, when as a young man I was studying Theology at Leuven, at the College of Pope Hadrian VI. These feelings affected me even later on in life, when in the course of my studies I traveled through France, which enjoyed an abundance of scholars who were great experts of antiquity. I greatly wondered how it could have happened that those mysteries of grace (mysteries that even in the opinion of learned men had been expounded with great clarity), which at one time had been transmitted with unwavering certainty and confidence by St. Augustine and his disciples and eventually by the Roman Church herself, the mother and teacher of all, had by now become hidden and engulfed and oppressed by a great darkness. As a result, such mysteries eluded countless learned scholars, who are zealous and intelligent people and who are used to passionately debating each other in order to attain the truth. Without a doubt, I came to the conclusion that the reason for such a situation had to be either one of the following: either such issues could not possibly be discovered and probed by the human mind, or there was a methodological error compromising the quest for truth. I thought the first option was totally incredible, due to the fact that it seemed really foolish to believe that those great teachers of the ancient Church, who were celebrated for the renown of their teachings, wasted their minds in the pursuit of things that could not possibly be investigated, or that they buried truth that had been uncovered in Democritus's "well"[13] at such great depth that it could not be recovered or exposed to the light again. Neither of these two hypotheses could reasonably be thought or upheld, when it came to such great men, without incurring remarkable imprudence and absurdity. Thus, the only other viable option was to conclude that for some reason modern scholars do not have a valid

13. Translator's Note: One of the sayings attributed to Democritus by Diogenes Laertius in his *Lives and Opinions of Eminent Philosophers* (IX, 72) was: "Of truth we know nothing, for truth is in a well."

method to seek this truth with, which is capable to lead them to the dwelling place of what is and remains mysterious.[14]

Chapter III

The discovery of the truth concerning divine grace and the difficulty for the Scholastics to reach an agreement, as they disagree with each other because of Philosophy. The problems that ensue from this situation.

On account of this, I began to pay more diligent attention to find out in what way most people were hard pressed to reach a decision concerning these difficult controversies and then to transmit it to others. Unless I am mistaken, I realized that most people who teach from universities' lecterns and attempt to explain the difficulties pertaining to Theology have first trained for several years in the practice of Philosophy and were not considered to be fit to teach controversial theology unless they first spent considerable time engaging in dialectical and metaphysical speculations. Even though this approach may serve a good purpose, namely exercises in these difficulties and the sharpening of one's mind, nonetheless we know from experience that when people spend the most effective part of their youth studying such matters they will hardly find any time to meditate upon and penetrate the authentic principles of real Theology. Thus, whenever they are at a loss as to what to think and say about the most serious and arcane issues, they do not care, as they should instead, to inquire what the authority of Sacred Scriptures or the venerable authority of the Church Fathers have to say; rather, they immediately seek the aid of Philosophy, which they regard as an arsenal for every solution, and use its rules to inquire about the value of the deepest mysteries. In fact, what else, I wonder, has generated those propositions if not Philosophy, which accommodated divine grace to the tyrannical commands of human freedom? What has so valiantly defended them if not Philosophy, which does not seem to

14. Editor's Note: Jansen here implicitly criticizes the scholastic method, which he eschewed in favor of a more historical positive theology. The move away from philosophical scholasticism toward positive theology, characteristic of Leuven, was yet another way that Jansen and his later disciples clashed with Jesuits, whose *Ratio Studiorum* gave pride of place to Aristotle.

admit any other kind of freedom than that which is dominated with absolute and indifferent power by all things that are either admitted by or rising against the will? What has produced good works to be obtained through the mere qualities of one's character, if not Philosophy, according to which the faculty of the will, informed by the habit of virtue, is regarded as the sufficient principle of a perfect action? What has originated, prepared, and constructed the state of pure nature if not Aristotle's philosophy, which even some pagans endowed with greater common sense have condemned? What has shown the real virtues of pagans and of damned human beings, who still produced some good works, if not pagan Philosophy? What has discovered natural faith, hope, and love for God above all things, despite the Sacred Scriptures' and their authors' silence about them, if not the most pure Philosophy? What has differentiated the various types of graces, a diversification that was completely unknown in ancient times, and what has eliminated God's pre-definitions, and the true and gratuitous predestination of created actions, if not Philosophy? People who are very well versed in Aristotelian disciplines debate in a confident and magisterial fashion about these theological issues, which for the most part are very arcane. Consider that in the various schools people defend with ease any point of view over and against others by means of dialectics. Sometimes it happens that they first claimed hesitatingly they had to defend an idea (unless it was expressly defined). But as soon as their intellectual audacity bestowed victory on them, and such victory instilled in them confidence, they upheld as true and transmitted to their followers their newly discovered truth. They are evidently far removed from observing the rule of St. Augustine, the most reliable teacher: "For now, by always observing a wise and religious sense of prudence, when it comes to such an obscure issue we must not believe anything rashly. We must do so in order to avoid the danger that if later on truth emerged (even though such truth could not possibly contradict the sacred books of both Old and New Testaments), we would not be inclined to reject it because we have grown fond of our error."[15]

15. Augustine, *De Genesi ad litteram libri duodecim* II, 18.38 (*The Literal Meaning of Genesis* II, 18.38).

Moreover, there is yet another danger to be considered, which is not any less harmful to morals (unless our minds were firmly rooted in a conscientious humility) and which is usually incurred by those who have engaged for a long time in this field of dialectical philosophy: I am talking about the danger that in the heat of the dispute such people sometimes appear to be yearning more for victory than truth. In such an instance, once a new proposition has been examined and outlined (since by then one appropriates it), they immediately wish others would adopt it too, as if they themselves had discovered it and taught it. This defect arises especially when in the process of debating contested issues some visible and known things are loved in an excessive manner. Such issues usually do not end together with classes of Philosophy once they are abandoned: rather, they are transferred together with a mixture of countless philosophical issues to lectures about most sacred Theology and find their way into theological treatises as a way to explain God's mysteries, as if they had been ratified by philosophical sharpness. We can see some troublesome examples of such foolishness in some of the writings of ancient scholastics, so much so that we may conclude that these people feared nothing more in life than the fact that theologians had quit reading Porphyry's *Isagoge*, or Aristotle's *Categories* and *Analytics*.

After considering these and similar things with greater attention than usual, I ceased wondering why the various schools were vexed by so many disputes and dissenting opinions concerning the aids of divine grace. I did not find necessary to seek or to investigate in a deeper way the reasons why some people found the discovery of truth and others a consensus of divergent opinions to be a hopeless enterprise. In fact, by adhering to those principles, which each of the two parties[16] regarded as undoubtable, neither truth can ever or hardly be discovered, nor an agreement be reached. In fact, we should not decide by means of philosophical principles those things that each of us has decided to uphold, on the basis of Aristotle's or Zeno's doctrines, concerning the following things: (1) God's way to intervene in human affairs; (2) the nature of free will; (3) the convergence of one's dispositions with

16. Translator's Note: The Jesuits and the Dominicans.

the will; (4) the indifference of the will; (5) freedom of the will's great power to resist all passions and temptations; (6) the limits of the use of reason; and all other similar things. It seems that all these things should have been investigated under the guidance of ecclesiastical authority and upheld by its judgment. In fact, Philosophy, just as it has always been the "mother" of all heretics, once it is employed in this fashion to define the arcane mysteries of divine realities eventually becomes the mother of errors.

Chapter IV

The difference between Philosophy and Theology. The intellect is at the former's service; remembrance is at the latter's service. Theology's beginning is unwritten tradition, and occasionally, even the written one. What Christ and the apostle Paul had in mind concerning the legacy of Theology.

What is commonly accepted and regarded as certain among true theologians depends on the foundation of the revealed principles of Christian Theology. Therefore, those paths through which either that original revelation or those same revealed principles are transmitted to the next generations must necessarily be sought after and faithfully followed. In fact, who doesn't know that both of them have been transmitted to people as authentic instruments of ecclesiastical tradition thanks to either the pen of writers or the tongue of preachers? These two instruments in turn faithfully entrusted the received deposit of doctrine in a similar way to both the disciples and their successors. Therefore, just as the intellect is the proper faculty to undertake the study of Philosophy, remembrance is the proper faculty to undertake the study of Theology. Thus, the intellect makes the Philosopher who he is by shedding light on principles that have been thoroughly understood; conversely, remembrance makes a Christian Theologian who he is by remembering those things that have been transmitted to future generations either in writing or by preaching. It shouldn't therefore come as a surprise or be regarded as nonsense to anyone that Christian wisdom arises from the recollection of transmitted revelation and divine words, except to those who do not realize that such eternal wisdom, namely the Word of the Father (from whom our wisdom derives as its source and exemplar), has sprung from the creative memory of God the Father.

Consequently, we may conclude that hearing, by which those things that are preached and transmitted are received (even though the intellect is absolutely unable to penetrate them) is the sense that better characterizes theological studies than Philosophy. In fact, the Philosopher is not one who commits to memory the many things that are pointed out to us by our senses, but rather one who perceives and understands with silent thoughts the things that are going on in his own mind. Thus, Saint Paul and the other apostles did not articulate various demonstrations in their preaching by which they either penetrated the divine realities or entrusted to their followers things that needed to be elucidated; rather, that which they themselves once heard they proclaimed as things to be equally heard and believed in: [St. Paul] "*heard secret words, which it is not granted to man to utter.*"[17] And: "*Hold the form of sound words, which thou hast heard of me in faith, and in the love which is in Christ Jesus.*"[18] And also: "*And the things which thou hast heard of me by many witnesses, the same commend to faithful men, who shall be fit to teach others also.*"[19] Paul's fellow apostle John said: "*And this is the declaration which we have heard from him, and declare unto you.*"[20] This was certainly the reason why not only the apostles, but their successors as well, namely the holy Church Fathers, transmitted most gladly to their disciples not only the things they heard and received (which is to say, those unchanging things that encapsulated the truth they conveyed), but also the very same words with which those teachings were conveyed to them. Augustine wrote to Honoratus, seeking to give him instruction on theological matters: "Do not think me silly for using Greek words. In the first place, because I have so received, nor do I dare to make known to you otherwise than I have received."[21] And also:

17. 2 Cor 12:4.

18. 2 Tim 1:13.

19. 2 Tim 2:2.

20. 1 Jn 1:5.

21. Augustine, *On the Profit of Believing*, trans. C. L. Cornish, in *Nicene and Post-Nicene Fathers, First Series*, vol. 3, ed. Philip Schaff (Buffalo, NY: Christian Literature, 1887), New Advent.org, revised and edited for New Advent by Kevin Knight, https://www.newadvent.org/fathers/1306.htm, 5.

"In the Catholic Church we teach through a special divine tradition that the soul must not worship any creature. I gladly use the words through which this teaching was transmitted to me" (*The Greatness of the Soul*, 34.77). He said this because allegedly the word "creature" was not found in the Latin language. Obviously, the holy Fathers regarded this with great devotion, namely that the Son of the Father said: "*The things I have heard of him, these same I speak in the world*";[22] and to the Jews in regard to the same matter: "*As I hear, so I judge.*"[23] Likewise, he said to the apostles: "*All things whatsoever I have heard of my Father, I have made known to you.*"[24] Finally, he promised in regard to his Holy Spirit: "*For he shall not speak of himself; but what things soever he shall hear, he shall speak.*"[25] Likewise, the apostles faithfully entrusted as an inalterable legacy to their successors those things that they heard from Christ's own preaching. Thus, those successors in turn transmitted to their listeners, both in writing and in an oral fashion, the teachings bequeathed to them by their elders, which had not been deduced from philosophical principles or altered by sophisticated argumentations. In fact, Christ the Lord, the apostles, and our elders did not care to derive the divine mysteries from the received pleas of the philosophers or to reduce such mysteries to their principles: rather, they resolved to simply transmit what had been accepted, and to refute the arguments of irreducible enemies concerning transmitted truth, which they presented as some kind of probable truth.

Therefore, as the entire Christian doctrine is derived from heaven, in other words, being accepted and believed through hearing from divine revelation, this too was the case, namely that neither the Lord Christ wrote anything, nor did He command His apostles to write down anything as they conversed with Him in this life. Instead, He was satisfied to bequeath these things by the simple preaching of His sacred mysteries, which were meant to be ruminated in people's hearts more than to be scrutinized by their intellect. The apostles followed this method with great precision. Thus, they too did not regard it as their

22. Jn 8:26.
23. Jn 5:30.
24. Jn 15:15.
25. Jn 16:13.

task to put in writing the Gospel as a body of doctrines; rather they saw it as their task to make sure that the heavenly doctrine would be poured into the hearts of the disciples as a compiled symbol of things to be believed, without adding or subtracting anything. However, as they addressed people and were subjected to human vicissitudes, since they too had to adapt to different circumstances and face adversities by which even the wisest human decisions are vexed, they were forced to put in writing in several chapters the main elements of the doctrine. They did this, not in order to transmit the proper method to attain the entire body of Christian teachings, but so as to exhort those who did not practice the works of faith by stimulating them with various exhortations, and also to refute the heretics who opposed the transmitted doctrine in their attempt to improve the Christian faith, or to lead them again back to the norm of abandoned truth. This is why, for instance, Saint John made manifest the mystery of the Son of God's generation at the time when Cerinthus disturbed the transmitted doctrine; however, he held back and omitted mentioning the mystery of the procession of the Holy Spirit since there was no pressing need to do so. This is why Saint Paul, as the Jews mistakenly attributed the grace and benevolence of God to the human will, decided to discuss the arcane mystery of divine predestination, which the writers of the Gospels had only briefly talked about, as if through a grate, since they did not have to confront any error about it. Also, this is why Saint James explained certain phrases of Saint Paul to some people who, because of a mistaken view, had rejected [the importance of] good works; phrases that uphold faith in a more glorious way thanks to the addition and praise of good works.

The reason why Christ the Lord and the apostles followed this way to spread the heavenly doctrine, and once they made it their own entrusted it to the following generations as something to be observed, is rather obvious. In fact, the new law does not require, in regard to itself and its own nature, to be written on paper, parchment, or stone, but only on the tablets of people's hearts. Thus, this is the essence of the whole difference between the new and old law: the old law, written on stone, intimidates people from the outside, while the new one, which according to the prophet Jeremiah is "written on the heart," delights people from the inside. Consequently, since the exterior Scripture is almost essential and proper of the Old Testament (which is why it has been appropriately called "written Law"), it cannot agree with the New Testament on the basis of its first consideration, but only by a certain adaptation to new errors or human weaknesses: therefore, not only human wisdom, but divine providence as well, is used to abandon and even modify its higher and more perfect resolutions. In fact, since God decided to give to the Jewish people only a brief compendium represented by the Decalogue and few more laws, as soon as they abandoned their creator by shamefully worshipping that [golden] calf, He broke their most stiff necks by imposing on them a massive amount of rituals and connected them to His worship with severe threats and punishments. As a matter of fact, some distinguished Church Fathers taught that this was the cause, which went beyond God's original intention, of that burdensome system of laws, ceremonies, and bodily punishments and rewards. Thus, we can truly say without hesitation that this practice of connecting to written characters the highest truths that the law of grace venerates, derived from the way human beings behaved: Scripture indeed uses it to accomplish and confirm all things.

Chapter VII

There are two ways to penetrate the mysteries of God: human reason and love. The former is dangerous and proper of philosophers, while the latter is the safe method adopted by Christians.

On the basis of what has been said so far, yet another substantial mystery is revealed. This mystery has been hidden by the vast majority of those who are inclined to argue in a very subtle and logical way about divine realities. In fact, there are two ways to penetrate the divine mysteries that are proposed by God's revelation as articles of faith: the first is through human reasoning, which has been followed by philosophers as well. This way is liable of running into many errors: this has been abundantly demonstrated in the case of many great thinkers, whether modern, medieval, or even ancient Church Fathers. These people, by inquiring immoderately about the majesty of the divine mysteries, eventually were overwhelmed by their glory. In fact, in such inquiry and exposition it is of the utmost importance to have a sense of moderation. This sense does not lead truly humble and Christian spirits to itch to solve new issues about the revealed mysteries (which I mentioned before),unless the need to say something against the onslaught of errors forces their hand, and to define them much less on the basis of the principles of human philosophy, but much more on the basis of revealed wisdom. In fact, it was for these reasons that the apostle Paul and the early Church Fathers disdained human philosophy.

The second way to penetrate divine mysteries stems from intense charity by which the human heart is purified and enlightened in order to penetrate the secrets of God, which are found in the "bark" of the Sacred Scriptures and in the revealed principles themselves. This way of understanding is very familiar to real Christians: through it, in both spiritual men and women, as charity increasingly grows, so does wisdom, until it reaches the perfect day. In fact, just as the tree grows from a seed, and vice versa the seed from the tree, and through this mutual production they both multiply endlessly, so does the knowledge of the Christian faith kindle love of charity and works through it. This charity continuously kindles the new light of knowledge, the light awakens the flame of love, and in turn the flame kindles the light: thus, this succession constantly leads the Christian spirit to the fullness of fervor and light, namely charity and truth, or wisdom. However, just as these two ways to attain knowledge differ greatly, so do the truths that each of them uncover. The truths proper of Philosophy are mostly prickly and dry, limited to mere speculation, and therefore frivolous and useless. The truths concerning God, human beings, and ethics are prudent and flow back deep into the affection that originated them. This doctrine, which is both most stable and certain, is quite often transmitted by Augustine and is the only one that needs to be taught to all those who strive to attain an understanding of divine things. Hence the claim Augustine makes in *Tractates on the Gospel of John* (96, 4): "For that cannot be loved which is altogether unknown. But when what is known, in however small a measure, is also loved, by the self-same love one is led on to a better and fuller knowledge."[26] And then he immedi-

26. Augustine, *Tractates on John* 96, trans. John Gibb, in *Nicene and Post-Nicene Fathers, First Series*, vol. 7, ed. Philip Schaff (Buffalo, NY: Christian Literature, 1888),

ately adds in what way one can grow in the knowledge of divine things: "If, then, you grow in the love which the Holy Spirit spreads abroad in your hearts, 'He will teach you all truth.'"[27] A little further on, he says that we must hope for growth in this matter: "Everything that will still happen concerning the attainment of that perfection [which will be given to us after this life], the Lord promised us through the love of the Spirit, when He said, 'He will teach you all truth.'"[28] As he upholds this truth, Augustine even quotes the apostle Paul: "*Rooted and grounded in love, you may have strength to comprehend* [i.e., by knowing] *with all the holy ones what is the breadth and length and height and depth . . .*"[29] He then ends his Tractate by saying what I mentioned before: "For in such a way will the Holy Spirit teach you all truth, when he shall shed abroad that love ever more and more largely in your hearts."[30]

And so that no one may argue that this must be understood in a precise manner from Aristotle's rules concerning the truths of morals that must be followed, Augustine himself applies it to the truths that are supremely theoretical, which we believe about God even though we may not understand them: "So shall the result be, that not from outward teachers will you learn those things which the Lord at that time declined to utter, but be all taught of God."[31] Augustine adds:

> The very things which you have learned and believed by means of lessons and sermons supplied from without regarding the nature of God, as incorporeal, and unconfined by limits, and yet not rolled out as a mass of matter through infinite space, but everywhere whole and perfect and infinite, without the gleaming of colors, without the tracing of bodily outlines, without any markings of letters or succession of syllables—your minds themselves may have the power to perceive."[32]

New Advent.org, revised and edited for New Advent by Kevin Knight, http://www.newadvent.org/fathers/1701096.htm, 4.

27. Augustine, *Tractates on John*, 4, trans. John Gibb.

28. Translator's Note: This is Augustine, *Tractates on John 96*, 5; however, it is my own translation.

29. Eph 3:17-18.

30. Augustine, *Tractates on John* 96, 5, trans. John Gibb.

31. Augustine, *Tractates on John* 96, 4, trans. John Gibb.

32. Augustine, *Tractates on John* 96, 4, trans. John Gibb.

He applies this view in other works of his to other most profound mysteries as well, including the arcane mystery of the Holy Trinity. Love, insofar as it diverts the affection of a Christian from other creatures and focuses it on God, purifies the eyes of the heart from the smoke and darkness of earthly desires by which human beings' hearts are darkened and hardened, making it impossible for them to understand the revealed mysteries. "The more the heart is made straight [by redirecting it through love to God], the more it becomes able to see what it could not see and successfully attain what it wasn't able to accomplish before."[33] And in another work of his: "Do you wish to see God? Jesus said: '*Blessed are the clean of heart, for they will see God.*'[34] Therefore, you first need to purify your heart: apply yourself to this task, encourage yourself to do it, persevere in it. What you wish to see is pure, but the means through which you seek this vision is impure."[35] But who ever doubts that the love of truth, which is to say, the love of God, is what purifies the heart? Augustine himself says: "Truth purifies, vanity pollutes."[36] And immediately after: "Love of truth is in accordance with the [second] commandment, but love of vanity is opposed to it."[37] In fact, all earthly desires are full of darkness, but love [of God], which is radically opposed to human desire, dispels this darkness so that it may discern in this light the eternal radiance by which everything can be clearly seen. Augustine says: "Once you dissipate the darkness of your unsubstantial desires you will see the light."[38] In the second book of his *The Lord's Sermon on the Mount* (3, 14), as he explains in a clearer way how this can be accomplished, he mentions in a most wonderful way the darkening and the brightening of the heart, and says that God "is always ready to give us his light, not of a material kind, but that which is intellectual and spiritual: but we are not always

33. Augustine, *Ennarations on the Psalms* 77, 10. Translator's Note: This is a translation of the quotation as Jansen has it and cites it.

34. Matt 5:8.

35. Augustine, *Sermon* 261, 4. Translator's Note: Translations from Jansen's quotations of Augustine's *Sermons*, found at http://www.augustinus.it/latino/index.htm, are my own.

36. Augustine, *Sermon* 8, 5.

37. Augustine, *Sermon* 8, 5.

38. Augustine, *Sermon* 216, 9.

ready to receive, since we are inclined towards other things, and are involved in darkness through our desire for temporal things."[39] Thus, he taught that such darkness can be dispelled by turning our minds to God: "In the very act of turning there is effected a purging of the inner eye, inasmuch as those things of a temporal kind which were desired are excluded, so that the vision of the pure heart may be able to bear the pure light, divinely shining, without any setting or change: and not only to bear it, but also to remain in it; not merely without annoyance, but also with ineffable joy."[40] Accordingly, it is particularly preposterous to suggest that human beings, who approach divine mysteries with blind eyes while they are still led astray by earthly desires, are able to scrutinize, understand, penetrate, and define such mysteries before that mysterious light, which a holy way of living is able to produce, arises in their hearts. This is indeed an example of proud presumption if not imprudence! Augustine says: "Isn't it injustice that oppresses your eye so that you would not be able to see this light? So now, what? Will you be able to lift your wounded heart up to God? Should it not first be healed in order to be able to see? But are you not being proud when you say: 'First I want to see and then I will believe?'"[41] In the same passage, by the verb "believe" he means the precepts of a good life or of love, since "*the just one lives by faith*."[42] Thus, elsewhere he writes in a more generic way: "the time of faith [i.e., of this life] lived righteously obtains the intelligence of unchanging wisdom, so that knowledge is consolidated not only by faith but also by understanding."[43] However, there cannot be any just life, nor can anyone attain it, according to the most truthful doctrine of this teacher, unless divine love granted or donated it to him. Therefore, nothing can be any more commonly found throughout his

39. Augustine, *On the Sermon on the Mount*, Book 2, trans. William Findlay, in *Nicene and Post-Nicene Fathers, First Series*, vol. 6, ed. Philip Schaff (Buffalo, NY: Christian Literature, 1888), New Advent.org, revised and edited for New Advent by Kevin Knight, https://www.newadvent.org/fathers/16012.htm, 3.14.

40. Augustine, *On the Sermon on the Mount*, Book 2, 3.14, trans. William Findlay.

41. Augustine, *Enarrations on the Psalms* 39, 21. Translator's Note: All subsequent cited translations of Augustine are based directly on Jansen's text, not on the original text of Augustine.

42. Rom 1:17.

43. Augustine, *Eighty-three Different Questions*, 81.1.

writings than the fact that the understanding of these things, which are proposed as things to be believed through faith, are indeed even in this life the *reward of faith*, just as Isaiah in the Septuagint version alleges: "*Unless you believe, you will not understand*."[44] Holiness of life is always enclosed in this faith, which issues from divine love and dispels the darkness of human hearts.

These statements issue from the very foundations of this unshakeable doctrine, through which Augustine constantly upholds the power of divine love in reference to the mysteries that our faith believes are supposed to be understood and penetrated. See for instance when he says that the Holy Spirit has been given to us human beings, "in order to contemplate with the breath and fire of love and charity not human and temporal realities, but rather divine ones."[45] Or when he says to the Manichean heretics who strove to penetrate the principles of revealed faith despite such impurity of heart: "We can attain the fullness of knowledge through love."[46] And to their bishop Faustus: "We do not arrive at truth other than through love."[47] Or when he addresses Catholics: "Good habits lead to understanding."[48] Habits indeed proceed from good affections. In his letter to Macedonius, Augustine writes: "Our habits are rendered good or evil by either good or evil affections."[49] However, a good affection is charity, which is something no Christian ever doubts. And finally, when Augustine says that faith "stirs up a more burning love so that the more ardently we love God, the more certainly and the more calmly do we see him."[50] For this reason, afterwards he uses expressions such as "splendor of pious charity" and "brightest charity."[51]

44. Isa 7:9.
45. Augustine, *Eighty-three Different Questions*, 81.2.
46. Augustine, *Two Books on Genesis against the Manicheans* II, 23.36.
47. Augustine, *Against Faustus the Manichean*, 32, 18.
48. Augustine, *Tractates on the Gospel of John* 18, 7.
49. Augustine, *Letters* 155, 4.13.
50. Augustine, *The Trinity* VIII, 9.13.
51. Augustine, *Letters* 145, 6.

2. Saint-Cyran and the Spiritual Life of Grace

Jean-Ambroise Duvergier de Hauranne, Abbé de Saint-Cyran

Translated by Richard T. Yoder[1]

The Abbé de Saint-Cyran (1581–1643) was, along with his good friend Cornelius Jansen and the reformer Angélique Arnauld, one of the three fountainheads of early Jansenist thought. For years he was closely connected to the theologian and reforming prelate Cardinal Pierre Bérulle (1575–1629),[2] who propelled him into the heart of the Parisian circles of *dévots*, pious Catholics committed to the reforms of the Council of Trent. In this capacity, Saint-Cyran became a famous spiritual director. In 1635, he became the chief confessor to the nuns of Port-Royal de Paris, and, two years later, started to advise and encourage men to retire from worldly business and enter a quasi-eremitic life at Port-Royal des Champs. These men were soon to be known as the *solitaires* of Port-Royal.

1. Jean-Ambroise Duvergier de Hauranne, *Lettres chrestiennes et spirituelles de Messire Jean Duverger de Hauranne, Abbé de St-Cyran* (Rouen: Jean Viret, Jacques Besongne, and Clément Malassis, 1645), 73–75, 161–80; Jean-Ambroise Duvergier de Hauranne, *Théologie familière, avec divers autres petits traitez de dévotion* (Paris: François Muguet, 1669; first edition 1644), 10–16, 56–58.

2. Translator's Note: Bérulle founded the French Congregation of the Oratory, a religious order that would, until its suppression during the Revolution, produce numerous Jansenist leaders, notably Pasquier Quesnel.

Yet he ran afoul of Cardinal Richelieu, who saw in Saint-Cyran a potential threat. Saint-Cyran taught that true contrition, which encompasses sorrow for sin based on love of God rather than a mere fear of hell, was necessary to receive absolution in the sacrament of confession; Richelieu disagreed. Additionally, and probably far more importantly, Richelieu distrusted Saint-Cyran's connections to Jansen, who had strongly criticized French foreign policy during the Thirty Years' War (1618–48) in his *Mars Gallicus* (1635). So Richelieu had Saint-Cyran arrested and held without charge in the Château de Vincennes. He would not be freed until after the Cardinal's demise in 1642, dying shortly thereafter.

We can best glimpse Saint-Cyran through his spiritual letters and the *Théologie familière* (1644), an influential catechism that, written before the *Augustinus*, advances proto-Jansenist theology in a simple, easy-to-understand way. In his letters we discover several central themes: the importance of seeking solitude, the Christian duty to read Scripture, the uselessness of propositional faith without charity, and the imperative to prepare the soul carefully for Holy Communion. Saint-Cyran's catechetical writings offer a markedly Augustinian interpretation of the Catholic faith. These texts, edited and read by the community at Port-Royal, had a formative influence on early Jansenism.[3]

Richard T. Yoder

From *Lettres chrestiennes et spirituelles de Messire Jean Duverger de Hauranne, Abbé de St-Cyran* (1645)

Letter XIII—To a person of condition, his intimate friend; he speaks of separation from the world, and of the happiness of solitude.[4]

20 June 1642

Monsieur,

I borrow another hand, so as not to miss writing to you, and to thank you for the charity that you have shown to those persons whom

3. Translator's Note: The *Théologie Familière* was used for catechetical instruction in the convent school of Port-Royal de Paris. See John J. Conley, *The Other Pascals: The Philosophy of Jacqueline Pascal, Gilberte Pascal Périer, and Marguerite Périer* (Notre Dame: University of Notre Dame Press, 2019), 46–47.

4. Translator's Note: Robert Arnauld d'Andilly (1589–1674), conseiller d'État,

you know. God desired that you should come to know these disorders so that you might judge with more assurance than all the others who are in the world. You can no longer doubt after this that towns and courts are the stumbling blocks of Christians, because they are such for the people there. For myself, I have no need to learn that by new experiences. It has been a long time since I saw it in the best people, whose virtue the world admired. But had I neither seen nor experienced it, I would know it rather by the Wisdom of God, who exhorts us so often in His Scriptures to withdraw ourselves from the world in order to serve Him in solitude, of which our Master[5] speaks, saying, it seems to me, of an excellent Bishop, *In solitudine poterat deificari.*[6]

When God will separate us from the world by death, the first regret we shall have will be that we had not thus separated ourselves in advance, to merit by a conversation with God this ineffable union of love and charity that we hope to have with Him in Heaven; apart from which, the Faith teaches us, we are eternally miserable—which is horrible, but very just, and authorized by all the Scriptures and the holy Fathers. The Christians who will not have passed their life in the love of God will have a greater share in that eternal misery than the Pagans, the Turks, and the Jews. Only heretics will be treated worse than bad Catholics. It is time that we think on it seriously, and that we break all the bonds and all the attachments that make us still love the world, so that we might be attached to God alone.

Necessary for this is a separation from the world that is entirely spiritual and that, by the exercises of an interior virtue, separates the soul from the body as much as the body separates from the exterior world, when it leaves all that it loves in the world in order to withdraw into solitude.

I know not how I have entered into this discourse: but please receive

---

translator, horticulturalist, and *solitaire* of Port-Royal. One of the most well-connected and prolific savants to retire in penance at Port-Royal; his translation of the *Confessions* of Saint Augustine is a literary monument of the *Grand Siècle*. Elder brother of Antoine Arnauld (1612–94) and Mère Angélique Arnauld (1591–1661). His daughter, Angélique de Saint-Jean Arnauld d'Andilly (1624–84), would become Abbess of Port-Royal-des-Champs.

5. Translator's Note: St. Augustine.

6. Translator's Note: "In solitude, he could be deified."

this effusion that comes from the fullness of my heart, in place of the thanksgiving that I owe you. Although it is not necessary that I should face you, as you wish for me to pass for another "you." I can truly say that I am so, and that I grant you a great testimony thereof in speaking to you as I speak to myself, and in desiring nothing else for you but an everlasting good, no more than I do for myself.

So much did I want to build palaces here below, and to remain ever in the most beautiful houses of the world, that I fled from them; and perhaps I would burn them in advance, as God will one day order his angels to burn them. For in the end they are nothing but the trophies of human vanity that must be consumed by the flames of the last conflagration, and which oblige us by their nothingness to search for our lodgings forever in the eternal Palace of Paradise, as St. Paul says, where we can only arrive by purifying ourselves in the flames of Divine love that ordinarily burn in solitude, and chill in commerce with the world.

Letter XXXII—To a person of condition, one of his friends; he speaks to him of the dispositions necessary to Commune frequently; of what one must do before and after Communion, and of the manner of reading Holy Books fruitfully, so as to grow in virtue as much as in science.[7]

From the Bois de Vincennes, 21 December 1642[8]

Monsieur,

I have placed myself before God for some time, before marking for you the order that you should follow in order to go to Holy Communion. One doesn't prescribe any rule for a man who carries himself well, to instruct him how he should dine and sup. The good health that he possesses leads him there at the right hours. And when he is at table, it causes him to eat with appetite, in keeping the rules of temperance, if he is as healthy in soul as in body.

But because there isn't any danger that we risk in going to eat too much at the Holy Table of the Church, there to receive the Body of the

7. Translator's Note: The recipient is Paul Le Pelletier, sieur [Lord] des Touches (1602–1703), close to Jansenist circles.

8. Translator's Note: This is one of Saint-Cyran's later prison letters. He was released from the Château de Vincennes in 1643.

Son of God, it suffices for all rules to have a healthy soul in order to be nourished from this Holy Meat, just as it suffices to have a healthy body for a sober and temperate man to go without any fear to the table where he eats so as to nourish his body.

All the difficulty, therefore, is in having a healthy soul so as to go to Holy Communion, not having any particular rule of temperance that one must observe when one actually eats this Holy Meat.

The health of the soul depends upon the common life that we lead in the Church. If we have a firm design to live as Christians and in the narrow way, beyond which there is no salvation, according to the Gospel—and if we countenance everything that the faith of Jesus Christ and the Church obliges us to do, so as truly to establish ourselves there—and if we have walked therein for some time, separating ourselves from the world, which is one of the principal conditions of this life—we have the true disposition that God demands of us to go to Holy Communion. For then our soul is in the state of a man with a healthy body, who can go at the ordained hours to take his meals every day.

This firm design of such a person to live as a Christian, and this testimony that it renders to him and to others by his public and particular actions, that he only wishes to live on earth so as to go unto God, excludes from his soul all sorts of attachment to the least venial sin. This can often serve as an impediment for Holy Communion in a soul who is otherwise good and virtuous, as would be the diversion that she[9] would wish to take with a man who would have no resemblance to her, to feel other things than what concerns God.

Nevertheless, to enlighten you a bit better as to this spiritual health of the soul, and this narrow way, in which a Christian must be established so as to be always disposed to Holy Communion, one must know:

That for a man to assure himself that he walks in this way, he must not involve himself, without a particular vocation from God—neither in the Priesthood nor in the Religious Life, which are the two most excellent Christian forms of life. And if he finds himself engaged in

9. Translator's Note: I render this feminine in line with the convention of Christian ascetical writing that genders the soul as female, a tradition that Saint-Cyran is clearly working from here.

the Religious Life by some vow, he must enter therein so as to be able to live as a Christian. As, on the contrary, if he has engaged himself in the Priesthood by a vow, or by a particular devotion, he must recognize that he does so ignorantly, not to say lightly; and that he needs other dispositions and a greater perfection to be a Priest than to be a Religious, and by consequence, this vow is not ordinarily good, nor agreeable to God.

The good and Christian life that one leads in the narrow way, even though one be neither a Priest, nor a Religious, is sufficient to have a healthy soul, and to give a Christian the right to go fearlessly unto Holy Communion every Sunday and all Feast Days.

If he's a man of your condition, and capable of handling books, every day he must read the Gospel, which is the rule of the Christian life, and which commands us to walk in the narrow way. It will teach him, to the measure of the grace that has grown in his soul, to make cuts rather than additions in his life, however good and Christian it be.

I would desire as well that he should join to this reading that of the rest of the Holy Scripture, and particularly to the Epistles of the Apostles, which are the first clarifications and, so to speak, the first commentaries on the Gospel, as one of the greatest preparations for the Holy Eucharist, if one joins to the knowledge of the divine truth drawn from these holy Books both action and practice.

I feel obliged to give you here an important piece of advice, which will perhaps remove the greatest impediment that one ordinarily finds these days in men of devotion, who pass a part of their life in the study of holy Books, and in the illustration [*éclaircissement*] of the principal truths of our Religion.

They ordinarily make great collections of the maxims of the Gospel, and of all the Mysteries and secrets of our Faith, and place in this a great part of their piety and their devotion. But if they do not grow as much in charity as they do in the knowledge of divine truths, they err greatly, according to Scripture and Saint Augustine, and fall into the same dryness of heart where fall the avaricious, who spend their lives in amassing great treasures and in filling their coffers without using it to win Heaven, and to advance their salvation in giving to the poor.

Money is called by the Greeks "use" [*l'usage*], because it does not deserve the name of money, if we don't use it as we must, and as God ordains. All truth, and principally that of the Gospel and of the holy Theology of the Son of God, has this in common with money—that it's useless to man if he does not avail himself of it for the good of his soul at the very same instant that he learns it.

Money that rests in coffers rusts by itself in the end, or at least it rusts the soul of the one who keeps it thus, without dedicating it to a good use. The divine truths, reduced entirely to memory or in books, even though they never rust *per se*, waste and swell the spirit of the one who doesn't take care to make a good use of them—that is, to turn them to good actions, following the words of the Apostle, who addresses Christians thus: *Veritatem facientes in charitate.*[10]

I see few men of learning and devotion who use it thus, and who become more pious in becoming more learned in the truths—not only of the human sciences, but also of the divine science of the Gospel and of all Religion. I don't believe that there's anything that so impedes the profit that one could draw from the Sacraments, and particularly from Holy Communion.

We see manifestly that they become more knowledgeable [*sçavans*] from day to day in the Scripture and in good Theology, but we never see that they become more considerate in their discourse and in their judgments, nor more fervent in their piety, nor that they advance in humility and in patience, which are the two most evident proofs of the growth of charity in a soul. One sign that this great number of truths does not serve them is that those truths we teach to the people in their Catechisms ordinarily help them very little in the practice of good works or to live better than the others who do not know about them. The Apostle reveals to us this impediment, in saying that "knowledge puffeth up; but charity edifieth,"[11] which is as if he said to us, that if one grows more in one than in the other, then necessarily the heart must rest there a bit swollen. For, to prevent one side of the scale from rising over the other, there must be an equal weight in both.

For myself, I can say that there is nothing that has so much instructed me, nor warmed me more to love God, than this grace that He has

10. Translator's Note: "Doing what is true in love" (Eph 4:15).

11. Translator's Note: 1 Cor 8:1.

granted me of applying myself to all the truths of each Philosophy—just as much of what the Faith teaches us, as that which nature has taught even more to Christians than to the Pagans, because of the marvels that the light of Jesus Christ discloses to us in the order of the world, which had been unknown to Aristotle and Plato.

It is this [light] which reveals to us that all of nature and the whole world are nothing but a painting of the truths of grace, and that we would not know how to learn anything by Chronology, Cosmography, Mathematics, and by the Meteors that one need not report here, and which cannot serve a good man to advance in true virtue and in the love that he owes to God.

I say more, and I am not afraid to affirm that the whole history of the world, and the course of the common actions of all men, particularly those of Christians, is a continuous instruction for a good man who watches over his faith, and who intends to husband all that he hears, what he sees, and what he reads for the good of his soul. I do not believe that God has a greater lesson for men to make them despise temporal things, and love the eternal, than those that He gives them by the common actions of all men, both great and small, rich and poor, ignorant and learned, good and evil.

. . .

I must say now, of science and of truths, that which the Apostle says of riches and the goods of this world, that although they do not harm a Christian, he must possess them as if he does not possess them. That is, he must feel no anxiety about having them, and he must not have any attachment to them. God has granted you the grace of detaching you somewhat from the goods of this world; that causes me to hope that He will give you an equal [grace] in the truths in which He instructs you, be it in reading, or in communicating with other men. And as there is no need to regulate you in that which pertains to worldly goods so to make you better disposed for Communion, I hope that I will be even less obliged in the future to regulate you in the truths that you are learning. For you will only use them as lights that cause you to see better from afar this admirable Body of Jesus Christ, toward which you desire to go so as to unite yourself to Him intimately [*étroitement*]. As the Gospel tells us that as soon as the eagles (that is, the Elect) will see him one day, they will rise above the earth to go join themselves to Him, by a blessed flight in the middle of the air. There is no affection like that by which a soul who is attached to nothing, and who is as suspended in her body as the Son of God is in the Eucharist, loves nothing as the Word, Spirit, and Body of Jesus Christ.

If you live with this detachment in your heart, your love for Jesus Christ alone, which is nothing other than that hunger and thirst for justice of which He speaks in His Gospel, will bring you to Holy Communion almost any day that you wish.

So that you remember what I have just said touching the manner of studying, you have only to bring back your spirit to these words of the Apostle—"to be wise unto sobriety"[12]—and to these other words to the Corinthians—"everyone hath his proper gift from God."[13]

I would prefer that a man might entirely renounce learning [*la science*] and live in Christian simplicity, which would lead him more surely to Holy Communion, than to see him badly use knowledge, as he stops and enjoys himself with it, like misers with their money. This impedes him from going as he should to the Holy Table and from profiting from that celestial nourishment.

When a man withdraws from worldly companions . . . which every man who has mortally offended God is obliged to do, leaving the liberty of haunting the world to innocents, he needs almost no other disposition to go every Sunday and Feast Day to Holy Communion. By which must be understood that he lives in solitude like you do, fleeing idleness, and attending always to God.

When it comes to venial sins—those that proceed from infirmity, and those in which the will has little share—they can be remitted by a single *mea culpa*, and a *dimitte nobis, etc.* Those that are born from a little more volition than infirmity, but which have no root in the soul, since all they do is pass, can be effaced by the sole recognition that we have joined in them, either by some alms or by some other satisfaction, whether by some light abstinence or by some prayer, even before the confession that we make of them to a Priest, which is very useful when

12. Translator's Note: Rom 12:3.

13. Translator's Note: 1 Cor 7:7.

we use it as we must, although it has only come into the ordinary usage of the Church very late for the erasure of venial sins, because for more than a thousand years, the Just who committed them were more often content to choose for themselves some light penances before going to assist at the holy Sacrifice of the Mass, and then to Communion.

For one needs no less disposition for the one than the other, according to Saint Chrysostom; and if you have led for one or two years consecutively the life that you lead now, I would not find it very difficult to advise you to Commune almost every day if you wish.

The other preparations, which consist in certain particular practices, do not seem so necessary for a solitary Christian [*Chrestien solitaire*]. As truths alone do not dispose us to Communion, so thoughts of devotion do not dispose us thereunto any more, if they are not the results of a good life and of continual vigilance over our actions, and of the movements that God stirs up in those who will participate in His Body in such a good preparation. I am assured that, living as you do, you will not miss them, neither before nor after Communion.

This good life and this continual vigilance that you have over yourself is sufficient to go to Communion, without these truths that are not enough by themselves. But for the present I do not command them to you, because those that I have prescribed for you elsewhere will have to suffice. So that you have only to hear the Mass with attention, without turning away your eyes or your spirit, and then to Commune with a profound reverence and all the holy affections that God may give you. I hope, however, in some time to send you some particular practices for hearing Mass, although the explanation that I have made to you instructs you enough, and gives you a means thereby to form some for yourself, according to the sentiment that God will grant you.

From *Théologie familière* (1644)

Lesson III—Of the Fall of Man

1. How did Adam use so great a grace?

Very badly. For he lost it in less than a day.

2. From where did this misfortune come to him?

From not having sufficiently honored and recognized God, who had created him so happy, and from being too pleased with his own excellence and in his own prosperity.

3. Was his sin therefore pride and vanity?

Yes, because the angel who became a demon by this same sin communicated it to him to make him a companion in his misery, counselling him to rise up against God in eating the fruit that He had forbidden.

4. What design did man have in committing this sin?

He wanted to lift himself above his condition, and no longer to recognize the submission that he owed to God, but to live independently like Him.

5. What effect did this sin produce?

It did everything contrary to what it pretended to do. It lowered him below all creatures; it raised them against him. It made him a slave of his passions and of the devil and subject to the eternal death of body and soul.

6. Did man thus lose his royalty?

Yes. For all his subjects banded against him and abandoned him, because he had abandoned God. Nor did he remain master of himself alone; all his senses and all his movements, whether of body or of soul, revolted against reason.

7. What consolation remained for him?[14]

None. For he had no means to defend himself against so many enemies, nor to deliver himself from his misery. Nor could he even merit God's taking pity on him, because having entirely lost His grace, he no longer had the strength to do any good work, nor even to pray to God to help him.

14. Translator's Note: A particularly "Jansenist" point, insofar as humanity after the Fall are left without anything to ameliorate our sorrowful condition.

8. Was this disgrace for Adam and Eve alone?

No, but also for their children, and for all their posterity. For as all the fruits of a bad root are bad, and as clean waters cannot come from a source that is infected, likewise, there can only be born from first parents soiled by sin, children who are sinners like their fathers.

Lesson IV—Of the Redemption of the World

1. Did God abandon man in this state?

No, for Adam had no sooner sinned, when God, touched by compassion, by His goodness alone, promised to deliver him.

2. Where is this promise written?

In the book of Genesis, where God, cursing the devil in the serpent because he had caused man to sin, tells him that the seed of the woman will crush his head—signifying by these words Jesus Christ, who having descended from Adam and Eve by the holy Virgin, delivered men from the tyranny of the devil who held them captive.

3. Did God soon accomplish this promise?

No.

4. How long did He wait?

Four thousand years, for there were so many years from the sin of Adam to the birth of Jesus Christ.

5. In what state was the world in at that time?

In the state where the sin of the first father had put it.

6. Were all men thus in a state of sin and damnation?

Yes. Outside of a small number[15] of chosen souls, in which God preserved His grace and the living faith in His promise.

7. Who were these souls?

They were particularly some of the race of Seth, firstborn of Adam after the death of Abel,[16] like Enoch, Noah, Abraham, the Patriarchs, and the Prophets.

15. Cardinal du Perron, *Traité de l'Eucharistie*, Lib. I, c. 13. Translator's Note: This citation and those following are found in the original text itself.

16. Cardinal du Perron, *Traité de l'Eucharistie*, Lib. I, c. 31.

8. Were not the Jews among this number?

Not all, but only[17] those who had a living faith in Jesus Christ, like the Patriarchs and Prophets. For the Law that Moses had given to them could not save anyone, but only the faith and grace of Jesus Christ.

9. Were there many just men among the Jews?

There were few, as St. Augustine frequently says.[18]

10. Were all the rest of the world damned?[19]

Yes. Apart from some particulars whom God favored extraordinarily among the Pagans, such as Melchizedek, Job, and his family. All the others were under the power of the devil, who treated them according to his will, and abused them even up to making them adore rocks and beasts as Gods.

11. Why did God wait four thousand years to deliver them?

So that men would recognize the greatness of the sin that they had committed against Him, seeing that it was the cause of the ruin of so many souls, and the greatness of His mercy and His grace, seeing from what misery He retrieved them by Jesus Christ. That is why we must have a joy and a perpetual recognition of God, for what He has caused to be born in us since the Incarnation of His Son.

Lesson XII—Of Grace

1. Is it enough to know the Commandments of God to keep them?

No. For beyond that we must have the Grace of God, without which we can accomplish not even the least of the Commandments, nor do anything good, whatever knowledge we may have.

17. St. Augustine, *Liber Contra Adim.*, c. 1.

18. St. Augustine, *Liber de Catech. rud.*, c. 19, 22. *Liber expos. Epist. ad Gal.*, c. 3. *Liber contra Adim.*, c. 17.

19. Translator's Note: Whether intended or not, this is a succinct response to the optimistic *De la vertu des païens* (1642) by the so-called "erudite libertine" François de la Mothe le Vayer. Antoine Arnauld attacked this treatise in *De la nécessité de la foi en Jésus-Christ*, published posthumously in the tenth volume of his collected works (1777).

2. What is Grace?

It is a gift of God, which is communicated to us by the merit of Jesus Christ to enlighten and fortify our soul, and to make it do everything that God desires of it.

3. Can we merit this Grace?

We can do nothing at all to merit the first grace, by which we enter into the service of God; it must come to us by His pure mercy, by which He precedes and attracts all those who approach Him.

4. Does it suffice to have this first Grace?[20]

No. For after we have entered by it into the service of God, we can do nothing, nor advance in any fashion, if He does not precede us at every step, and does not send us a new help and a new grace.

5. Do we thus always depend upon the mercy of God?

Yes. For at whatever degree of justice that we have come to, we have need of continual assistance from God to keep us there and to do good works.

6. From where does this great necessity come?

It comes from that which we have always in ourselves while we are in this life, a natural corruption that the Scripture calls concupiscence, which always carries us against the Law of God, and stirs up in us temptations and movements that cannot be surmounted but by the Grace of Jesus Christ. And all the virtue and exercise of a Christian in this world consists in combatting and diminishing this concupiscence, little by little.

20. Translator's Note: One of the most "Jansenist" parts of the catechism, insofar as Saint-Cyran here opposes the Molinist idea of a "sufficient grace" that is made efficacious by the cooperation of the free will. Both Thomists and Jansenists disagree(d) with this theology.

3. Angélique Arnauld and the Reform of Port-Royal

Mère Angélique Arnauld

Translated with an Introduction by Elissa Cutter[1]

Before the posthumous publication of the *Augustinus* by Cornelius Jansen (1585–1638) in 1640, Mère Angélique Arnauld (1591–1661, née Jacqueline Arnauld) had already made a name for herself. She had become abbess of the Cistercian convent of Port-Royal in 1602, just after her eleventh birthday—an appointment obtained for her by lying about her age and drawing on family connections. At this time in her life, as she described in her autobiographical account of her reform of the convent, she did not have a vocation to religious life and was not particularly dedicated to following Cistercian traditions. In 1609, inspired by the sermon of a visiting preacher, she had a conversion experience and began to reform the convent according to the teachings of the Council of Trent and the Cistercian interpretation of the *Rule of Saint Benedict*. Her reform put her into contact with many of the great reformers of this period of French history, including François de Sales (1567–1622),

1. A critical edition of this letter can be found in Angélique Arnauld, *Œuvres completes*, vol. 1, *Lettres*, ed. Jean Lesaulnier, Françoise Pouge-Bellais, and Anne-Claire Volongo (Paris: Classiques Garnier, 2020), 121–28; it can also be found in the eighteenth-century collection of her letters, *Lettres de la révérende mère Marie Angélique Arnauld, abbesse et réformatrice de Port-Royal*, vol. 1 (Utrecht, 1742), and in a manuscript copy at the Bibliothèque nationale de France (BNF f. fr. 17791).

Sébastien Zamet (1588–1655), and Jean Duvergier de Hauranne (1581–1643), known by his title as the Abbé de Saint-Cyran.

Mère Angélique's reputation for reform led to her correspondence with many other female religious communities undergoing reform. The letter translated here is an example of such correspondence. She addressed her letter to Louis Macquet (d. 1671),[2] a frequent correspondent, who had requested comments on the 1635 version of the Constitutions of the Annonciades. This letter is significant because Mère Angélique's comments on the Constitutions come from her own experience of reforming the convent of Port-Royal and give us a glimpse into convent life at this time, prior to the outbreak of controversy following the publication of the *Augustinus*. Although responding to Macquet's request, this letter also includes gendered rhetorical structures—such as the repetition of "it seems to me" instead of directly stating her comments—showing how women in this era of history needed to strategically structure their writing, especially when corresponding with men.

Elissa Cutter

A Letter of Mère Angélique Arnauld to Louis Macquet

4th January 1635

Monsieur,

In order to obey you simply, I read several times the Constitutions that it pleased you to send to me and will say to you that I was delighted to see the good nuns[3] in the so true and narrow practice of religious

2. Louis Macquet was the superior and confessor for the Annonciades of Boulogne-sur-mer and drafted the Constitutions for that convent. This community was originally associated with the Franciscan order but had become associated with the Order of the Annunciation of the Blessed Virgin Mary (or Annonciades), and established the cloister in the early seventeenth century.

3. Translator's Note: The term that Angélique uses here is *filles*. In seventeenth-century France, this term was used to designate women who were consecrated to God, either in a convent or under spiritual direction. In the context of monastic life, nuns used familial names to refer to each other—the nuns were "sisters" to each other, the

observances, in which I have not found any to fail. It seems that God has given to you a vocation to establish His grace in this convent,[4] without which we can never succeed in what we undertake. But, since you wish it, I will say to you some small remarks that I made, although it might not be necessary and that all might be able to remain as it is.

First of all, it seems to me that it would be better to not put the punishment that the transgression of the statute warrants in each, but to make of them a chapter at the end, because this has a hint of harshness to see this repetition, and that it is necessary to presuppose that they will keep them with so much affection and charity that it does not need the threat. I am sending you a copy of our fragments where you will see an example of it and will be able to adjust there all as it pleases you.

It seems to me that it is possible to add something to the [article on the] reception of nuns. You will see in the articles that I am sending to you if it is particularly true [that one should] receive a nun if she is very virtuous although she might not have wealth, for the rest is nothing. But for this one, I find it important, in having received—among others—four who were so extremely useful to the house that they might have been meant to be not only received for nothing but bought. And you will note that so few of such [girls] are found, that others than [these girls] can be made responsible. It is not necessary to fear the great number of them. And you will notice, if you please, that these nuns of which I speak, they were not of great spirit, but docile, simple, having good judgment, humble, penitent, and who seek religious life in order to be continually sacrificed there. Souls ordinarily carry grace on their faces and their words make known their heart. But, if this article[5] is in the Constitutions and it might be well known to everyone, then you will never receive a girl if she is not of wealth—these good ones will never present themselves, believing it impossible to be received.

---

abbess their "mother," and they were her "daughters," the latter of which is a possible translation of the term *fille*. I have chosen to translate this as "nun" in many cases because that term best fits the context of the women referred to in this letter, given that they had been cloistered since 1629.

4. Translator's Note: Although the term here is *monastère*, I have chosen to translate this as "convent," as it was an enclosed community of women.

5. Translator's Note: That is, an article in the Constitutions that indicates that girls must come with a dowry.

You say that they will not go outside in order to receive the habit, as they practice in all well-reformed houses. Ours leave—and also in several other reformed convents—in accordance with the old ceremonies of the Church, which must not be neglected. And this exit and return is agreeable, because after the first trial putting them outside in the freedom to not return, it seems better; their first entrance being sometimes secret and ordinarily with few people, this second, public one is of greater edification.

You do not speak about the examination that the vicar general must do, according to the holy council.[6] You will see the manner that we provide to do it. You will find possible that during [it] one might give a lot of freedom to the nuns. But if they are well founded in the spirit of grace, this will not harm them and is for edification with the seculars[7] who see how honestly and freely they consecrate themselves to God.

You say that they will not be able to be sent to the parlor except for three times during the year of the novitiate.[8] There, there should be some exception—being able to have there some novices possessing their wealth, who would be able to conduct business, or nuns so dear to their parents and to others of some consideration that one should not deny to them this consolation more often. Besides that, the discussions of the novices in the parlor must recognize their spirit, and sometimes the great austerity of the novitiate makes them succeed at hiding it.

You do not say how much time the superior is in charge—three, six, or nine years—[and] if all the community elects not only the discreet,[9] but still all the other offices.

6. Translator's Note: That is, the Council of Trent (1545–63), which addressed reforms of ecclesiastical practices, including monastic life, in responding to the Protestant Reformation. Angélique's reform of Port-Royal—and the comments she made in this letter—were based in part on the directives of the Council. For more on this, see Elissa Cutter, "Monastic Reform in Seventeenth-Century France: The Cistercian and Tridentine Influences on Angélique Arnauld's Reform of the Convent of Port-Royal," *Cistercian Studies Quarterly* 52, no. 4 (2017): 425–51.

7. Translator's Note: "Seculars"—in relation to the clergy—refers to those clergy who were not associated with the vows of monastic life. Members of the clergy who were also monks were known as regular clergy.

8. Translator's Note: The novitiate refers to the initial period of religious life, a type of probation period for the novices before they make their formal vows.

9. Translator's Note: Angélique here uses the term *discrète*, which was used both as

It seems to me that in order to leave the choir by necessity, it would not be necessary to say anything, but only after having made the reverence to the Holy Sacrament, to go to make the inclination before the superior or the president and, at the first assembly after, to say what was the need. Because it is not then the time to examine things, nor to distract oneself with anything but what [is] absolutely necessary.

It was found, by the way, by some very capable persons, not to compel the nuns to confess to an extraordinary confessor, because it would be possible to find among them [those] who would not be in the disposition [to confess]. But, in order to not appear different, all might enter into the confessional, and those who do not wish to confess might content themselves with asking the blessing from the confessor.

For the recreation, I find that the manner in which it is prescribed would be the most difficult and the most uncomfortable exercise of the day, and which would accustom the sisters to question unceasingly and to know the dispositions of each other, which is not appropriate. I am sending to you the manner that we manage here with great liberty. We never speak in twos here, but we sit in a circle, even in the garden, where we never walk during the recreation because we would not be able to hear each other. We do not speak, however, very loudly, but reasonably, and we rejoice modestly.

You have pensioners[10] and I do not see rules for them in there—neither who must be their teacher, [nor] their lodging, exercises, food, corrections, and how to direct them in the parlor, at what age you can receive them and until what age to keep them.

For the extern sisters,[11] you say very well all that they owe to the convent, but you do not say what the convent gives back to them—what assistances in sicknesses and old age, what recompense if one might

---

a title of honor for the superiors of convents and as a way to refer to the other executive officers of the convent, that is, the positions that assisted the superior.

10. Translator's Note: In this context, "pensioners" refers to female students paying a pension to live at the convent and be taught by the nuns.

11. Translator's Note: Angélique uses the term *les tourières du dehors* here. The *tourières* were those in a cloistered convent who were designated to do all the external business for the nuns. As her explanation indicates, these were not professed nuns, but local women hired to do such business for the convent.

dismiss them. Justice is necessary for all, and religious houses are subject to being ungrateful.

There is also something to say on this point about the confessor, if he is a secular priest.

It seems to me that it would be better to never speak during the refectory, this not being possible without some indecency. And, that it is not necessary to wait that one might have read a little in order to start to eat; the blessing[12] suffices for the recollection.[13]

For the converse sisters,[14] I strongly favor that they continue to go without them if it is possible. But in the article on the suffrages[15] for the deceased, there are those who do not know how to read. Yet if there might be some sisters who do not know how to read, it is necessary that they might be converse [sisters], not being able to be of the choir since they might not be able to assist there. So, if there are not any of them, I would like to remove this word from the Constitutions, because it will help those who will have the temptation to not choose it someday. Yet the reason why I strongly favor that there might not be any of them is because one has great difficulty in finding these girls such that they would be necessary, and that most often they enter religious life in order to find that which they do not have in the world and to insure their life. Moreover, the nuns of the choir might be used more courageously in work when there are no lay sisters and serve among themselves more charitably. I would like better to decide some other austerities than work. The Capuchin Poor Clares do not have it.

For prayer, you say that they will always read a stage of the Passion. Would it not be better to follow the order of the mysteries of the Church and to designate which book?

12. Translator's Note: Angélique uses the Latin term *benedicite* here.

13. Translator's Note: The term recollection (*récollection*) here refers to what is done to place oneself in the disposition of composure and calm for prayer.

14. Translator's Note: Converse sisters, also called lay sisters, were nuns who did not make formal vows and were responsible for domestic chores and services in the convent. The distinction between converse and choir nuns often reinforced class distinctions within the convent.

15. Translator's Note: The term here is *suffrages*, which refers to the prayers of the Divine Office for the commemoration of the saints and the deceased.

It says in your Constitutions that the superior[16] will give the order that the community might often make spiritual conferences with the father-confessor. The frequency of these things might bring in no time contempt and boredom, and might distort many of the ordinary exercises. And there will not always be found confessors who might have the capacity to do them well, so that it seems that some limitation of time would be necessary, and to say that it will be with the confessor or another person.

It says in the article on the duty of the superior that she will always have in hand the statutes while she will hold the chapters,[17] in order to confront by them the transgressions of those who are deficient and to regulate penances with them. It seems to me that this process has a feeling of secular justice, and to judge by writing is a great difficulty. It appears to me that it will suffice to say that she will often read the rules, statutes, and regulations in order to observe them promptly in all things and to make them observed by others. About the penances, I will say to you, that it seems to me that it is necessary to give freedom to a superior to act ordinarily by her opinion, that she must try to take from the Spirit of God and not to regulate them all herself. The letter kills and the spirit gives life.[18] There are certain girls for whom it is necessary sometimes to conceal transgressions, even important [ones], or you cause them to do worse and to mock all the penances. Of themselves, after some time, they make even greater ones than those that you might have had imposed on them, and with great edification. For other good and docile girls, it is necessary to give great [penances] for the least faults, in order to give a good example and to lead them to merit. Yet this does not have a certain rule. Sometimes you make the good ones do penance for those who are not disposed to do it,

16. Translator's Note: This term is feminine in the French in this paragraph and the next, indicating the superior within the convent or the abbess.

17. Translator's Note: The chapters were community meetings of the convent, during which the nuns dealt with matters related to life in the convent. As this section of the letter indicates, the superiors could give out penances to nuns who were deficient in some way. This was also where voting would take place, whether for the elections of the superiors or to decide which novices to accept as full members of the convent.

18. Translator's Note: 2 Cor 3:6.

or even for those who might desire it in order to mortify them more strenuously.

In article V, on the bursar,[19] it says that she will obtain the signature of the mother on her account every evening. It is a great constraint for both of them. We only sign it every month after having examined it.

In III, the article on the extern sister, which is very good and important, I would prefer that the penance might be other than to not go to the parlor, principally for the kin. For it is to make known this penance to seculars. And, on the contrary, it seems to me that it would be necessary to make [them] to do some other devout penance, and to try to reduce that [penance] which would have made a transgression to atone for when she would speak to the seculars, trying to remove the impressions that she would have given against the reputation of the convent, or of some particular [nun], and even formally recanting it if the thing is important, as the conscience obliges there. The incorrigibles must be deprived of all conversation until one might have known them in the disposition to no longer abuse it.

In the seventh article on the mistress of novices and youths, whom I believed always to be the same person, [one must] give her an assistant—well-chosen and entirely submitted to her—who might serve as example in this virtue of submission to the novices as in all other things. You say that they will assemble three times a week in the novitiate, but you do not say what they will do there. Ours assemble there every day, if there is not a sermon or some other conflict for the mistress. On some days, they say their faults before the mistress, and she makes them to read with her help a point of the rule and explains [it] to them. On other days, she gives them a virtue to practice during the week. She discusses the catechism with them if they have need of it. If there are any among them who might need to learn to read, it is the assistant who teaches them in the novitiate, at a designated hour. The same shows to all together the rubrics of the breviary and tells them all the days on which one says the office, and what the brief orders.

19. Translator's Note: The term in French here is *la dépositaire*, which just means a caretaker or keeper of something. The bursar was responsible for keeping the accounts of the convent, paying the bills, collecting payments, etc.

In the third article on the pantry sister,[20] it says that the mother will name every week a sister for the kitchen. It seems to me that there would need to be two of them, yet again that the community might not have been too big, because there are always difficult things where one needs assistance, and that it would be better that they might not be so rushed with work in the meal times, when ordinarily there is too much for one; and in the hours when they will find themselves in leisure, one could give them some occupation.

The infirmary, article 2: one should not go except rarely to visit the sick all together, nor even individually, if it is not the mother, vicar, discreet [officers], or someone to whom the mother might give particular obedience for it. And the professed, except the above-named, might not visit the novices.

In [the article on] the sacristan[21] [it] is ordered that the turning box of the sacristy will have two keys. You do not say the same thing about the turning box of the supplies, nor of the conventual door, although I believe that it is practiced thus.

In the laundry, we have been accustomed to say how much one gives by week of veils, of tunics, of handkerchiefs; and one might not increase [them] without some particular necessity.

Article twenty-nine on the extern sisters, that they might ask the blessing of the mother every night—it is a great oppression for the mother, who otherwise has so much to do that I do not know how she can do enough there. And, [it says] to ask for pardon every Sunday from the extern sister—if nothing happens against her, it seems to me that it is not necessary. This might turn on custom and might prevent that one does it with sentiment when they have failed.

Of the mistress of the choir, fourth article: in place of this announcement in the refectory—which is a bit annoying and amusing (for all things might take some time)—there is a table like that which

20. Translator's Note: *La dépensière*, in this context, refers to the person who took care of the consumption of the community. *La dépense* can refer to a pantry, so I have chosen to translate this term as the "pantry sister."

21. Translator's Note: Angélique uses the feminine term *la sacristine* here. This term referred to the nun who was responsible for the sacristy, which is where the sacred vessels and other items for use in the liturgy were kept.

you have depicted for the Holy Communion, where she writes all the offices of the choir, and on Saturdays each might check what it requires. The mother has another table where she writes in the same way the offices of each week and the assistants of the offices.

Fifth article. I have just found this table which seems to me to suffice in this annunciation and we have found no difficulty in this practice.

There is, my father, the small remarks that I made, which are not important. I have just received your second letter from the first day of the year. I received no inconvenience in this reading; on the contrary, I was consoled by it. What I can say to you of the greatest necessity is that the girls be truly spiritual and solidly virtuous, in order to not keep all the good laws like Jewesses,[22] but as Christians; that the servants be charitable and supporting; the weak humble and patient toward themselves, not losing heart. Finally, it is by the interior that the exterior must be formed, and not by the exterior to make the interior.

All this is so muddled that I do not know how you will be able to read it, and your Constitutions very sullied. Forgive me for all; I am so often interrupted that I most often do not know what I do. Another time, we will speak of your own and of ours.[23] However, I beg you very humbly to pray to God for us and to obtain for us [the same grace] from your good nuns, whom I honor with all my heart in our Lord, from whom I exist.

22. Translator's Note: Such comments, which today we would see as anti-Semitic, were common in Christian writings of seventeenth-century France, especially in this contrast of Christian and Jewish religious life.

23. Translator's Note: This comment refers to the spiritual direction that Mère Angélique offered to Louis Macquet in their correspondence. She did engage in the practice of offering spiritual direction to men through her correspondence, as this indicates, but later opted to stop this practice—a decision that caused controversy between her and Sébastien Zamet. This decision was made under the influence of the spiritual direction of the Abbé de Saint-Cyran, though it ultimately remained her decision. As she explains in her autobiographical account of her reform, part of her reason for this decision was that Saint-Cyran had reminded her of her desire—as a nun—to flee completely from the business of the world.

4. Agnès Arnauld and the Spirit of Port-Royal

Mère Agnès Arnauld

Translated by Philip Porter[1]

In many ways, the reform of Port-Royal was a family affair. Mère Angélique Arnauld was aided and seconded by her sister, Catherine-Agnès de Saint Paul Arnauld (1593–1671), née Jeanne, commonly known as Mère Agnès. More mystically inclined than her sister and less polemical than her brother Antoine, Mère Agnès nevertheless played numerous roles at the convent before eventually serving twice as Abbess. She was one of Port-Royal's leaders during its most intense period of persecution in the seventeenth century, the Formulary Controversy of the 1660s. Many of the nuns, Agnès included, refused to sign a formulary condemning the propositions of Jansen without any reservations. As historian John Conley notes, for this conscientious refusal, "the convent school and novitiate were closed; the chaplains were expelled. Foreign nuns hostile to Jansenism were imported to govern Port-Royal, now surrounded by an armed guard. The most recalcitrant nuns, including Mère Agnès, were exiled to foreign convents."[2] In 1669,

1. Agnès Arnauld, *L'Esprit du monastère de Port-Royal*, in *Les constitutions du monastère de Port-Royal du Saint Sacrement* (Mons: Gaspard Migeot, 1665), Internet Archive, 297–420.

2. John J. Conley, "Agnès Arnauld (1593–1671)," *Internet Encyclopedia of Philosophy*, IEP.utm.edu, accessed 2 June 2022. See also John J. Conley, *Adoration and Annihilation:*

a tentative truce was restored, known as the Peace of Pope Clement IX, and two years later, Mère Agnès died in the good graces of the Church.

Given her prominence at the monastery, Mère Agnès left behind several writings which represent the reform of Port-Royal. One important work was *L'Esprit du monastère de Port-Royal*, published along with the convent's Constitutions in 1665. This text presents the ideal "spirit" of the convent as a community of female monastics. The selections included here focus on monastic seclusion, the admission of novices, patience, and prayer. Yet for all her moralizing language, Agnès remains quite practical. She provides a window into life at Port-Royal, and how the nuns strove to live a common life.

Richard T. Yoder

The Spirit of the Monastery of Port-Royal

Since in *The Image of a Perfect Religious*[3] we did not want to portray a particular person who possesses all the qualities of this religious, but to form an idea which could serve as a model to the good souls who aspire to the perfection of so holy a state, we do not claim that everything that one will see in this *Spirit* [the present work] is practiced at Port-Royal in complete perfection. But this is what we were striving for, and the goal that the superiors who led it proposed, to satisfy their duties according to the lights that God had given them.

1. The spirit that we attempt to keep in this monastery is difficult to explain because it is neither affected by nor formed upon human reasoning, even though it sometimes leads one to the most perfect things. It is a spirit that strives to seek God and to follow Him in all things. It learns to conceive of God in an inconceivable way, not only because He is incomprehensible in His infinite grandeur, but also because we

---

The Convent Philosophy of Port-Royal (Notre Dame, IN: University of Notre Dame Press, 2009).

3. Editor's Note: This text is *L'image d'une religieuse parfaite et d'une imparfaite, avec les occupations intérieures pour toute la journée* (Paris: Charles Savreux, 1665), in which Agnès depicts the ideal nun of Port-Royal as an *individual*. By contrast, *l'Esprit* is more concerned with the *community*.

are not able on our own to form any thought to raise ourselves up to Him, and even less to have one that is worthy of Him. That is why this one thought that faith gives, that He is God, is enough to give souls the impression of a reverence which makes them entirely dependent on His divine Majesty, and which leads them to expect everything—but according to the order of His providence, not of their desires.

This foundation being established, these religious do not promise that they will become most perfect, even though they have the will to work with all their strength to become so. They know that nothing is perfect except what God approves, and that they could greatly deceive themselves by believing something would be very useful for their progress which would perhaps be the cause of their ruin through the complacency they would have to adopt to possess this virtue and to attribute it to themselves, as if they had acquired it through their work.

. . .

5. What sustains the spirit of this Religion the most is the lack of communication with people within and without: there is no friendship, no special confidence of one with another.[4] We practice the maxim of the prophet: *my secret is for myself* [Isaiah 24:16], because pouring out good thoughts dissipates them, and the ease of speaking about things that are not good impresses them more in the mind.

We content ourselves with the direction of the people that God has provided and in whom we find everything that we can desire when we seek only to go to God by their guidance.

We seek that same thing in sermons and in readings, since everything that is more pleasing to the spirit when it gives way to curiosity does not nourish and enrich the soul, as Scripture says, by the good use that it makes of the most solid truths, which are often the most common.[5]

4. Editor's Note: Agnès certainly has in mind her sister's famous "Journée du Guichet." On the 25th of September 1609, Angélique forbade her lay family entrance behind the grille of the monastery, as was then customary. This conflict marks the beginning of Angélique's reform of Port-Royal, to which Agnès was strongly committed.

5. Editor's Note: Opposition to "curiosity," understood as the cupidity of the intellect, was a common point among Jansenist moralizing. Jansen denounces it in his *De Interioris Hominis Reformatione Oratio*, translated into French by Arnauld d'Andilly

We seek even less to visit secular people in the parlors, and we have no inclination to go there except by order of obedience, having rendered the affection to parents entirely spiritual, in order to see them only in God and for the sake of their salvation. But because this attitude is not reciprocated on the part of the parents, we see them when it is ordered, and we speak to them as best we can, so as to injure neither our natural duties nor the obligation we have to preserve our heart without division for God, who wants to possess it entirely.

6. In this house, we do not desire to increase by a great number of girls. And although the desire that God be served leads them to wish that an infinity of souls would prefer God to all things, they know that they can contribute nothing by their hard work [*industrie*] to give this disposition to anyone, because it is only the Eternal Father who has the power to draw souls to His Son [John 6:44].

When He presents some girls who want to enter into Religion, we investigate as much as possible whether they come from this part, that is to say, if it is the inspiration of God that sends them. This is the only thing that makes an impression on the mind of those who must test them. The most advantageous human qualities are nothing to them unless it seems that grace will use them for these ends; without that they are instead weapons against Religion.[6] This is why we treat these persons with less sweetness than others, even though it is necessary to let everyone know how narrow the way is that leads to God.

We do not run unreasonable tests on Novices to overthrow their spirit, because we know from experience that this method can result in a contrary effect, which would be to prepare them for all this by human effort. We are trying to imitate the conduct of God, who asks some difficult things of souls, but softens them by the anointing of His grace, which makes them embrace those things with joy. And although the people who require of others the very tedious things that Religion demands do not have the power to convey this gentleness to them, they

---

as the *Discours de la réformation de l'homme intérieur* in 1644. St. Augustine himself has similar ideas throughout his work, including, *inter alia*, in *Confessions* 10.35.54-55.

6. Editor's Note: "Religion" here principally means "the Religious Life," that is, the vowed life.

are in a certain way sending them to God to ask it of Him and reminding them of the graces they have received from Him, which ought to be a strong reason not to refuse anything He asks of them. If we encounter solid virtue in a soul, and find that she bears the mark of God's elect upon her forehead, because we notice in all things the rectitude of her intention, then this is the one we embrace, even though she has very little natural talent, because God has chosen the weak things of this world to confound the strong [1 Corinthians 1:27].

But the greatest number of those who seek Religion is not composed of those souls who have God alone before their eyes. There are also many others who seek God first, but not exclusively, having many shortcomings that distract them. Still, it is not permitted that we reject them, since, as Our Lord says, it is not the healthy but the sick who need a doctor [Mark 2:17]. It is therefore with a view to these [sick] ones that Religion is a charitable mother, who does not consider so much what they are in themselves as what God does on their behalf—not wanting to heal them (since that belongs to God alone), but she [Religion] treats their sicknesses and brings them all the remedies that are in her power. Not by gentle guidance, which would only encourage their weakness, but instead by persecuting with charity whatever in them is contrary to their vocation. If this sort of guidance is not a burden to them and they join in loving it, then even though they always make mistakes, it is enough that what is good prevails over what is bad. This is the case when they desire that we continue to give them this guidance and that we do not give them rest in the war they must wage against their inclinations. The same is true when they do not tire of the rebuke and chastisements that wipe out their defects as they commit them, but receive them with the spirit of humility and a genuine desire to benefit from them.

If it is an advantageous thing for individuals not to be completely delivered from their defects in order to keep them in humility and contempt of themselves, it is also an advantage for the well-regulated community to have this counterweight of a number of imperfect persons who keep it from being lifted up by the virtue of others. Besides, Religion is more for the weak than the strong. The one purpose we should have in admitting the people who present themselves should be to contribute to their salvation and not to take advantage of the perfection that could be in them.

7. This is what obliges the Sisters of this Monastery not to lay claim to the esteem of creatures, and which gives them a higher opinion of other religious, who they prefer to themselves because they feel their own defects and they presuppose more virtue in others, which is a reason to put themselves beneath them and to want them to be more approved and praised than their own community. But this is still a small thing since it is necessary that they even be willing to be unjustly blamed without proof by the world, and even by some spiritual persons, who are able to be beguiled and believe things to be otherwise than they are when they are told by others, and they do not bother to consider them or to inform themselves fully. God allows this because it has pleased Him to choose this way to test this house and to preserve it from the acclaim of creatures, in which one can become complacent and be carried imperceptibly to want to please them to keep oneself in their esteem, instead of being drawn by patience and humility to want to please God alone and to forget and despise the world, regarding it as crucified as we are crucified to it [Galatians 6:14].

8. In this house, we try to be in a state of perpetual thanksgiving for what He has done for it in giving it teachers of solid truths and sure maxims in order to go to God, who preserve from illusion and from disorders of spirit, which are found in many people who believe themselves to be truly serving God when they are in fact serving themselves with holy things to nourish their self-love. If human weakness makes us fall into the same faults of self-seeking, we have a way to recognize our error and to not continue in the folly of those who want to square God with nature. We try not to be attached to the holiest things, like prayer, Holy Communion, or spiritual communications. We prefer all these things to the satisfaction of the senses, and we deprive ourselves of all other consolations in order to merit to take part in them. Yet we know that they are not our final end, even though they lead us there. This is why we put God in Himself above all, and we expect from His will, His order, and His action upon us what will make us be His, without fearing that we lack anything because of that.

9. We do not desire with impatience and with anxiety a degree of

perfection higher than the one in which we are, which could be only an effect of pride and self-love. It is not that we do not work daily to progress in the way of God, as all Christians are obliged to. But we would fear to lose the sense of our unworthiness if we did not bear with patience the common state to which we are reduced, which can nevertheless become in a certain way a perfect state, if we are devoted to ceaselessly fighting its imperfections.

. . .

13. The spirit of this house is still a spirit of prayer—not that many have some of the extraordinary graces in prayer that God imparts to whom He pleases, but because everyone knows that it is necessary to await everything from the grace of Jesus Christ as a result of the continual prayers we offer Him as our one mediator, who has made Himself the liberator from all our ills, from which He delivers those who have recourse to Him. We do not go to prayer to receive spiritual consolation. Fear and respect toward the Majesty of God does not allow us to expect that He must look exclusively at us. It is enough that He assures us by His Holy Scriptures that we should not lack confidence in His goodness, since He says that those who call on the name of the Lord will be saved [Romans 10:13].

14. We make little of the difference between vocal and mental prayer, as long as the former is done as it should be—that is to say, not only from the mouth, but from the heart—since in both of them we address ourselves to God, we submit ourselves to Him, we thank Him for His graces and ask Him for new ones, and we are touched by different movements toward God depending on the inspiration that it pleases Him to give. And although this is experienced with a more palpable contemplation in mental prayer there is also more to fear for one who only seeks there more pleasure for oneself. On the other hand, praying with the mouth and particularly in the public prayer in which the whole Church is united with us, the spirit is borne toward God without being turned back toward itself, and it uses words that it sometimes cannot understand, but that God understands, and which are more pleasing than those that we might choose, because these are the words of His Holy Spirit, who makes souls holy when they speak them by the same Spirit.

This maxim makes them prefer the Divine Office to their individual prayers in accordance with the spirit of their Rule, which desires that the choral office should be the most essential of their prayers, and that their private prayers always come from the movement they will receive from God, and not from a routine or technique in which one exerts oneself to indulge one's spirit, which sometimes takes pleasure as much and as humanly in spiritual things as in profane ones.[7]

15. Devotion to the word of God, that is to say to Holy Scripture, ought to follow the spirit of prayer. They have great respect for the holy books in which God Himself has spoken to humans. They prefer this reading to everything else, and although they do not understand most of the mysteries that are locked away there, they stop at what they grasp and leave to God the knowledge of what they cannot grasp. If they sometimes ask that we instruct them about the meaning of these words, so hidden and so mysterious, this is not out of curiosity but only to benefit from the light of others. They try to bear, in imitation of Saint Cecilia, the Holy Gospel in their breast, having nothing so precious to them as the words that the eternal Word Himself spoke. And since it has pleased Him to do it in a very simple way, they revere this simplicity above all the elevated expressions that He Himself gave to the Prophets, to St. Paul, and to the other Saints who have written by His inspiration. This is why they never tire of the most common Gospels that are read in Church, always listening to them with a new attention, because they are springs that can never be exhausted.

. . .

18. We have as a rule to fear above all things the odd one who would endeavor to be more austere than the others, or more withdrawn and more solitary, except insofar as one needs these particular means to strengthen oneself to return to the shared spirit.

We desire to be neither known nor seen in the house, and to be as though hidden by the shadow of God [Psalm 91:1], placing all our hope in remaining under His wings [Psalm 91:4], having no other safe place to escape the terrors of the night, as the prophet says, nor the arrow

7. Editor's Note: This preference for liturgical devotion, as opposed to the affective and visionary personal devotions promoted by the Jesuits, is characteristic of Jansenist piety more broadly, as is the devotion to Scripture reading in the following section.

that flies by day [Psalm 91:5]. Nor do we have any other place to escape the tricks of the malign spirit, which are all the temptations he gives us, or the cowardice to remain in worldly good, or vanity when we have remained in it, or the deceptions by which he bedazzles the soul, but especially those illusions which the same prophet calls the noonday demon [Psalm 91:6]. But these illusions have no way into those who do not claim to have particular graces over and above their Sisters, believing that there is no other joy than to hide oneself in the hiding places of God, since Our Lord promises that He will be in the midst of those who will be gathered in his name [Matthew 18:20].

5. Antoine Arnauld on Frequent Communion

Antoine Arnauld and Martin de Barcos

Translated by Richard T. Yoder[1]

For over fifty years, Antoine Arnauld (1612–94) was the theological leader of the French Jansenists. Brother of the Abbesses of Port-Royal, Robert Arnauld d'Andilly, and Bishop Henri Arnauld of Angers, the man known as "le Grand Arnauld" did battle against the Jesuits and the Calvinists with a polemical verve and prodigious output virtually unmatched in his century. He was a doctor of the Sorbonne, a major Cartesian philosopher and logician, and, alongside Pierre Nicole, an apologist for Catholic sacramentology. Though once living as one of the pious *solitaires* at Port-Royal, under pressure from Church and state authorities Arnauld eventually went into exile in Belgium, where he died in 1694. When his *Oeuvres Complètes* was edited in the eighteenth century, it stretched to a massive forty-two volumes. It can be said without exaggeration that Arnauld was one of the dominant intellectual forces of *Grand Siècle* Catholicism. Given his prodigious output, he was the undisputed master of theological Jansenism.

1. Antoine Arnauld, *De la fréquente communion, ou les sentimens des Pères, des Papes, et des Conciles, touchant l'usage des Sacrements de Pénitence et d'Eucharistie, sont fidèlement exposez: pour servir d'adresse aux personnes qui pensent sérieusement à se convertir à Dieu, et aux Pasteurs et Confesseurs zelez pour le bien des âmes*, 7th ed. (Paris: Pierre le Petit, 1683; 1st ed. 1643), 10–12, 17–18, 19–20, 33–35, 183–87, 580–82, 612–15, 626, 628–30.

Arnauld made his début as a controversialist with his first major publication, *De la fréquente communion* (1643). His chief target in this work was the Jesuit Pierre de Sesmaisons, whose *Instruction sur la fréquente communion* attacked the rigorist spiritual teachings of the Abbé de Saint-Cyran. As Saint-Cyran only saw the text upon his release from prison, he asked his young disciple, Arnauld, to answer Sesmaisons. *De la fréquente communion* is that extended reply. A collaborative work, it features a preface by the priest Martin de Barcos (1600–78), Saint-Cyran's nephew and secretary, which epitomizes Arnauld's argument.[2]

The book advances two key points of sacramental discipline. First, that absolution can and often should be delayed until after the completion of penance and the attainment of true contrition, and second, that it can be salutary and even necessary for a soul to withdraw from receiving Communion for a time, so as better to cultivate a spirit of penance. Arnauld charges that the Jesuit position, which encouraged frequent Communion, implicitly mirrored Protestant arguments about the requirements needed to take the sacrament. To make these points, Arnauld appeals frequently to the Church Fathers, the Council of Trent, and more recent authorities of the Catholic Reform, such as Carlo Borromeo and François de Sales. Although *De la fréquente communion* was widely lauded upon its release, it also stirred up bitter controversy. Its rigorism was, for instance, the last straw that alienated Vincent de Paul from the Port-Royal circle, to whom he had previously been linked by a long personal friendship with Saint-Cyran. Along with Jansen's *Augustinus* (1640), *De la fréquente communion* became one of the defining texts of Jansenist thought.

Richard T. Yoder

2. Frédéric Delforge, "Barcos, Martin de," in *Dictionnaire de Port-Royal*, ed. Jean Lesaulnier and Antony McKenna (Paris: Honoré Champion, 2004), 143–45.

De la fréquente communion

From the Preface by Martin de Barcos

Authority of the Fathers as Considerable on the Disposition Required for the Blessed Sacrament, as Regarding Its Essence

Isn't it strange that, as all Catholics are obliged to resort to the authority of the Fathers to prove to the heretics[3] that this Sacrament is not only a holy thing, as they believe, but that it is the Holy of Holies, and God Himself enclosed invisibly under the visible species, this author[4] nevertheless wishes us to abandon the authority of the Fathers when it comes to regulating the disposition with which we must approach this Sacrament, in shoving to the altar and to the sanctuary those who had separated themselves from it as unworthy for many years?

If we desire that the heretics would believe St. Basil when he says that "those who commune, touch the body of Jesus Christ,"[5] why do we not believe him when he says that "one must be dead to sin, to the world, and to one's self, to merit participation in this Sacrament"?[6]

If we wish that they believe St. Ambrose when he says that "after the words of consecration the bread becomes the flesh of Jesus Christ,"[7] why do we not believe him when he says that "whosoever desires to eat life must change his life, because if he does not change his life, he will eat life to his condemnation, and it will lose him in place of healing him, and kill him in place of reviving him"?[8]

If we wish that they believe St. John Chrysostom when he says that "this table is the table of the King of Heaven and Earth"; that "the ministers who serve there are the angels"; that "the King Himself is present there in His person";[9] why do we not believe him when he says that

3. Translator's Note: Protestants.

4. Translator's Note: The "author" in question is the Jesuit Pierre de Sesmaisons (1588–1648).

5. Basil, lib.2. *De Bapt.*, c.2. Translator's Note: All patristic and canonical citations, unless otherwise noted, come from the original.

6. Basil, lib.2. *De Bapt.*, c.2.

7. Ambrose, *De Sacr.*, lib. 4, cap. 4 & 5.

8. Ambrose, *Serm. Dom. 4. Advent.*

9. John Chrysostom, *Hom. 24 in 1 Cor. & alibi passim.*

"those who have the honor of being seated at this royal table, and of drinking from the cup of the King, must be adorned magnificently"? That "they must have a robe of pure white,"[10] and that "this table is not the table of crows, but of eagles, that is to say, of souls sublime and elevated, who have nothing in common with the earth, who do not hang down low, who do not creep in the love of creatures, but who fly without ceasing toward the things on high"?[11]

If we wish that they believe St. Augustine when he says that "we immolate upon our altars the holy victim who has by His blood erased the writ of our condemnation,"[12] why do we not believe him when he says that "the one who does not remain in Jesus Christ, and in whom Jesus Christ does not remain, does not eat this flesh spiritually, but he receives the Sacrament to his condemnation, because being impure, he has had the presumption to approach the mysteries of Jesus Christ, which no one approaches worthily but the one who is pure, and of the number of those of whom it is said: Blessed are the pure of heart, for they shall see God"?[13]

If therefore we employ the testimonies of these great men to establish the truth of this Sacrament against the heretics who deny it, why do we not employ them to establish the true disposition toward this Sacrament against those Catholics who combat it? If we wish for the heretics to believe the first, then why do we not want to believe the rest? Must the Fathers only have authority with the enemies of the Church, or must they also have it among her children? And if the truth of the Scripture, which they teach, gives us weapons for the defense of our faith, does it not also give us laws for the regulation of our *mores* and for the conduct of our life?

And certainly, it is clear that our disposition to the Sacraments must be proportionate to the eminence that we encounter there; for the manner by which we must approach a private person or a prince is different according to their different quality. This is what renders this disposition immutable according to the theologians, because it has an essential

10. John Chrysostom, *Hom. 17 in Ep. ad Hebr.*

11. John Chrysostom, *Hom. 24 in 1 Cor.*

12. Augustine, *Confess.* lib. 9, c.13.

13. Augustine, *Tract. 26 in John.*

rapport with the substance of the Sacrament, which is immutable. If therefore this Sacrament were nothing other than the figure of Jesus Christ, as the heretics pretend, it is certain that it would not demand so particular a disposition in approaching it. But being God Himself, as we prove to them by Holy Scripture and by the Fathers, and God become living and immortal bread for the nourishment of our immortal souls, how then can we suffer Him to be treated so unworthily as to judge as well-disposed to frequent His awesome table those who are in a state so unhappy and far from Him, according to the same Scriptures and the same Fathers?

And truly, it seems that this author had wished in his writing to set up as the disposition for the Sacrament that which the heretics have for the same Sacrament. And just as they have thereby destroyed all the essence and the truth established by the faith and by the tradition of every century, in rendering it no more than a figure and a simple sign, he desires as well to ruin entirely the true disposition confirmed by the same tradition and by all the Fathers in rendering it no more than an image and a shadow of that which the Saints have demanded and have established by their works. Because, provided that a man testifies outwardly to the reverence and respect which [the Fathers and Saints] desire he should have engraved in the depths of his soul—provided that he makes an apparent act of piety, which they desire he should make by a sincere and true affection toward Jesus Christ—he finds himself well and truly disposed to commune frequently.

It is enough for him to give outwardly the kiss of peace to the Son of God, like that unhappy Apostle, although he must betray him a few days after, or perhaps the same day. It is enough that he approaches there the face and countenance of a man whom he loves, although the world possesses all his affections. It is enough that he honors the Savior with his lips, and that he receives Him on those lips, although his heart is as far from Him as heaven from earth.

But who, on the contrary, would not approve and esteem the zeal of those persons who, thinking seriously of converting to God, and being touched by the pain and regret of having profaned for so long a time this so holy and inviolable pledge of His love, prepare themselves for some time by humility and by penitence, only then to approach this holy table with more purity and respect, according to the opinion and the precept of all the Fathers? . . .

But, when I speak of separating ourselves thus for some time from the Body of the Son of God, the better to dispose ourselves to receive Him, I do not pretend to authorize the criminal negligence of those who would be glad to have a pretext of piety to exempt themselves from communing frequently, and who, by a tepidity that the Scriptures menace with a great torment, would do what the others do by a profound humility and by an affection toward Jesus Christ as ardent as it is respectful.

As there was once a manner of deferring baptism, which was approved by the Church, when one did it to prepare one's self by all sorts of good works, and another that the Church condemned, when men separated themselves therefrom to remain yet in a worldly and licentious life, which they knew they could not lead after baptism, there is likewise a manner of deferring Communion that the Church approves, when we retire therefrom to dispose ourselves by the fruits of a veritable penance. And there is one that the Church rejects and that she condemns, when we do so by an indifference and an insensibility toward holy things—which is so formidable in souls that there is nothing for the Church to do but oppose it, because it leads to impiety and irreligion. One cannot separate one's self from this bread of life as rivers separate from the sea, which tend toward it even when they leave it, and which approach it by another way, at the same time that they separate from it. Hence, the Councils have defined penitence as a pathway to the Eucharist, which shows rather that one advances toward it in retreating from it. . . .

That This Book Does Not Tend to Turn Souls away from Frequent Communion

The Son of God desired to give to us His Body under the accidents of visible and material bread, to make us understand, by this rapport and this proportion to sensible things, the manner by which we must approach Him in this Sacrament. This bread of heaven is the food of souls, as the bread of earth is the food of the body. As bodies fall into languor if they are not sustained by the bread of earth, souls fall into weakness if they are not sustained by this bread of heaven. But, even though the bread that we use every day is useful to us, we can nevertheless equally injure our health, whether we use it or not. If we eat it when we are in an extreme weakness, we thereby render ourselves still weaker, and it hurts us greatly in place of helping us. And if, being sick, we keep ourselves voluntarily in our ill humors, without intending to put ourselves in a state in which we can eat, we make our illness not only greater, but incurable.

Do we not see clearly in this so sensible image how we can sometimes separate ourselves usefully from this divine Sacrament, even while we must always tend toward it? And is there anything more injurious to the truth and to the respect that we owe to Jesus Christ on His altars, than to assert that we are drawing the faithful away from Communion, because we declare to them the true disposition to be able to commune usefully, according to the Fathers, as necessary for the glory of God as for their salvation? Do we remove them from Holy Communion when we teach them the means of approaching it, in always proposing it to them as the end of their exercises? Will you accuse a doctor of diminishing food for men, who cannot subsist without it, because he does not give them solid food when they are sick? Will you accuse him for exhorting them to take beforehand some bitter potions to drive away the cause of their sickness? And would he be guilty for removing from them in their weakness the bread which he gives to them in their health, because he knows that as it strengthens those who are strong, it further weakens those who are already weak? . . . It is thus not to draw men away from this adorable Sacrament, but to teach them the manner of approaching it, and to imprint in them the respect and reverence with which they must receive it . . . lest it cause their death, instead of healing them. . . .

The Council of Trent Did Everything It Could to Reestablish Penance

It was only time that prevented the bishops from restoring things again to a more perfect state, as this reason is expressly marked in the discourse by which the Council [of Trent] was ended, in which one of the Prelates, chosen to speak for all the others and to recite all the most remarkable things that had passed in that Assembly, spoke on these terms: "Having been obliged to do two things—first to defend the doctrine of the faith, and secondly to reestablish the discipline of the Church, because the heretics affirm that they are separated from us principally due to the disorders of our discipline—we are acquitted of our charge in both the one and the other, insofar as it is in our power and as the circumstances of the times have permitted it to us."[14] Let us remark three very considerable things in these words.

The first is that the Council recognized that the discipline of the Church can become disordered, as it was then effectively disordered, and that these irregularities are the source and cause of heresies. So then, it is not to cause schism in the Church, as some falsely imagine, but on the contrary, to imitate the conduct of the Church herself and of the Holy Spirit that animates her, if we mark the disorders born within her and work ceaselessly for the reestablishment of her discipline, lest the corruption of many members beget a dangerous malady for the whole body.

Second, with the bishops of the Council assuring us that they had regulated all things that had been in their power, they note rather clearly that they would have been delighted to be able to restore them to a still more perfect state, as they testify in various places in the Council. And so, we cannot better second their so holy and praiseworthy intentions but by always bringing the faithful into the path that is most canonical and most conformed to the guidance of the Holy Spirit, authorized by the experience of more than twelve centuries. For, even though it had not been commanded in the following centuries, as it had been in the others, nevertheless it had always been approved and even commanded in certain cases, and the marks thereof are still conserved in many Churches.[15]

Third, that if they had not restored the discipline of the Church to the highest point, it is because they had been prevented by the circumstances of the time, so dismal and deplorable. And certainly, how could

14. *Orat. Habit. In Sess. Ult. Conc. Trid.*

15. Translator's Note: The use of the capital for "Églises" here suggests Barcos is referring to different Sees. However, it is not clear which dioceses in particular he means.

they have been able to act otherwise? That holy Assembly, illumined by the Spirit of God, beheld that the whole of the Catholic Religion, as Pope Paul III said in the Bull of the Council's convocation, was "overwhelmed and almost oppressed by the multitude of her woes."[16] Seeing that there had been formed an overflowing deluge of heresies that had come all of a sudden to melt over her; that this general pestilence and this contagious air of error had passed over lands and seas, and had spread almost in a moment into Germany, into Hungary, into Transylvania, into Norway, into Denmark, into Sweden, into England, into France, into the Low Countries; seeing the Turk inflated with the new prize of Rhodes, and menacing the Christian Provinces, as the same Pope says;[17] seeing that her enemies grew every day in force and number; that her children had fallen into a prodigious laxity, in which they had languished for a long time; seeing license among the people, ignorance among ecclesiastics, factions among princes, wars among kings, disorder and dissolution in everyone.

Therefore, what otherwise could that holy Assembly do in so wicked a time, than what it did? Considering beyond that, that the Devil had stirred up against it the heresy of Luther and Calvin, proportionate to the weaknesses of Catholics, the more easily to seduce them. A heresy entirely sensual, wholly of flesh and blood, that, pushing men into the satisfaction of their passions, next promised them Paradise—that destroyed both the sovereignty of princes and the hierarchy of the Church—and that altogether ruined the penitence of sinners, the virginity of virgins, the vows of religious, the celibacy of priests, the fasts of the faithful, the good works of the whole Church.

We must therefore admire the wisdom of those pastors for not having obliged all Christians to the penance contained in the canons by the express words of the other Councils, because in that state they neither could nor had to do so. We must admire their zeal and their firmness, in that they had taken the care always to maintain it in a way—less clear, in truth—but still intelligible nevertheless to those who had ears to hear it, like St. Charles Borromeo, and to so many others with him.

16. *Bulla indict. Conc. Trid.*
17. *Bulla indict. Conc. Trid.*

They heard it very well.[18] And at last we must admire this marvelous and divine artifice that the Holy Spirit used to establish discipline in a time when it seemed that all things conspired to its ruin.

From Part I

Chapter XXII—The Necessary Dispositions for the Frequent Communion of Those Who Only Commit Venial Sins. In which is also explained the opinion that Monsieur de Genève[19] gave regarding weekly Communion.

We have seen how those who are guilty of mortal sins must purify themselves, before presenting themselves before the Eucharist. From that I leave you to judge what one must think of a man who wishes to assure us that "it was never the practice of the Church that these persons had several days to do penance before communing."[20] It remains now to consider how one must proceed for that which concerns venial sins in the reception of the Eucharist, which is the other chief proposition of Gennadius.

The consideration of the extreme purity that the participation of these sacred mysteries warrants causes this author [Gennadius] not to wish to counsel Communion every day to souls who live in piety, and who find themselves entirely exempt from mortal wounds, although they should feel some light wounds, that is, the bites of those offenses for which the holiest saints strike their breast daily, as Saint Augustine says. He is content to exhort them to commune every Sunday; and still with two extremely considerable conditions. One, that before approaching this sacred table, they purify themselves of their faults, howsoever light, by prayers and by tears. And the other (which is of an

18. Translator's Note: I have separated this last short clause from the foregoing sentence for the sake of clarity and flow.

19. Translator's Note: François de Sales (1567–1622), Bishop of Geneva. This Savoyard cleric was extremely influential on French Catholicism through his *Introduction to the Devout Life* (1609), also known as the *Philothée*. Along with Jeanne Françoise de Chantal, he cofounded the Visitandine Order. Both he and Chantal, eventually canonized, were personally acquainted with Port-Royal. He was for a time the spiritual director of Mère Angélique Arnauld; several of his letters to her are extant.

20. Translator's Note: A quotation from Sesmaisons.

extreme importance for the conduct of souls, and which by itself ruins all your maxims), that their will is not engaged in these venial sins. . . .

Which Monsieur de Genève [François de Sales] had also perfectly well understood, having established on this passage of Gennadius the rule that he gives for Communion, and having expressed in the terms that I believe myself obliged to bring back. For many people strive to authorize their disorders by his doctrine. And separating, at your example, the counsel that he gives to commune each week from the dispositions that he judges necessary thereto, they imagine themselves by a deplorable blindness to follow the maxims of this holy bishop, in whatever state in which they commune, provided that they do it often—just as the Jews believed themselves very religious observers of the law of God, in observing some of its precepts according to the letter that kills, and not according to the spirit that gives life.

See how this holy man speaks: "To receive the Eucharist every day, I neither praise nor condemn it. But I recommend communing every Sunday, and exhort it to everyone; provided that the spirit be without any attachment to sin; these are the very words of Saint Augustine" (that is to say, of the *Book of the Ecclesiastical Dogmas*, which is often cited under the name of Saint Augustine) "with whom I neither praise nor absolutely blame the one who communes every day, etc. But, Philothea, you see what Saint Augustine encourages, and counsels very strongly, that one communes every Sunday: do this therefore as much as it is possible for you, if, as I presuppose, YOU HAVE NO KIND OF AFFECTION FOR MORTAL SIN, NOR ANY AFFECTION FOR VENIAL SIN, AND YOU ARE THUS IN THE TRUE DISPOSITION THAT SAINT AUGUSTINE REQUIRES."[21]

Therefore, it is only to those who find this disposition in their heart, and this purity of conscience, that Monsieur de Genève counsels Communion weekly, and not indifferently to all sorts of persons as you say, without leaving it to the judgment of the confessor to dispose otherwise, according to the state of the sickness. And so that you might not believe that he had followed this sentiment without having well weighed it, he repeats in the conclusion of this chapter, and establishes

21. François de Sales, *Introduction to the Devout Life*, Part II, Ch. 10. Translator's Note: Emphasis in Arnauld.

as a certain and indubitable rule, THAT TO COMMUNE EVERY WEEK, IT IS REQUIRED TO HAVE NEITHER MORTAL SIN NOR ANY AFFECTION FOR VENIAL SIN, AND TO HAVE A GREAT DESIRE TO COMMUNE.[22]

You see that this holy bishop is not content that a man should be exempt from mortal sin, to judge him in a state to commune every Sunday. Instead of which you judge capable those who commit these sins in every encounter, provided they confess themselves of it as often as they commit it: but that he desires, besides that, two conditions as absolutely necessary. . . .

The first is to have no attachment to venial sin; which does not consist in fooling one's self, as many people do, and throwing back upon our fragility all the effects of our lack of virtue and our negligence. But, to judge sincerely whether our heart is truly detached from affection for venial sin, it is necessary that our own actions, which are the fruits of secret passions that we nourish in the soul, serve as testimony—that, as much as we can we avoid these sins, we carefully flee all occasions which could bring us there, and that we embrace all that gives us a means to escape them. This consists principally in loving solitude and a retreat at home, and little company with the people of the world, which such a person must see only by necessity and by force; to acquit ourselves of true civil duties, and not of those that are superfluous. It "being impossible," as Saint Teresa remarks very well, "that a person entangled in the world should advance in virtue; see well that she remains without danger in the state where she is, if she does not retire from all unnecessary affairs, as far as her condition can permit: because," she says, "it is impossible to be among so many and such venomous beasts without being bitten rather often."[23] Thus, in order to believe one's self reasonably disengaged from affection for venial sin, it is necessary to avoid its occasion as well as any negligence. . . .

The second disposition that this holy bishop demands is "to have a great desire to commune," by which he marks for us two extremely important points. The first, that to exhort a man to commune, even on Sundays, one must have a great consideration of the particular

22. Translator's Note: Emphasis in Arnauld.

23. Teresa of Avila, *The Interior Castle*, I, Ch. 2.

movement that carries him to desire to take part in this holy Banquet. For this kind of conduct and particular grace is like the temperament of each of the faithful, which must regulate our ordinary food. The other, that for this weekly Communion, one must have a soul in great health. For this great desire to commune of which Monsieur de Genève speaks, and which Saint Bonaventure calls "an excessive thirst produced by the Holy Spirit, which makes us desire to receive the one who alone can refresh the ardor and the alteration of the soul who loves Him," is nothing other than the effect of the health of the soul, as the appetite is the effect of a good disposition of the body.[24]

From Part III

Chapter IV—Of the Strange Maxim of This Author: That the More One Is Denuded of Graces, the More Boldly Must One Approach Jesus Christ in the Eucharist.

But you go much further. I am astonished that your hand did not tremble when you were writing these words, so contrary to the first sentiments of Christian piety and to the respect that we owe to Jesus Christ: "The more that I find myself stripped of graces, I must more boldly approach the one who has no greater contentment than to make largesse of his favors. While our Savior conversed among men, did he separate Himself from sinners? Truly He was not wary. It was for them he had come."[25]

If I wanted to take this proposition in the sense that the terms bear, I could say to you that it contains the heresy of Luther and Calvin, against the necessary preparation for reception of the Eucharist, and that it gives space to all the impious who approach this Sacrament, having a conscience charged with a thousand crimes, to excuse themselves of their sacrileges. Because from this they can learn to respond to those who would rebuke their criminal temerity, that the more they find themselves stripped of grace, the more they believed they must boldly approach Jesus Christ. And the example that you bring, of the

24. Bonaventure, *De profect. Relig.* l, 2, 6, 77.

25. Translator's Note: A quote from Sesmaisons.

sinners that the Savior of the world never separated Himself from while He conversed with men, would fortify again this interpretation. For, because the greatest part of those sinners were in a state of sin and out of the state of grace when they approached Jesus Christ, is this example not capable of easily causing carnal men to imagine that in staying in all their sins, where their corrupt inclinations engage them miserably, they will do much better to commune, and that the Son of God will take no insult that they approach Him in this state? Which is so easily concluded, as Saint Thomas offers the same example of these sinners who approached Our Lord when He was in the world as an objection against the Catholic doctrine of only approaching the Eucharist when in a state of grace and charity.[26] And Luther made of it one of the principle foundations of his heresy against this same doctrine of the Church.[27]

Nevertheless, to show you that I do not wish to treat you with rigor, I will restrict myself to the best sense, and the least criminal, that you could give to these words, by which we must only understand them with this modification that you have expressed in the preceding article: "Provided that there is no mortal sin." That is to say, according to your doctrine, provided that having committed it, one has confessed beforehand. That's all you can offer for your defense, to say that by these graces (of which you assure us that the more we lack them, the more boldly we must approach Jesus Christ), you have only meant those movements of grace by which God illumines us, warms us, fills us with devotion, and renders us attentive to these Mysteries. All the subtlety of the world would not know how to give to your terms a sweeter and more favorable explanation.

And yet, who would be the Catholic to whom this very explanation does not give horror? And who could endure that in the Church of Jesus Christ, taught of the dignity of this Sacrament by His very mouth, as the Council says—taught by the mouth of His Apostle of the punishment that menaces those who do not approach it with enough reverence, taught by so many Saints of the extreme care that one must

26. Thomas, III part. Q. 80. Art. 4.

27. Roberto Bellarmino, *De Euch.* L.4, c.19.

have to prepare oneself for it, and to present oneself only in holy dispositions and in a profound humility—one could teach as an excellent maxim, that the more we find ourselves lacking devotion, lacking fervor, lacking charity, lacking feeling of God, lacking attention to the things of Heaven, so much the more must we boldly approach Jesus Christ? That is to say, that the audacity with which we commune must grow in proportion that we feel ourselves less well-disposed to do so? I say no more. One loses time by refuting what you need only propose to those who have the least piety, for it to be rejected as impious. One need only report these maxims to destroy them. The blasphemy that they contain is so visible, that it strikes the eyes first, and the impiety thereof is so gross and so clear, that there is no need to be convinced of it.[28]

Chapter IX—Of the Devotion That Is Necessary to Commune Fruitfully

Then, as it is at the same time the preparation and the effect of the Eucharist to remain in Jesus Christ, as we have already said, the best and most assured rule to recognize those who deserve to commune often is not to stop so much at what they say as at what they do, and how they follow the footsteps of the Savior of the world. To understand easily the obligation that we all have to imitate the life of Our Lord, as the Gospel describes to us, one must only consider that we are all religious in the general religious order[29] that Jesus Christ instituted, and obliged to the observation of His rule. Just as, in the fashion of all the instituters of particular religious orders, who learned it from Him and His Spirit, He desired to practice [it] Himself before having it be written, so as to engage by His example, before all other persuasions, those who would wish to embrace it.

It is for this reason that the Savior of the world desired to lead a common life, and to live as a man among men, and not only as Saint

28. Jerome, *Epist. ad Ctesiph.*

29. Translator's Note: The exact word is "religion," which here and elsewhere I have chosen to translate "religious order" to more accurately reflect the metaphor that Arnauld is using. However, I have also at times used "religion" in English to denote when Arnauld seems to speak of the concrete and specific virtue lived out in those religious orders.

John, who lived like an angel in the desert and a penitent out of the desert. So that, His life being more like that of other men, it was more proper to serve as a model for the life of all Christians, of whatever condition and profession.

And yet, we see today that the greatest part of Christians who are engaged in the religion and rule of Jesus Christ persuade themselves that it is easy to bear exterior marks, without taking any pain to walk in His footsteps, to imitate His life, and to observe His rule, which is entirely in charity, in contempt, in the hatred of the world, and in separation from all things that can cause offense to God; in which they are like unto those religious who have degenerated from their rule, and who lead a life contrary to that of their first institution.[30]

The only difference is that men, however unreasonable, find it well that one should reform particular religious orders, and that one should bring them back to the observance of their rule, and to the imitation of the life of their first instituters, however universal and however inveterate may be the contrary laxity. But there is almost no one who would tolerate today that we should return the religious of the general order of Jesus Christ to a serious observation of the rule that they had avowed, that is to say, the Gospel, nor that one should oblige them to conform to the life of their divine Instituter, and to walk as He walked. They believe themselves dispensed from it by custom. They persuade themselves that the times prescribe against the laws of God. They content themselves with seeing that one lives like this; they do not ask themselves if one must live otherwise. All are ready even to accuse of pride and singularity those who endeavor more than they do to conform to the teachings of the Gospel, to walk in the narrow path of Heaven, and not to follow blindly all the irregularities and all the disorders that seem authorized by a long usage.

The gross vices do not pass any more as legitimate, but at least as very pardonable. Those who are exempt from them pass for Saints, whatever vices of spirit they possess, whatever vanity inflates them, whatever ambition burns them, whatever avarice gnaws them, whatever hatreds and

30. Translator's Note: A pointed metaphor, given the context of Mère Angélique's reform of Port-Royal.

envies tear them apart. We no longer judge devotion but by frequent Communions. And we judge worthy for frequent Communion those who confess their crimes often, whether or not they ever leave them. It is enough that they should make "an intention of detaching themselves therefrom." And we believe that these people, buried in vices, "have effective wills to please God" every time that they say so to their Confessor—whether or not we ever behold any effect.

Saint Ambrose says excellently that, "as the Saints are the members and body of Jesus Christ, so sinners who do not leave their sins, are the body and members of the dragon. This is why," he adds, "as the first eat the body of Christ, the others eat the body of the dragon."[31] But today we desire to join two foods, so contrary. Those who eat every day the flesh of the serpent and the dragon, weekly eat the flesh of Jesus Christ just as boldly as the Saints.

I say more. Is it not a horrible thing that we should push to feed on Jesus Christ those who, according to the language of the Scriptures and the Fathers, we must take as Antichrists? Ask the Beloved Apostle "who is the one who is Antichrist," and he will reply to you, "that it is the one who denies that Jesus is the Christ."[32] And we do deny this, says Saint Augustine, in denying it by our works, when we confess it with the mouth: "We look," says Saint Augustine, "for those who deny Jesus Christ, and let us not stop at words, but at actions. For, if you interrogate those who profess Christianity, all with one common voice confess the name of Jesus Christ. But make them quiet their tongue, and interrogate their life. Since the Scripture testifies to us that we renounce God by our works, as well as by the tongue, we must recognize as Antichrists all those who confess Jesus Christ with their mouth, and who combat Him with their *mores*: *Qui ore confitentur Christum, et qui moribus dissentiunt a Christo*. Whosoever denies Jesus Christ by his actions, is Antichrist. I do not hear what they say, I see what they do: *Opera loquuntur, et verba requirimus*. Their works speak, and we do not stop at their words."[33]

31. Ambrose, *In Ps. 37*.
32. 1 John 2.
33. Augustine, *Tract. 3 in 1 John 2*.

Chapter XI—Whether Jesus Christ Receives a Great Happiness from the Frequent Communions of Those Whom This Author Brings to Commune Often

To imagine that all exterior actions, however holy they seem, can please God, if they are not sanctified by His Spirit, is to be a Jew.[34] And it is Pelagian to believe that these acts of faith, of hope, charity, and humility, of which you speak, could be made other than by a particular gift of the grace of Jesus Christ, which forms them into the movements of our hearts. And so, we deceive souls in persuading them that they should only commune frequently in order to exercise those acts of grace frequently—as if they necessarily accompany all Communions, and produce themselves every time that it pleases us to recite certain formulas to which, we imagine, we can reduce them. It is as if they depended entirely on our own will, and that to make them we needed only to bestir ourselves to do so.

But who can pretend to believe that a man makes great acts of faith in receiving the Eucharist, if all his actions and all his works are rather the marks of a dead faith, similar to that of Demons, rather than of a faith at once lively, active, and animated by charity? Is it hoping greatly in God to be attached prodigiously to the world? Is it having much love for Him to be filled with the love of self? Does one have a great humility in presenting one's self all the more boldly to the most terrible of Mysteries, when one is all the more stripped of graces? At last, do we "give a great contentment to Jesus Christ," if I may use your words, to recognize Him on the altar and to disavow Him in His *mores*?

Certainly, as much as the Communions of those whose hearts truly belong to God and who live according to the Gospel are agreeable to the Savior of the world, so much does He hold in horror all the Communions of those lovers of the world who by an impious error desire to separate religion from morality, and to be Christians only in church. They persuade themselves that frequenting the Sacraments is very compatible with their disordered passions. And who, after a confession of the lips that has zero marks of a true conversion, grant

34. Translator's Note: In the Pharisaical sense. This kind of casual anti-Jewish rhetoric was common in the early modern period.

as a place of retreat to the Son of God a house that seems clean on the surface, as Saint Bernard says, but which within is entirely full of mud.

They flatter themselves for some good thoughts that fill their spirit when they commune, and they imagine, as you attempt to persuade them, "that they exercise there a quantity of acts of virtue, of faith, of hope, of charity, of humility," not perceiving that all these acts are nothing but illusions. For, while good people sometimes have their hearts covered with wicked desires and the movements of sin, but nevertheless keep the depths of their heart pure, on the contrary, these worldly people believe they have a heart full of good desires on approaching Communion—and always the depths of their heart remain very corrupt. The Devil excites the evil thoughts in the first without harming them, and the good ones in the others without helping them; and it is by the same token that he often bears the wicked to Holy Communion to cause them to commit sacrilege.

This is why, as Saint John Chrysostom prefers a share in the happiness of the faithful to that of the Magi—in that the former adore on their altars what the latter adored in a manger, and possess Him vested in the glory of His Father, where the Sages only saw Him clothed in infirmity, and they have not only the right to make Him their offerings, which must be the riches of good works, but also to take and eat Him—he is not afraid on the other hand to compare those Christians who commune unworthily to the barbarous and impious King who wished to kill Jesus Christ under the pretext of going to adore Him with the Magi. And as it must be the guidance of the Holy Spirit that brings the just to the Eucharist, just as the light of Heaven brought those Princes to Jesus Christ, this Father assures us that "it is the Devil who sends sinners to commune, to adore Jesus Christ in appearance, but to kill Him in effect as much as they can."[35]

Thus may you see that it is not a stratagem of the Devil to prohibit those who are unworthy of these Mysteries, lest they approach it to their condemnation, but it is rather to take up the duty of the Devil to send them there in that state.

35. John Chrysostom, *Homil. 7 in Matt.*

6. Blaise Pascal's Conversion

Blaise Pascal

Translated by C. Kegan Paul[1]

The only Jansenist who is widely read today, Blaise Pascal (1623–62), has long been regarded as a spiritual master for his unfinished apologetic work, the *Pensées* (first published posthumously in 1670). Pascal was one of the leading mathematical and scientific minds of his generation, and was connected to the same intellectual circles that included such thinkers as René Descartes and Pierre Fermat. His contributions included proof of the existence of vacuums, much of the groundwork for probability theory and fluid dynamics, and even an early form of calculator.

Pascal was also a committed Jansenist. His posthumous *Écrits sur la grâce* evinces an extreme Augustinian soteriology, in which Christ only died for the elect. His polemical *Lettres Provinciales* (1656–57) defended Antoine Arnauld and viciously satirized the Jesuits for their practice of casuistry. The *Pensées* were originally intended to defend Christianity, and the Jansenist cause specifically, after the miraculous healing of his niece, a nun at Port-Royal, in 1656. His sister, Jacqueline (1625–61), a formidable intellectual in her own right, was also a nun at Port-Royal, where she strongly opposed signing the condemnation of Jansen.

1. Blaise Pascal, *The Thoughts of Blaise Pascal, Translated from the Text of M. Auguste Molinier*, trans. C. Kegan Paul (London: Kegan Paul, Trench and Co., 1885), 1.

While Pascal had been familiar with Jansenist circles for years, the turning point in his spiritual life came on November 23, 1654. We do not know what happened that night, but Pascal left behind a record. Known as the "Mémorial," it describes a profound encounter with God. It marked him for the rest of his life. After Pascal's death, this short, scriptural document was found sewn into the lining of his jacket, so that he might always carry it over his heart. The last three lines have been translated from the French and added here to Kegan Paul's translation, as they are usually included in modern editions of the text.

Richard T. Yoder

Pascal's Mémorial

†
This year of Grace 1654,
Monday, November 23rd, day of Saint Clement, pope
and martyr, and others in the martyrology,
Eve of Saint Chrysogonus, martyr, and others;
From about half past ten at night, to
about half after midnight,
Fire.
God of Abraham, God of Isaac, God of Jacob,[2]
Not of the philosophers and the wise.
Security, security. Feeling, joy, peace.
God of Jesus Christ
Deum meum et Deum vestrum.[3]
Thy God shall be my God.
Forgetfulness of the world and of all save God.
He can be found only in the ways taught
in the Gospel.
Greatness of the human soul.
O righteous Father, the world hath not known thee,
but I have known thee.[4]
Joy, joy, joy, tears of joy.

2. Editor's Note: A phrase used throughout the Bible, but in this context most likely an allusion to Exodus 3:15, the theophany of the Burning Bush.

3. Editor's Note: "My God and your God" (John 20:17).

4. Editor's Note: John 17:25.

I have separated myself from Him.
Dereliquerunt me fontem aqua vivæ.[5]
My God, why hast thou forsaken me? . . .[6]
That I be not separated from thee eternally.
This is life eternal: That they might know thee
the only true God, and him whom thou hast sent, Jesus Christ,[7]
Jesus Christ,
Jesus Christ.
I have separated myself from Him; I have fled, renounced,
crucified him.
May I never be separated from him.
He maintains himself in me only in the ways taught
in the Gospel.
Renunciation total and sweet.
Total submission to Jesus Christ and to my director.[8]
Eternally in joy for one day's exercise on earth.
Non obliviscar sermones tuos.[9] Amen.

5. Editor's Note: "They have forsaken me, the fountain of living water" (Jer 2:13).

6. Editor's Note: Kegan Paul's translation, though capturing one important connotation of this line, is not strictly correct. Pascal writes in the future tense, literally, "My God, will you leave me?"

7. Editor's Note: John 17:3.

8. Editor's Note: The director in question is Antoine Singlin (1607–64), the Jansenist chaplain and confessor at Port-Royal des Champs until the Formulary Controversy forced him to leave in 1661. He was a disciple of St. Vincent de Paul and, subsequently, the Abbé de Saint-Cyran. Pascal did spend some time at Port-Royal after this "Night of Fire."

9. Editor's Note: "I will not forget thy words" (Psalm 118 [119]:16).

7. Jean Hamon on the Saints of Grace

Jean Hamon

Translated by Richard T. Yoder[1]

Port-Royal was not, for the most part, a major center of mysticism. However, Jean Hamon (1618–87) was an exception to that rule. A physician who retired to lead a life of penance, prayer, and education as one of the *solitaires* of Port-Royal des Champs, Hamon became one of the spiritual luminaries of the community. He theologized the eremitic life in *De la solitude* (published posthumously in 1734). He wrote extensive treatises on prayer in both French and Latin, including a commentary on the Lord's Prayer and another on the Song of Songs. But Hamon was not just a contemplative. From his arrival at the monastery in 1650, he became one of the community's chief memorialists, composing beautiful Latin epitaphs for the dead nuns, *solitaires*, and servants. He taught at the Petite École de Port-Royal, continuing to ply his medical art. And besides serving as a doctor for Port-Royal and its environs, he stepped into the role of ersatz spiritual director during the persecution of the mid-1660s, when he alone of the *solitaires* was allowed to stay and have contact with the nuns.[2]

Much of his *oeuvre* was published posthumously, including his

1. Jean Hamon, *Entretiens d'une âme avec Dieu; qui comprennent un grand nombre de prières pleines de l'esprit des divines Écritures et des Saints Pères, et exprimées pour la plûpart dans leurs propres paroles, nouvelle edition* (Avignon, 1740), 357–60.

2. Jean Lesaulnier, "Hamon, Jean," in *Dictionnaire de Port-Royal*, ed. Jean Lesaulnier and Antony McKenna (Paris: Honoré Champion, 2004), 504–9.

Entretiens d'une âme avec Dieu (1740). This book of prayers covers the central mysteries of the Christian faith as well as numerous saints. At times, as in the excerpt below, Hamon gestures toward the controversy surrounding Port-Royal. His "Prayer to the Holy Defenders of the Grace of Jesus Christ" packs a tremendous amount of Jansenist theology into a relatively small space. Hamon praises God's almighty, efficacious grace, while deprecating the powers of the human will. Although he does not mention them by name, there can be no doubt that Hamon regarded Port-Royal and its allies as belonging to the "zealous and intrepid lovers of the magnificent glory of [God's] empire over hearts." In that sense, these prayers become an aspirational self-portrait of the greater Jansenist community.[3]

Richard T. Yoder

Entretiens d'une âme avec Dieu

To the Holy Defenders of the Grace of Jesus Christ

Great Saints, who have so faithfully defended the interests of the justice of God, and uncovered to men the scope of His mercies;

who have recognized with sincerity and established with force the weakness and the infirmity of our nature, and posed by this means the unshakable foundations of Christian humility, which is so necessary to us;

who have highly preached the grace of Jesus Christ, by which we are saved, and generously fought for true liberty against those who, *under the pretext of elevating it by great elegies, only extend it above its just boundaries*;[4]

who, full of zeal for the defense of our rights, which are nothing but the totally gratuitous love of our Judge who wishes to grant us mercy, are pressed by the movement of charity, with which you are ignited, to vindicate against the heretical enemies of the grace of Jesus Christ the

3. The translator would like to thank Joshua Caminiti for his assistance in locating the citations of St. Augustine below.

4. Translator's Note: Emphasis in original. All italics in the text reflect the emphasis of the source.

price of our redemption, which they strive to take away from us, and to preserve for us, as well as for all the Church, the spiritual bread that they dispute;

who, in recognizing the testimony that the Holy Spirit gives us that we are children of God, have reciprocally given witness unto Him that it is He who makes children of God, and who alone discerns them from the children of evil;

who, at the example of the twenty-four elders of the Apocalypse, which with a lively sentiment of piety and humility cast their crowns at the feet of the throne of the Lamb, have done on earth and in view of the whole Church what they did in Heaven, in publicly sustaining that *God crowns only His gifts in us, when He crowns our merits,*[5] and that thus it is He alone who causes all of our glory, as He is all of our strength;

pray for us, so that, being nothing and capable of nothing by ourselves, and capable of everything in the One who strengthens us, we may have a firm hope in the grace of our Savior.

Prayer to God

O God, who after Saint Paul, the first Preacher of Thy love and Thy grace, hast given unto us again as defenders and masters, Saint Augustine, Saint Prosper, Saint Fulgentius, Saint Germanus, Saint Loup, Saint Prudentius, Saint Bernard,[6] and all the other zealous and intrepid lovers of the magnificent glory of Thy empire over hearts, and of the victorious grace that submits them to it; give us by their charitable intercession, *the knowledge of that Christian grace which alone discerns wise from foolish virgins,*[7] and grant that it make us equally humble and courageous, so that, as far removed from the presumption of those who believe themselves capable of all, as from the cowardice of those who do not wish to undertake anything, we might keep

5. Translator's Note: An opinion appearing throughout St. Augustine's works, as in *Enarratio in Ps.* 102 (103), 7; *Ennaratio in Ps.* 98 (99), 8; *De Gratia et Libero Arbitrio*, Book I.6, 15; *Tractatus III in Evangelium Ioannis*, 10; *Epistola* 194, 5.19.

6. Translator's Note: A golden chain of anti-Pelagian exemplars. Saint Bernard of Clairvaux is also important as the spiritual father of the Cistercians, the order to which Port-Royal once belonged.

7. Translator's Note: A reference to the Parable of the Ten Virgins, Matthew 25:1–13.

ourselves ever in dependence on Thee, to receive justice from Thee, and that rendering glory to the grace by which we are saved, and *full of the recognition for what preceded us, we might admire like true Israelites*, in the sentiment of a profound adoration, *the infinite mercy that has redeemed us for eternity*, and that we might ceaselessly edify ourselves, in causing [them] to see by the changing of our life, and by the ardor of a holy love, what is the efficacy of the cross of the Savior, and the all-mighty power of Thy name.

If it pleases Thee, Lord, grant that, humbly recognizing the gifts that we receive from heaven, we might respond to the testimony that the Holy Spirit gives us that we are children of God, in giving Him reciprocal testimony, and in truly confessing that if we are called sons of God, and if we are thus effectively, it is the work of mercy, and not the fruit of our own efforts. Thus do we beseech Thee by Jesus Christ, our Lord. Amen.

O God, who givest *grace for grace*[8] so liberally, grant by Thy mercy, that, well convinced that the crown of justice and the recompense of the just are pure gifts of the Holy Spirit, we might sincerely recognize that we will be able to do nothing to share in them but by the help and grace of this same Spirit.

O God, who punishes the ungrateful by the subtraction of Thy grace,[9] grant, if it pleases Thee, that never fearing anything else than making ourselves guilty of ingratitude toward Thee, we might offer Thee ceaseless thanksgiving proportionate to the grandeur of our deliverance, and to the extent of Thy benefits.

All the Glory of the Strength and Virtue of the Saints Belongs to God

I recognize, O my God, *that to thee alone is due all the glory of the virtues*[10] that have shone in Thy Saints. For it is not by the efforts of human will

8. John 1:16.

9. Translator's Note: Antoine Arnauld was stripped of his doctorate by the Sorbonne in 1656 for maintaining, in his *Seconde lettre . . . à un duc et pair* (1655), that St. Peter denied Christ because, in the moment of temptation, he was deprived of the grace to avoid doing so.

10. Translator's Note: If meant as a quotation, Hamon errs in attributing this to Psalm 88:17; however, it may just be an interpretation of the same.

that they have been saved, which is on the contrary the unique cause of all the maladies of our soul, but by a pure effect of the divine mercy, which alone can heal us. No, it is not by the strength of their free will, but by the grace of the Holy Spirit, that they are sanctified.[11] They are only agreeable to Thy Father because Thou art Thyself the object of their complacencies. They have only vanquished the world because Thou hast triumphed over it. Their victory is that of Thy cross. *For they have not been put in possession of the land of the living, by the means of their sword, and their arm has not saved them. But it is Thy right, it is the power of Thine arm, it is the light of Thy face; for Thou has placed in them Thine affection.*[12]

11. Translator's Note: This is a characteristically Jansenist view, against the Molinist opinion that the cooperation of the free will is necessary to make sufficient grace efficacious for salvation.

12. Translator's Note: Psalm 43:4.

8. Angélique de Saint-Jean Arnauld d'Andilly and Jansenist Imprisonment

Mère Angélique de Saint-Jean Arnauld d'Andilly

Translated by Elizabeth Huddleston[1]

Although many of the nuns of Port-Royal signed the formulary with a note of mental reservation as to whether or not the five propositions were actually in Jansen's text, this signature was unacceptable to both Rome and the French King, Louis XIV. In 1664, Archbishop of Paris Hardouin de Péréfixe (1606–71) ordered the nuns of Port-Royal de Paris to sign the formulary condemning Jansen once again, this time without any reservations. Though originally well-disposed toward the nuns, several visits to the convent left the Archbishop infuriated. Expecting to find docile obedience, he instead discovered a house full of intelligent, fiercely conscientious women who could parry his every argument. It was after one such session that Péréfixe famously accused the nuns of being "as pure as angels, but proud as devils." And so he removed twelve of the most recalcitrant nuns from Port-Royal to face imprisonment in various other convents.

The most famous first-person account of this period comes from the pen of Mère Angélique de Saint-Jean Arnauld d'Andilly (1624–84). Perhaps the greatest intellect among the nuns of Port-Royal, Angélique

1. Angélique de Saint-Jean Arnauld d'Andilly, *Relation de captivité d'Angélique de Saint-Jean Arnauld D'Andilly*, ed. Louis Cognet (Paris: Gallimard, 1954; 1st ed. 1711), 143–51, 190–95.

de Saint-Jean had grown up in the monastery alongside her aunts, Angélique and Agnès. She was a militant Jansenist who adamantly refused to sign the formulary, encouraging others to stand fast and fiercely excoriating any who compromised. From 1678 until her death, she served as abbess, the last Arnauld to hold the position. It was under her tenure that Louis XIV banned the convent from taking students or any new postulants, sanctions that would condemn Port-Royal to a slow death.

But first, she faced imprisonment. For a year, she lived at the Annonciade convent in Paris, after which she and other "*non-signeuse*" nuns were moved under heavy guard to Port-Royal's old property in the country, Port-Royal des Champs. Her account of this period was published posthumously as the *Relation de captivité d'Angélique de Saint-Jean Arnauld d'Andilly* (1711). By then, it was a monument to a dead community; Port-Royal was dissolved in 1709 and razed over the next few years. The excerpts selected here demonstrate Angélique de Saint-Jean's antipathy toward the Jesuits, her relations with her captors, and, above all, her own view of the persecution she endured.

Richard T. Yoder

Relation de Captivité d'Angélique de Saint-Jean Arnauld d'Andilly

Jesuit Sermons

I have come a long way, but I must recount the retreat where I had spent Advent. I thought I had to leave at Christmas to return to the choir and not excommunicate myself. During all of Advent, I was told of the beauty of Fr. Nouet's sermons,[2] and it was always to make small reproaches for not wanting to hear them. Madame des Hameaux, who often visited the convent and who did me the honor of waiting to see me several times, was practically angry with me—though with courtesy, for she always treated me civilly—although she took the freedom everyone acquired at this time to exhort me for my salvation to prepare

2. Translator's Note: Fr. Jacques Nouet (1605–80) began writing against the Jansenists as early as 1632.

myself to receive Holy Communion, and, to achieve this, to obey the Church. By the grace of God, I found myself so calm in mind at that time that, in truth, I did not fear that the sermons of this priest would make any impression on me, as I had first feared. Thus, after seeking counsel from God, to whom alone I could have recourse in all my doubts—which, however, is not a small problem because one does not know if one is worthy of hearing His answer properly—I concluded that it would be a scandal not to remain for the sermon on Christmas Day and to leave the church where I would have attended Vespers. For this reason, it was better for me to resolve to hear it. I told this to these good Mothers, and this was the reason that compelled me to attend. They insisted that it would have been wrong to do otherwise and that everyone would find it very strange that I had a problem with this, which none of our Sisters in other convents had had.

So, I concluded that I would go. But, God once again wanted to spare me this trouble. The goodness of the Mother Superior dispensed me from [the sermon] for that day, when I had enough mortification from being separated from the altar of Jesus Christ, without adding that one. I don't know where this good impulse came from in her. Before Vespers, she came to ask if I would prefer to go pray, during the sermon, before the Blessed Sacrament, which was exposed on their side of the chapel, although there was already a deaf sister assigned there. I told her that I was infinitely obliged to her for this grace she offered me, and that she gave me two pleasures at once, but she would have been more at ease if I had not felt this favor so deeply. In passing, I noticed what I experienced in several encounters during our affliction: that it is almost always true that one suffers more from the anticipated apprehension one has of things before they happen, than of the things themselves when they happen. There is no advice more important and more useful to practice on these occasions than that of the Gospel: Do not think of tomorrow. I remember that, long before Christmas and before Easter, I dared not think that I would spend these holidays separated from Holy Communion without feeling some strong emotion and self-pity that made me dread that time. Not only would I have the pain of being deprived of such a great grace—because on this subject faith convinced me well enough that God could fill this void and give me as much strength by the communication of the sufferings of Jesus Christ as by the participation in the divine sacrament that is their memorial—but mixed with this was a human fear of humiliation: that I would appear at such feasts like a poor dog being chased from the table to which all the others approach. In the choir I would be exposed to judgment and to the glances of all the sisters, little novices, and servants, who looked on me as a wretch whom God rejects and whom the Church abandons. I nevertheless accepted it wholeheartedly and commended myself to God on this occasion, without stopping to consider that it was the least I could do. However, he has helped me so much in these moments that I didn't know if I have ever spent these holidays with more spiritual consolation. As a result, I didn't even feel this outward humiliation as much as I thought I would. Through reason and reflection, I discerned that I was not affected by it because I was much more moved by the advantages of our persecution and by the part it gave me in the annihilations[3] of the Son of God.

I had not yet attended the New Year's sermon. I asked for a dispensation until Epiphany, when the preacher took his leave. So, I heard him for the first and last time. I don't need to say how he preaches: it is well known. But the best thing about it was that he didn't say a word concerning the arguments of the time. His sermon was all about the love of God and was quite full of feeling. However, this great ardor with which he speaks warms his listeners less when they know that his Order, the Society of Jesus, are not certain if we are obliged to love God, except, perhaps, at the moment of death, or at most on feasts and Sundays.[4]

Since I am on this subject, I must mention the other occasions on which I have heard these priests speak. There was a rumor that one of them had spoken to me at the choir gate against my will, but that is false. I only heard them in the pulpit on three occasions. The first was

3. Editors' Note: The word used here, *anéantissement*, is a technical term referring to the kenotic humiliation and "annihilation" of the Son of God in his incarnation, passion, and resurrection. It is used frequently in French spiritual and theological literature of this period due to the pervasive influence of Cardinal Bérulle.

4. Editor's Note: Here, Angélique de Saint-Jean accuses "laxist" Jesuits of using casuistry to undermine the duty of the Christian to love God, an accusation which was put most forcefully by Pascal in the tenth of his *Lettres Provinciales* (1656–57).

Father Nouet. The second time was a priest who had returned from Canada, whose name I was not told. He preached on one of the Shrove Days and delivered a sermon I found very useful. It was about the necessity and of the advantages of suffering: that it is the mark of the elect, that persecution was the reward of justice, that whoever wants to make the horoscope of a Christian has only has to consult the star and the sign that presided at his birth. You will find that he was baptized into the death of Jesus Christ, that the cross with which he was marked was the dominant sign of his second birth, and thus, in his whole life he can expect only the influences of these signs that necessarily lead him to all kinds of crosses, humiliations, and sufferings, even unto death.

The eve of this sermon, I heard another, from a Picpus[5] monk or another order—I do not know him. He preached against the disorders of these days to encourage us to pray to God for the many people who forget their salvation. I think these good Mothers liked this sermon because this good priest was very animated and spoke with great zeal. Madame de Rantzau,[6] who was ill at the time, and whom I was taken to see, asked me which of the two sermons I had valued more. I understood her intentions, and replied that the subject matter of the latter was more useful and relevant to me than that of the other sermon. In saying this, I said nothing but the truth.

The third time I heard another Father speak again was on a day of Lent, at a private conference given to the nuns on the renewal of their vows, which they were obliged to make on the day of the Annunciation. They often had these conferences and have had several since, but I was never asked to go. So, I don't know how they decided to come ask me that day if I wanted to go to the conference held before Terce. I saw no problem with it because I did not see any new reason to refuse, both because they did not tell me that he was a black-robed preacher [Jesuit] and because I had already agreed that they had not spoken in any way about anything of which I could complain.

5. Translator's Note: A Franciscan community founded by Vincent Mussart in 1600. It was named for the neighborhood in which their house was located in Paris.

6. Editors' Note: Madame de Rantzau, widow of the Maréchal de Rantzau, was the superior of the Annonciade convent in which Angélique de Saint-Jean was imprisoned. She was a convert from Lutheranism.

So, I heard a good man who still speaks his old Gaulois,[7] but who basically gave them a completely solid sermon, and who presupposed the right maxims of grace. This was either because he had not yet renounced them or because he is one of the oldest in the Society and may not have engaged in the heat of the last disputes. Perhaps it was because the strength of the truth compelled him to yield to the authority of the Gospel he had taken for his subject, and that he was not afraid that it would be to the prejudice of the opinions of his Society, because he thought he was speaking only in front of women who did not suspect any fault in what he said. I had such a distinct satisfaction in seeing grace victorious on the lips of its enemies. Even if this good man were not personally opposed to it, he wears the habit of those who are.

His theme was the words of the Gospel of the day: "Ye shall seek me and find me not, and in your sins you shall die."[8] He wanted to prove to them that there is often a need in the Christian life for renewal, and, to establish the principle, he compared the life of the soul with that of the body. He told them that, as the body necessarily falls into old age with the long course of years, so the soul is subject in the life of grace to grow old; the same causes which produce old age of bodies also produce old age of souls. He showed that what causes weakness in old age is when the head and the heart cease to deliberately influence the vital and animal spirits, which must provide vigor to all the members. Likewise, the source of the chilling and weakening of souls is when Jesus Christ, who is our head, ceases to shed his light in our spirit and when the Holy Spirit, who is the heart of the body of the Church, ceases to animate our will by the movements of his charity. Just as the body becomes heavy, sight darkens, and hearing and the other senses weaken in old people, so in the withdrawals of interior graces we see the most fervent virtues fall into cowardice and languor, because God is withdrawing.

This was taken so far that I couldn't be more astonished that it was a black-robed Father speaking like this. But I did not try to conserve his sermon, nor would I claim to be writing it here. I add only one comparison he used to express the helplessness to which we are reduced by the withdrawal of the interior lights, when God takes them away from us.

7. Editors' Note: The implication here is that he is an honest man, who has no guile.
8. Translator's Note: John 8:21.

He attributed to a soul in this state the words of the prophet: *Posuerunt me in obscuris, sicut mortuous saeculi.*[9] He said it was similar to those dead of the world who are given a great funeral ceremony. The dead are put in a bright chapel. It is entirely covered in cloth and surrounded by light. All those who are far away are illumined by it, but this poor dead man, who is very close and for whom all this has been done, is alone in the darkness and cannot see the slightest amount of light that surrounds him. This is the true image of this poor soul, he added. She has lost the light of her eyes because Jesus Christ, who was accustomed to spreading the knowledge of the truth within her, no longer illuminates her inwardly. No matter how much you preach to her, exhort her, threaten her with the words of God, she herself tries to read the writings, meditations, and books that touched her before, but she no longer has a taste for all this. She no longer hears any of it, she is not touched by it, *quaeretis me et non invenietis.*[10] She seeks and she could not find him. He was committed to this theme before, because of the conclusion of the Gospel: *Et in peccatis vestris moriemini.*[11]

In the end, I believe that he realized he was going to go out of the bounds of the almighty free will of his Order, and that he passed on the side of the freedom of the children of God, which consists in recognizing our dependence on the voluntary grace of the Savior. For suddenly, he abandoned his proofs and principles to reflect that it was not God's fault that we did not have the help and the lights that we need; rather, it was our negligence that was the cause, and we could always get out of this state. And, as it would have taken a long speech to clarify all this and combine it with everything he had just said, he did not attempt it. Rather, he ended rather abruptly, having left this hanging in the air. Among all the good things he said, he mixed in some ridiculous terms and tales. These women laughed about it almost aloud during our conferences. But I was not shocked as much as I would have been with someone else, because it seemed to come from simplicity; the rest was solid and serious.

We said the Office and Mass afterwards, and after Mass the Superior

9. Translator's Note: "They have placed me in the shadows, like they place the dead" (Ps 142:3).

10. Translator's Note: "You will search for me, but not find me." (Jn 7:34)

11. Translator's Note: "You will die in your sins." (Jn 8:24)

took me on a tour of the garden. She did not fail to ask me how I felt about this exhortation. I simply replied that I had found it very good, and then I asked her who this Father was. She told me that it was Father du Breuil, who had been the Superior at La Flèche for a long time. They had taken him thence after the death of Father de Saint-Jure to put him in the deceased priest's place, because he was a very spiritual man and provided spiritual direction for many notable people and was the confessor of the black-robed Fathers with Father Nouet. This last piece of information gave me compassion for him because, if he takes on his conscience the sins of everyone else in his community, what good will he do if he himself is more innocent than them? She then told me how she had come to know him by accident. Lacking a preacher for a great feast, and the black-robed Fathers having promised her a priest, they later sent him because a bishop requested they do so. Madame des Hameaux, who takes an interest in everything concerning these nuns, complained so much to the black-robed Fathers that they were forced—so as to remain on good terms with her—to send them Father du Breuil immediately. He came by obedience but could never resolve to take the pulpit and speak in front of everyone. He apologized to the Mother, saying he was not fit to preach, and that he also had difficulty speaking, due to a paralysis of his tongue. This made him even more incapable of the task.

He offered only to give a special exhortation behind closed doors. The nuns enjoyed it so much that they asked him to return several times since. According to them, he seems to be humbler than the others. That is why he maintains a little more light than the others, so as not to ignore completely the sovereignty of God and the baseness of humanity. That's all I have to say about them, because I haven't seen any of them in private.

The Bull *Regiminis Apostolici*: Threats of Excommunication[12]

I have already mentioned what happened during Lent and how I wrote to the Archbishop for Easter Communion. My good Sisters began to

12. Editors' Note: The bull in question, *Regiminis Apostolici*, was promulgated by Pope Alexander VII on 15 February, 1665. It mandated that all clergy and religious sign the formulary, now defined as condemning "the five propositions taken from the book of Cornelius Jansen . . . in the sense understood by that same author," and thus definitively ruling out Arnauld's *fait/droit* distinction. See Denzinger-Hünermann 2020.

urge me again so that I might not let this feast pass like the others. One day, the Superior came to tell me on behalf of Madame des Hameaux, who sent me her compliments and added that she made sure to pray for me, that it was time for me to think about taking Communion at Easter. The Mother Superior urged me to make a reply. I told her I was astonished that she would offer me such an honor and that they would still have faith in me, given my position. Since the time I had told them my feelings on the signature, which I regarded as a mortal sin, they could have easily judged that I had more repugnance from committing it on the feast of Easter than at any other time. I would not want to shed the blood of Jesus Christ with his executioners so I could eat his body with the faithful. I think I didn't say this last phrase on this occasion and that I stuck to mortal sin. I must have used it in another meeting. Afterward, the Mother Superior said nothing to me for a while, except that she sighed because of the hardness of my position. But, a few days later, she brought up my words in the presence of Madame de Rantzau, exaggerating the blow to her heart it had given her to see me guilty of placing the legitimate obedience that I owe my superiors in the rank of mortal sins. I replied that if she had wanted to take the trouble to consider the reasons I had told her several times to make her understand that in my current disposition, I could not sign without committing a public lie in a very serious matter without wounding the reputation of my neighbor, she would have had no difficulty in judging that I regarded the signature as a crime. She would have no reason to be surprised that I had expressed this "mortal sin" to her because I had always spoken to her about it in this sense if it were not in the same terms. Nevertheless, since this term caused her pain, I promised her that I would no longer explain myself so forcefully, and that it would be enough for me that she understand how insignificant it is in comparison to the great feasts or the desire for Communion that leads me to do something that would make me unworthy of Communion for my whole life.

As they saw me so firm in my position, they began to scare me of the brand new evils that awaited us. At first they explained nothing. Finally, they told me about a papal bull coming out, and I testified that I was expecting it and that it did not surprise me too much. I was not told then what this bull said. But, another time when the Mother Superior was alone with me, she opened this discussion and demonstrated a strange apprehension about the things to which I was going to expose myself, without telling me what they were. I asked her what it could be. She sighed and tears filled her eyes as she told me she didn't even dare to think about it. I pressed her many times without her being able to tell me. I thought she dared not speak the word "excommunication." Finally, it was I who asked her if it might be that we would be excommunicated. "Unfortunately, yes! The horrible thing!" she said to me. "They say this bull comes for you and excommunicates you all if you don't sign. After that, my dear Mother, if you allow yourself to be excommunicated, I tell you now that it will be impossible for us to keep you with us. We will beg the Archbishop to remove you. Never did I see such a possible outcome!"

I replied that I belonged to God, that He would do with me whatever He pleases, and that I was more afraid of separating myself from Him by offending Him than of being excommunicated for having been faithful to Him. Moreover, disturbing as this news was, it was less surprising to the people who knew that it was only the fulfillment of wishes that the Jesuits stated publicly a long time ago. They have worked unceasingly to make it succeed. If God will allow them to arrive at their plan, things will go even further, since it was many years before any mention of the formulary that they wrote that the royal sword had to join the sword of the Church to destroy those who displeased them. Seeing the way things were developing, and where the violence had already broken out, it was not unthinkable that in the long run we could die from it.

She exclaimed, "What a thought!"

I told her that this thought was truly horrible, but that it had already occurred to the Jesuits. I told her they themselves had printed it in their writings, and that it was by no means a tale. As for the excommunication, they had not waited for the bull to declare excommunicated those who refused the signature and to urge the King to banish them from the kingdom. This I read in a writing by Father Ferrier[13] shortly before

13. Editors' Note: Probably Jean Ferrier, a Jesuit, disciple of the anti-Jansenist polemicist Père François Annat. From 1670, he was Louis XIV's confessor, before

leaving Port-Royal. So, there is no doubt who is requesting the new bulls and from where the inspirations come to the Pope, who cannot know from so far away everything that is happening except according to the reports that are made to him. She could see in my face that I was speaking with conviction. I didn't think it wrong to express more strongly than usual, since it was a question of excommunication, and it was important that she see that I thought of this excommunication as a strange injustice, which I do not attribute to the Church, but to enemies determined and wicked enough to ambush her ministers and make them instruments of their vengeance. The good Mother wanted to soften things, but she did not have all the facts needed to do so, except that she could not believe these good Fathers capable of such a strange obsession.

It is true that the news of the bull did not surprise me, because I thought things were even worse. I imagined that everything would be destroyed, especially after January, when I tempted fortune by asking if the Mother would kindly allow me to ask Petit[14] for the *Homilies of Saint Chrysostom on Saint Matthew*. I told her that he would give the bill to me because my father would pay for them. I did not see how she could civilly refuse my request, but either to find an excuse or because she believed it to be true, she answered that the King had forbidden all the books and all the translations of these Messieurs.[15] When I told her that the book I asked for was not among these, she replied that if the bookstore I named had printed it, I could not have it, because they had seized everything from that bookstore, and that several booksellers were imprisoned. I simply believed it and convinced myself that the war had begun, that there was some bloody declaration, and that

---

eventually being succeeded by Père La Chaise. The text in question is probably either *L'idée véritable du jansénisme* or *Relation fidèle et véritable de ce qui s'est fait depuis un an dans l'affaire des jansénistes*, both of which were published in 1664.

14. Translator's Note: Pierre Le Petit, a Parisian printer, was the primary publisher of works by Jansenists. The work in question is *Homélies de Saint Jean Chrysostome sur l'évangile de Saint Matthieu*, 3 vols., trans. Paul-Antoine de Marsilly (Paris: Le Petit, 1665).

15. Translator's Note: The "Messieurs" here are the *solitaires*, the community of male scholars at Port-Royal des Champs.

people were shouting: *Exinanite, exinanite.*[16] I was concerned about it, but I was not anguished, for God, by his grace, had already strengthened my peace.

Since I had been told about this new bull, from time to time I asked for news. I was told once that it had arrived, but was not received in *Parlement*. Then, I was told that the King had carried the bull to *Parlement* and that it was received, but that it was not published. I told them that it would not be long before it was published and that the Archbishop would waste no time. From day to day I awaited this news, which gave me a glimpse of a necessary change in our affairs, and especially for me, since these good Mothers kept telling me that if I excommunicated myself absolutely, they would not keep me. I knew that for some it was not only the horror of excommunication but also the pity they would have had to see me abandoned, not daring to look at me, because they imagined that such was the outcome. Among others, the Subprioress told me the day before I left that in speaking of this, she had declared that she never would have had the courage to treat me in this way, and that she could not prevent herself from coming to see me. The Subprioress mentioned that Madame de Rantzau had instructed that no one should approach me, except the one who has permission to deal with excommunicates, as she does every day with Lutherans.

Finally, on the Sunday in the octave of the Ascension, when I heard the Gospel at mass, *absque synagogis facient vos*,[17] and all the rest, I said to myself: "Surely they are publishing the bull today," and I was impatient to be told it was true, but I could not learn anything from it until the following Tuesday. When I saw in the accompanying pastoral letter that indeed it had been published that day, I had a real consolation to think that Jesus Christ had foreseen it and had looked at us on this occasion when He had said these words: *ut, cum venerit hora eorum, reminiscamini quia ego dixit vobis.*[18]

16. Translator's Note: "Destroy it! Destroy it!"

17. Translator's Note: "They will put you out of the synagogue" (John 16:2).

18. Translator's Note: "When their hour comes, you will remember what I have told you" (John 16:4).

9. Pierre Nicole on Enduring Persecution

Pierre Nicole

Translated by Daniel J. Watkins[1]

Pierre Nicole (1625–95) was one of the most prolific writers among the *solitaires* of Port-Royal. Born at Chartres and originally destined for the priesthood, Nicole became an educator and philosopher at Port-Royal des Champs, where he taught the future playwright Jean Racine. Nicole was a close collaborator with Blaise Pascal and Antoine Arnauld; with the latter, he wrote *La Logique, ou l'art de penser* (1662), more commonly known as the *Logique de Port-Royal*, which would become a standard textbook for centuries. In an apologetic and controversial key, he wrote numerous treatises against the Calvinists, the Jesuits, and the troubled mystics known as the "Quietists." He played a major role in helping to set up the Boîte à Perrette, a fund to assist Jansenists. And he, too, had a share in the persecution of Port-Royal. In 1679, the Archbishop of Paris came to Port-Royal des Champs to disperse the *solitaires*, close the schools, and forbid the nuns from taking any more postulants. Nicole went into exile in Belgium, where he lived for some time with Arnauld. Eventually he was allowed to return to Paris, where he died in 1695.

In the Anglophone world, Nicole is best remembered as a moralist due to his monumental *Essais de morale* (1671), translated into English

1. Pierre Nicole, "Règles pour les tems d'épreuve et de persécution," in Jean Hamon and Pierre Nicole, *Principes de conduite dans la défense de la vérité par Monsieur Hamon, avec des règles pour les tems d'épreuve et de persécution par M. Nicole* (n.p., 1734), 161–77.

as early as 1677. It is as a moralist that he writes here, in the context of Port-Royal's suffering under Louis XIV. This short treatise, which teaches the reader how profitably to endure persecution for Christian truth, was published with a similar text by Jean Hamon in 1734. By then, Jansenists faced renewed attacks by Cardinal Fleury's royal administration, including imprisonment. It thus forms a link between the crisis of the 1660s and the ongoing affair of the appeal against *Unigenitus* in the early eighteenth century.[2]

Richard T. Yoder

Règles pour les tems d'épreuve et de persécution

I

It is necessary to prepare to suffer all manner of violence so that, as Saint Peter says, we are not surprised or shocked, as if it were something unexpected, when we are tested by fire.[3] The Fathers warn us that the persecutions that will come at the end of the world will be more dreadful than those of the first centuries because Satan, retaining all of his cruelty, will transform himself into an angel of light to deceive us.

II

We will soon know from experience whether we have truly renounced the world, if we no longer love anything in it and if the only thing that we seek is to leave it. It is nothing, says St. Cyprian, to have promised God to renounce the world in one's baptism if one doesn't truly renounce it while suffering. Suffering, says St. Chrysostom, is solid proof of our faith. It is in vain that Christians say that they believe in the resurrection of eternal life if they do not love the crosses through which alone they are able to enter it. St. Ignatius[4] was in chains and ready to

2. The translator would like to thank Diane LeBouille for her assistance on the translation.

3. Translator's Note: This is likely referencing 1 Peter 1:7.

4. Translator's Note: St. Ignatius of Antioch (died between 98 and 117 CE), not the founder of the Jesuits.

be devoured by beasts, and in this state he assures us that he was not yet a perfect Christian, that he was only beginning to be a disciple of Jesus Christ, that he would become one by fighting against the beasts and becoming through death a host following the example of Him who offered Himself to His Father for our sins. It is an error to believe that we are ever able to understand Jesus Christ crucified without crucifying ourselves with Him.

III

It is necessary to suffer in silence following the example of Jesus Christ. He was the Word of His Father. He was able to defend Himself honorably, and He was able to confound His enemies, but He prefers to appear guilty and obey rather than justify Himself and be less obedient. He conceals His wisdom and His strength, and He lets himself be taken to the cross like a lamb. He opens His heart, and He closes His mouth forever; He lets the snake speak all sorts of lies and calumnies. He no longer talks to him, but He crushes him and puts him to death. And we, who are in danger of committing so many indiscretions through our words, how much do we have to place a faithful guard on our lips!

IV

What is the use of speaking when God no longer speaks? Believe me, anything more that we can say only serves to weaken us if God does not make us say it. However correct our speeches may appear, they are often only born out of the sickness of our mind. We speak under the pretext of healing our brothers who have been harmed by lies, but instead of relieving them we make their wounds incurable, and perhaps we even harm ourselves. Our Lord commands St. Peter after he struck Malchus and cut off his ear to put his sword back in his sheath because whoever will strike with the sword will die by it.[5] This sword, says St. Bernard, is our tongue, our words; when we use it against the direction of Jesus Christ, even though it is to defend Him, we are only striking our brothers in the ear—that is to say, making them more deaf to the

5. Translator's Note: See Matthew 26:52, John 18:10.

truth and wounding ourselves sometimes with a mortal wound. We believe we are right to contradict unjust people, and yet we resist the will of God who intends to use their injustice to train us.

V

As Saint James said, one is perfect who does not sin with his tongue. We can say that one suffers with perfect patience in a manner worthy of Jesus Christ who does not amuse himself with words that are often only vanity or pride and which are always useless when we are committed by the command of God to bear witness to the truth through our suffering, by the loss of our freedom, and even by the shedding of our blood. It seems to me that it is such a precious gift to participate in the passion of Jesus Christ, that when God grants us this grace, we ought no longer apply ourselves toward anything other than remaining in a profound admiration for such an extraordinary favor. This astonishment should keep us in respectful silence[6] and make us withdraw within ourselves in order to rejoice in our crosses in the presence of God and to give to Him continual acts of thanksgiving for them. *Parum est christiano pati, nisi etiam glorietur & gratias agat.*[7]

VI

Silence is necessary for us in this time during which every moment ought to be precious for us, so that we might watch over all our actions in order to do them with such Christian prudence before the world and fidelity before God that we might not give to men any actual reason to mistreat us, and so that it might be true, at least with regard to them, that we suffer only for justice, and that they only persecute the truth when they persecute us. Without this we put ourselves in danger of

6. Editor's Note: The Jansenist strategy of "silence respectueux" toward the question of *fait*, or fact, was condemned by the Papal Bull *Vineam Domini Sabaoth* in 1705. This left no room to assent to the condemnations of Jansen's propositions while denying that they were actually in his text, even for those who had signed the Formulary of Alexander VII with this restriction in mind.

7. Translator's Note: "It is not enough for a Christian to suffer, unless he also gives [to God] glory and thanks."

making our sufferings useless, or at least very imperfect, of dishonoring the Cross of Jesus Christ, of scandalizing men and making them blaspheme, and at last of making ourselves unworthy of the help of God, without which we can only fail. I admit, however, that it is very hard to be so attentive to ourselves that we will not fall into some sort of imprudence. It would be pride to be flustered by this. If we cannot be without faults, at least let us attempt to correct them by humbly asking God for forgiveness.

VII

The strength of the people of the world only comes from their passion and pride. Ours, in order to be wholly of God, ought to have for its foundation an interior silence, perfect peace, and deep humility. If these are in our heart, we have nothing to fear from anything that can happen outside of us. Let us be humble, gentle, and peaceful like Jesus Christ, and we will be strong like Him. *Pax sit intus & non timebit foris.*[8]

VIII

The greatness of the tribulations into which we are heading ought not terrify us. Let us not fear the devil, and he will flee before us; let us not fear men, and we will be stronger than them. It is usually only the fear of persecutions and not the persecutions themselves that make us weak. Let us increase our charity until we banish all fear from our souls, and we will be assured of the help of God; our strength will increase in the tribulations that the truth will bring us to suffer, and a humble patience will make of our crosses a perfect work.

IX

If one knocks down this earthly house and drives us out of it, do we not have an eternal one in heaven? And from this hour on, who could prevent us from living in Jesus Christ, entering into His wounds, and having Him live within us? It does not grieve a Christian to be banished

8. Translator's Note: "If peace be on the inside, one will not fear the outside."

from his country; he only seeks God, and he finds him everywhere.[9] The only exile that we should fear is to be banished forever from the presence of God, from His house, and from our heavenly home by these terrible words: *Go, cursed ones, to the eternal fire that has been prepared for the devil and his angels. Ite maledicti, &c.*[10]

X

If it is true that Truth has delivered us and that Charity has made us slaves of Jesus Christ, then we will not fear losing our freedom. Prisons are not prisons for those who can and must raise themselves up above the earth in order to converse with God.[11] We ought to bless the chains, which do not prevent us from walking in the way of truth and which even help us walk it more faithfully. On the contrary, prison is like a retreat for Christians. It separates them from the world. It is a solitude where God leads them, where He dwells with them, where He speaks to their hearts, where they listen to Him, and where they respond to Him: *audiam quid loquatur in me Dominus Deus.*[12] He speaks to them internally by pouring His Spirit into their hearts, and they respond to Him by continual acts of thanksgiving.

XI

The prison that we ought to fear is the world. The slavery that we ought to worry about is being in concord with it. There is no dungeon that has such thick darkness, since it blinds the soul. Its teachings are the chains that make us captives of Satan. Its spirit extinguishes the Holy Spirit in us. Everything in it is full of crimes and criminals who are often all

9. Editor's Note: Many Jansenists did in fact go into exile. Nicole himself fled for a time to the Spanish Netherlands (modern-day Belgium) alongside Antoine Arnauld, though he eventually returned to France.

10. Translator's Note: Matthew 25:41.

11. Editor's Note: Starting with the Abbé de Saint-Cyran, many Jansenists did face imprisonment (including conventual imprisonment) in both the seventeenth and eighteenth centuries.

12. Translator's Note: "I will hear what the Lord God says to me." This comes from the Vulgate's version of Psalm 84:9.

the more guilty the less they appear to be so before men and who are always guilty enough to be condemned by their own conscience before the eyes of their sovereign Judge.

XII

Although we might not find in the dungeons and in the chains the temporal joys and delights that the people of the world seek with eagerness and by which the servants of God are horrified, we will not however be without pleasure. Our joy will be to despise all kinds of joy, if not to suffer for the truth. *Voluptas Christiani fastidium omnis voluptatis.*[13] We will have the consolation of knowing that we might never have entered into it if the Holy Spirit were not entering into it with us, and we are assured that He will accompany us as long as we have the courage to remain there.

XIII

The abandonment of and separation from all things will not be difficult to endure for those who have entirely renounced this age and who desire to die at peace with themselves. We find God's help as His creatures abandon us, and if it is true that we have left everything for Him, He will give Himself in place of all that we have given Him. *Te da ei, & habevis illum; unde derelinquimus, inde juvamur.*[14] We will be rich because our hearts will be full of God, of His charity, and of His light. His promises will be our abundance—His word, our treasure; His spirit, our company; and His grace, our supreme happiness. Estrangement from people who can sustain us by their lights and example is a terrible thing. But it does not matter if we no longer have a master on the earth. How lucky is this privation which obliges God Himself to be our master! What happiness to have that master in heaven who no creature could take away from us and whose anointing will teach us all things.

13. Translator's Note: "The pleasure of the Christian is the loathing of all pleasure."

14. Translator's Note: "Give to him, and you will have him; from where one leaves behind, there one is helped."

XIV

But even in this state we would fool ourselves, and to our great danger, if we thought that there is nothing left to do. We are then obligated more than ever to watch over ourselves, so that the injustices and excesses of our enemies do not get in the way of the charity that we owe them. On the contrary, compassion obliges us to redouble it, as we see that they are doing themselves so much harm, and to not consider at all the harm that they are doing to us. What consolation to be assured of conquering our invisible enemy, who is the devil, if we love with all our hearts our visible enemies, who are our brothers.

XV

There is nothing that separates us so much from the darkness of those who persecute us than to have a great compassion for them, to groan for them, to ask mercy for them, to pray to God that He pardons them, because they know not what they do. They do not know the damage that they do to the Church, because they are in darkness; and they know still less the wounds that they are inflicting on their own souls, because the hardness of their hearts has taken away their feeling.

XVI

We must consider these days as a time of harvest. We will reap a good crop; we will pick fruits that we have not sown into the ground. This is what ought to give us joy, at least an inner joy if it does not reach our outer feelings, since the great happiness of the Christian is to suffer. The best proof that we are friends of the Bridegroom is to bear the marks of His Passion.[15] The great secret that He will teach to His dearest disciples is that we can only follow Him by taking up our cross, that it is necessary to be lifted up onto it [the cross] in order to be taken to heaven, that it is necessary to be glorified on this Tree of Life by which the world is crucified to us and we are crucified to the world.

15. Translator's Note: The allusion of the bridegroom here is likely to the so-called Parable of the Ten Virgins in Matthew 25:1–13.

XVII

If we ought to try to edify those who want to destroy us and to have peace with those who have no peace, how much more must we keep it with our brothers? And when we live in the same house, this house becomes the house of God. What joy when we are of one and the same heart, one and the same soul! We become one with Jesus Christ as He is one with His Father. What consolation, what fellowship *in uno estote, unum estote, unius estote.*[16] Let us be of the same mind without anything able to divide us. Let us be of the same substance and one and the same creature formed by Jesus Christ. Let us be the same person by the uniformity of our actions, which ought all to derive from the same Holy Spirit.

XVIII

The unity of Christians makes them invincible. The devil can do nothing against them when he cannot divide them, and if the bond of charity unites them perfectly with one another, they are assured that nothing is able to separate them from Jesus Christ. How efficacious are our prayers when they come from many who make themselves into one! Whatever helplessness each of us may have in particular, we are strong with our brothers; let us even say with the Scriptures that we are in some sense stronger than God. We oppose His anger; we stop His arm; we resist Him; and we even force Him, as Jacob once did, to give us His Holy Blessing.

16. Translator's Note: "Be one, of one, and in one."

Section Two
The Storm of *Unigenitus*, c. 1679–1760

10. The Jansenist Critique of Jesuit Missions

Sébastien-Joseph du Cambout de Pontchâteau

Translated by Richard T. Yoder[1]

The battle between the Jansenists and the Jesuits was not simply a question of soteriology. It encompassed a wide number of issues, including ecclesiology, ethics, politics, and even foreign missions. The Jansenists were not alone in criticizing Jesuit missionaries. Major controversies erupted over the Jesuits' culturally accommodationist strategies in China, Japan, and South India. Jansenists were minor but persistent players in these dramas, known as the "Rites Controversies," in which Dominicans, Franciscans, missionaries under the papal *Congregatio de Propaganda Fide*, and members of the *Missions Étrangères de Paris* took the lead.

The most important contribution that Jansenists made to the Rites Controversies was *La Morale pratique des Jésuites* (8 vols., 1669–93). Begun by Sébastien-Joseph du Cambout de Pontchâteau (1634–90), Cardinal Richelieu's nephew and a *solitaire* of Port-Royal, the *Morale pratique* borrowed heavily from other anti-Jesuit works while offering a distinctly Jansenist perspective. Pontchâteau was well-connected with

1. Sébastien-Joseph du Cambout de Pontchâteau, *La Morale pratique des Jésuites, second volume, divisé en sept parties, où l'on représente leur conduite dans la Chine, dans le Japon, dans l'Amérique, et dans l'Éthiopie, le tout tiré de Livres très-autorisez, ou de pièces très-authentiques* (Cologne: Gervinus Quentel, 1683), 352–62.

figures in Rome who were opposed to the Jesuits. He forcefully (if not always fairly or accurately) attacks the missionaries for compromising the most important truths of the Gospel and undermining Catholic bishops abroad.[2]

Although Pontchâteau was lead author on the first two volumes, his death in 1690 caused his collaborator, Antoine Arnauld, to take up the project for another six volumes. The "Remark" below, taken from volume 2, may in fact have come from Arnauld himself. Regardless, it presents a clearly Port-Royalist attack on the Jesuits. The author's emphasis on vernacular worship and Bible reading, suspicion of Jesuit motives, and skepticism toward pagan learning all reflect broader "Jansenizing" tendencies.

Richard T. Yoder

La Morale pratique des Jésuites, Vol. II

Remark III—The Pope, having found it wise that the Jesuits translate the Holy Scriptures into Chinese, and that they say the Mass, recite the Breviary, and administer the Sacraments in this language, they instead judged it better not to do so, by a spirit opposed to the spirit of the Church.

Nothing better confirms what we have just said in the preceding Remark against the ridiculous obstinacy of the Jesuits in wishing to make the St. Thomas Christians change the language of their service,[3] than what they themselves said about the permission which the Pope had given them to say Mass, to recite the Breviary, and to administer the Sacraments in the Chinese language. For how does it look, that the popes who desired that they say the Mass in Chinese, would not

2. Bruno Neveu, *Sébastien Joseph du Cambout du Pontchâteau (1634–1690) et ses missions à Rome, d'après sa correspondance et des documents inédits* (Rome: Publications de l'École Française de Rome, 1968).

3. Editor's Note: The previous remark attacked the Jesuits for their demand that the St. Thomas Christians of southern India switch their services to Latin, and that, finding them intractably attached to their ancient liturgical language of Syriac, they were unable to reconcile them to Rome. The author attributes this "unreasonable" requirement to the Jesuits' nefarious desire to make the Indian Christians "entirely dependent upon the Society."

have wanted it said in Chaldean,[4] which is one of the three languages consecrated by the title of the Cross? Or that, having approved that the new Christians celebrate the mysteries in a language in which no one had ever celebrated them, [the popes] had considered it bad that the Christians converted by an Apostle should continue to celebrate them in the same language in which that Apostle first instituted them?

But let us see as well that the Jesuits are always the same; that they only follow their own caprice, and that they deign not to apply themselves to the best things, most in conformity with the spirit of the Church, when they don't find it to their advantage—even when the Pope proposes it to them.

For that is what the same Father Bartoli[5] teaches us in his *La Cina, terza parte dell'Asia*, printed at Rome in 1663. On page 702, he treats rather badly Father Nicolas Trigault[6] of their Society, who returned to China in 1619. Bartoli says that he had given more hope than he showed of advantageous effects for this mission: that he brought back some privileges more honorable than useful, without the consent of the Visitor and Provincial, his superiors, both of whom knew nothing about it. It is not clear if what he then says about the translation of Scripture into Chinese, and of the use of this language in the divine service, is part of those privileges more honorable than useful, which were not to their taste. Whatever it may be, here's what he says:

> The Pope also granted them the power of translating the Holy Scripture into the vulgar tongue; not only that of the people, but also that which is understood only by the men of letters. But whatsoever knowledge they had of it, seeing that this enterprise was long, difficult, perilous, and hardly necessary,

4. Editor's Note: Believed to be Aramaic, though actually Syriac.

5. Editor's Note: Daniello Bartoli (1608–85), Italian Jesuit historian and writer, noted for his histories of Jesuit missionary work. The full title of the work cited here is *Dell'historia della Compagnia di Giesú, La Cina, terza parte dell'Asia* (Rome, 1663). He had previously published volumes covering Jesuit missions in other Asian countries, including Japan and India.

6. Editor's Note: Nicolas Trigault (1577–1628), Flemish Jesuit missionary, scholar, and translator in China who was an enthusiastic proponent of Matteo Ricci's methods before eventually dying by suicide, perhaps due to his unsuccessful defense of using the Chinese term *Shangdi* for the Christian God.

the superiors did not wish to provide anyone to work on it, nor did they avail themselves of another permission that the Pope had given to say the Mass, recite the Breviary, and administer the Sacraments in the language of the learned, by which is meant also the Chinese-born priests.

We are obliged to the Jesuits for having given notice of the power which they had received from Rome to translate the Holy Scriptures into the principle of the two vernacular languages which are current in China, that of the men of letters. For here is an excellent proof in defense of the Holy See against what the heretics reproach her for with such sourness, namely, condemning all versions of Scripture in the vernacular. But what a shame for the Jesuits not to have responded to the expectation that we had of them! Were they able to do anything more glorious for their Society than producing a learned and exact version of all the Holy Books, and to add to the many languages by which God has desired that the truths which He has revealed to the canonical writers might be known by men, the tongue of this great Empire? But they did not merit that God should grant them the grace of rendering this service to the Church. Their conduct was too human and too far removed from His spirit. Their heads were full only of mathematics and the philosophy of Confucius, and they believed it much more important for the establishment of the Christian Religion among the Chinese to reform their calendar, than to give them knowledge of what is contained in the divine books which the Holy Spirit dictated to the Prophets and Apostles.

Therefore, they desired that everyone should know that the Pope had judged them capable of translating the Holy Scriptures into Chinese. This increases the reputation of the Society. And they declare that he had not erred, because they had in effect "enough knowledge of that language" to come to grips with this work. For they would have been angry if we believed that it was by incapacity that they had not undertaken it. They even insinuate that there were some among them who would have been happy to apply themselves to it. But they tell us at the same time that their Superiors, who had the secret knowledge of the Society's politics, did not judge it *à propos*, because this enterprise was "long, difficult, perilous, and hardly necessary," which meant that they "did not wish to provide anyone to work on it."

Behold the four reasons that, they say, brought their superiors, not only to have no zeal for so important a work, but even to oppose the zeal of the individuals who would have gladly worked on it. The enterprise was "long, difficult, perilous, and hardly necessary." But who cannot see that these two last pretexts, that it was "perilous and hardly necessary," are injurious to the Pope and to all antiquity? Would the Pope have proposed to them a project of this importance, and which would surely require much work, if he had judged it "perilous and hardly necessary?" They thus accuse him of erring in his judgement, and they condemn along with him all the ancient Fathers, who had so often recommended to make the faithful read the Holy Scripture, and to instruct them in it from their infancy, as St. Paul approves of doing to Timothy. They cannot save themselves by saying that this was good for the countries where the preachers condemned with the Scripture all sorts of idolatry, or for the times where one does not fear to preach Jesus Christ crucified, even though it be a scandal to the Jews and a folly to the Greeks—but that they, using a contrary practice (because they had judged it appropriate to permit to the Chinese many idolatrous cults, and to speak to them as little as possible of the Cross of Jesus Christ), had reasonably judged that the reading of the Holy Scripture translated into Chinese would have been perilous to their new Christians, in that it would give them scruples touching the idolatry that they wanted to preserve, and that it would have shown them the poverty, humility, and ignominious sufferings of Our Lord, Jesus Christ, as well as his death on a gibbet. All of which, by a great prudence, they had hidden from these people, because they have too great a horror of it.

But as they would have the shame presently to defend themselves thus, their false prudence having been condemned by a Decree of Rome in 1645,[7] the only thing they could allege today would be the length and difficulty of the enterprise. Why therefore do they tell us that they could do it, but that they do not want to? And how do they respond if we say to them that they must at least begin with the New Testament, and that they would not need even half the time for this that they

7. Editor's Note: The Papal Congregation for the Propagation of the Faith (*Propaganda Fide*) condemned the Chinese rites in 1645 on the advice of the Dominican missionaries who opposed the Jesuits' methods. In 1656, however, Rome lifted this ban in favor of the Jesuits, though it was later reimposed.

took to translate or to compose such books of mathematics, of which Fr. Kircher[8] left us such a long enumeration in his *China Illustrata* (including only those of Fr. Matteo Ricci),[9] which he catalogues under the heading *Sequentes post se libros in bonum Ecclesiae Sinicae reliquit*?

One expects by reading this that they must need translations of the Gospel and other parts of Scripture, or the works of the Fathers. But we are a tad surprised when we see that which follows:

1. The *Practical Mathematics* of Clavius[10]
2. Six books of Euclid with annotations by the same Clavius
3. The Sphere of the same man (who had had Ricci as a pupil)
4. A General Map of Geography with the history of peoples, etc.
5. A treatise of Physics
6. A method for making sundials
7. The manner of making and using an astrolabe
8. The use and manner of making spinets[11]
9. A Moral Philosophy that contains a treatise on friendship and twenty-five conclusions that comprehend the sap and spirit of all the discipline of morals, so as to moderate the passions, and to live well and happily in following the conduct of reason.[12]

Finally, they boast that since their entry into China until 1636 their Fathers had composed in Chinese some 340 volumes, as many on religion as on morals, physics, and mathematics. For everything was good

8. Editor's Note: Athanasius Kircher (1602–80), the German Jesuit polymath who wrote on numerous subjects. His book *China Illustrata* (1667) is an important early work of European Sinology.

9. Editor's Note: Matteo Ricci (1552–1610), the Italian Jesuit missionary and scholar who, though not the first Jesuit in China, definitively shaped it by initiating a strategy of *accomodatio*, or adaptation to local circumstances and cultural norms. Ricci brought the Jesuits into close contact with the Confucian literati and the imperial court, where they served in a scholarly capacity. This association would continue (though not without controversy) until the era of the international suppression of the Jesuits.

10. Editor's Note: Christopher Clavius (1538–1612), the German Jesuit mathematician and astronomer who, as a professor at the Jesuit Collegio Romano, taught Matteo Ricci.

11. Editor's Note: A small form of harpsichord.

12. Editor's Note: The foregoing list is very much in keeping with Jesuit evangelical strategy in China, which relied heavily upon scientific, geographical, and philosophical exchange with the Confucian elites.

to them, and there was nothing in which they did not wish to make themselves seem useful. It was only the Gospels and the Apostolic writings (not to mention the other parts of Holy Scripture) that they did not believe worthy of the trouble to which they would apply themselves, to give a means to their new Christians of nourishing themselves with the Word of God.

They made no more of the power that the Pope had given them (and to priests born in China) to say the Mass, recite the Breviary, and to administer the Sacraments in the Chinese vernacular spoken by the men of letters.

The Pope only did this in imitation of the wise conduct of one of his predecessors, John VIII [d. 882 CE], who permitted the newly-converted Slavs to celebrate the sacred Mysteries in the Slavonic language. . . . These are without a doubt the same views that Paul V had in finding it appropriate that they should celebrate the Divine Office in Chinese—and great benefits would have come of it. This would have closed the mouths of the heretics, in causing them to see that the Church is not far removed from permitting (for good reasons) celebration of the Mass in the vernacular, and that she well desires that we do so in the new establishments of the Christian Religion in this great country, which she has always done in other times, as Cardinal Bona recognized in his *Books on the Liturgy*, book 1, ch. 6,[13] where he supposes as a constant thing, "that the Divine Office is said in each country in the language which is vulgar in that land, when the Christian Religion was first established there by the Apostles or by their disciples."

Moreover, there would have been a great consolation to the vast majority of the newly converted Chinese, who do not know Latin, in being able to understand what is said in the Holy Sacrifice, and to be able as well to recite the Divine Office in a language which they would understand. . . . But to convince the Jesuits by their own words of the fruit that the Chinese Christians would draw from the celebration of the Mass in their language, we need only report here what they themselves said in their history of Ethiopia, of which we have already spoken in a previous Remark; that having promoted some Ethiopians to Holy

13. Editor's Note: This is certainly a reference to Giovanni Bona, *Rerum liturgicarum libri duo* (Rome, 1671), sometimes known as *De rebus liturgicis*.

Orders, this was to them a great help. "For in celebrating the Mass," they add, on page 224, "*in their literary language*, but according to our use, it is a very efficacious start, as much for the priests themselves as for the parishioners, who rejoice to see and to hear the Mass said in their language, and with our ceremonies." Why therefore do they not wish to do the same thing in China?

Finally, one of the greatest advantages that this would bring to that new Church [of China], is that we would more easily find among the Chinese converts to the faith, persons capable of being elevated to Holy Orders, because it would no longer be necessary that they should know Latin, or we could content ourselves that they had just a light knowledge of it. For it is certain that there is a great utility in these new establishments of Christianity in having more priests in these countries themselves, because they know better by what manner we must undertake the conversion of their fellow citizens, have more use of the language of the country as well as more access to enter into conversation with those of their nation, and who in persecutions hide themselves better and are more difficult to discover than foreigners—as we have seen in the last Chinese persecution, where there was only one sole Dominican who was a Chinese national able to assist the Christians, all Europeans being relocated or hidden.

But the Jesuits were not men to be moved by similar reasons. There are many other encounters where they did not trouble themselves to do what might have edified the heretics, or at least not put an obstacle to their conversion. They didn't care at all about giving the Chinese this means of understanding what is said in the Most Holy Mysteries [the liturgy]. The Jesuits preferred that the Chinese ignore it, so that being less instructed, they might depend more upon them, and the ignorance of the disciples might be a means for the masters to further dominate their faith. And in terms of being able to ordain more Chinese, so far are they from regarding this as an advantage, that they do as little as they can for it, as we are going to see in the following Remark.[14]

14. Editor's Note: In the next remark, the author contrasts the Jesuits of Japan with the French Bishops of the *Missions Étrangères de Paris* in Southeast Asia, who cultivated a native priesthood.

11. Four Poems against the Jesuits

Translated by Jean-Pascal Gay[1]

Jansenists were appealing to an increasingly literate public sphere in France long before the flood of polemical literature in the wake of the bull *Unigenitus* (1713) and the launching of the *Nouvelles ecclésiastiques* in 1728. By the final decades of the seventeenth century, Jansenists had honed a strategy of engaging the public with poems, fictionalized conversations, and songs. This strategy followed in the footsteps of Pascal, whose *Provincial Letters* (1656–57) had delighted and scandalized France. A favorite target, of course, was the Society of Jesus.

We present four samples of such popular literature below. The first, a "Sonnet to the Jesuits," attacks the Society's alleged moral laxity and their accommodation to non-Christian religions, concluding that only "errors and lies" lay at the heart of the Jesuits. The second text, a printed "Letter on the Chinese Rites," brutally satirizes Jesuit missionary efforts in China. The "Chinese Rites" controversy centered around Jesuit attempts to adapt Catholicism to Chinese culture by admitting Confucian and other Chinese rituals that missionaries believed could be compatible with Christianity. The letter sarcastically advises the Jesuits to use their influence in Rome to create a "feast of Confucius" as a holy day of obligation, so that all can say "pray for us Confucius." In such a case, the author asks, why not just bring back pagan Roman religion? The ultimate Jesuit *coup d'état*, the letter claims, would be the

1. We are grateful to Jean-Pascal Gay for selecting and translating these poems (cited below) and for assisting us in writing this introduction.

canonization of a non-Christian and the imposition of silence on all who disagree with Jesuit syncretism.

The third poem argues that "the Molinists" (i.e., Jesuits and their theological allies) have become "deaf to the truth." They became Pelagians to fight Calvinism and pagans out of fear of becoming rigorists. The antidote to such error is the solid doctrine of saints Augustine and Thomas Aquinas.

The fourth text is an exceedingly dark satirical song, sung to the tune of a popular Christmas carol. Taking the form of a dialogue between a slick Jesuit confessor and a vile "sinner," the song showcases the absurdities of extreme moral laxity (it should go without saying, of course, that this hypothetical conversation is a polemical distortion). Employing ridiculous distinctions, the Jesuit confessor assures the penitent that he is still in a state of grace, despite having murdered his parents and raped his sister. Through the medium of songs and ballads such as this one, the illiterate could exercise a measure of agency in the ideological battles rending French society. Through memorized words put to a well-known tune, one could show support for an embattled Jansenist *curé* or bishop or express antipathy for Jesuits passing by in the streets of Paris.

The first and fourth texts were in the possession of the Jansenist Louis Fouquet (1633–1702), bishop and *comte* d'Agde. Such collections of Jansenist news and documents were ancestors of the *Nouvelles ecclésiastiques* weekly journal, and are now housed in the Bibliothèque nationale de France (BNF). Texts such as these poems were sent to friendly patrons like Bishop Fouquet, to aid their dissemination around Jansenist networks. However, the readership for such polemical texts, at least in some cases, extended beyond friends of the Jansenist cause and could include the royal court and important sections of the urban public in Paris and the provinces. Copies of the second and third texts below are in the Bibliothèque de l'Arsenal (part of the BNF since 1934). While the authors of many of these texts are unknown, it is likely that, especially in Paris, identities of prominent polemicists might have been apparent or at least suspected. For example, it was known that Jean de La Fontaine (1621–95) wrote the anti-Jesuit poem *Ballade sur Escobar*.

These selections are evidence of the wider "literarization" of polemics in seventeenth-century France.

Shaun Blanchard

1. Sonnet to the Jesuits[2]

Companions of Jesus, how insolent thou art
You speak of the law as would libertines
And what is even more fright'ning to the courts,
You dare to deny your obvious deed.

Mohammed and Jesus with you weigh the same.
When you betray God, what should the King think?
Infidel children lacking honor and faith,
Against this attack, what defense can you make?

You claim that the culprit's expelled, it's enough.[3]
But are his writings erased from your hearts?
Wicked men, should we not expect their fruits?

Behold what terrorizes the good folk;
Each starts to see what a Jesuit is.
One discovers only errors and lies.

2. A Letter on the Chinese Rites[4]

To the good reverend Fathers
The Jesuits of China,
Under the banner of the Machine,[5]
Near the Emperor and the Great.

O mitigated Apostles and politic Directors,
Who lead to the Faith by Mathematics,

2. Translator's Note: "Sonnet aux Jésuites," BNF Ms.fr. 23503, *Nouvelles ecclésiastiques* 1693, f°89–90.

3. Editor's Note: The precise "culprit" in question remains unidentified. The reference to "courts" and "the King" here may refer to the charge that Jesuit moral teaching justified regicide.

4. Translator's Note: "Sur les Cérémonies Chinoises Épître," Bibliothèque de l'Arsenal, Ms. 1145 (printed).

5. Editor's Note: This is probably a reference to the mathematical and scientific scholarship of the Jesuits in China.

Wise Engineers, do you know what we fear?
That on your *Elements* the Anathema might fall,
And that one would wish for the love of you
That Confucius were a saint.
Or rather that the whole of China,
Which is still going its own way under your discipline,
Had for this vain object of infatuation
A little less devotion.
For, we say, to treat this background of Idolatry,
Of external, political, and civil worship;
To want to make a mere trifle of it,
Is not to reflect on the heart of a Gentile.
It is to conceal the deadly wound,
It is to foment evil by accommodation;
By dint of being good, it is to make villains;
Of two opinions it is to follow the less sure:[6]
Indeed whatever turn one could give to it,
We cannot understand how by your maxims
One can in security canonize crimes,
Surrender to the Devil for fear of being damned,
Set up altars and temples for the reprobates,
Make them Patrons, emulate their examples,
Honor their portraits with prostrations
Lighting candles, genuflecting,
With perfumes, incense prayers, sacrifices,
And by a thousand other ways try to make them propitious:
And to Confucius, above all others, resort,
To invoke his spirit, to wait for his help,
As holder of all sorts of graces,
To believe him to have come down and be present there,
To show one's gratitude by accompanying him;
All these words, you say, are anything but pleasing.
But if the intention excessively flatters the model,
If in the heart there is an unfaithful spirit,
The motives of a Chinese man are always suspect;
No matter, these motives are but simple respects;
And on this point of honor, even if it takes several volumes,
You shall not want arguments nor pens,

6. Editor's Note: The author is implying that Jesuit errors about Confucianism are bound up in their lax moral system of probabilism (following "the less sure" of two opinions).

Whose specious lines will know how to combine
The spirit with the flesh, the earth with the heavens,
And by long calculations joined with experiments,
Place consciences under happy ascendants.
But if one wants reasons, and not speeches,
Bold Sophisms are not proofs;
And yet in all your Authors this is what we find.
Lies, errors, insults, contempt,
The blind persuasion of their own merit,
The pride hidden under hypocritical zeal,
Are the faithful leaders of the party they have taken;
Unfortunate defenders of their own vain chimeras,
In a shadowy maze they run without making progress;
The truth hurts them and their reckless eyes
From the side where it shines and never stops.
Look therefore if you please elsewhere than in your School,
For some entrenchment that would provide you cover;
For if Confucius passes for an Idol,
China is idolatrous, and that is your undoing.
But since it is unfortunate that one in such a case
Might be able to disarm probability,
Do you know what I would advise you?
Have recourse to authority.
Make by the credit which you have in Rome
That the feast of Confucius be a day without work,
That we may say one day, which will please you most,
Pray for us Confucius.
You will then argue that the famous Manes[7]
Dispel the darkness in the hearts of his devotees
And make them discover the natural secret,
To turn their worship to the universal Being;
Then this coup d'état, my most Reverend Fathers,
By imposing silence on all your adversaries,
Will raise the honor of the great Confucius;
You will walk triumphant, preaching in his favor;
Soon the story of his great deeds will appear,

7. Editor's Note: The divine *Manes* ("di manes") were the deified spirits of the dead in Roman religion (see Charles W. King, *The Ancient Roman Afterlife: Di Manes, Belief, and the Cult of the Dead* [Austin: University of Texas Press, 2020]). The author here further stigmatizes the Chinese Rites as heathen with a reference to ancient pagan practice from a pre-Christian context that an educated French audience might know.

And then you will argue, all full of his spirit,
That a Hero can sometimes rise to glory
Without having known Jesus Christ,
Our only Savior, our sovereign Master,
In whose name I write to you,
And whom I pray at last to make you know
The error of your minds.

3. Sonnet—"What Sort of People the Molinists Are"[8]

What sort of people the Molinists are!
What a new kind of Christian!
They make themselves Pelagians
To fight the Calvinists.

Today these Probabilists
Agree with the Pagans,
And now they have become Confucians
Out of fear of being Rigorists.

But what remedy for this venom?
Saint Thomas and Saint Augustine
In vain against them hold Chapter,[9]

The superb[10] Society
Jealous of its free will
Makes itself deaf to the truth.

8. Translator's Note: "Quelles gens que les Molinistes," Bibliothèque de l'Arsenal, Ms. 1145.

9. Editor's Note: "Hold Chapter" here is a reference to the formal deliberative meetings of monks. The author is probably implying that neither current Augustinians and Dominicans nor even Saints Augustine and Thomas Aquinas could convince the proud Jesuits to change course.

10. Editor's Note: The author is being sarcastic, but also alluding to the deadly sin of *superbia* (a haughty or arrogant pride).

4. Interview in Verse between a Sinner and a Jesuit on the Matter of Philosophical Sin[11]

The Sinner:
O Father, I hear say
There is nothing you ignore
Would you but teach me
How to become a man of good?

The Jesuit:
You would find nothing better to do
Than to come to us.
There is not one of us
Who is not but all yours

Sinner:
I fear that when my soul
Shall appear bare to you
You will think me vile
And frankly a villain.

Jesuit:
This is a vain terror
We are not of the kind
Who cause so much pain
To such poor penitents.

Sinner:
I have committed every crime
That one could imagine
How would you have maxims
To forgive me for them?

Jesuit:
One often can do wrong
Without being a criminal
And what we call mortal sin
Is a great mystery

11. Translator's Note: "Entretien en vers d'un pécheur avec un jésuite sur le péché philosophique," *Nouvelles ecclésiastiques*, January 1690, BNF Ms.fr. 23500, f°34 et sq. The editor of the *Nouvelles* clarifies that this text is to be sung to be tune of the Noël, or Christmas song, "Or nous dites Marie." The public gave this song the nickname "Justified Parricide" (that is, the murder of the father). See the same manuscript, f°49.

Sinner:
But I have killed my father
To inherit his wealth[12]
I have poisoned my mother
For fear that she'd talk

A Sister, young and wise,
Escaped the dagger,
But the outrage I did her,
Amnon did Tamar[13]

Jesuit:
Everything you say
Is assuredly wrong
But can you know if it merits
Eternal chastisement?

Sinner:
Now Father do tell me
where you have found
that one could act so wretchedly
without reprobation

Jesuit:
Nowhere but in our Schools
Can one learn the secret
And two or three words
Will tell you how this works

12. Editor's Note: This horrific and amazing scenario is presumably based on the "justified parricide" propositions condemned by the Holy Office under Pope Innocent XI in 1679, numbers 14 and 15 (see Denzinger-Hünermann 2114–15). Proposition 14 reads: "It is licit with an absolute desire to wish for the death of a father, not indeed as an evil to the father, but as a good to him who desires it, for a rich inheritance will surely come his way"; 15 reads: "It is licit for a son to rejoice over the parricide of his parent perpetuated by himself in drunkenness because of the great riches that came from it by inheritance." Proposition 14 is from Tommaso Tamburini, SJ, *Explicatio decalogi* [*Explanation of the Ten Commandments*] (Lyon, 1659). Proposition 15 is without citation.

13. Editor's Note: As recounted in 2 Samuel 13, Amnon, son of King David, raped his half-sister Tamar. He was later killed on the orders of his brother Absalom.

But for me to teach you well
Do pray open your heart,
So that I shall lead you
As a wise director

Brother, pray tell me
When you actually sinned
Did you think you were doing anything
That would the Heavens offend?

Sinner:
I had nothing in mind
But my own ambition
And the beast that I am
But followed mad passion

Jesuit:
So much the better, God is only offended
when we do think of Him;
behold the ignorance
of the sinners of this day

Sinner:
But, Father, I believe
that by breaking His laws
My crimes where inciting
His anger against me

I am a guilty man
One worthy of His wrath
a loathsome sinner
Whom I myself detest

Jesuit:
You are deceiving yourself
by this humility
the grace of baptism
has not abandoned you

Sinner:
How can I be in grace
after so many misdeeds?
What then erases it
from the souls of sinners?

Jesuit:
This is the mystery
You should be aware of
Listen well, brother
Let me make it plain

Philosophical sin
is against reason
theological sin
is of another fashion

The latter does not offend
and God is only wroth
because we think of Him

12. Pasquier Quesnel's Biblical Commentary

Translated by John Meinert[1]

There is perhaps no figure more important in the history of eighteenth-century Jansenism, or, for that matter, anti-Jansenism, than Pasquier Quesnel (1634–1719). Quesnel, expelled from the French Oratory, fled to Brussels in 1684 where he lived with Antoine Arnauld before ultimately settling in Amsterdam. Author of many works, the most important was an immensely successful biblical commentary called *Le Nouveau Testament en français avec des réflexions morales sur chaque verset*, often known as *Réflexions morales sur le Nouveau Testament*. This work, first published in French in 1693, was a revision and expansion of two earlier biblical commentaries. Celebrated by Jansenists as the "Elisha," or anointed successor, of Arnauld, Quesnel's fiercest opponents saw him as a heresiarch in an infernal chain running back to Luther and Wycliffe.

French and Roman condemnations did nothing to harm Quesnel's popularity, and the watershed bull *Unigenitus* (1713), which condemned 101 propositions taken verbatim from the *Réflexions morales*, catapulted Quesnel into celebrity and infamy. By the end of the eighteenth century, Quesnel's commentary had gone through numerous editions and was translated and diffused around Europe. In certain contexts, such as

1. The translation below is taken from Pasquier Quesnel, *Le Nouveau Testament en français avec des réflexions morales sur chaque verset* (Amsterdam: Joseph Nicolai, 1727), 4:331–38.

Anglican England, a condemnation from the pope was taken as proof positive that Quesnel's biblical exegesis had merit. This "right kind of papist" was translated and read outside of the Catholic world and admired by figures like John Wesley.

The excerpt below, commentary on John 15:1–11 for "a Tuesday in the time of Easter," is exemplary of Quesnel's style and of the Jansenist commitment to the doctrine of efficacious grace. The extreme Augustinianism summarized in the final three sentences of the entry on verse five was condemned in *Unigenitus* article two.[2] An emphasis on personal salvation and direct contact with Scripture appealed to many devout readers. The constant themes of resisting immorality, pride, schism, and heresy are balanced with an intense personal spirituality based on love of Jesus that is at times moving and beautiful.

Shaun Blanchard

The Gospel of John Chapter 15

Following the Discourse on the Last Supper

Jesus is the Vine, the faithful his branches. Life and Joy in him alone.

I am the true vine and my Father is the vinegrower.

1. Jesus is the true vine, the excellent, spiritual, and divine vine, of whom the others are nothing more than figures and shadows. He is the vine planted by the hand of God in the womb of the virgin, in the field of the world, and cultivated by the same hand. She does not carry a bitter fruit like the synagogue, but a wine that redeems, washes, sanctifies, nourishes, and strengthens the world here and inebriates in heaven. Jesus abandoned Himself to the hand of His Father to be cultivated and pruned according to His will. Let us adore this heavenly vinegrower; and because we are the branches of this vine, let us permit Him to do what is pleasing to Him. If He does not cultivate us in this way, we are useless branches.

2. See Denzinger-Hünermann 2402.

He will cut off all the branches that never bear fruit in me. All those who bear fruit, he will trim so that they will bear more.

2. The faithful without works are the branches without fruit. This is to have no faith: to prefer even one day cut off from the body of Christ rather than to be strengthened by the afflictions of this life and thereby to bear the fruit of good works. Both the good and the evil branches are joined to the vine, but not all of them bear fruit. Yet it will not be until the day of the great separation that the evil will be separated forever. Every branch will suffer the pruning knife; but woe to them who are not pruned by the vinegrower in the current life. They will only undergo the pruning knife to be cut off from the vine. The suffering of the good and the evil have very different effects. The evil become worse; the good become better. The one who does not want such a pruning does not want to bear fruit and wants to be cut off. Let us be careful not to push away the hand of this loving vinegrower.

You are already pure because of the word I have spoken to you.

3. The word of Jesus Christ purifies the heart of the Christian by enlightening it, showing it the true good and the means of arriving there, and inducing it to renounce its faults. This is the knife which trims the superfluities of the branches and which is always necessary to have on hand during this life. When God does not prune His vine by afflictions, then He prunes it by His word and His grace, moving it to prune itself by mortification and penance. We are already pure when Jesus Christ has washed us in His blood through baptism or justified us by confession. But there is always something, even in the most beautiful branch, to prune and trim. We must fear this above all else: thinking oneself to be totally pure in this world and imagining that Jesus Christ has finished His work in our hearts.

Remain in me and I will remain in you. As the branch cannot bear fruit on its own, but only when it remains attached to the vine, neither are you able to produce anything unless you remain in me.

4. Two things are necessary. The first is to remain intimately united to Jesus Christ by faith and charity so that we may live in Him and of Him. The second is to receive the power of doing good from Him,

because we are not able to do any good work of ourselves without the influence of His grace and His Spirit. It is not enough to be united through baptism to Jesus Christ our head. It is also necessary to be united to Him by prayer, desire, meditation, and the practice of His gospel, all of which make Him even more present to us. It is good to pray the prayer of the first Christians on every occasion to renew the spirit of baptism: I renounce you, Satan, and all your pomp, and all your works. I unite myself to you, O Jesus, and give myself to your Spirit. To separate oneself from his Church, which is His body, is to separate ourselves from Him and His Spirit. And what fruits can one bear outside of this body and without this Spirit: only the fruits of death and cursedness.

I am the vine and you are the branches. The one who remains in me and I in him bears much fruit because without me you are able to do nothing.

5. Jesus Christ is one with His Church in the admirable unity of head with members, who are not members except in this unity: a single body, a single man, a single vine. Jesus Christ causes His members to bear much fruit when He makes them lead a good Christian life, when He animates all their actions by His Spirit (even common and ordinary actions), and when He applies them to good works. To accomplish this, He continually pours His virtue into His members, as the head into His members and as the vine into its branches, a virtue which always precedes, accompanies, and follows their good works and without which they would not be able, in any way, to be pleasing to God, nor to merit. The grace of Jesus Christ is the efficacious principle of every kind of good. It is necessary for each good action (great or small, easy or difficult) in order to begin, to continue, and to finish. Without it, not only would one not act at all, but one would not even be able to act.

The one who does not remain in me will be cast out as a useless branch. It dries out and when it is picked up it is cast into the fire and burned.

6. Whoever is not in Jesus Christ and dies in that state is not good for anything except to be cut off and thrown into the fire as a dry branch. Whoever is not united to the head: 1. Will be separated from the body and will not share in its good. 2. Will be deprived of the juice

and sap of grace. 3. Will be abandoned to the devil. 4. Will be cast into the eternal fire. 5. Will be burned forever without being consumed. Whoever assumes that he can bear fruit by himself is not connected to the vine. He who is not connected to the vine is not in Jesus Christ. He who is not in Jesus Christ is not a Christian (St. Augustine). Is it possible to think about this threat of the Son of God without terror? And yet the world is full of dry branches: the impious, atheists, bad Christians, schismatics, heretics. Let us grieve for these blind people who do not even wish to take the trouble to examine whether they are connected to the vine or whether they are cut off, flattering themselves in thinking that they are connected to the vine and bearing fruit when, in reality, they are nothing but dry branches ready to be thrown into the fire. Let us grieve, or at least fear, for ourselves.

If you remain in me and my words remain in you, ask whatever you want and it will be done for you.

7. Three sorts of unions or conditions are necessary to obtain what you desire from God. 1. It is necessary to be united to Jesus Christ by a living faith and by charity. 2. One must be united to Him by love of His truth, meditation on His word, which is the rule [*règle*] of our desires (as it is the book of God's designs, to which we ought to conform our desires and prayers). It is not enough to have faith and charity. One must nourish them by the word of God. To read it carelessly and for fashion's sake is contrary to the respect we owe to it and our own advantage. It is necessary to engrave and imprint Scripture deeply into our hearts, so that it dwells there. There is nothing except love that can make it dwell there just as there is nothing except love that can put it into practice. 3. The third condition to be fulfilled is prayer. For it is by prayer that the branch is attached to the sap and the sustenance of the vine, so that it might be nourished more abundantly. God allows those who love Him the liberty of demanding anything and commits Himself to giving every gift to them. This is because the one who loves God will not ask or love anything except God's will. It is the same Spirit who prays in them and who grants their prayers.

The glory of my Father is that you bear much fruit and that you remain my disciples.

8. Three motives cause our prayers to be granted: the glory of God, the building up of the Church, and the sanctification of souls. These are three conditions that are always included in the prayer of a good Christian. Concerning the first, which encompasses the others, God always grants that which is asked of Him—all the glory that God wants to have outside Himself reduces principally to that which He gives Himself by the operation of His grace in the hearts of men on earth and by the outpouring of His glory in the heavens. Indeed, the production of fruits of the Holy Spirit in a soul and the formation of a Christian are more glorious than the creation of the material world and the production of the massive diversity of flowers and visible fruits. It is by the former that the Mystical Body and the spiritual world are formed, in which and by which God wants to be eternally adored—with His Son as the head and His Spirit as the soul [of the Mystical Body]. Let us never be at a loss to find ways of glorifying God. There is nothing greater or more necessary than working on our sanctification and our salvation, as well as that of others. No one can neglect these without also failing to obtain the glory of God.

I have loved you as my Father has loved me. Remain in my love.

9. We owe everything to the gratuitous love of Jesus Christ for us just as Jesus owes everything to the gratuitous love of His Father, by whom Jesus has been filled with all the fullness of divinity. He chooses us to be His members and to accomplish in us and by us the good works that we do, just as the Father has chosen Him to be our Head and to accomplish miraculous works in Him and by Him. God loves His Son and us in His Son. Jesus loves His Father and us for the sake of His Father. Let us love this same God in Jesus Christ and Jesus Christ for God. The love of God, of Jesus Christ, and of the Christian form a triple knot which will never be broken in heaven, for it is eternal life and the grand mystery of eternal happiness. He is unhappy, even in this world, who does not give everything to remain in this love! God of my heart, who loved me first, make me remain perfectly in your love, so that your love will remain eternally in me.

If you keep my commandments you will remain in my love as I have myself kept the commands of my Father and remain in his love.

10. The observance of the commandments of God is the unique means for eternally establishing God's love in us. God has attached His love and the eternity of His love to the accomplishment of His law, even in Jesus Christ Himself. The love and obedience of the Son toward His Father cannot cease to be; it cannot be interrupted for a moment. Jesus Christ, nevertheless, merits the eternal continuation of His Father's love for the Son. The more the command of the Word concerning the human will of Jesus Christ is infallible and sovereign, the more the operation of the Holy Spirit in His heart is efficacious and all powerful, the more His will is free, His love worthy of God, and His actions meritorious. The fidelity of my love for God and the attachment of my heart to His law can only be the effect of your all-powerful grace, O Jesus: deign to accomplish this in me for the honor of that which your Father has worked in you.

I have told you all these things so that my joy may remain in you and that your joy might be complete.

11. Just as the love of God is always followed by the accomplishment of His law, the accomplishment of His law is inseparable from the heart's joy. This is the joy of Jesus Christ, Christian joy, the effect of His grace and the fruit of His Spirit. It is the seed and germ of eternal joy that He scatters in His members. He inebriates His elect and floods their hearts. This joy will not be full and perfect until charity is too, and the law is fully and perfectly accomplished and ineffaceably engraved in the heart. If we want to rejoice as true Christians, let us make the law of God our joy and delight. This is not the passing joy of sterile and fruitless reading, but the solid joy of a sincere and true love, of a correct and persevering practice. The foolish one sacrifices this joy and the hope of heaven for a carnal joy, the joy of the moment, for the joy which is the source of a thousand sorrows and inquietudes in life!

13. Defending the Right of Women to Read the Bible

Ursule de La Grange (pseudonym)

Translated by Elizabeth Huddleston[1]

The condemnation of Pasquier Quesnel's biblical commentary by Pope Clement XI's bull *Unigenitus* (1713) caused a firestorm of outrage and protest. Some of the many grievances stemmed from the bull's condemnation of eight propositions concerning Bible reading and liturgical participation.[2] These condemnations shocked and embarrassed many Catholics and seemed to confirm the worst prejudices of Protestants.

Jansenists, led by Antoine Arnauld and the women of Port-Royal, had long insisted on the right of women to read the Bible and participate in the liturgy. In October of 1713, soon after the publication of *Unigenitus*, a pamphlet appeared titled *Lettre d'une dame française au pape Clément XI, sur sa constitution contre le Nouveau Testament du Père Quesnel* under the name of Ursule de la Grange. This pseudonym was probably an allusion to the environs of the recently destroyed Port-Royal (*les Granges*). The author might have been a man, perhaps Nicolas Le Gros (1675–1751). However, the author could certainly have

1. Ursule de la Grange, *Lettre d'une dame de Paris au Pape sur Constitution de 8. Septembre 1713 contre* Le Nouveau Testament, avec des Réflexions morales. *Nouvelle edition* (n.p., 1714).

2. See *Unigenitus*, numbers 79 through 86 (Denzinger-Hünermann 2479–86).

been a Parisian woman like Françoise-Marguerite de Joncoux (1668–1715), an intellectual and Jansenist.[3]

Alternating between pleading, bitter sarcasm, and searing wit, the letter displays real erudition along with genuine pathos. The examples gathered from Scripture and the tradition and history of the church are unanswerable. One finishes the pamphlet with the distinct feeling that it is those seeking to restrict the access of women to the Bible who should be embarrassed, and not the women of France.

The pamphlet includes a nod to the Gallican method of so-called positive theology (basing arguments on Scripture and tradition). A common trope of Catholic reformers in this period is also employed when the author asks how it could be possible that Christians have "less advantage" than Jews, who enjoy the "sweetest consolation" of access to divine Scripture in word and song. This letter was reprinted many times, sometimes with slightly different titles like the one given below from the "new edition" of 1714. It was popular as late as the 1780s, when the letter was translated into Italian and printed in Pistoia in Bishop Scipione de' Ricci's *Raccolta* series (1783–90) of Jansenist and philo-Jansenist texts.

Shaun Blanchard

Letter of a Woman of Paris to the Pope on the Constitution [*Unigenitus*]

Most Holy Father,

Although Saint Paul commands women to keep silent in the Church, I do not believe that I am disobeying the Apostle if I throw myself at the feet of Your Holiness to say the same words that the wise Abigail once said to the Prophet David: "May this fault, my Lord, fall on me. Only allow your servant to speak to you, and do not refuse to hear her."[4] For you are the common Father of the faithful, and you are beholden to the wise, as well as the foolish.

3. Benvenuto Matteucci suggests Le Gros in *Scipione de' Ricci: Saggio storico-teologico sul giansenismo italiano* (Brescia: Morcelliana, 1941), 127n21. I am grateful to Simon Icard for the plausible suggestion of Joncoux.

4. Translator's Note: 1 Samuel 25:24.

The Bull condemning Father Quesnel's *New Testament* causes such great embarrassment in this kingdom, and above all among people of my sex, that I believed you would not find it inappropriate if I asked you for an explanation of two propositions, which cause me extreme embarrassment. The first is number eighty-three, conceived in these terms, which I have taken care to have translated: "It is an illusion to persuade oneself that knowledge of the mysteries of religion should not be communicated to women by the reading of sacred books. Not from the simplicity of women, but from the proud knowledge of men has arisen the abuse of the Scriptures and have heresies been born."[5] I only ask concerning the first half of this proposition, Most Holy Father, was it not to a woman of Samaria that Jesus Christ explained the profound mystery of grace? Was Mary, sister of Martha, not seated at the feet of the divine Savior, where she listened to the words of Truth? Was the great mystery of the resurrection not first announced to [Mary] Magdalene? Did she not announce the resurrection by the very order of Jesus Christ to those [the Apostles] who in the course of history announced it to all the earth? If the Epistles of St. Paul—so difficult according to St. Peter—were only for men, why then does this Apostle order them to be read in front of everyone? Why does he so often mention women, such as Priscilla or Mary, and many others? Finally, did not the Beloved Disciple write one of his canonical Epistles to the Elect Lady? What can be said now, Most Holy Father, of Saint Thecla, that worthy disciple of Saint Paul, to whom no other treasure was found after her death, but a wooden bowl, and the *Acts of the Apostles*? What about Cecilia who, according to the Roman Breviary, carried the Gospel of Jesus Christ in her heart, a mystical seal of which the Bride speaks, and who spent days and nights in meditation on the truths that this book contains? What about Paula, Melanie, and Euxodia, to whom Saint Jerome recommended so strongly the reading of Scripture, so much so that, according to the Holy Doctor, they no longer needed his advice? What can be said, finally, of so many virgins who only replied to the tyrants who questioned them, and to the judges who put them to death, with the words of Scripture?

5. Editor's Note: Denzinger-Hünermann 2483 (*Unigenitus* 83, condemning Quesnel's commentary on John 4:26).

Moreover, Most Holy Father, does not God sometimes choose the strongest? Was it not Deborah, seated under a palm tree for so long, who wisely judged the people of Israel, and who, armed with the sword of the Lord, overwhelmed the enemies of His name? Was it not Huldah who prophesied such great misfortunes to the nation and to the holy city?[6] Was it not Judith who, by her resistance to the priests, glorified Israel? Was it not the widow of Zarephath who fed the Prophet of the Lord? Add to all these beautiful examples the pious widow whose charity God praised; this good woman, from whom the same Savior received such beautiful praise; the holy women who followed Him in His missions, and who were more faithful to Him at death than the disciples and Saint Peter himself; the daughters of Saint Philip, so full of the spirit of God; and so many other women of whom Scripture speaks. And yet, you want to deprive those who, following Saint Augustine, the Church calls devout, from reading these stories which are so glorious and so edifying for the faithful. What model, then, should we imitate for our life? If Christian mothers are to be saved by the education of their children, if faithful women are to sanctify their unfaithful husbands, if they are to love them, strive to please them, flee luxury and vanity, adorn themselves with decency and modesty, like the wives of ancient Patriarchs, where can they find better than in Scripture the instructions necessary to fulfill all these different duties? Where are the Christian virgins, the richest portion of the flock of Jesus Christ, who must put their trust in Him? The sinful women, who must drown their iniquities in their tears—where will they find each other, the help they need, better than in these holy books, especially if they have the misfortune of falling into the hands of [spiritual] directors who seek only their own interests? Or, to hear from preachers who preach too often in the manner spoken of in another proposition (prop. 95)[7] condemned in the same Bull? To whom then should your servants have recourse, if

6. Translator's Note: 2 Kings 22.

7. Editor's Note: *Unigenitus* 95, condemning Quesnel's commentary on 1 Corinthians 14:21 (see Denzinger-Hünermann 2495). The commentary reads: "Truths have descended to this, that they are, as it were, a foreign tongue to most Christians, and the manner of preaching them is, as it were, an unknown idiom, so remote is the manner of preaching from the simplicity of the apostles and so much above the common grasp

you take from them the bread of life and of understanding, which the faithful soul, according to the pious author of the *Imitation* [*of Christ*], can do as little without as the living bread which came down from the heavens? What will they go back to? Dreams? Visions? "The wicked have told me fables," said the Prophet, "but nothing, my God, comes close to your holy law."[8] I can assure you with all truth, Most Holy Father, that the pious women in France are struck by this prohibition, as Your Holiness himself would be, if someone deprived you of reading Saint Gregory, Saint Leo, and generally all the other writings of the Holy Pontiffs, whose place you hold on earth, and with whom you will one day be, if it pleases God, associated in heaven.

I now come to the other half of the proposition. "It is not from the simplicity of women, etc."[9] I am not reckless enough to disagree with a proposition, the clarification of which depends on a full knowledge of the history of the Church. On the contrary, remembering that a woman was the first to be seduced, I could not fear enough for my own fragility, especially when I reflect that Abelard had Heloise, that Luther kidnapped a nun, whom he called his Bride of Canticles, and that Montanus and several other heretics brought after them several women loaded with sins. But to know the truth, if ever any woman produced immediately and by herself any error, it is a fact which I would relate to Your Holiness without difficulty, although I was born in a time and in a country where one is often obliged to doubt, in spite of oneself, all that is not based on the Word of God or on the Tradition of the Church. What surprises me the most, Most Holy Father, is to see that you have condemned a proposition which says little good about our sex, while there are an infinite number of *libelles*[10] around the world

---

of the faithful; nor is there sufficient advertence to the fact that this defect is one of the greatest visible signs of the senility of the Church and of the wrath of God on his sons."

8. Translator's Note: Psalm 119.

9. Translator's Note: *Unigenitus* 83 (see Denzinger-Hünermann 2483).

10. Translator's Note: A *libelle* is a political pamphlet or book that slanders a public figure. *Libelles* held particular significance in France under the Ancien Régime during the eighteenth century, when the pamphlets' attacks on the monarchy became both more numerous and more venomous. See Robert Darnton, "The Forbidden Best-Sellers of Pre-Revolutionary France," in *The French Revolution: The Essential Readings*, ed. Ronald Schechter (Malden, MA: Blackwell, 2001), 110–37; and Darnton,

charging us with atrocious invective, outrages, calumnies, blasphemies, and curses. May one day your zeal be animated against works so pernicious and so detestable!

The second proposition, which is the eighty-sixth in the Constitution, worries me no less. "To snatch from the simple people this consolation of joining their voice to the voice of the whole Church is a custom contrary to the apostolic practice and to the intention of God."[11] Alas! Most Holy Father, what did Saint Paul mean when he exhorted us to edify ourselves with songs and hymns? What did Saint James mean when he ordered us to sing when we were in pain? What did Saint Ambrose mean when he told the people to sing in the Church at times of persecution? Finally, what did the churches of East and West intend, when in celebrating solemn services, the psalms were chanted by the faithful of one or the other sex? Why, Most Holy Father, with one stroke of your pen would you close the mouths of so many pious souls who praise the Lord? Would you like to destroy what so many saints have perfected? The Christian people would have less advantage in this than the Jewish people, whose sweetest consolation was to sing the praises of the divine mercies. What? The daughters of the Church will no longer be able to sing the hymns of the daughters of Zion, not even the *Magnificat*, that excellent and divine canticle of the Most Holy Virgin! We have been happily doing so in France for a long time. Neither our prelates nor your predecessors have ever faulted this holy practice. Thus, Most Holy Father, I am afraid that you will not have much satisfaction with this article, nor with several others of your Constitution. I fear even that this spark will someday cause a great fire. The schism of England proves only too well that one often plucks the wheat without realizing it. May your wisdom, therefore, correct at an early stage all unfortunate things that could happen. Receive, for this purpose, your servant's humble protest. Saint John Chrysostom did not think it was unworthy of him to receive and benefit from the advice of a good woman on an occasion much less significant than this. And, to demonstrate an example of more interest

---

The Literary Underground of the Old Regime (Cambridge, MA: Harvard University Press, 1982).

11. Translator's Note: *Unigenitus* 86, condemning Quesnel's commentary on 1 Corinthians 14:16 (see Denzinger-Hünermann 2486).

to you: Was it not Saint Catherine of Siena who made one of your predecessors leave the See of Avignon? I must admit that I have none of the merit of this servant of the Lord. I will, however, end this letter, Your Holiness, with the very words of the admirable woman of whom I spoke at the beginning (and might it please God that I be answered in the same way): "The Lord has set you up to be the head of his people, and to destroy the enemies of his name; take care therefore that there is no evil in you all the days of your life; may your heart not be exposed to these scruples and remorse, for having shed innocent blood."[12] Being overwhelmed with blessings, may you always remember your dearest daughter and obedient servant.

URSULE DE LA GRANGE
21 October 1713.

12. Editor's Note: This is a direct translation from the French of the letter and does not clearly correspond to a particular verse in 1 Samuel 25. The woman mentioned here is Abigail.

14. The Appeal of the Bull *Unigenitus* to an Ecumenical Council

Translated by Guido Stucco[1]

On March 5, 1717, four French bishops entered the Sorbonne in Paris and read out this formal appeal of Pope Clement XI's 1713 bull *Unigenitus* to a (future) ecumenical council. These "Appellant" four were Pierre de La Broue (Bishop of Mirepoix), Charles-Joachim Colbert de Croissy (Montpellier), Pierre de Langle (Boulogne), and Jean Soanen (Senez). They had the support of 97 of the 110 doctors of theology at the Sorbonne, and much of the faculty of Nantes and Rheims. Soon, ten more French bishops joined the Appeal. The papacy—not to mention the French government—had a full-scale ecclesial crisis on its hands. Perhaps five percent of eligible French clergy formally appealed the bull, though at times sympathy for the Appellants was surely much higher than this. Paris was particularly full of dissent: a full three-fourths of Paris's 450 *curés* (parish priests) were Appellants.[2]

Though the proximate cause of the *Unigenitus* crisis was the condemnation of Pasquier Quesnel's popular Jansenist scriptural

1. The text of the appeal translated below (with minor omissions) is reproduced in full in Jacques Parguez, *La bulle Unigenitus et le jansénisme politique: Avant-coureur de la Révolution français* (Paris: Maurice Glomeau, 1936), 203–10. Bracketed verses placed immediately after a condemnation from *Unigenitus* refer to the passage in Scripture that Quesnel was commenting on. They were inserted by the editors of the present anthology, following the convention in Denzinger-Hünermann.

2. See Van Kley, *Religious Origins of the French Revolution*, 86; Cottret, *Histoire du Jansénisme*, 158.

commentary, we should place this conflagration in continuity with centuries of French strife with the papacy stretching back to the late medieval era. References to conflicts with Boniface VIII in 1302 and Leo X in 1517 help us understand why many "Gallicans" and other anti-ultramontanists around Europe who were not Jansenists were still troubled by *Unigenitus*.

While issues surrounding divine grace, penance, moral casuistry, and access to Scripture were all of importance, the Appeal helped crystallize the ecclesiological issues that ultimately made "the cause of Quesnel" and the Jansenists of interest to statesmen and clergy around the Catholic world. In a revealing statement, the Appeal argues that the conduct of the papacy "seemed to leave to the bishops only the ministry of executing the Pope's decrees, even though they received immediately from Jesus Christ the power to judge matters concerning faith, morals, and discipline."

Clement XI responded with censure in the bull *Pastoralis officii* of August 28, 1718. Ultimately, however, it was the power of the French crown and state to control and shape the French clergy that forced resistance to *Unigenitus* underground. After the bull became state law in 1730, opposition to it was severely marginalized, at least for clergy (not necessarily for laity, such as members of the *parlements*). The most important result of *Unigenitus* and the Appeal was a fusion between Jansenism and Gallicanism. Elements of this imperfect but very real union were eventually exported to the rest of Europe and reverberated into the nineteenth century.

Shaun Blanchard

Text of the Appeal of March 5, 1717

Pierre, bishop of Mirepoix; Jean, Bishop of Senez; Charles-Joachim, bishop of Montpellier; Pierre, bishop of Boulogne: to all those who will read this letter, greetings in Him who is the true Salvation of all men.

The bitter pain that pierced our hearts on the occasion of this sad affair, which has already troubled the whole Church of France for a long time, is not a pain that just affects us. Rather: "We share it with many others, and mainly with those who have a love and a most sincere veneration for the Apostolic See."[3]

It is indeed the case that after the Constitution that begins with the words *Unigenitus Dei filius* was promulgated, all good people were not able to read it without shedding tears for the following reasons: that it is a subject of joy for the enemies of the Church; that the faithful are exposed to the continual insults of the impious and of heretics; that the still feeble faith of new converts is shaken; that the salvation of many is in danger; that it [*Unigenitus*] excites disastrous divisions everywhere; that the turbulent promoters of a pernicious and corrupt morality see in this document a triumphant vindication; that the pure light of heavenly doctrine is obscured by the clouds of profane novelties; that all of the orders of the Kingdom [of France], the Magistrates, the Ecclesiastics, the Faculties of Theology (especially that of Paris, so commendable for its scholarship, the first of all Universities), the *curés* [parish priests], the bishops, and finally the entire Kingdom is troubled and embittered.

In these circumstances, so disagreeable and so fraught with dangers, the holiest priests are left in dismay before the altar of Jesus Christ, and the multitudes of the faithful raise their hands to Heaven. As far as we are concerned, we have not ceased to pray, imploring the One from whom we have received the *deposit of faith* and who entrusted us to safeguard that which He Himself wanted to be retained in its integrity and purity according to His immutable promises. At the same time, we have exercised all care and application in the way that pastoral solicitude demands of us, so as to avoid, as much as it is in our power, failing to display the proper respect due to either the authority of the Sovereign Pontiff, who has received from Jesus Christ the primacy in the whole Church as the indivisible link of ecclesial unity, or to the sacred rights of Christian Truths.

The entire Christian world knows that for three years there were no efforts, requests, or supplications that we failed to employ with Our Holy Father, Pope Clement XI, to convince him to remedy these ills.

3. St. Bernard: Letter 178 to Pope Innocent II, etc. . . .

We had hoped that according to the example of his predecessors,[4] he would graciously receive those who, motivated only by love of truth and justice, laid in his bosom the public lamentations of the faithful and the sentiments of their own grieving hearts. Then he might finally realize that the truth has been hidden from him, and he has been deceived by false suggestions.

However, we have not been able to achieve anything, because preemptive ideas [*préventions*] formed by unfaithful reports have not yet been dispelled. Scandals grow day by day, and disagreements are increasingly getting heated, such that the peace of the Church is disturbed and Christian truths are altered. We who are *established by the Holy Spirit to govern the Church of God*[5] in truth and charity, according to the portion of authority that has been confided to us, are obliged to have recourse to the remedy that the present circumstances make necessary, a remedy that is both certain and efficacious.

This is why we walk in the footsteps that our fathers have marked out for us to preserve the truth and reestablish the peace of the Church. We refer[6] this whole affair to the judgement of the Universal Church, which is the Sovereign Tribunal of Spiritual Authority, the unshakeable Pillar of the Truth[7] and the Sanctuary assured of peace and charity.

Far be it from us to have any intention of prejudice, or to demean the honor, the authority, or the unity of the Holy Apostolic See. We believe, on the contrary, following the general tradition of the most holy Fathers, that this is indeed the most proper and suitable means to conserve and defend them.

Therefore, we the undersigned Bishops who make recourse to the remedy of the said Appeal[8] state, put forward, and offer to prove at the appropriate time and place that which follows:

4. Pope Alexander III, etc. Editor's Note: Alexander III convoked the Third Lateran Council in 1179.

5. Editor's Note: This quotation comes from Acts 20:28, a verse often used to highlight the God-given (*de iure divino*) authority of bishops.

6. Editor's Note: The French *déférer* is a verb used in legal contexts, meaning to refer a case to the competent court or judicial authority.

7. Editor's Note: This descriptive image of the church is taken from 1 Timothy 3:15.

8. We have followed the Act of Appeal of 1517.

First of all,[9] the censure of some of the propositions condemned by the aforementioned Constitution [*Unigenitus*] have the effect of undermining the foundations of the Ecclesiastical Hierarchy, the Sacred Rights of Bishops, the Freedom of the Kingdom, and the unanimous sentiment of the Most Holy Fathers, who teach that "it is the Church that has received the keys of the Kingdom of Heaven; because," as St. Augustine says, "it is not one man alone but rather the unity of the Church that has received these keys."[10] Also, such censure undermines the authoritative word [*oracle*] of St. Peter, the prince of the apostles, and of the other apostles as well, who say that "We must obey God rather than human beings [Acts 5:29]." These propositions are the following:

§90: "The Church has the authority *to excommunicate*, so that she may exercise it through the first pastors with the consent, at least presumed, of the whole body [Matthew 18:17]."

§91: "The fear of an unjust excommunication should never hinder us from fulfilling our duty. . . . Never are we separated from the Church, even when by the wickedness of men we seem to be expelled from her, as long as we are attached to God, to Jesus Christ, and to the Church herself by charity [John 9:22–23]."

§92: "To suffer in peace an excommunication and an unjust anathema rather than betray truth is to imitate St. Paul: it is far from rebelling against authority or destroying unity [Romans 9:3]."

Second, in this whole affair, the Constitution has violated the legitimate authority of all the bishops, in general, and the Sacred Liberties of the Kingdom. This has occurred regarding many points: in the manner in which this text has been redacted, in regard to the things that are included in it, and, after its publication, in regard to a certain brief of our Holy Father the Pope. . . .[11] Against the dignity of the Bishops and

9. Editor's Note: Beyond this initial "first of all," the Appellants did not number their grievances. However, we insert numbers into the text to help orient the reader, when the authors instead begin new paragraphs with other transitional phrases such as "what is more."

10. Translator's Note: See for instance Augustine, *Tractates on the Gospel of John* 124, 7.

11. Editor's Note: A papal "brief" is an official and authoritative letter, though less so than a bull. The brief is titled *Brief of Our Holy Father Pope Clement XI Dated*

of all the Laws of the Realm the pope's brief was printed, made public, and inserted in the acts entitled *Verbal Proceedings of the Assembly of Cardinals, Archbishops, and Bishops Held in the Paris Archdiocese in the Years 1713 and 1714*. This brief seemed to leave to the bishops only the ministry of executing the Pope's decrees, even though they received immediately from Jesus Christ the power to judge matters concerning faith, morals, and discipline.

Third, the said Constitution condemned propositions that express nothing but the true sense and pure spirit of the most holy canons on Penance, containing by consequence the authentic rules of Penance, confirmed by the authority of Popes, the clergy of France, and of the most holy Bishops, on which depend the legitimate administration of this sacrament and the eternal salvation of the faithful. We must indeed delay reconciliation[12] in the case of sinners who do not yet have a spirit of repentance and contrition, who do not behave with humility, and do not feel the state of sin. These propositions are the following:

§87: "It is a method full of wisdom, light, and charity to give souls time for bearing with humility and for experiencing their state of sin, for seeking the spirit of penance and contrition, and for beginning at least to satisfy the justice of God before they are reconciled [Acts 8:9]."

§88: "We are ignorant of what sin is and of what true penance is when we wish to be restored at once to the possession of the goods of which sin has despoiled us and when we refuse to endure the confusion of that separation [Luke 17:11–12]."

Fourth, the aforesaid Constitution overturns the most solid foundations of Christian morality, and even the *first* and the greatest *of the Commandments*, namely the first one, concerning the love of God. This is done by the condemnation of expressions[13] that emphasize the need for such love both in order to bring about the conversion of the will and

---

March 17, 1714, Addressed to the French Cardinals, Archbishops, and Bishops Gathered in Paris in 1713 and 1714 concerning the Acceptance, etc. (title taken from the original text of the Appeal).

12. Editor's Note: This is a reference to delaying absolution in the confessional.

13. "Fear restrains nothing but the hand, but the heart is given over to sin as long as it is not guided by a love of justice." Editor's Note: This original note references the proposition condemned by *Unigenitus* §61 (Denzinger-Hünermann 2461).

to carry out our deeds in the manner which we were commanded to, which is to say by relating actually or virtually to God as our final end. This is made manifest in the condemnation of some propositions[14] such as §44, which is conceived in terms entirely similar to those expressed by Pope St. Leo,[15] several other Church Fathers,[16] and Cardinal Stanislas Rochus [*sic*],[17] one of the presidents of the Council of Trent:[18] "There are but two loves from which are born all that we will and all of our actions: the love of God that does everything for the sake of God and that God rewards; and the love of ourselves and the world, which does not relate to God what ought to be related to Him, and for this reason becomes in itself evil."[19]

Fifth, the said Constitution stigmatizes other propositions, which the scope of our present Appeal does not allow us to describe in more detail, but which nevertheless convey nothing but instructions on the necessity, excellence, fruits, and effects of charity, *which is the end of the precept* [to love God], and without which *everything else is of no use*. In those propositions the term *charity* is taken in the same sense in which one finds it commonly employed in the Scripture and in the Holy Fathers;[20] that is to say, in reference to all chaste love, even that which is only present and begun.

Sixth, the condemnation of various propositions tends not only to extinguish the sacred fire that our Lord Jesus Christ came to spread on earth, but also to snatch away this divine Light that the faithful of every age, sex, and social condition may derive from a devout reading of Holy Scripture, *which is generally proposed to all* (see St. Thomas, etc.).

14. Propositions 44, 46, 47, 49, and 53.

15. St. Leo, Sermon Five, concerning fasting on the seventh month. There are two loves, etc. . . .

16. St. Augustine, St. Fulgentius, St. Gregory, etc. . . .

17. *Confession of the Christian Faith*, etc. . . .—Peter Lombard teaches, etc. . . .

18. Editor's Note: The reference here is to the Polish cardinal Stanislaus Hosius (Stanisław Hozjusz) (1504–79), author of the work cited in the note above, *Confessio fidei catholicae christiana* (published 1553–57). This work was an anti-Protestant apologetic written by Hosius at the behest of the Synod of Piotrków (1551). Made cardinal in 1561, Hosius was appointed a presiding papal legate of Trent's third and final session in 1562–63.

19. Editor's Note: See Denzinger-Hünermann 2444 (*Unigenitus* 44).

20. St. Augustine, *On the Spirit and the Letter*, etc. . . .

Seventh, the said Constitution condemns and disapproves of various propositions, some of which present nothing other than what the Prophets, the Apostles, and the Holy Fathers taught us concerning the difference between the Old and New Covenants. Others merely teach what St. Augustine said in his *Enchiridion*[21] in regard to the first article of the Creed: "that the effect of the will of the Almighty is not blocked by the will of any creature." Finally, some other propositions contain the same doctrine that the Holy Doctors and the Sovereign Pontiffs[22] have taught us concerning various points, and in particular on the help *that is necessary for each action, and that derives its efficacy from the omnipotence of God, and from the sovereign dominion that the divine Majesty has over the wills of men, as over all other creatures that are under Heaven*. These are helps by which, to use the very same language of General Councils,[23] God, by means of "Jesus Christ unites us efficaciously to Himself by the gift of His grace alone," though He nevertheless "always leaves us the free power not to give our consent" (Council of Trent).

Eighth, the said Constitution indiscriminately stigmatizes, with the harshest and most atrocious qualifications, certain propositions that for the most part are expressed in the very terms of Scripture, the Councils, the popes, and the Church Fathers.

This is the case, for instance, of Proposition §27: "Faith is the first grace and the source of all the others." This proposition is entirely alike and conformed to these words of St. Augustine's:[24] "What is the grace that we received first? Faith"; to these words of the Council of Trent: "Faith is the beginning of man's salvation, the foundation and root of all justification";[25] to these words of Pope Boniface II:[26] "It is a truth

21. Editor's Note: The Appeal parenthetically cites here "Manuel à Laurent, ch. 96, etc. . . ."

22. Pope Clement VIII, St. Thomas, etc.

23. Editor's Note: The Appellants parenthetically cite here "Tome XII des Conciles du P. Labbe." This is a reference to Philippe Labbe's monumental *Sacrosancta concilia ad regiam editionem exacta*. The twelfth volume covers the period 1414–38.

24. Augustine, *Tractate Three, on John*. Translator's Note: the reference is to Augustine's *Tractate on the Gospel of John* 3, 8.

25. Chapter 8. Translator's Note: see Council of Trent, *Decree on Justification*, 8 (Denzinger-Hünermann 1532).

26. Letter to St. Caesarius of Arles. Translator's Note: see Pope Boniface II, *Per*

certain and Catholic that in all goods, of which faith is the first, the mercy of God precedes us, when we do not yet want it"; and finally to the words of many other Fathers which are conformed to the expressions of Holy Scripture.

Another example is Proposition §12: "When God wishes to save a soul, at whatever time and at whatever place, the undoubted effect follows the will of God." The proposition here is word for word from St. Prosper (*Poème des ingrats*), according to the translation that has been made in French verse of the Latin poem of this Holy Doctor. It was cited under his name in the very book from which [this condemnation] has been extracted.[27] [This proposition] conforms to the constant tradition of both the Western and the Eastern Churches (see the Liturgy of St. Basil).

Such are many other propositions that present nothing but the language used in Holy Scripture, consecrated by the perpetual tradition of all the ages, and confirmed by the constant use of the faithful.

Ninth, those who have presented these propositions for condemnation to our Holy Father the Pope have twisted the words of the author [Quesnel] into senses foreign to them. These propositions have neither been faithfully translated from the Latin nor extracted from the book in good faith. They have defamed the author with the most atrocious notes. He has therefore been misunderstood, and he could not defend himself even though he never ceased to request the opportunity to be understood. They did not show the proper respect due to the most eminent and illustrious men who approved this book. And finally, this Constitution has been introduced in such a manner and in such form that if it is admitted once, there will be no more books or authors who can remain secure from the reach of attaint in the future.

FOR THESE REASONS and many others which we are ready to present at the proper time and place: "We lift our spirits up to the Lord, placing our trust in the same Truth that we follow, not wishing to omit any of the things that we believe with the help of the grace of God can be useful, until the tempest formed by these storm clouds has been

---

filium nostrum, 2, to Bishop Caesarius of Arles, January 25, 531 (Denzinger-Hünermann 399). Boniface II was pope from 530–32.

27. Editor's Note: The reference here is to Quesnel's book *Réflexions morales*.

quieted, and the truth spreads its rays everywhere."[28] And [we are] assured by a firm faith that "the protection of God has never and will never abandon His holy Church."[29] We have made express protestations previously, that we would never say or even think anything that is contrary to the One, Holy, Catholic, Apostolic, and Roman Church, nor to the authority of the Apostolic See, to which we protest that we remain united in an inviolable communion to the last breath of our lives. Neither will we ever depart from the respect which is due, according to the sacred canons [*les saintes règles*], to our Holy Father the Pope. *For the glory* of Almighty God, for the preservation and exaltation of the Catholic faith and the ancient doctrine, for the peace and tranquility of the Church and of the Kingdom, for the defense of the rights of the Episcopate and the Liberties of the Gallican Church: We, both ourselves and all those who have joined us or will join us in this endeavor, are Appellants, and we appeal to a future General Council[30] that will be legitimately assembled in a safe place, where we or our deputies can go freely and securely, along with those to whom it belongs to judge concerning the sorts of issues [connected to] the aforesaid Constitution. . . .

And in the fear that our Most Holy Father Pope Clement XI has been driven, by the ill insinuations of some persons, to proceed or cause the beginning of proceedings of any kind whatsoever, by his authority or any other authority such as it may be, against Us, our Churches, our *curés*, and the Faithful who are subject to us, by excommunication, suspension, interdict, deposition, deprivation, or by any other way whatsoever: and so that our State,[31] and that of those who adhere to Us or who wish to adhere to Us, remains safe and sound in all things: We, on behalf of ourselves, our Churches, our *curés*, and the Faithful who are subject to Us, as well as those who adhere to Us, or wish to adhere to

28. St. Leo, Letter 44. Editor's Note: St. Leo is Pope Leo the Great, who reigned 440–61.

29. *Idem*, Letter 45.

30. This is in conformity with the act of appeal of 1517 concerning the concordat [the Concordat of Bologna of 1516], and with the act of appeal of 1460, etc.

31. Editor's Note: the bishops are here referring to their "State" as bishops, that is, to their office.

Us, are all Appellants. And we appeal by this Act to said future General Council, and to anyone or anything to whom or to which by law it is necessary to appeal each and every aforesaid grievance which has been made or will be made. And We ask with the authority which is due to the letters called *Apostolos*: We place our Churches, our *curés*, and the Faithful who are subject to Us, as well as those who adhere to Us, or want to adhere, with their state and their rights, under the protection of God, and of the universal Church, and of the said General Council.[32]

We will protest to renew this present Appeal, where, when, and before whom we see fit.

Made in Paris in the presence of the undersigned Notaries public, the year of the Incarnation of Our Lord 1717, the first day of March.

32. This conforms to the Appeal of 1303, under Boniface VIII, etc. . . . of Benedict XIII [pope of the Avignon line, excommunicated at Constance, d. 1423], etc., of 1460 etc. . . .

15. The Abbé d'Étemare on the Conversion of the Jews

Jean-Baptiste Le Sesne des Ménilles d'Étemare

Translated by Luke Togni[1]

From the beginning, Jansenists were associated with diligent scriptural study and a turn to patristic exegesis. In the wake of *Unigenitus*, a distinctively Jansenist method of apocalyptic biblical interpretation arose. Jansenist "figurism," popularized by a circle connected to the Oratorian seminary of Saint-Magloire, sought to make sense of the myriad political and ecclesiastical defeats that Jansenists had suffered and encourage and embolden the flock. Typological interpretations that connected the Old and New Testaments to each other and to subsequent historical events certainly go back to the first days of Christianity. What gave Jansenist figurism its unique strength, however, was an evolving typological vocabulary in which every new persecution or setback could be interpreted within the matrix of scriptural symbolism and become a cause for hope rather than despair.

The work of the Oratorian Jean-Baptiste Le Sesne des Ménilles d'Étemare (1682–1770) responded to the seeming failure of the various means of recourse Jansenists had sought against "the Bull." To this

1. The excerpts translated below are taken from *Explications de quelques prophéties touchant la conversion future des juifs, et spécialemente de celle du ch. 11. de l'épître aux romains, avec une Réponse à des difficultez qui ont été proposées sur cette Explication* (n.p., 1724), 3–4; 9–10.

end, the Abbé d'Étemare retrieved and reinterpreted an old apocalyptic trope: the future conversion of the Jews, especially as prophesied by St. Paul in Romans chapter eleven. Though apostasy may seem to surround the faithful (Jansenist) Catholic, the "living branches" of the Appellants and others who cling to "the Truth" are the chosen instruments of God to convert the Jews. Hopeful confidence in the return of the Chosen People became a central theme of convulsionary Jansenism: this spectacular triumph would vindicate Jansenist "Truth" as well as restore "the losses and weakening of the Church" of the present day.

Despite the overwhelming odds faced by those clinging to "the Truth"—caught between the hammer of papal and episcopal condemnation and the anvil of the French state—God is ultimately in control of all of these events. The sympathetic reader or listener is inserted into a grand biblical drama, one in which dispiriting current events are actually part of God's plan to vindicate His righteous few. Herein lies the appeal of figurist exegesis and preaching for the persecuted Jansenists.

Shaun Blanchard

An Explanation of Certain Prophecies Concerning the Future Conversion of the Jews.

And especially that of the eleventh chapter of the Epistle to the Romans

St. Paul, in the ninth chapter of the Epistle to the Romans, raises the difficulty of harmonizing the abandonment and hardening of the Jews with the promises of God contained in the Old Testament. He gives three answers that mutually support one another. These must all be put together if one wants the difficulty to be resolved entirely.

He gives the first in the same chapter [nine], verses six, seven, and eight, and in the rest of the chapter. Paul's first answer consists in saying that the promises refer to none but the true Israelites. All those who are children of Abraham according to the flesh and according to the order of nature are not [necessarily] true Israelites; but only those which have been given to Abraham by a special providence and by the predestination of God, which God had in mind when He made the promises to Abraham. This is carried to the conclusion that all those among the Jews who have not believed would not be included in the promises, and therefore one would not be able to maintain on any basis that their abandonment is contrary to the promises, because these promises do not pertain to them. This first response is very well known and widely used.

The second response is found at the beginning of chapter eleven. [This position maintains] that it is not true that God has rejected entirely the carnal race of Abraham; this Paul manifestly proves by giving his own person as an example, and in yoking all those among the Jews who have believed and who have not ceased to be a great number, although they were few in comparison with the rest of the Nation [the Jewish people].

But the Apostle does not go a long time before realizing that these two responses, however true they may be, are not sufficient. He comes soon to consider that the promises with which the Old Testament is replete are applied in too particular a manner to the race of Abraham according to the flesh, and too closely linked with that family. These promises are too often addressed to the Nation as a body, too often addressed according to the universality of that [Nation] to totally reduce their accomplishment to the calling and conversion either of a very small number of the children of Abraham according to the flesh, or to the conversion of the Gentiles, who are not children of this Patriarch except in a spiritual manner.[2] This is why he has recourse to the third response.

[That third response] consists in saying that a day shall come when the Jews shall convert in full, and when the body of the Nation will

2. Editor's Note: D'Étemare is here arguing that Paul correctly interprets the Old Testament promises as referring to the Jewish people as a totality, and thus the hope of future conversion in Romans chapter 11 must refer to the entire "Nation" of the Jews rather than just to a righteous Jewish "remnant" or to Gentiles becoming part of the people of God. Addressed to the nation as a "body," it applies to the integrity of the nation as indivisible and distinctive, in its universality, to the full extent of its members across time and space. A remnant would not account for the universality, while a replacement by the Gentiles would not account for this distinctiveness and integrity of the Jewish nation.

recognize Jesus Christ. St. Paul opens this third and last response at verse eleven of the eleventh chapter: *What then should I say? That the Jews have fallen to such an extent that their decline should be without any redress? This would not please God.* And he continues to develop for us his third response, by expounding the secrets of the marvelous work of God. Their fall, he continues, has become the opportunity for the salvation of the Gentiles, who did not come in except to repair the breach that the Jews made through their fall. They [the Gentiles] were zealous to imitate the faithful Jews who had preceded them in the service of God. And through this the Gentiles became, in turn, an example worthy of being offered to the unbelieving Jews, and appropriate to give them a fitting model for emulation.[3] Therefore, the Jews will one day profit from their example and so will also be able to enter, in their turn, into the way of salvation. This will happen at the occasion of the fall of the Gentiles, threatened by St. Paul. . . .

Therefore, Malachi teaches us that that which will delay the Day of the Lord, connected by Isaiah and St. Paul to the destruction of the Antichrist, will be the conversion of the Jews. This must take place beforehand. And St. Paul, as we have seen, presented to us the reason for the delay of the day of judgment and the coming of the Antichrist in the Epistle to the Thessalonians. The apostasy, otherwise known as the mystery of iniquity, had to occur beforehand and begin in its own time. And St. Paul teaches us in the Epistle to the Romans that there was an apostasy whose effect would be to open the doors to the Jews, in order to bring them into the Church. I inquire about all of this. Let us see the truly wonderful harmony between the Apostle, Malachi, and Isaiah.

This is not all, because Malachi makes us understand the horrible state in which all the Earth shall be when Elijah will come to convert the Jews. Effectively, there will be nothing left to happen except for Jesus Christ to descend to strike the Earth because of the anathematized, and to take up from it the few just that will remain, as Lot was rescued from Sodom before God struck because of the anathema. "Lest I come," says the Lord, "and strike the land because of the anathema." This accords very fittingly with this apostasy of which St. Paul speaks,

3. See the passages of St. Chrysostom, of Oecumenius &c.

which will be very widespread at the time when the Jews will come in, restoring the losses and weakening of the Church.[4]

One thing more must be remarked. The two verses of Malachi that we have come to relate are preceded by another, where he has spoken of Moses without us knowing why [he does so] and without the rest of the discourse of the Prophet that he appears to quote: "Remember ye, says the Lord," Malachi 4:4, "the Law of Moses my servant, which I gave to him on the mountain of Horeb so that he would bring my precepts and my ordinances to the entire people of Israel." Moses, in being joined unexpectedly to Elijah in such an extraordinary circumstance, assuredly gives an opportunity to recall that one has seen him with Elijah, speaking together with Jesus Christ on the day of the Transfiguration, and in the Apocalypse chapter eleven[5] where it spoke about the two prophets to whom the Holy City was given. The person of Moses appears no less explicitly designated than Elijah. And so, if Elijah is indicated by the power to seal the heavens, so that it does not rain at all during the times in which he forbade it, times which St. John [in the Apocalypse] reduced to three and a half years, Moses likewise is indicated by the power to change water into blood and to strike the Earth with all kinds of plagues.

St. John sees these two witnesses under the figure of the olive trees and of the two candelabras placed before the God of the Earth [Revelation 11:4]. This brings us back explicitly to the fourth chapter of Zechariah, where he spoke about the candelabra or seven lamps, and of the two olive trees that are present before the Ruler of the Earth.

Do these two olive trees not strike the imagination, and do they not make us inevitably recall the olive trees of St. Paul[6] and the mys-

4. See in the *Tradition* the passage of Elijah according to Monsieur Hamon, to Monsieur Bossuet, and to Monsieur Chétardie. Editor's Note: Joachim Trotti de La Chétardie (1636–1714) was a famous biblical commentator known for his writings on the apocalypse and fulfillment of prophecy.

5. Editor's Note: The Apocalypse of St. John is otherwise known as the Book of Revelation.

6. Editor's Note: Romans 11:17–18 reads, "And if some of the branches be broken, and thou, being a wild olive, art ingrafted in them, and art made partaker of the root, and of the fatness of the olive tree, boast not against the branches. But if thou boast, thou bearest not the root, but the root thee."

teries that he has uncovered for us thanks to this metaphor? And he finds rightfully that Zechariah is one of the prophets who has spoken most clearly about the conversion of the Jews, and that the two men that he saw under the figure of the two olive trees were Jesus the son of Josedech and Zorobabel, both destined to restore the Temple after the Babylonian Captivity. In this they were a figure very expressive of the two prophets, who will be employed to reestablish the Tribes of Jacob, and to make them reenter the walls of the Temple of God, after a long captivity where we have seen them groan, of which the Babylonian exile was but a shadow. The return from the Captivity of Babylon was the figure of the conversion of the Jews, which will be the return from this other captivity, one that has been longer and more fatal. It is this that gives us the key to the great extent of space [given to] the Prophets. They make wonderous pictures of the return from the Babylonian exile, which we would not be able to stop ourselves from finding hyperbolic and exaggerated if they had not wanted us to cast other events under the idea of the return from Babylon; among others, that which concerns the general conversion of the Jews, which we await.

16. The Biblical Drama of Figurism: *Jesus Christ under Anathema*

Abbé Jacques Gudvert

Translated by Luke Togni[1]

One of the most aggressive publications of the figurists bears the unsubtle title *Jesus Christ under Anathema and Excommunication.* Authored by the Abbé Jacques Gudvert (d. 1737), it was published in Amsterdam in 1727, shortly before adherence to *Unigenitus* was, by royal decree, made the law of the French nation and not just of the church. Gudvert's pamphlet of around seventy total pages reflects this deteriorating situation. It is tinged with anger, wit, sadness, and intense desperation.

Gudvert's thesis was that *Unigenitus* had put Jesus Himself under excommunication and thereby anathematized the gospel: "Behold, thus, an accurate likeness obtains between the judgment of Caiaphas and this Bull." Seeing the contemporary rejection and condemnation of Jansenist "Truth" in the figure of the tortured and crucified Christ was Gudvert's primary typological image. The Jesuits are decried openly as heretics. Bishops who accept *Unigenitus* are successors of Judas. The Synagogue is a figure of the Roman Curia. Gudvert's attack on papal infallibility is scathing: "It is necessary that the Truth should perish rather than the least stain fall on [the pope's] pretended infallibility."

1. This excerpt is taken from Abbé Jacques Gudvert, *Jesus-Christ sous l'anatheme et sous l'excommunication* (Amsterdam: Nicolas Potier, 1731), 19–24.

Pasquier Quesnel is honored as a kind of Christ-figure who was martyred for his faithfulness. For example, just as those examining Quesnel's writing ripped his words out of context, so also did the corrupt accusers of Christ. Ultimately, Quesnel and the Truth he defended were condemned "with as much injustice and lawlessness as Christ was before him." While Gudvert's work reads at times like a bitter, violent polemic, it also offers an uncomfortable critique of the powerful. In the contemporary age, as in the time of Christ, the powerful are ready to condemn the innocent and ignore the truth lest they risk their own authority. It is no wonder that this provocative pamphlet was soon placed on the Index of Forbidden Books and publicly burned.

Jesus Christ under Anathema helped create a distinctively Jansenist theology of history. Along with the work of Duguet and d'Étemare, Gudvert influenced the narrative of church history put forward by later Jansenists, for example those at the Synod of Pistoia (1786), who translated *Jesus Christ under Anathema* into Italian and diffused it among parish priests.

Shaun Blanchard

Jesus Christ under Anathema and Excommunication

We see now the proportional likeness that obtains between the sentence of death pronounced by Caiaphas against Jesus Christ and the Constitution by which Clement XI condemned the book of Fr. Quesnel and the 101 Propositions which are drawn therefrom, and then excommunicated its defenders. In this lies that likeness in its entirety, and respects both its foundation and its form.

With respect to its foundation, as Caiaphas condemned Jesus Christ, the Constitution has condemned His Truth. Jesus Christ calls himself the Truth, and so to condemn the Truth is to condemn Jesus Christ Himself. But, further, which truths are condemned by the Constitution? The truths more precious and dear to Jesus Christ than His earthly life: the right, which He purchased by His blood, to choose and form His Elect Himself; the power and effectiveness of grace; the necessity of the mediation, faith in, and hope for His merits; the obligation to love Him and His Father, to direct all our actions thence, and to approach Him with faith and love rather than with brutal passions, by sheer fear alone like a beast, and other similar truths. Is condemning such holy truths that form the soul of religion not condemning Jesus Christ Himself? And this is just what the Bull has done. Behold, thus, an accurate likeness obtains between the judgment of Caiaphas and this Bull.

But if the injustice of one or the other judgment is the same, so it is likewise for the form. We see the same passions, the same plots among the Pharisees and the latter-day promotors of either affair: the same character in the judges, the same weakness in the people. Envy, hatred, and a false zeal for religion moves the Pharisees against Jesus Christ as against the purity of doctrine. The same passions move the Jesuits against the doctrine of the Gospel, against the grace of Jesus Christ and the obligation to serve God with love; against Fr. Quesnel and against those luminaries who have endorsed him. The Pharisees, by decrying the Savior, became impious and blasphemers, while the Jesuits, by decrying the truths they hate, have given themselves to heresy. On every side we goad, warn, and stir up these judges. We are resolved that, regarding these vague accusations, they would collapse even before they have been examined. Therefore, we seek crimes that could have offered the pretext for condemnation and find none. What shall we do? Shall we send back the accused absolved? Nay, rather, we have committed to this matter and would be ashamed to retreat from it. Passion blinds us so much that we have forged crimes for [the judges] against Him who is most innocent and holy. Jesus Christ confesses that he is the Messiah—what a consolation for the Jews who were burning with expectation through so many ages! And [yet] we say: He has blasphemed! Fr. Quesnel taught that God is so powerful that He can convert and save a sinner however hardened he may be; [he taught] that man was made to love God, and that he ought, consequently, to sacrifice through love all the movements of his heart and every action of his life to Him. What is yet more wonderful? What is more capable of raising Christian joy? And the Bull has condemned him as a *teacher of error, a seducer, and a son of the ancient father of lies.*

But, further, on what foundation have we been able to pronounce such a judgment to Rome? For some time, the Roman Curia has consulted neither Scripture nor Tradition for their decisions; betaken with its arrogant opinion of its own infallibility, it adjusted them based upon previous developments, irregular and reckless as they may have been, and so it was necessary [that the Roman Curia] should have a resemblance to the Synagogue. The Pharisees had bound the Chief Priests to forbid the recognition of Jesus Christ as the Messiah—without an examination—under pain of excommunication and expulsion from the Synagogue. That is the reason why, when [Jesus] had confessed that He was the Messiah while being interrogated by Caiaphas, they believed that it was needless to pursue any further investigation. People full of themselves and who believe themselves to be the only infallible oracles have no concern to step back: this would be to recognize themselves capable of mistakes. It was better that the Messiah should die than to examine whether Jesus Christ was actually the Messiah; that would have sullied their authority.

Behold the spirit of the Roman Curia laid bare. It never retreats. The least little note is made a great affair, a decree of the Inquisition, a Bull drawn up against all rules, like the Bull against Baius—which was never published nor received according to canonical forms—is for [the Curia] an infallible oracle. [Such documents] it prefers to Scripture, to the decisions of the Councils, and to the unanimous agreement of the Fathers. The Jesuits obtained a note from Alexander VII favorable toward the sufficiency of fear without love in the Sacrament of Penance. They also obtained a Bull for the formula that condemned the five famous propositions [of Jansen]. The five propositions were no longer condemned only in themselves (no one held them) but, this Bull said, they were condemned in the sense that Jansen held them. [The pope] had not previously made an examination of Jansen. However, he had condemned him. Those who will study Jansen's text with the greatest attention that they can give, will declare that they find in it nothing but the dogma that grace is efficacious by itself, upheld by St. Augustine, St. Thomas, and the whole of the Tradition. The partisans of Molina will often make a similar declaration. What will happen? Will the Roman Curia confess its fault? Hardly. It is necessary that the Truth should perish rather than the least stain fall on its pretended infallibility. Fr. Quesnel dared to uphold the insufficiency of fear and the necessity of the love of God in the Sacrament of Penance and the efficacy of grace on its own. Granted, he has Scripture, the Councils, and the Fathers on his side. Still, the Roman Curia held it necessary that Fr. Quesnel and the Holy Truths that he protects should be condemned with as much injustice and lawlessness as Christ was before him.

Some false witnesses, by changing certain sayings of Jesus Christ, change the sense of that which He had said. They accused [Jesus] of saying that He could destroy the Temple made with human hands, as if He had spoken of the material Temple in Jerusalem rather than the Temple of His body, which was the true Temple of God. Destroy this Temple and in three days I will rebuild it, Jesus said. In the same way, some have maliciously shortened and mutilated certain propositions of Fr. Quesnel, in order to make them more likely to be poorly understood. The Gospel says that the witnesses who testified against the Savior did not agree among themselves. The bishops, moreover, who are the witnesses as well as the Judges of doctrine, do not agree among themselves regarding the meaning of the propositions of Fr. Quesnel. For these reasons we have challenged them [the bishops] a hundred times, I would dare to say it, to see that they have made a false witness against him in the Pastoral Instruction of 1714, in the Body of doctrine of 1720, and in their *mandements* [episcopal decrees]. One Apostle handed Jesus Christ over for a sum of money. Would to God that there were only one of those who call themselves successors of the Apostles who, with an eye to self-interest or ambition, has imitated the faithlessness of Judas. After the sentence of death was pronounced by Caiaphas against Jesus Christ, the Chief Priests bound Pilate, despite himself, to condemn and crucify Him. After the Bull, the Pope and the Bishops bound the Princes and Magistrates, willingly or not, to lend their hand strongly to make sure the Bull was received. How many times did the Emperor resist and refuse to authorize the unfortunate Bull, and the models which were at last settled to be accepted? Behold thus a striking likeness between the condemnation of Jesus Christ and that of the doctrine of Fr. Quesnel, as much in its form as in its foundation.

17. The Miraculous Healing of Anne Lefranc

Anne Lefranc

Translated by Maxwell Pingeon[1]

In 1727, a young Jansenist deacon named François de Pâris (1690–1727) died in the Parisian slum parish of Saint-Médard. Almost immediately, miracles began to be reported at his grave. Yet it was not until 1731 that the growing cult of François de Pâris began to attract serious controversy. While Jansenists had previously pointed to similar miraculous healings as a sign of divine favor—starting with the so-called Miracle of the Holy Thorn at Port-Royal in 1656—the miracles of François de Pâris were different. The reports of cures engendered a sensation in the capital, drawing enormous crowds to the little cemetery of Saint-Médard. Soon, the devotees began to shake and convulse at the gravesite. Hence they came to be called *convulsionnaires.*

One turning point that helped provoke the shift away from more conventional forms of Catholic piety to convulsions was the public controversy over the healing of Anne Lefranc. A poor, unhealthy woman who had been lame and partially paralyzed for many years, Lefranc went to the cemetery with a mission. Her Jansenist pastor, the

1. Anne Lefranc, "Relation de la maladie et de la guérison d'Anne le Franc," in *Recueil des Miracles opérés au tombeau de M. de Pâris, Diacre, avec les Requêtes présentées à Monsieur de Vintimille Archevêque de Paris, par Messieurs les Curés de cette Ville, et un Discours Préliminaire sur les Miracles,* vol. 1 (Utrecht, 1733), 301–9.

somewhat erratic Abbé Lair, had just been removed from his title by the Archbishop of Paris, Vintimille du Luc (1655–1746). Lefranc hoped for a miracle that would vindicate the cause of her "lawful pastor." Her healing in November of 1730, which was publicized by the clandestine Jansenist press, shocked the authorities into a response. In the summer of 1731, the archbishop ordered a team of physicians to investigate. They never examined or questioned Lefranc, but, basing their conclusions largely on the account in her "Relation," declared that her illness was mere hysteria, and that her "healing" was neither complete nor miraculous. Vintimille added fraud to the accusations against Lefranc and used the doctors' verdict to condemn the entire cult of François de Pâris.[2] And in August, under increasing pressure from the Church, devotees started to convulse during their own healing experiences.

Anne Lefranc's account of the healing traces the full length of her illness, compounded by many chronic symptoms. It shows not only a faith in the miraculous work of François de Pâris but also the attachment of ordinary laypeople to their local clergy. This latter motivation was sustained theologically by a broader Jansenist turn toward Richerism. Named for the Gallican author Edmond Richer (1559–1631), Richerism emphasized the rights and dignities of the lower clergy at the expense of an increasingly "apostate" hierarchy. It became widespread among Jansenists as more and more of the French Episcopate turned against them.

Richard T. Yoder

The "Relation" of Anne Lefranc

To the Greater Glory of God:

An account of a sickness I had for twenty-eight years, and for which I was healed by the intercession of the Blessed deacon François de Pâris, buried at Saint Médard.

At nine years old, on June 15, 1703, I had my first fainting spell. I fell unconscious for two hours, and my tongue receded into my gullet,

2. B. Robert Kreiser, *Miracles, Convulsions, and Ecclesiastical Politics in Early Eighteenth-Century Paris* (Princeton: Princeton University Press, 1978), 124–30.

staying locked there for an entire day and night such that I could not feel anything with my mouth; the doctor of body and soul was called to treat me. After bleeding me multiple times in the arm and the foot—and twice at the throat—he gave me some medicine, and little by little my tongue released and regained its usual place in my mouth.

I was then seized with convulsions of the nerves so violent that even though lying flat on the bed I began to bounce up and down, flying so high that I hit the canopy of the bed. I was flailing about so wildly that multiple people needed to take positions by my side to catch me lest I hurt myself on the way down. These convulsive fits lasted three months, getting worse by the day, and I sometimes had as many as sixty a day. The many treatments I took did not relieve me, but only weakened me further.

As soon as these nervous convulsions ceased, I grew swollen from head to foot, and burned constantly with fever, often clutching my sides and my heart, which was almost continuously beating out of my chest. I remained in this state until 1707, and though I could from time to time leave the house, I was in such bad shape that I was often taken for dead, having received last rites a total of seven times in the space of four years.

I then felt better for a period of two years, and could freely go outside, but my body was always swollen, with a lingering fever and palpitations when I attempted to walk even a little.

In 1709, I was fifteen. On May 19th, the day of Pentecost, I suffered a relapse that lasted into the month of August. I was so ill I needed to use the chamber pot up to twenty-five times a day. Painful chest pains followed, my sides ached, and I shook with a violent fever. Meanwhile, my swelling had not gone down, and on top of it all, I began to cough up blood. Monsieur de Fresne, who was my doctor since the beginning of my illness, gave me all the known treatments. But rather than relieve me, they only served to weaken me more and more, leaving me in such a low state as to inspire compassion in all those who came to see me. On an ordinary day, yet another in which there was not much hope for me, I was bled from the foot from ten in the morning to two hours past noon, to draw out of me five *palettes* of blood. Monsieur Duplessis was my surgeon then, and it was he who performed the bleeding. He is well disposed to attest that I stayed in this state for nine years, abandoned by all my doctors, each one lamenting my condition more than the last—I being so young—and telling me I would never get well. There were moments of relief during this period, but they did not last long.

Finally on April 17, 1718—Easter Sunday—I had such a bad choking fit that I needed to be bled from the arm and the foot and given an emetic.[3] I then lost the use of my legs, and on the Pentecost which followed, I lost my sight for four hours. Though I regained the use of my left eye a little bit, I could not work or read without glasses. As for my right eye, I could not tell the difference between an *écu* and a *liard*,[4] and stayed that way until the time of my healing.

Three years later, in September of 1721, I saw an Irish doctor who proposed bath treatments to regain the use of my legs, adding that he would be unable to cure me of my other ailments. Indeed, I was soon able to walk a little bit around my room after that, and feeling slightly better, I wanted to try to attend Mass.

On the first Sunday of Advent that year, I went outside for the first time in several years. But I began to suffocate so badly that immediately upon my return I needed to be bled from the arm and foot and given an emetic. The following year, on February 22nd, the first Sunday of Lent, I wanted to try and return to Mass, against the advice of those doctors and surgeons who prohibited me from ever going out again, and all the same things as described above happened again. Finally, on April 13 of the same year, the day after Quasimodo Sunday, I made a third attempt, but I found myself in such an awful state that there was not even time to bring me back to my room. I was bled from the arm and foot at a neighbor's house, and given an emetic. Another time I merely wanted to visit with a neighbor,[5] but I was struck down in the same way as before, and since that last attempt I did not leave the house.

These past thirteen years, I've hardly been able to walk at all, and then only by artificial means—that is to say, by taking baths—but in

3. Editors' Note: A medicament intended to induce vomiting.

4. Editors' Note: Coins of the *Ancien Régime*.

5. Source Note: The neighbor in question is Monsieur Foucquet, an armorer by trade, who is now dead. Below the reader will find the affidavit of his son-in-law, Monsieur de Roussy.

the long run, far from providing relief, these baths only weakened me, so much in fact that I have not been able to go down a flight of stairs for the past five years, and have not even been able to get out of bed for the past two years. To report here all the diverse situations in which I have found myself would exceed the space I have been allowed. I would only add that, during my illness, I received last rites twenty times, I've been bled one-hundred and forty times from the foot and twice at the throat. When you factor all the times I was bled from the arm, I must have been bled at least three hundred times in all. In recent years, my blood has been of very poor condition. I wasn't sleeping for more than an hour at a time; I'd lost all sense of taste; I was always acutely swollen, with terrible pains in my chest and sides, coughing up blood, and in being transported from one place to the next I would often faint and lose consciousness.

One might have difficulty believing that what I report here is in no sense exaggerated, for I am convinced that those who will read this account will fail to perceive how one could possibly endure such a situation. But the Lord is my witness that I have been entirely accurate and that persons of recognized probity could not testify otherwise, having seen what I endured with their own eyes.

In 1728, a person in whom I had the greatest confidence, and who had seen me from the beginning of my illness, exhorted me to seek the Lord's help through the intercession of the Blessed Pâris, but I told her frankly that I was not a believer. Though she told me of God's strength bursting through this saintly deacon, I confessed that I had little faith in him, and she never spoke of him again.

After that, I could only think of preparing myself for death, which I saw as the only possible remedy for my illness. I got very little relief from my pain, excepting the moments when a few charitable people would come to console me, and especially the curé[6] of Saint Barthélemy,[7] my pastor, who came as often as he could to encourage me in my suffering and was always nearby when I needed him.

6. Editors' Note: A curé was a canonically-installed pastor. With the Jansenist turn toward Richerism in the eighteenth century, the moral role of the lower clergy became increasingly important.

7. Editors' Note: The cleric in question is the Abbé Lair, an outspoken opponent of

A year ago, last Ascension Day, as I began to hear more of the miracles taking place at the Tomb of the Blessed Pâris, I felt pained by my former lack of faith in the man. Touched by the marvelous events that were happening day after day, I bid someone to pray a novena for me at Saint Médard. But either because the Lord was punishing me for my former faithlessness, or because it was not yet my time to receive His mercy, I experienced no relief. Nonetheless, I trusted that if I could go to the tomb in person I would be healed, even though my situation would not yet allow me to be transported there.

In the end it was the events surrounding Father Lair, my pastor, that renewed my confidence. On the 4th of October I was shocked to learn that he was going to be replaced by another parish curé, and I resolved on the spot not to recognize his successor. To rely on that man's ministry was so repugnant to me that I would rather die than submit to it. I therefore asked of God, in the bitterness of my heart and my eyes brimming over with tears, that He would heal me through the intercession of His Servant, such that I would not be made to participate in injustice by receiving the sacraments from someone whom others had appointed to replace my legitimate pastor. For in all other things that were rightfully his I was ready to communicate with this other curé, and any other who thinks like him, such that I would happily attend Masses celebrated by him, and even receive the sacraments from him, not only in other churches but even in Saint Barthélemy, on condition that they be administered to me as from a simple priest and not as my pastor. It was with this commitment in mind that I resolved to pray a second novena at Saint Médard to implore God that He heal me, and in so doing vindicate my own curé.

In the meantime, the same person who had first told me of the Blessed Pâris came to see me, and I told her of my designs. But unlike the first time, when she offered to carry me there on the spot, she told me she would come back and see me in a little while, that we would have to wait and see. I told her I could not wait, and I pleaded with her to go to Saint Médard the following morning, October 26, 1730, and told her

---

Unigenitus whom Archbishop Vintimille removed in 1730. For a full discussion of the controversy around Lair's removal, including Lefranc's healing, see Kreiser, *Miracles*, 115–22.

that if she would not accede to my request I would send another person to pray in my stead. After my pressuring her in this way, without exposing my motive, she yielded to my demands.

I forgot to add that the evening before I began the novena, I attempted to walk in my room, supported by two people, but my legs could not bear any weight at all. The following day, I tried again, and nearly fell backward, almost sending one of my helpers tumbling down the stairs. But from the first day of the novena, I began to feel the use of my legs again as I crossed from one room into the other, still supported by two people, and day by day I began to feel better.

On October 28, the third day of the novena, two clergymen of the parish who were guided by the Truth came to see me, and as it is customary to transport the Blessed Sacrament to the sick of the parish on the four great feast days of the year, they wished for me to receive it on Saint Marcel's day from the hand of the new curé, who was the designated celebrant for the feast. They gave me several reasons why I should accept: among others, that refusing would put me in great danger. But I could not overcome the repugnance I felt toward the side they were encouraging me to take, and I told them with tears in my eyes that I would expose myself to anything rather than recognize my pastor's successor.

On the night of the Day of the Dead, Saint Marcel's Day, the final day of my novena, I had planned to go to Saint Médard, but I was in such a sorry state that I did not expect to be able to get there in the morning. When I arose that morning, however, I tested my legs to see if they would support me. Realizing that I was able to stand, I wanted very much to go. I left at seven in the morning, very swollen still, with my usual chest and side pains, and aching throughout my whole body, especially in my legs, and blind in my right eye. A neighbor of mine who accompanied me along with my sister feared this day might be my last, but I was increasingly confident I would be healed.

As soon as I was in the carriage, I seemed to no longer be in pain. But as soon as I arrived at Saint Médard, and I had to make my way to the tomb of the Blessed Pâris, I was in incredible agony, and arriving on the spot, I cried out to the Lord, "My God, Thou who canst read the secret hearts of men, Thou knowest why I am doing this. Lord, I ask for neither health nor sickness, neither life nor death, for I know not which of these things I should ask of Thee. I therefore pray to Thee, Lord, if it be Thy will, to choose me, despite my unworthiness, to manifest the glory of Thy truth by the intercession of Thy servant, and that Thy holy will be done."

Barely had I finished my prayer when all my aches and pains ceased. I then went to Mass, but in between the elevations of the Host and the Chalice my condition deteriorated again, and I could not stand up, feeling weak all over, and my clothing underneath my arms was drenched in sweat. But nothing could prevent me from taking Communion unassisted and on my knees. My strength came back as soon as I had joyfully received the Host. After Mass, since I had been fasting, someone gave me a morsel of biscuit and something to drink, which fortified me somewhat, and I walked without difficulty to the carriage. I then noticed that my swelling had gone down, that I could see clearly out of both eyes, and that I no longer felt any pain. I still felt weak in the legs, but I was able to walk unassisted up the stairs to my fifth-floor apartment.[8]

The next day I was sick to my stomach and I evacuated a large quantity of bad humors. Since then, however, I have felt fine, and I presently feel no pain in my chest or sides. I eat and sleep again, and I can work and read without glasses. Indeed, I no longer even feel any strain around the eyes at all. I can walk; I go to Mass; and the more I move along, the better I feel. God even gave me the strength to abide the fatigue and affliction of the six months during which my aunt, who had taken care of me since I was a girl, sickened and died. And since the beginning of Lent, the Lord has granted me the grace to fast without difficulty, something I have never been able to do in my life.

I pray that those reading this account join me in thanking the Lord for having chosen me, someone so unworthy, to manifest His wonders.

To Him alone do we owe the glory of the ages.

Signed, Anne Lefranc, Paris, 6 March, 1732

8. Source Note: She currently lives on Rue de la Barillerie near the Palace at the Botte de Cour.

18. In Defense of Convulsionary Jansenism

Louis-Basile Carré de Montgeron

Translated by Marie Giraud[1]

In January of 1732, royal authorities decided to close the cemetery of Saint-Médard. But in spite of this setback, the cult of François de Pâris continued. In small conventicles that met in private rooms, worshippers of all classes gathered around relics of the wonder-working deacon to continue their devotions. A new element emerged. While convulsing, devotees began to attack each other: they consensually crushed, beat, burned, branded, dragged, stabbed, and crucified each other, often with no apparent injury. These acts, which were also taken as "miracles," were called the *secours*—or "help"—and dramatized the preservation of the Truth (i.e., Jansenist Catholicism) in the midst of persecution. Women were the most prominent recipients of *secours*, with men ordinarily administering the blows. And in the midst of it all, *convulsionnaires* of both genders would prophesy.

These rites, forbidden by law and condemned by ultramontanes, split the Jansenist community. Although the early miracles had been warmly welcomed by most Appellants, the turn toward convulsions and the *secours* provoked an enormous controversy. Many accused the *convulsionnaires* of demonic possession, hysteria, fraud, sexual

1. Louis-Basile Carré de Montgeron, *La vérité des miracles opérés par l'intercession de M. de Pâris et des autres appellans, démontrée avec des observations sur le phénomène des convulsions*, vol. 3 (Cologne: Librairies de la Compagnie, 1747), 224–28.

impurity, or some mixture of all four. In 1735, thirty Jansenist divines issued a "Consultation" condemning the *convulsionnaires*. But others disagreed. The jurist Louis-Basile Carré de Montgeron (1686–1754), a wealthy and enthusiastic *secouriste* who had been converted from libertine Deism at Saint-Médard, took up the task of defending the cult of François de Pâris. In 1737 he published the first volume of *La Vérité des miracles*, which he personally presented to Louis XV at Versailles. This act of *lèse-majesté* landed him in prison for the rest of his life.

Yet Montgeron continued to write. With a team of collaborators, he released a second volume in 1741, and a third in 1747. By then, most of his old allies had died or abandoned him. He became increasingly concerned with defending the divine character of the most violent aspects of *convulsionnaire* worship, the *secours*. This excerpt, taken from volume 3 of *La Vérité des miracles*, shows how one young woman became a *convulsionnaire* as a result of her miraculous healing.

Richard T. Yoder

La Vérité des miracles, Vol. III, Part VII—"Examen de l'Autorité des Théologiens Antisecouristes"

Article XVI

This new *convulsionnaire* whom God uses today for His great works is only a poor peasant from the village of Méru, in the Diocese of Beauvais—where she has, where she has remained, nearly since her birth, in suffering, crying out in pain. That is, until the 8th of July 1743, when she came to Paris, or to be more accurate, until the 31st of July, when she experienced convulsions and was miraculously healed.

Having lost her mother at the start of 1726, when she was only eighteen months old, she was put into the care of her paternal grandmother, where she was not able to receive the care she needed, although she was always, until her miraculous healing, of a weak constitution.

There was every reason to believe that from birth there was something inherently wrong with the stomach of this child. She was always sick, never able to eat solid foods without suffering tremendous pains.

But above all, from the age of fourteen, her stomach became a continual torment, and the top of her sternum was so often uncomfortable that it had to be put back into place with an operation which was extremely painful.

In 1741 when she was about sixteen or seventeen years old, her increasing pains became even more abnormal, her stomach constantly bloated, in which all her muscles were completely distended to the point where she was barely able to eat any kind of food at all. Scarcely had she finished swallowing when she was forced to vomit. We were surprised that she was able to live like this, without any kind of nourishment staying in her body. She was of a delicate constitution and had the paleness of death painted on her face, which seemed to announce every day that she was going to be death's latest victim. But God, who had destined her for great works, had other plans.

In the month of March 1742, Providence brought a relative to Méru who had been staying in Paris. This relative, well informed on her Religion and devoted to the Truth, was moved by compassion to see the degree to which the body and the soul of this poor sick woman had been neglected. Not only was no one offering her any remedies for her continual pains, which seemed to diminish her extremely, but even worse, they had raised her in such ignorance that she was unable to read or write. Without informing her of the importance of the major Truths of Religion, they had barely taught her the first principles of catechism.

The relative, who was staying in Méru for a year, took in the poor sick woman and used all her knowledge and remedies to heal her body and enlighten her soul.

With regard to her body, the relative's efforts were futile. She called the surgeon, who exhausted in vain all of his knowledge and remedies; this bore no fruit, which is again proof that the pain was a congenital defect. The relative was driven to abandon the sick woman without knowing how to relieve her of her suffering. Even if they could stop her vomiting for a few days, she continued to be sick every day with even more intensity after short intervals, just like she had experienced previously.

Even if the charitable relative did not succeed in this respect however, her cares had a very happy success with regard to the most important undertaking. The sick woman eagerly accepted all the advice she was given. Having experienced in this world only continual suffering and the rebukes of men, her heart opened up with joy at the hope of eternal life in the bosom of the Son of God. Her relative taught her to accept her pains and to receive them with total submission, and to pray with fervour to the Savior of the World so that they could be joined in His sacrifice.

The sick woman quite quickly made use of this submission and was able to bear this considerable burden without limit: she needed to experience a remarkable test. It was not only the redoubling of her pains, but what was more painful was that her relative returned to Paris in April 1743 without her. She had pleaded and tenderly insisted, without success.

Once the relative returned to Paris, the woman became almost inconsolable. It had seemed that her pains were in some ways halted when she heard the relative speak of the goodness of saints, and she looked upon her as a guardian angel who was carrying her up to heaven. But in losing the pleasure that she had found in those kinds of conversations, she was no longer able to bear the burden of her pains, which became stronger and more aggressive day by day—she was feeding herself only on her tears.

Finally, having suffered for so long, she made the decision to find her relative in Paris, despite the overwhelming state she found herself in, and the excessive weakness which made the idea of such a journey totally impractical. But she put all her belief and trust in the Almighty, and sustained by her faith, she began her journey in July 1743.

Despite the pain she endured, and the extreme fatigue that overwhelmed her, she finally arrived in Paris in the same month of July.

As soon as her relative saw her, her initial reaction was of spite toward her, to the point where her door remained shut, but on further reflection, she soon expressed gestures of goodwill. She saw that it was utterly out of the question that she should return to her province in the state she was in, and the goodness of her heart made her at least try to give her some of her strength back before sending her home.

The relative first went to a doctor, who did not hide from her that this illness was going to be very difficult to cure, and that the treatment would be very long and very expensive.

The relative, who was not able to pay expensive fees, was determined to place her in the Hôtel-Dieu, if only she was able to acquire a bed where she could be alone. But unable to succeed in this task, and unable to leave her to sleep with complete strangers, she made the decision to keep the sick woman with her. Rather than giving her remedies, she put her under the protection of the Holy Deacon, and the relative made her swallow the soil from his graveside mixed with water and ashes, following the advice which she had received from an ecclesiastic of the "Truth."

Nonetheless on the sixteenth day of the same month of July 1743, a violent fever took hold, and gave her such repulsion against all sorts of foods, and at the same time an insatiable thirst devoured her, which made her drink water almost without limit. As a result, she became incredibly bloated, especially in her stomach, which blew up in an extraordinary fashion.

From time to time she fell into long fainting spells, and on the 22nd of July, she looked, for three hours, as though there were no signs of life left in her, except a little warmth that seemed close to extinction. It was in vain that they rubbed her temples, her nose, her lips, with all the liquors of the most spiritual kind; she remained immobile, unconscious, and so pale that she seemed dead. They tried to make her swallow the liquor but her teeth were so clenched that they were unable to open her mouth. They started to fear the worst, until a *convulsionnaire en convulsion* came to her aid, and declared to those assisting that she would bring her back to the here and now. To that end, she put in a spoon a few pinches of precious soil gathered from the grave so fertile in miracles, with a few drops of water, and presented this mixture to the lips of this suffering victim. She suddenly opened her mouth, and before she had even opened her eyes, had swallowed the entire spoonful greedily. In that moment, she came back from her fainting spell. And with the *convulsionnaire* having made her then drink two glasses full of the same remedy, the sick woman received considerable relief.

This favorable experience clearly showed that this was the remedy to give to the sick woman. She never stopped making use of it on all occasions, and many pious people joined her and prayed that the Blessed Pâris might be her intercessor before God.

Each time she swallowed the beneficent healing mixture, she found herself relieved for a few moments, but was not completely cured, and it did not stop her from falling back into long stretches of lethargy and weakness.

Among other things, on 28 July she lay still unconscious and without movement, with eyes blank, fixed and open just as though she were dead, from eight o'clock at night until one in the morning, despite all the efforts that were made to bring her out of this state. And then, her abnormally bloated stomach began to be agitated by quick movements, and with such violence, that it scared all those by her side. One could see a huge growth rising from her throat ready to choke her. As she was unable to speak she made a sign indicating that this growth was choking her, but there was no cure available; her teeth were still so clenched that it was impossible to make her take anything. Thus, the color of her face started to change, so that from moment to moment, the color would come and then go, which expressed the degree of suffering she endured. They finally found a way to make her swallow the mixture, so beneficial for the effects that God Himself produced. And as quickly as the fit had come, her symptoms subsided, although she was not fully cured.

God delayed the cure, because He wanted to wait for the *antisecouriste* theologians to disseminate their *Response* to the Public, to refute it Himself by this miracle which He operated visibly by means of the *grands secours.*

On the 30th of the same month of July, the moment the sick woman came out of another fainting spell, another *convulsionnaire* arrived who came close to her with her fist raised, and said "Do you want me to strike you in the stomach?" "No," replied the sick woman. But despite this rejection, the *convulsionnaire* struck her in the belly as quickly and as strongly as she could.

A few of the spectators were annoyed; but in an instant, their anger changed to admiration, when they heard the sick woman cry out the same sounds as the *convulsionnaires*—"*Ah! Que c'est bon!*" And they saw her open her arms and present her belly to the *convulsionnaire* saying, "Again, again." Without the need for her to ask a second time, the *convulsionnaire* struck her again with even more force, and without complaint, the woman asked for even stronger blows.

After this intervention the woman seemed almost completely healed. Her belly no longer bloated. Every strike she received spread a healing balm across her entire body so particular that it drove away all her pains. She was only missing her strength, but she would soon receive this in abundance.

The next day, July 31, she herself fell into convulsions, at two o'clock in the afternoon. A certain assured expression was visible on her face, in her demeanor, and in her body language, which were completely different to her previously shy temperament, showing that something extraordinary was taking place in her, and the answer to this riddle was soon to be revealed.

Suddenly an involuntary and convulsive movement forced her to hit herself in the belly with all her strength. This girl's simple nature, growing up in ignorance, and the sheer fatigue and exhaustion caused by her ailments had held her in an almost continual silence, in which she only spoke in very few instances. At that very moment she shouted at the top of her voice to deliver an animated speech that was clearly beyond her natural capabilities.

Around five o'clock in the evening she fell into fits of convulsions and struck her own belly with anything she found at hand. Around her there were only three other people of her sex; of the three, one was very tall and strong. She begged them to strike her, but her strikes were too weak. She lay on the ground on her back and one after another invited them to take turns to climb up and stand with both feet on her belly. And because this weight did not seem enough, they were forced to sit on her all three together, one on top of another. Who would ever think that this would be the specific [medicine] by which it pleased the Almighty to give her healing the final seal of approval? She got up from this heavy charge with such healthy demeanor, not only in perfect health, but also with extraordinary strength.

From this day forward, until now, she receives the most terrible and astonishing *secours* several times a week without showing any signs of fatigue. On the contrary, for her, they give her an abundant source of strength and inconceivable vigor.

Sat down on the floor with her back to a wall, she receives up to two thousand kicks one after another in the pit of her belly, by all those who come to see the *convulsionnaires*, and no one is capable of kicking as hard as she would like. "This is why" she says, "the more the 'Truth' is trampled on by the children of the world, the more it will receive strength from it."

She orders a man to stand on her head with both legs and supports him without any pain.

Splayed out on the floor, she is struck by logs all over her body, and mainly on the chest and stomach. She causes the most robust men to break a sweat, who soon tire of the blows they give her, and that she never tires of receiving. With every violent strike, an air of joy takes hold of her face, and her eyes, turned heavenward, express the happiness of a soul who, suffering death for the Truth, already considers going to heaven as her infinitely great reward.

Held up straight against a wall, she takes a spit roast, the strongest she can find, and she places the sharp end in the pit of her stomach, or between her ribs, and then has four, five, six people push hard against the other end with all their strength, so that the spit bends and folds in on itself with such violence.

God had placed an inconceivable force, visibly above anything else imaginable in a human body, in this woman's stomach, which for nineteen years had been so weak and so distended from the tip of her sternum down to every fiber in her body, that she was unable to handle the smallest amount of solid food! But it was not only in the stomach of this girl that God had placed these superhuman qualities.

Sometimes, she places the point of the spit to her throat, or on her forehead. Two people try to push with all their might, and she never feels any pain, nor does she receive harm.

It seems that God takes pleasure in reversing all the laws of nature, to simply convince those who are seeking the Truth that only His omnipotence is capable of producing such miracles!

Finally, after several months, she received strikes by sword all over her body, and even on her throat attempts were made to push as hard as possible. But there was no harmful impact. Even if her skin folded on the points, and there was sometimes a small red mark left behind, her flesh was never pierced. Many people all at the same time gave her strikes by the sword without reprieve for two to three hours, and a great number of the swords broke from being pushed with great inflexibility and difficulty. And during all this time, she gave impassioned speeches far beyond her reach.

19. Jacques-Joseph Duguet on a Christian Prince

Translated by Luke Togni[1]

Jacques-Joseph Duguet (1649–1733) has rightly been called the father of Figurism. One-time Oratorian and professor at Saint-Magloire, it was Duguet, the teacher of d'Étemare, who first popularized Jansenist hopes of a mass conversion of the Jews that would purify the Catholic Church. Duguet was troubled, however, by increasingly extreme manifestations of Jansenist resistance like the *convulsionnaires*. His career represents a different fork in the road for the Francophone Jansenist community. Duguet's biblical exegesis and ecclesiology appealed to Catholics around Europe, including many who were not invested in the Jansenist struggle in France.

One of Duguet's most important contributions was a political work: the *Institution d'un prince*. In 1711, Duguet began writing a manual of instruction for the ideal Christian ruler at the behest of Victor Amadeus II, Duke of Savoy, who wanted it for the education of his eldest son. Originally kept only for private use, the *Institution* was first published in Leiden in 1739. It went through many editions and was widely acclaimed around Europe, by Catholics and non-Catholics (it was translated, for example, into English).

1. The excerpt below is taken from Jacques-Joseph Duguet, *Institution d'un prince, ou Traité des qualités, des vertus & des devoirs d'un souverain. Par la M. l'Abbe Duguet. Nouvelle edition. Avec la Vie de l'Auteur* (London: Jean Nourse, 1750), 4:35–42. Also translated is the summary paragraph that begins chapter 3 (page 20 in vol. 4).

The excerpt below, from chapter three of volume 4, deals with the sovereign's duties vis-à-vis the church. It is not difficult to see why Duguet's text appealed to so many as the eighteenth century wore on. Clashes between Catholic states and the papacy, supported by the Jesuits and ultramontane clergy, became more and more directly confrontational. Duguet's theses regarding church and state rested on the claim that "ecclesiastical authority and royal authority were complete before the conversion of the Emperors [to Christianity]." This claim was not unique to Jansenism, and reached back to the great medieval struggles between popes and sovereigns.

The so-called "indirect power" of the pope to depose excommunicated sovereigns and release their subjects from allegiance is systematically rejected as a chimera. Duguet argues that this theory, formulated in the counter-reformation period by Cardinal Roberto Bellarmino as a moderation of more extreme hierocratic views of papal power, ultimately falls apart for the same reasons a theory of direct power of church over state does. The church "cannot remove what it cannot give" to the sovereign; that is, temporal authority. Ultimately, the church has rights over the person of the sovereign as one of the faithful, but no rights whatsoever over "the royal authority." While the church has the right to excommunicate anyone, Duguet cautions employing this extreme penalty against heads of state. It is as an "infinitely dangerous" measure that does more harm than good.

Shaun Blanchard

Institution d'un Prince

Volume Four, Chapter Three

The Kings, by becoming faithful,[2] have recognized another power besides their own, but one yet still very useful to them. Ecclesiastical authority and royal authority were complete before the conversion of the Emperors. These two powers are independent from each other. The sole means of preserving their mutual independence is to the guard the

2. Editor's Note: This refers to the conversion of kings to Christianity; through baptism, kings became part of the body of "the faithful."

limits Scripture has placed between one and the other. Tradition establishes the same limits. It is an error contrary to Scripture and Tradition to attribute to Ecclesiastical authority a power, however indirect, over the temporal authority. It is necessary to distinguish the character of the King [as such] from his character as one of the faithful. The Church has rights over the faithful man, but none over his royal authority. *There is a necessary union between the Ecclesiastical authority and the royal authority, since one supplies what is lacking in the other.*

Article Six

It is an error, contrary to Scripture and Tradition, to attribute to the Ecclesiastical authority an indirect power over the temporal authority.

1. We have seen that the Popes have not only recognized these important truths, but that they have strongly established [these truths] themselves, and that consequently there is nothing more opposed—and I am appealing not to modesty but to the constant teaching of the Popes solidly instructed by the Gospel—than the pretension direct or indirect of those whom flattery has seduced over the temporal authority of the Kings. This pretension is, it seems, less odious if considered as nothing but indirect and as a result of the scandalous obstinacy of Kings regarding morals or doctrine—or if the Ecclesiastical authority is constrained to repress, by this extraordinary way, when all other ways were proved useless.

2. But this indirect power over the temporal power of Kings, whether of Bishops or of the Pope or even of a Council that presented itself as general [ecumenical], is just as contrary to Scripture and Tradition, and just as pernicious to the Church and the State, and just as capable of filling the Republic with rebellions and other troubles, and just as fatal to religion as the chimera of a direct authority over the temporal authority of Kings. One necessarily supposes the other,[3] because one must have received that [direct authority] to use it, and it is impossible to use it with wisdom and legitimate power, however indirectly, if one has not received it in substance. The greatest of all defects is that of [the

3. Editor's Note: Duguet here means that appealing to the indirect power necessarily implies a direct power.

lack of] power. No good intention can compensate for it, nor can it cover it up, and it is clear that to use [that power] in specific occasions, it is necessary to have it in substance and reality.

3. The adjudications that the ancients made between the Ecclesiastical authority and the royal authority either absolutely destroyed the indirect power of the Church over the temporal power of Kings, or they equally authorized the indirect power of Kings over spiritual matters and over the sacraments. "As it is not permitted for us to have temporal Empire," said Hosius in the name of all the bishops, "nor is it any more permitted to Emperors to assume for themselves the right to offer sacred things or to participate in the ministry of them."[4] Pope Gregory II said that "as the Pontiffs have no right to mix themselves up in the affairs of court, nor to grant offices of state, so neither does the Emperor have any right to mix himself up in the affairs of the Church, nor to select and ordain the ministers of the Church."[5] The equality of the two sides is the same: no more can the priesthood lord over human matters; nor can the Empire over spiritual matters. It is necessary to hold to these limits, or to confess that the Empire has an indirect power over the sacraments and things divine as much as the priesthood claims a like power over the temporal authority of the King.

4. How, then, would it be possible for Churchmen to have such power over royal authority since Scripture submits them to [the temporal power] and bids them to teach others to submit to it as well? The Holy Spirit says through St. Paul that "each person is subject to the superior powers, since there is no power which does not come from God, and it is He who has ordained those powers that are on earth."[6] The general phrase *omnis anima*, "every person," does not exclude anybody, but includes all. "Although you are an apostle," says St. John Chrysostom on this point, "although you are an evangelist, or a prophet, although you are honored by some other distinction or ministry, you are included in this general rule: since this kind of submission is

4. Hosius, in his Letter to the Emperor Constantine. Editor's Note: Hosius, bishop of Córdoba, Spain, was an important advisor to Constantine and played a prominent role at the Council of Nicaea in 325.

5. Editor's Note: Gregory II was pope 715–31.

6. Editor's Note: Duguet footnotes here the Latin Vulgate text of Romans 13:1.

not at all contrary to piety and is, rather, compatible with the greatest virtue.[7] Therefore, one cannot avoid [that submission] by pretending to be a solitary priest or bishop, since the Apostle subjects every state of life to the temporal authority of Princes and the magistrates sent by the Princes."[8] It is with this intention that St. Peter names not only the Emperor and the King, but also the governors and magistrates who share in their authority: "Be subject (he says without distinction), in order to obey God, to every man who has power over you, be he King, as the sovereign, or be they governors sent on his part."[9]

5. These sacred laws are not only general and without exception for all people, but even for all time. These laws cannot be bracketed in situations where the Kings are infidels and enemies of the Church: they suppose, on the contrary, that the Kings will one day submit to the Gospel, and it is with this viewpoint in mind that St. Paul besought powerfully "that we make supplications and prayers for the Kings and for all those who have been elevated in dignity, because God wills that all men be saved and come to the knowledge of truth."[10] This great Apostle knew well that these supplications and prayers would be granted one day. It was, therefore, natural that he would give rules to the ministers of the Church, who agreed at that time that the Princes would receive the sacraments from them and would submit to their spiritual authority. It was even an absolute necessity that [the ministers] were aware of the limitations that would then be placed upon the submission that was due to the temporal authority. And he [the Apostle Paul] would not have left the ministers under the impression that they had no way to impede abuses other than purely spiritual means, if it was true that they had received from others the entitlement to remove the sword from those who received it from the hand of God. But very far from giving them any such thought, the Apostle declares in absolute terms,

7. Editor's Note: Duguet cites here and gives part of the Latin text of St. John Chrysostom (c. 347–407), "Homily Two to the People of Antioch."

8. Editor's Note: Duguet cites here in support a similar passage in Latin from the commentary of Theodoret of Cyrus (c. 393–c. 458) on Romans 13 (verse 1): "Whether one is a priest, or a bishop, or a monk, these all must submit to the commandments of the magistrate."

9. Editor's Note: Duguet here gives the Latin Vulgate translation of 1 Peter 2:13–14.

10. [1] Timothy 2:1; 4.

"that whoever resists the authorities, resists the order of God,"[11] and that those who so resist draw condemnation upon themselves. And he [St. Paul] gives no other rule for all the ages to come, than the obligation to submit oneself, not only in fear, but moreover conscientiously, to those whom God has charged with caring for society.

6. As the usage of indirect power has the same consequences as the direct and immediate power, namely, that it causes the same wars and the same rebellions, and that it bathes the world in blood and carnage, there is nothing that should be more disallowed by Scripture than this indirect power over the royal authority. Before spilling a single drop of blood, it should be necessary that the righteousness of our cause at hand be more evident than the sun. Since all the fatal consequences following from an enterprise whose basis is doubtful would come crashing down on the temerity of those who would be its authors, they would be culpable before God for all the blood that would be spilled all about on both sides. But far from this usurpation of an indirect power over the temporal power of the Kings having a sure and indubitable basis in Scripture and the Tradition, just the opposite is manifest there. The Princes and their subjects have the right to oppose it as an evidently unjust pretension. Thus, on the side of the Princes, all [their actions] are just and necessary. As for the usurpers, it is their actions that are entirely unjust and criminal.

7. It is, therefore, impossible to doubt that the Empire is absolutely independent from the priesthood, that the priesthood submits to it in all human and temporal matters—as Ecclesiastical writers and the Popes[12] themselves have recognized—and that when the Prince uses his power well, it behooves us to submit to it in conscience. When he abuses it, it is necessary to prefer the will of God—who established [the Prince as] His minister to protect the good and punish the bad—to [the Prince's] unjust commands, but never to resist the legitimate authority of him who has no judge upon this earth and knows none but God as his superior, and who renders account of his conduct to none but Him.

11. Editor's Note: Duguet is here quoting Romans 13:2.

12. *Regibus nos etiam subditos esse sanctae Scripturae praecipiunt* (Letter of Pope Pelagius I). Editor's Note: "We also are to be subject to Kings, as the holy Scriptures commands."

According to Tertullian, "He who speaks in the name of all Christians, whose defense he takes upon himself, has been established by God. He is in the second place after God. He is inferior to none but God. He is the first after God. Nothing but the heavens rest above his head, and he holds all that he has from the same one who gave him life. Men have given nothing to him, neither existence nor the power to command, nor do they have any power at all to take it away from him."[13]

Article Seven

It is necessary to distinguish the characteristics of a King as such from his character as one of the faithful. The Church has rights over the faithful person, but it has none whatsoever over his royal authority.

1. But, some will say, when the Emperors became Christian, did they not become children of the Church by their baptism? Was it not from her [the Church] that they needed to receive instruction and the sacraments? Did they not owe her obedience? And when [the Emperors] were not docile, surely she did not lack the means to recall them to their [Christian] duties?

2. One ought to admit that they are the children of the Church and her disciples in respect to religion, and that the Church has every right to use all legitimate means to correct them when they fall into sin, and to carry them back to penitence. She can even cut them off from the sacraments in a manner that is more or less public. But she does not have the right to fall into crime to remove them [from office], nor to become culpable for sedition and revolts. This would brush up against an authority which [the Church] should hold for herself to be inviolate, as well as for everyone else, and which is therefore, from her point of view, independent, just as the priesthood is independent from the Empire.

3. It is therefore necessary to distinguish [in one person] the character of the King as one of the faithful, or, what really amounts to the same thing, the royal authority from the person. The Church has rights over the man as one of the faithful, but it has none over the royal authority. She can forbid the Prince's use of sacred things, but she can

13. Editor's Note: Throughout this quotation, Duguet gives seven citations from the original Latin of Tertullian's *Apology*.

never make an attack on a power that depends upon God alone. The Church cannot remove from him what it cannot give to him. She will respect the sword that God has placed in his hand, and she must never bring herself to this outrageous act, equally contrary to piety and reason, that is, to tear that power out of [the Prince's] hands under the pretext that he abused it. She will use powerful weapons, but spiritual ones; God has entrusted her to instruct, to draw back, and convert. But she must never usurp those things that are forbidden to her. Among these [spiritual weapons], she looks upon the sword of excommunication, very useful for the particularly difficult, but infinitely dangerous to use when it has to do with Princes, so that even one such severe action might engender bitterness, and the resulting resentment and indignation [at its use] could result in very fatal results for their subjects, and for the whole Church.

20. Underground Jansenist Journalism: The *Nouvelles ecclésiastiques*

Anonymous

Translated by Keanu Heydari[1]

The clandestine journal known as the *Nouvelles ecclésiastiques* was one of the chief organs by which the Jansenist cause stayed alive. Running from 1728 to 1803, it entered into and shaped the nascent public sphere of eighteenth-century France. Replete with complaints about Jesuits, *philosophes*, and the persecution of Jansenists, the *Nouvelles* kept up the struggle against *Unigenitus* for decades after it had largely faded from public interest. Yet it was also one of the few cultural sites where the voices of ordinary people were taken seriously. The words of underrepresented figures—including working-class people, uneducated women, and minors—all appear in the pages of the *Nouvelles*, which relied upon these voices as proof that a righteous remnant of the people would preserve the "Truth" of Jansenist Catholicism.

The article selected here demonstrates that tendency, and covers one of the many episodes that Jansenists lamented. It details the struggle between Jansenists and Ultramontane clergy at the Hôpital général de Paris, an institution which served as a hospital, asylum, orphanage, school, and prison across several different locations. This particular battle takes place at the Hôpital de Bicêtre and concerns the education

1. "De Paris," in *Les Nouvelles ecclésiastiques*, 7 août 1749, 125–28, https://gallica.bnf.fr.

and sacramental life of the "choirboys," mostly orphans, living there.[2] The novelist Nicolas Restif de la Bretonne (1734–1806) was one of these "Enfants de Chœur" and remembered the Jansenists there fondly, if not without some criticism. He eventually left Bicêtre alongside his half-brother, the Abbé Thomas, for the Appellant stronghold of Auxerre in 1747.[3]

These conflicts of the late 1740s were an opening salvo in what would become known as the Refusal of Sacraments Controversy. The Archbishop of Paris, Christophe de Beaumont, instructed his clergy to refuse Communion and last rites to anyone in the diocese who could not produce a *billet de confession*, a signed document accepting the bull *Unigenitus*. Beaumont's measure implied that Jansenists would die in perdition. Eventually, this policy led to a legal battle with the *Parlement* of Paris, which included several prominent Jansenists in its ranks.

Richard T. Yoder

Suite des Nouvelles Ecclésiastiques, 7 August 1749—From Paris

In the last issue, we gave an idea of the great advantages that the Master of the Altar Boys and the Governors of Bicêtre brought to this house. The Administrators were extremely satisfied. Only the priests found fault with it. They said that the Hospital was being turned into a Geneva.[4] Their proof was that the poor recited Psalms in French in their dormitories (what a misfortune!), and that their Governors did not commune (which is very false). The pulpit was used to decry them; they were called preachers;[5] and they had, they said, orders from the Vicars-general to prevent (these gentlemen) from speaking their errors.

2. Editor's Note: See Henry Légier-Desgranges, *Du jansénisme à la Révolution: Mme de Moysan et l'extravagante affaire de l'Hôpital général, 1749–1758* (Paris: Hachette, 1954).

3. Editors' Note: See Nicolas Restif de la Bretonne, *Monsieur Nicolas, ou le cœur humain dévoilé*, vol. 2 (Paris: Isidore Liseux, 1883), 1–77.

4. Editor's Note: Implying that the Governors were turning the boys into Protestants.

5. Editor's Note: The term *prédicant* refers here to a Protestant minister.

They were careful to tell the archbishopric that these Governors were priests in disguise: as if it would have been a crime for persecuted priests to take on a layman's habit to serve the poor in a hospital! It is true that two of them withdrew because of these denunciations, of which they were informed. One was a priest and the other a deacon. The latter returned sometime later, and died in the service of the prisoner's infirmary, the most tiresome [death] of all. The poor incorrigibles complained bitterly about those who wanted to correct them; and they found only the priests willing to allow them to complain. Hence a multitude of memoranda were presented to the Archbishop, to the Attorney General, to the First President, to the ministers themselves, as if it had been a matter of state. The Administrators and the Rector (M. Vierne) still parry the blows. But how to ward off all those which the destructive spirit can deliver?

The Master of the Altar Boys, who was regarded as a simple clerk, and who was effectively nothing more when he consecrated himself in 1735 to the service of this Hospital, performed the office of subdeacon in Christmastide; and for this serious case, he was ordered by the Archbishop to give an account of his conduct to M. de St. Exupery. He did so, and could not be proven guilty. However, they did not want him to be innocent, and his examiner advised him to leave the hospital for a few days. He obeyed; and, learning nothing new, he returned to his post. No sooner was he there than he was told of a letter from M. Boyer, who absolutely demanded his departure. He wanted to wait for a formal order; but the Administrators, while showing much regret at losing him, strongly urged him to leave, for fear, they said, that something worse might happen to him. One feels the full force of such an exhortation. As a result, M. Fuzier, after having done so much good for nine years, of which we saw a small sample during the [reign of the] last Ordinary, withdrew completely on February 16, 1745, and the Master mentioned in the first part of this report was happily appointed in his place. As he had the same zeal, the same views, and almost the same talents as his predecessor, he had the same persecution to suffer; and the change of Archbishop and Rector put the drafts out into the open.

M. Vierne, who had been working in the Hospital for forty years, and who had held the office of Rector for twenty years, had been thinking for a long time of resigning from it, because he found, he said, that his situation was beyond his strength and his conscience. In fact, in addition to all the other inconveniences, the details of which would take us too long to relate, what he found most difficult to bear was to see in the houses of the hospital the bad priests who were placed there in spite of him; real murderers of souls, whom he could only see going to the altar with a shudder, and who, in order to have the Archbishop set against him, said that he only liked the Jansenists; even threatening him sometimes to let him die without the Sacraments, if he fell ill in Bicêtre. He therefore relieved himself of this heavy burden in December 1746 and was replaced by a priest (an ex-Lazarist, it is said) who, without any disguise, took the opposite route to that taken by M. Vierne. His first reform fell on the altar boys, whom he wanted to force to go to Confession with the priests of the house. He spoke to them in particular and did everything he could to intimidate them and seduce them. "What!" he said to them one day in anger, "Messrs. the Priests of Bicêtre confess more than two thousand souls of Devils[6] who are in this house; and they will not be able to lead small souls like yours!" Shortly afterwards it became all too clear that this new reformer himself needed a great reform in his morals. M. de Bellefond[s],[7] then Archbishop, was convinced of this at the Salpêtrière, the place of residence of the Rector, where this prelate went on purpose.

We will not dwell further on this fact, to which we will be able to return when we have been put in a position to speak about the ravages of the Salpêtrière.

During seven or eight months of vacancy in the rectorate, the Hospital enjoyed a peace which in truth was never disturbed except by the zealots of the Constitution.[8] This delay would undoubtedly have been very sufficient to make a good choice, if good subjects were not excluded from these kinds of places. The day after Easter 1747, M. Malbosc, the new Rector, who had been [in this position for] fifteen

6. Editor's Note: The adult inmates of Bicêtre.

7. Editor's Note: Jacques Bonne-Gigault de Bellefonds (1698–1746), who served as Archbishop of Paris for less than a year before succumbing to smallpox.

8. Editor's Note: That is, the papal bull *Unigenitus* (1713).

days, asked the Master for confession tickets[9] for his children. He answered that they had not taken the precaution of providing themselves with them, because it was not the custom to require them, but that they had satisfied the precept. The Rector, for this first time, went by his word, as had been done until then. One would have said that these fourteen children were the sole object of the solicitude of a man who was at the head of thirty priests, charged first and foremost with the care of 15,000 souls. Even if it had been to edify, it was only to destroy.

Basically, it was the Master who was being blamed. On the eve of the feast of the Blessed Sacrament, May 31st of the same year, the Rector returned to the charge and told the Master, "I forbid you to take your children to Confession outside the house." He also forbade the children to go to Confession and added: "I will confess you myself; you will find in me a good father and a good confessor." The Master opposed this defense with the reasons already set out in the previous issue, and the dismayed children very strongly expressed their personal opposition. On June 23rd, the Master was summoned to the Rector's office at the Salpêtrière, to put an end to this great affair. He explained the dispositions of these poor children and asked that they at least be allowed to finish with confessors who had known them for five or six years, and who had their confidence. The embarrassment to which such a change would throw them, in the circumstances in which they found themselves, was easy to feel.

But he was talking to a man who was insensitive to such considerations. "The children," he said, "will certainly go to confess to me, or to the priests of the house. I have," he added, knocking on a table, "I have the court, the archbishopric, and the administration for me." He said too much. The Administrators were not for him.

Finally, he said that the next day he would go to Bicêtre to confess these children. He went there, went up to them, asked a few questions from the catechism, and said that he was coming to confess them. One of the older children asked him with tears that they "at least be allowed

9. Editor's Note: The *billets de confession*, required by Archbishop Beaumont for the reception of the Sacraments. These requirements were at the heart of the Refusal of Sacraments Controversy, which began, in part, at the Hôpital général.

to finish with the confessors to whom they had been going for so long, and who had all their confidence."

"No," said the Rector, "you must show an example to the poor,[10] who, on the pretext of going to Confession, go to the cabaret."

"You are quite sure, Sir," said the child, "that we are not going there (to the cabaret) because our Master is leading us and bringing us back."

"Don't be obstinate," said the Rector. "You must do as I order you."

The child's answer: "It is not because of stubbornness that I am making these requests; it is because Wisdom says that one must choose a counsellor among a thousand."[11] All of them responded likewise.

The Rector looked at the Master and said to him, "Isn't it surprising that children as old as these have not yet made their First Communion?" Then addressing one of them, "How old are you?"

"I'm seventeen."

"Seventeen years old! And you haven't made your First Communion yet!"

Answer: "Sir, allow me to tell you that my age has nothing to do with it. Those who lead me want me to have instruction and piety."

"I can see," said the Rector with emotion, "that you are breathless." He went out at the same time and went, without warning, to the Confessional. Seeing that no one was there, he left, and took it as an affront. It was a game on his part to make the Master guilty.

However, several of the relatives or protectors of these children, who had only put them there to train them in piety, [having been] informed of what was going on, withdrew them. The Rector complained about this to the archbishopric, saying that it was the Master who was taking them out, which was false. He did not fail to blame the Master for the invincible reluctance of the children themselves to change their confessor.

At about the same time a small incident occurred, from which the Rector and the priests took great advantage, to achieve their ends. A prayer to M. de Pâris was found in the sacristy in the book of one of these children.[12] The Rector was informed of this, and he made

10. Editor's Note: Another allusion to the adult inmates of the Hôpital général.

11. Editor's Note: The orphan here reportedly quotes Sirach 6:6.

12. Editor's Note: That is, the Deacon François de Pâris, the Jansenist "saint" at

a great deal of noise about it, and on this occasion went to visit their little library. *L'Idée de la conversion du pécheur*[13] was the first book that fell into his hands, and which he put in his pocket, although the Master claimed it as his own. He did the same with the Catechism of Montpellier,[14] and the *Instruction dogmatique sur la première communion.*[15] The latter was no less uselessly claimed by the Master than the former had been. Thus, approved or not approved, Privilege[16] or not, he found that everything was contraband: two New Testaments in French, *Histoires choisies*, the Catechism in verse by the Abbé de Heauville (approved by a great number of bishops and doctors, and so often reprinted),[17] and a few other works. A small book entitled *De L'Hospitalité*,[18] for the instruction of those who serve the poor: everything was confiscated.

"Is this what you told us, Sir," said those poor children, crying loudly, "that we would find in you a good father and a good confessor? You take the Word of God out of our hands. You want us to make our first

---

whose tomb the *convulsionnaire* movement began. See "The Miraculous Healing of Anne Lefranc" and "In Defense of Convulsionary Jansenism."

13. Editor's Note: A treatise on penance by Jan Opstraet (1651–1720), a (philo-) Jansenist of Leuven, originally published in 1730.

14. Editor's Note: A famously Jansenist catechism written by François-Aimé Pouget under the auspices of Charles-Joachim Colbert de Croissy (1667–1738), Bishop of Montpellier, who was one of the original four Appellants (see "The Appeal of the Bull *Unigenitus*")

15. Editor's Note: Almost certainly the *Instructions dogmatiques et morales, pour faire saintement sa première communion* (1690). The 1739 edition appears in the second volume of the *Dictionnaire des livres jansénistes* (1752), which at least indicates how it was received. See Dominique de Colonia and Louis Patouillet, *Dictionnaire des livres jansénistes, ou qui favorisent le Jansénisme*, vol. 2 (Antwerp: Jean-Baptiste Verdussen, 1752), 273.

16. Editor's Note: The "privilège du Roi" was the authorization of the French censors.

17. Editor's Note: The *Catéchisme en vers, dédié à Monseigneur le Dauphin*, by Louis Le Bourgeois d'Heauville, Abbé de Chantemerle (1st ed. Nantes, 1668).

18. Editor's Note: Possibly the *Idée du devoir de l'hospitalité* (1739); it appears in the second volume of the *Dictionnaire des livres jansénistes*, which argues that the book's only purpose was to "engross the finances of the Sect [of Jansenists], and to find easy asylum for Apostates and all the Intriguers of the Party." See de Colonia and Patouillet, *Dictionnaire*, 2:245.

Communion, and you take away from us the books that serve to prepare us for it. How can we have confidence in you?"

The Master himself could not hold back his tears, so the Rector mocked him, saying, "Ah, see how he cries: are we not doing him great harm?"

Nevertheless, as the cries and tears of the children did not cease, the Rector changed color several times, and abandoned the visit, or, to put it better, the plundering of the books. He went out and removed those he had taken. Then, ashamed no doubt of the excess to which his blindness had led him, he had the New Testament, the Catechism of Montpellier, and the *Histoires choisies* put back on the lectern in the church, so that the Master might find them on his way to Vespers, which was to be sung. It was the eve of St. John the Baptist, Patron of Bicêtre.

After this sad scene, the Master wanted to withdraw; but he was advised to wait for a precise order. He therefore remained for some time, during which time the Rector absolutely obliged the children to leave their ordinary confessors and to address themselves to a priest of the house. The Master soon realized the harm this change of guide was doing to his little flock. But until we found him forced to give up the game at last, let us move on to the Governors and see how the Rector behaved with regard to these restorers of good discipline in the Hospital.

Although M. Vierne had recommended them to the new Rector, the latter only considered them as people from whom the house should be freed. He and his priests replied that the Archbishop wanted *peace* and *unity*; that only one *religion* was needed; that there were many *suspicious* people (in Bicêtre); that they would not be tolerated if they did not change, etc. They began by worrying the poor in Confession and said out loud that they would not pass any of them, without making sure of their submission, especially those who were under Governors suspected of Jansenism. They kept their word and showed that there is hardly any extravagance to which a false zeal does not precipitate the blind partisans of the Constitution. We will cite only two or three examples.

A young man of fourteen or fifteen years of age was on his deathbed and did not want to bring his confessor from outside for fear of committing him, so he turned to the priest of the house who was [there] on weekdays. The first thing this priest did was to ask the patient to accept the Bull, but the patient defended himself with all his might. The priest turned him around, tired him out, threatened him, came back several times, finally made him succumb, and gave him absolution, forbidding him, *under penalty of mortal sin*, to tell his *Governor*. He was then given Extreme Unction and Holy Viaticum. (It was his First Communion.) When he was communicated, he was made to make the same abjuration word for word that is required of Protestants who return to the bosom of the Church, and to this was added a formal acceptance of the Constitution, by making him lay his hand on the Holy Gospel. Word of this spread throughout the house. It was said that this young man had to be a Protestant, even though he seemed to be a good Catholic. The Governor, strangely surprised by this rumor, went to see the sick man, and found him sad and dismayed, sinking into bed to hide his tears. He asked him what was the matter with him, and at first all he could get out of him was sobs. He pressed him; and the young man finally replied that he could say nothing, *under penalty of mortal sin*.

The Governor, who did not understand anything, went to one of his colleagues and asked him to go and see if he could find out what was at issue. This colleague went and received the same answer, that he had been forbidden to do so. He said to the patient, "This prohibition," he said, "is only for your Governor; you can tell me everything without any fear."

He did so and found himself at ease. His Governor came in his turn, consoled him, boosted his confidence, and proposed that he recant in the presence of the same priests who had seduced him. The young man, full of joy, sent for them without delay, and his Governor withdrew. The priest who had confessed him arrived and, thinking that he had been brought in for some secret purpose, signaled to those present to withdraw.

"No, no," said the patient, "there's not one too many." At the same time, he clearly and firmly expressed his regret at having received the Constitution.

"Ah! but, my child," said the priest in a benign tone, "I didn't speak to you about it."

The patient, without breaking down, reminded him so expressly of all that had happened, that it made him blush, and disconcerted him to the point that he went away all confused, saying: “Go, my friend, think of your soul.” (Didn’t he himself have a great need to think of his?)

The other priest (the one who had administered the Sacraments), came in his turn, and the sick man made the same statement to him, to which he added well-founded and well-expressed reproaches for the fact that he had made him look like a heretic in public. “You are a little wretch,” replied the priest, more wretched than he was. “You have been advised,” he added, “to do what you have just done: it must have been your Governor.”

“Yes, sir,” said the sick man, “but I do it with all my heart, to put my conscience at rest: and no one forces me to do it.”

The priest was very happy with a confession that had escaped the poor child, and left, thinking only of making the most of this discovery. He and his confrère left immediately to complain to the Rector and the Archbishop’s office that they were being disturbed in their ministry. The next day the Rector went to Bicêtre and proposed to the dying man a new profession of faith, in which (he said) there would be no question of the Constitution. It was the one in the Ritual, to which he added this question of his own: “Are you subject to the Church *and the Pope*?” (It must not be forgotten in all these movements that we are dealing with a poor man from Bicêtre who is about fifteen years old.)

The young man hesitated and feared a new trap, because he had not seen in his Catechism this addition of the Pope. “But, Sir,” he says, “a Pope can make mistakes, and the Church cannot.” Finally threatened with the Censures of the Church, and being treated again as a heretic, he answers “Yes,” without knowing whether he is doing right or wrong.

He had reason to fear the artifice of the Rector, who, on leaving, spread the word that this young man was imbued with a very bad doctrine, and that he had *great difficulty in making him say* that the Pope is the visible Head of the Church. (We see here more than artifice.)

All of this, moreover, was to fall on the Governors, and in particular on that of the patient. The Rector, on leaving the latter’s house, had them all assembled in the Presbytery and told them that with regard to the poor, they must confine themselves absolutely to the letter of the Catechism.

"But shouldn't we explain to them what they don't understand?"

"No: that is none of your business. The letter, and nothing more." It was all very well for him to say that *the simple letter is enough* (even if it is not understood). He then spoke many commonplaces and threatened a great storm.

He was told of the wrongdoing of the priests in worrying the poor about the Constitution. "What do you want?" he said. "You are suspicious to them."

"But in what way?"

"You make the poor pray in French."

Answer: "That makes them understand what they say. M. de Vintimille (who was not suspicious) had the Psalter put in French for the poor; we follow his intentions."

Another grievance: "You speak badly of the cult of the Blessed Virgin, and you keep the poor away from her."

A[nswer]: "We tell the poor that the Blessed Virgin is truly the Mother of God; that she has always remained a Virgin, that she is elevated above all creatures, and that we must have great confidence in her intercession, because she has much charity for us and credit with God; we invoke her several times a day with the poor, and we say her Office together every Saturday."

"However," the doctor resumed, "you do not make them say the Rosary."

A[nswer]: "This is not the custom of the house, but it does not mean that we keep the poor away from devotion to the Blessed Virgin, since we say the prayers of the Rosary, the Our Father, the Ave and the Creed, with them several times; and we believe that attention to the prayers is more essential than their repetition."

Since, in spite of this, the Rector kept repeating that they were suspicious, they made all sorts of requests that he ask them about their faith and about all the articles of Christian doctrine; but the zealots of the Bull never accept this. This one "had not come for that," he said. Then he added with a sigh, that it was necessary to submit "to the King and the Church"; and that for him, he received the Constitution and was submitted to it "in heart and mind."

The Governors protested to him and proved to him that without receiving the Constitution they were subject to the King and the Church with all the fullness of their hearts, and more subject than if they had received it.

"How is that?" said the Rector, astonished.

Here it is: it is a consequence of the Constitution that the very fear of an unjust excommunication[19] can or must sometimes prevent us from being submissive to the King: it is therefore a sign of our submission and fidelity to him not to receive such a Bull. In the same way, the Church orders her children to reject everything that is contrary to her doctrine: thus, they obey her and are very submissive to her by rejecting a Bull which in its proper and natural sense is obviously contrary to her doctrine.

"Ah!" replied the Rector to these two demonstrations, "that would take us too far. . . . I came to the Hospital *to make peace reign there*." (Precisely as M. de Beaumont came to bring peace to the Diocese of Paris. Whereupon it would be quite natural to ask these gentlemen who is waging war.) "I recommend," added this peaceful person, "that you live in peace with the priests." It was the priests who should have been advised to live in peace with the Governors.

One of these priests who was present was taken as a witness that the Governors had never failed to do anything that was required of them; and this priest expressly agreed. "I believe it," said the Rector, "but it would be better to get closer, to meet with the priests: we would not see cases like the one today" (that of the sick man mentioned above, who died a day or two later).

It should be noted in passing that these zealots of the Bull do not dare to name it. Not long ago we saw a curé in Dax say to a lady, "Do you receive *this*?" Here, the Rector of the Hôpital général de Paris does not dare to pronounce this fatal name either. One would not see, he says, *affairs like the one today*. He speaks of submission and fidelity; but he does not name the Bull.

19. Editor's Note: A reference to the 91st condemned proposition in *Unigenitus*, "The fear of an unjust excommunication should never hinder us from fulfilling our duty; never are we separated from the Church, even when by the wickedness of men we seem to be expelled from her, as long as we are attached to God, to Jesus Christ, and to the Church herself by charity." See Denzinger-Hünermann 2491.

The Governors, to make up for this, testified in very energetic terms to their sincere desire to be united in everything with the priests; but they declared no less clearly that if the acceptance of the Bull was the point of reunion, they could not consent to it. Beware, the Constitutionalists have neither truth nor good faith on their side. The Appellants have both.

The Rector, after this discussion, went to the Archbishop's palace. He went there (if we are to believe him) to settle the matter; and on his report the Archbishop's Council decided that the Governor in question should leave, and that his confrères should be warned to be wiser. The order was served by word of mouth alone on Sunday, April 23rd, by one of the Administrators or directors of the Hospital. For these gentlemen had no difficulty on this occasion (and on the following ones) in overturning what they had established, or what had been established only in concert with them, under their authority, with their approval, and with their applause. As they were angry in spite of this at the Governor's departure, they asked the Archbishop, as a form of compensation, that they at least be freed from the two priests who were causing all this disturbance, and who were causing trouble in the Hospital. The prelate seemed to agree to this; but he said that there had to be other places vacant for two subjects so worthy of a good position. This was basically only a defeat. For these priests are such as the Archbishop wants them to be, and they were sure to please him by setting fire to this house. Indeed, this event further increased their courage. They looked for new opportunities to report it, and they found them. But the rest of this narrative must be left to the next issue.

As we finish this issue, we come across a letter from a gentleman from the provinces (who knows M. the Archbishop and is known to him) who, having learned of all the devastation and desolation of Bicêtre and the Salpêtrière, writes to one of his friends: "They want to take away the resources of the Hospital from good people. God will have to open His bosom to us when we will no longer find any asylum on earth."

21. Le Paige Protests the Refusal of Sacraments to Jansenists

Louis-Adrien Le Paige

Translated by Timothy Troutner[1]

The life and career of Louis-Adrien Le Paige (1712–1802) displays important lines of continuity running through eighteenth-century French Jansenism, from *Unigenitus* to the Civil Constitution of the Clergy. A jurist and member of the *Parlement* of Paris, Le Paige was the leading theoretician of a fecund ecclesiastical and political perspective that combined the Jansenism of the *parlements* ("judicial Jansenism") with radical Gallicanism and "patriot" resistance to Bourbon absolutism.[2] Le Paige published prodigiously and provocatively, protected as he was by King Louis XV's cousin, the Prince de Conti, who employed Le Paige as his personal librarian and named him judicial bailiff of the Order of Malta's Paris Temple.

The selection below comes from a 48-page pamphlet titled *Paradoxes, Sophisms, Disguises, False Principles, Principles Dangerous to the Tranquility of the State . . .* (1756). Published at the height of the

1. The excerpt below is taken from *Paradoxes, sophismes, déguisemens, faux principes, principes dangereux pour la tranquillité de l'État, calomnies, fausses citations, qui sont contenues dans une Instruction Pastorale que M. l'Archev. de Paris a signée & adoptée, qu'il a lûe publiquement dans l'Église de Conflans, lieu de son exil, qu'il a fait imprimer à Chartres, et qu'il a distribuée dans Paris et au dehors* (n.p., 1756), 34–39.

2. See the introduction to this volume.

"Refusal of Sacraments Controversy" in France, Le Paige here rebuts the Pastoral Instruction, an apparently ghost-written letter of the vehemently anti-Jansenist Christophe de Beaumont (1703–81). Archbishop of Paris from 1746, Beaumont led the zealots of the *dévot* party who were committed to refusing the sacraments of Holy Communion and last rites to opponents of *Unigenitus*, which reinflamed the debate over the bull and caused a chain-reaction of crises.

Fortunately for Le Paige and the philo-Jansenist cause, King Louis XV lost his nerve in the face of the internecine conflicts that highly publicized refusals unleashed. Louis exiled, but did not depose, Archbishop Beaumont, and the king issued a royal declaration of 2 September 1754 that the *Parlement* duly "registered" (that is, legally received and confirmed). This "Declaration of Silence" was a sweeping victory for the philo-Jansenist position because, in effect, it banned the refusal of sacraments by shifting the burden of proof onto the anti-Jansenist zealots, who could be accused of "schism" for causing division in the Church by *refusing* the sacraments.

Additionally, the ecclesiology that Le Paige presents in this tract shows the inevitable appeal of "Gallican" doctrine for anti-ultramontane statesmen and clergy around the Catholic world. Le Paige argues that the four Gallican articles of 1682 represent not just the particular tradition of the Church of France, but rather the ancient constitution of all the churches, before the usurpations of Gregory VII (pope from 1073–85), when "new pretensions of the Court of Rome" were fraudulently put forward.

Shaun Blanchard

Principles Dangerous to the Tranquility of the State

I. Absolute Power of Bishops

It's not enough for the author of the Pastoral Instruction[3] that the bishops be in the Church what a king or a monarch is in his states.

3. Editor's Note: Le Paige parenthetically notes here pages 10, 12, and 21 of the Pastoral Instruction.

Let one say that the spiritual authority is free and independent of the temporal power in matters which uniquely concern spiritual things; all well and good. But to speak of this free and independent power as an *absolute* power, as the Pastoral Instruction does not cease to do, is to introduce into the Church a despotism which runs counter to the tranquility of the state, and which affects its police powers. This will be made manifest in the articles that follow after this first one.

This despotism, moreover, is diametrically opposed to the spirit of the gospel and to this great maxim established by Jesus Christ: *The princes of nations lord it over them; it will not be this way among you.*[4] What difference, indeed, will remain between the kings of the earth and the ministers of the Church, if the power of the latter is *absolute* like the power of the first? The *absolute* power of a monarch consists in commanding without having to consult anyone, without being accountable to anyone, without being able to be constrained in his wishes or judged in his actions. Would not a bishop thus be on the same footing, if his power is *absolute*?

The writer[5] would doubtless say what our prelates say: that this is not what they claim, and that it is fitting that the bishops can be judged by their superiors in the order of the hierarchy. But these are big words which have little reality, at least for the age in which we live. For if one complains about a bishop, one cannot have any recourse to these superiors in the order of the hierarchy, no longer having either councils or synods. And what if we must even complain about a bishop's ecclesiastical superiors—if the appeal to these superiors proves in the event impracticable, or of too difficult an execution—what becomes of that dependence on their hierarchical superiors which the bishops so wish to recognize? And during this time the subjects of the State molested by a bishop will be without resort and will remain oppressed. Let us agree that the word *absolute* is too much, in the mouth of a bishop who has the evangelical spirit and the heart of a citizen.

4. Editor's Note: Le Paige evokes here Jesus' words in Matthew 20:25–26.

5. Editor's Note: Le Paige is referring here to the author who ghost-wrote the Archbishop's letter.

II. Independence in Civil Things and of Policing

What an uprising in the high clergy, or at least one party among them, against the Declaration of 1754! We have seen with what indecent affectation they draw a parallel with the *Ecthesis* of Heraclius and the *Typos* of Constans.[6] However, if it differs from these two evil documents as day differs from night; if it scarcely touches on the interests of the truth; if the silence that it imposes falls only on a scrap of paper[7] that spreads trouble everywhere and upsets the state, allowing full and entire liberty to profess, to teach, and to defend all catholic truths, why could a prince by a wise law not forbid, at least for a time, those interminable disputes, which set his states ablaze, which arm his subjects against each other, and which can cause riots and seditions? To make it a crime for a prince to do this smacks a little of anarchy.

III. Little Esteem for the Maxims of the Realm and for Our Liberties

My suspicions increase with a word that I read in a section of the Pastoral Instruction (p. 32): "national pretensions, assertions revered in one country and despised in another." What does the author mean by what he describes thus? It looks like a reference to what we call the maxims of the nation.

If one was content with saying the pretensions of individuals, or the pretensions of bodies and associations, everything would be clear as day. But the term *national pretensions* clearly refers to the principles received in an entire nation. [It expresses] the sentiment and desire of the whole nation, that which has the force of law in this nation, and that which characterizes it and differentiates it from others. It would be no

6. Editor's Note: In 638, the Byzantine Emperor Heraclius (575–641) issued a statement of faith (*Ecthesis*) attempting to make monothelitism—or the belief that Jesus Christ had only one will, a divine will—the official doctrine of the Empire. This attempt to conciliate "monophysites" who rejected the two-natures Christology of the ecumenical Council of Chalcedon (451 AD) was a failure, and rejected by both the Western and Eastern orthodox-catholic churches. Similarly, the "Typos" of Emperor Constans II (630–68) was a decree of 648 that attempted to suppress debate on Christ's will or wills.

7. Editor's Note: A reference to a *billet de confession*.

mere guess to understand by this phrase in the Pastoral Instruction the maxims of the realm of France, the liberties of the Gallican Church. This is blindingly obvious. And lest we get confused, the writer took care to designate more clearly, by adding "assertions revered in one country and despised in another." It is apparent that this feature can only refer to the Four Propositions of 1682 on the fallibility of the Pope, the superiority of a general council, the independence of the crown of sovereigns, etc. For these are the only maxims which are revered among us and despised, or at least unrecognized, in other places. Isn't it nice that after this we hear the Archbishop of the Imperial city [Paris] describe these maxims in the most unseemly fashion: "opinions," he says, "born out of the deterioration of the centuries, first hazarded by some man of authority, then adopted by passion, maintained by flattery; the maxims of innovators, of national pretensions, and the rest." Certainly, the portrait does not flatter, but it is also as unfaithful as it is hideous. Who does not know that what we call the maxims of the Kingdom, the liberties of the Gallican church, are nothing other than the ancient doctrine recorded in the ancient canons, maintained against the new pretensions of the Court of Rome since Gregory VII? They are as necessary to the Church as to the State, since they effect the safety of the throne and public tranquility. How then has my Lord the Archbishop been able to adopt a Pastoral Instruction which rises up against these maxims and these liberties? How can so many bishops of the realm league together to adopt this Instruction? Let it finally be seen where they [the bishops] wish to lead those who put their trust in them! It is the bishops who abuse them so outrageously in service of their own passions; they make them receive their novelties which favor the troubles and divisions they do not cease to stir up in Church and State.

Calumnies

I. A First Imaginary Heresy of the Appellants

I apologize in advance to my Lord the Archbishop of Paris, if I initiate criminal proceedings against his Instruction, and if I carry my reproaches to the point of a charge of calumny. But this is what I owe to my brothers, and this is what I owe to myself. The offended truth demands it, as does the honor of the Church, [which has been] dishonored in the most meritorious of her children. So demands the conscience of my Lord the Archbishop, which an unworthy writer[8] charges with this sin before God, and the spiritual good of the writer himself, who cauterizes his own [conscience] in such a criminal manner. Such are the motives which commit me to expose the turpitude and baseness of his calumnious imputations. He does not hesitate. He speaks bluntly: the Appellants are clearly heretics. It is true that the demonstration that he claims to make of their heresy is not extensive like the rest. The lack of proofs has apparently rendered him laconic this once: the *et cetera* speedily comes to the tip of his pen. I want to follow his example. Our whole business will be finished in a few words.

What, then, is this heresy of the Appellants? It is the doctrine of the Five Propositions. This is said quickly. He is hardly the first. Many others have said it before him and have been booed in Paris and in Rome. Perhaps he has forgotten the famous Five Articles presented to the Holy See under Alexander VII [pope from 1655 to 1667], where the supposed Jansenists presented their sentiments on the Five Propositions, and emerged from the examination with honor? If he knew this fact, he at least should not abuse the trust of my Lord the Archbishop,[9] who to all appearances ignored it.

But as if he doubted himself regarding this imputation of the Jansenist heresy, he made us heretics provisionally in another spot. The Appellants, not heeding authority, do not submit themselves to the Bull; this resistance is a heresy. As I have already discussed this point in the section on false principles, I do not believe that it is necessary to tarry longer here. Everything comes down to this. Even if it were true that the Bull was a decision of the universal Church, I would only be obliged to obey it to the degree that the thing seemed evident to me. If it was evident to me, and I did not submit to it, from that moment on I would be convicted of not wishing to recognize the authority of the Church in itself; this would make me a heretic. But, if I were disposed

8. Editor's Note: The ghost writer.

9. Editor's Note: Le Paige is, presumably, speaking sarcastically. Of course Beaumont knew very well the history of the conflict over *Cum Occasione* and *Unigenitus*.

to obey when I had the evidence of the voice of the Church, and I only refuse to submit because I do not have this evidence, it is extravagant and puerile to transform me into a heretic and to say to me, "Your heresy is your disobedience." To wish to make the world believe this is a calumny.

Section Three
The Jansenist International, c. 1760–1810

22. The Jansenist Church of Utrecht

Translated by Shaun Blanchard[1]

In September 1763, the Catholic clergy of the so-called "schismatic" Church of Utrecht held a Provincial Council. The goals of this small synod were ambitious and far-reaching, and the resulting *Acts and Decrees*, published in French, ran to over 400 pages and helped elicit hundreds of "letters of communion" from supportive Catholics all over Europe. Since their excommunication by the papacy in 1723, the "cause of Utrecht" already functioned as a *shibboleth* for anti-ultramontane Catholics. More important than any of the many specific doctrinal issues that the synod addressed, the *Acts and Decrees* provided a public ecclesial manifesto for an anti-ultramontane, Augustinian, and anti-Jesuit reformist Catholicism. The Utrecht clergy boldly asserted the orthodoxy of their small, "persecuted" church, by positioning it between Jesuit excesses on one hand while also, on the other hand, condemning the views of an extremist in their own ranks, whose Jansenism had blurred into Protestantizing positions.

In the selection below, Johannes Bijeveld, Bishop of Deventer, presents part of the synod's lengthy and scathing rebuke of the Jesuit

1. The excerpt below is from *Actes et décrets du ii. concile provincial d'Utrecht tenu le 13 septembre M.DCC.LXIII. dans la Chapelle de l'Eglise Paroissiale de Sainte Gertrude, à Utrecht* (Utrecht: Aux dépens de la Compagnie, 1764), 283–92. We have not included the footnotes original to the text that contain lengthy references to the works of Hardouin and Berruyer (the Acts of Utrecht are available online in French, for those who wish to consult these footnotes). All remaining footnotes are by the translator, and all italics are original.

Isaac-Joseph Berruyer (1681–1758). Berruyer, author of the *Histoire du peuple de Dieu*, an extremely popular biblical paraphrase, had courted controversy for years, and already been condemned by two popes and numerous ecclesiastical authorities in France.[2] The synod's detailed and lengthy rejection of the thought of Berruyer, along with that of his predecessor, another brilliant and controversial Jesuit scholar named Jean Hardouin (1646–1729), was not just a dog whistle to philo-Jansenists and anti-Jesuits around the Catholic world. It was also a genuine attempt to assert their own orthodoxy and regain the full ecclesiastical communion that they earnestly desired. The Utrecht clergy were capitalizing on a time when attacks on the Jesuit Order were reaching a fever pitch. Along with the myriad "friends of Utrecht" around the Catholic world, leaders of the synod were genuinely optimistic about a reconciliation with the papacy, especially when Clement XIV was elected pope in 1769.

The excerpted selection below shows the enduring importance of debates over divine grace, penance, and morality. Bishop Bijeveld relates the synod's position, a common one in Jansenist and Augustinian circles, that bad doctrine on grace leads to corrupt moral teaching and practice. Jesuit Molinism is just repackaged Pelagianism, and this heresy opens the door to moral confusion based on perverse scriptural interpretation. Not given to understatement, the fathers of the Utrecht synod accuse the works of Berruyer and Hardouin of "destroy[ing] the principal Mysteries of the Faith" and "overthrow[ing] from top to bottom all the Christian Religion." Though the ecclesiological debate was taking center stage in Catholic Europe, the initial Jansenist critiques of Molinism and moral casuistry were still vital concerns.

Shaun Blanchard

The Second Provincial Council of Utrecht (1763)

§9. Fruit of the Redemption: Grace and Predestination

According to St. Augustine, the only difference between grace and predestination is that "predestination is the preparation of grace, and grace

2. See Daniel Watkins, *Berruyer's Bible*.

is the effect of predestination." If the one is free, then the other must be likewise. If, on the contrary, grace is given for merit, it is not possible that the preparation for this grace—that is to say, the predestination of the Saints—is free. The Brothers [of the Society of Jesus] Hardouin and Berruyer, attached to their false principles on grace, maintain that the predestination of a certain number of Elect to eternal glory, before the foreknowledge of their merits, is nowhere in the Epistles of Saint Paul, nor in all the books of the New Testament. They hold only that a destination to this glory is in consequence of foreseen merits; they add that the predestined of whom the Scriptures speak are none other than *all the Faithful* without exception who, *because of their Faith*, have merited to be chosen to form the Church of Jesus Christ, and who are destined to enjoy eternal life, presuming *they wish to persevere*; this is a commentary perfectly in accordance with that of the Socinians,[3] who admit no other predestination than that *which contains no Mystery*.

These two impious writers carry these erroneous principles so far that they extend them even to the predestination of Jesus Christ himself (which, according to the Fathers and the theologians, is the foundation and model of ours). And thus, they teach that the predestination of this divine Head is not gratuitous. It was suitable, according to their doctrine, that God chose the humanity of Jesus Christ in preference to all others to make his Son out of it.[4] For this reason, Jesus Christ was, by right of his human birth, the first born of all men, and in this capacity *the King* of all the earth, *the Christ, the Messiah, the Pontiff, and the Mediator for men*. With this title of firstborn, he was still in common with all those over whom he had successively passed as head.[5] Jesus Christ was chosen, preferred over the other *firstborn* who had preceded him, only because God had foreseen that he would fulfill better than any of them the sublime and important functions attached

3. Translator's Note: This reference is to the non-Trinitarian or "Unitarian" theological system adopted by some Reformation groups and associated with the Italian Fausto Sozzini, or Socinus (1539–1604).

4. Translator's Note: The phrase "to make his Son out of it" is a reference to the created humanity of Jesus Christ. The implication here is not that Jesus was the "adopted" Son of God.

5. Translator's Note: The sense here is that Jesus is "firstborn" *of humanity* and thus still "in common" with those over whom he has Headship (the human race).

to the quality of Messiah and Mediator of men. Finally, the Brothers Hardouin and Berruyer not only fight against the Catholic dogma of predestination, gratuitous and before any foreseen merit, but they also treat that dogma with the utmost impudence, *error*, and heresy. According to Bellarmine, following St. Augustine, St. Fulgentius, & c. [that dogma] "must not be regarded as the opinion of a few particular Doctors, but as the faith of the Catholic Church."

§10: Morality

The grace of Jesus Christ is the principle of all good and of all the virtues. It is thus not possible that one's doctrine on grace will not influence one's doctrine on morals. Consequently, errors on grace give birth to an infinity of other errors on morals. If the Church's doctrine on grace, in making known to man the corruption of his nature, the weakness and the powerlessness of his will left to itself, the continual need of the helps of God for each and every one of our good works, inspires in us feelings of mistrust of our own strength, of humility, of confidence in divine mercy, of groaning, of prayer, of love, and of thankfulness, that [doctrine] (of Pelagius and of the Jesuits his followers) by flattering man regarding his own alleged strength, serves only to nourish his pride, presumption, and ingratitude, and to take away the feeling of indigence, unworthiness, and continual dependence with regard to God. It extinguishes in the heart the spirit of prayer and the action of grace, causing one, by the most wicked contempt, to mistake Pharisaic justice for true justice; that is to say, one will mistake the wide road to hell for the narrow way which leads to Heaven. But the Brothers Hardouin and Berruyer not only stifle the inner feelings of Religion and piety in hearts. By their principles on matters of grace, they also establish other maxims which destroy the whole body of Christian morality. First of all, they overthrow *the Eternal Law*, the first and sovereign rule of morals, by denying that there are any *eternal truths*, immutable, *independent of any kind of establishment*. Then, in excusing the sins of *ignorance*, they loose men from the obligation of the Law, because they regard as sin only that which is done against the *conscience*. They give as virtuous actions all those which it [the conscience] approves, whether it is itself regulated by the Law, or even if it is not. What an immense path they open up to the vilest and blackest crimes, under the pretext of *good intention*! The great precept of love of God and of neighbor is not spared. They combat, with all their strength, this obligation [to love of God] and the scope of it. But, at the same time that they thus restrain the first Commandment, they drop the bridle by unsettling understandings of concupiscence, arguing that all its movements [the movements of concupiscence] are not *vicious*. They assure us of a most impudent lie, claiming that Jesus Christ does not exactly condemn attachment to earthly goods, *but only attachment that is excessive, when one gives preference to temporal needs over the needs of the soul*. They even add that the divine Master *had nothing to say against magnificent meals*, nor against a certain *abundance*, and finally that *His presence showed His agreement with the pleasures that He had not condemned*. They do not even fear praising the cruel vengeance which the children of Jacob exercised on the inhabitants of Shechem.[6] They assure us, against the testimony of Scripture, that this action was approved of by the holy Patriarch Jacob.

Who would believe it! They even go so far as approving *suicide* in the person of Saul. Lying is no longer a sin, according to them, when the deceived person had some cause to suspect the sincerity of the speaker [who lied to them]. Finally, they close the door of salvation to sinners and deprive them of all the resources that Religion offers when they propose to them a false penitence for the true one. They represent these [false penitences] to sinners as *sincere and solidly proven conversions*, as *spectacles worthy of Heaven* and with which the Lord is *delighted*. But these are phantom conversions that are *followed soon after* by relapsing into the greatest crimes; such as, for example, that of idolatry. They even undertake to render Saint Paul an accomplice in their criminal laxity, pretending that the holy Apostle found penance for the incestuous too lengthy, and that he *desired* that the Church of Corinth might *seem to repent, in some way, of its severity*. It is thus that these unhappy writers do violence to the Sacred Text. They make it say anything that pleases them, and thus tear in pieces the divine Scriptures.

6. Translator's Note: This is a reference to the massacre of the men of Shechem by the sons of Jacob in vengeance for the rape of their sister Dinah (Genesis 34).

Note: Here the Most Reverend Bishop of Deventer read and presented to the Council several of the principal texts of Brothers Hardouin and Berruyer, which were mentioned in his Report, and he added:

At the sight of this overflowing impiety and blasphemy, who among you Fathers of this holy Council is not seized with horror? Who is there who did not desire to be able to plug his ears, if the interest of the truth did not oblige us to consider the entire magnitude of the evil, in order to bring in the most effective remedies? Bad speech corrupts good morals, as the Apostle says. This is why the opinion of the Deputies is:

§1. That the Council repress this horrible scandal with a summary exposition of Catholic doctrine which the Church, like an impenetrable shield, always puts up in opposition to the poisonous traits of these masters of error.

§2. Then he [the Bishop of Deventer] recommended the reading of several Pastoral Instructions against the impieties of Hardouin and Berruyer, which, especially in France, had made the truth triumph: among others, that of the most illustrious Bishop of Soissons.[7] [This pastoral letter] is very well known to us, and we do not cease to read it, and to deepen our understanding of it with a satisfaction that is always new. This Instruction is very solid, providing us all with invincible weapons against error, weapons that will be very precious to posterity. Also, the recently published [Pastoral Letter] of the illustrious Archbishop of Lyon[8] we regard as a monument worthy of perpetuating the venerable Tradition of that Church so ancient and so distinguished among the others [the Church of Lyon]. Finally, [we recommend] the first part of the Censure of the Sacred Faculty of Theology of Paris, which has been very well received by Catholic theologians.

§3. The Decree of the Council is to be drawn up in such a way that it ends with the solemn condemnation of the work of Brother Hardouin,

7. Translator's Note: François de Fitz-James (1709–64), bishop of Soissons (1738–64) and grandson of James II Stuart. Fitz-James was a diligent and irenic reformer of philo-Jansenist convictions.

8. Translator's Note: Antoine de Malvin de Montazet (1713–88) was consecrated bishop of Autun by Fitz-James in 1748. In 1758, Montazet became Archbishop of Lyon. Though he was never formally an Appellant, Montazet was lauded by Jansenists for his strongly philo-Jansenist positions.

and the work of Brother Berruyer, which the Most Eminent Migazzi, Archbishop of Vienna in Austria,[9] so well described in his Pastoral Instruction of July 3, 1760, as an *impious and very wicked work*. Both of these works were forged in order to destroy the principal Mysteries of the Faith, and to overthrow from top to bottom all the Christian Religion.

9. Translator's Note: Christoph Anton Migazzi (1714–1803), Archbishop of Vienna (1757–1803), was made cardinal in 1761. Migazzi was initially a supporter of a moderate, Muratorian "enlightened Catholicism" and Augustinianism in Austria. Increasingly perturbed by attacks on the Jesuits and by the rise of Josephinism, Migazzi rallied around the papacy.

23. A Mass in Honor of Port-Royal

The Abbé Jean-Antoine Gazaignes

Translated by Richard T. Yoder[1]

From shortly after the time of its physical destruction in 1711, Port-Royal des Champs became a site of pilgrimage for Jansenist sympathizers. Stones and bits of dirt were taken away by many devotees as relics of hallowed ground. The persecutions of the decades following *Unigenitus* (1713) expanded the sacred landscape of Jansenism. The Abbé Jean-Antoine Gazaignes (1717–1802) gave both voice and guidance to these devotions in his *Manuel des Pèlerins de Port-Royal* (1767). Gazaignes writes, "It is very praiseworthy and most edifying to make a pilgrimage to Port-Royal, when one has devotion to it, and when one can."[2] He envisioned a set of stations across and beyond the greater Archdiocese of Paris, where one could venerate the various relics of both the Port-Royalist circle and the later Appellants, such as Bishop Soanen of Senez.

He also wrote a Mass and Office for the "relics of Port-Royal" themselves. The propers of the Mass, which we have included here in Latin and English, emphasize several key themes. Port-Royal, now once again a "desert," had formerly been turned by God into a "garden" of heavenly praise. This transformation, which mirrors the Jansenist-Augustinian theology of efficacious grace converting the soul, is borne out in the

1. Jean-Antoine Gazaignes, *Manuel des Pèlerins de Port-Royal* (Au Désert, 1767), 106–16.

2. Gazaignes, *Manuel*, 71.

particular virtues that Gazaignes highlights: love of Truth, acts of penance, fortitude under persecution. And although the *Manuel* honors the *solitaires* as well as the nuns of Port-Royal, here the emphasis is decidedly on the latter. The Preface borrows gendered language from the Common of Virgins, strongly suggesting that the women of Port-Royal are Virgin Martyrs.[3]

Richard T. Yoder

Manuel des Pèlerins de Port-Royal— "Office des saintes reliques"—"À la Messe"

Introit

Dabo eis cor unum, et spiritum novum tribuam in visceribus eorum, et auferam cor lapideum de carne eorum, et dabo eis cor carneum ut in praeceptis meis ambulant, et judicia mea custodiant, faciantque ea; ea sint mihi in populum, et ego sint eis in Deum.	And I will give them a new heart, and put a new spirit within them: and I will take away the stony heart out of their flesh, and will give them a heart of flesh. And I will put my spirit in the midst of them: and I will cause them to walk in my commandments, and to keep my judgments, and do them. And they shall be my people, and I will be their God.[4]
Psal. Cantemus Domino, gloriosè enim magnificatus est. Gloria Patri, etc. Dabo, etc.	Psalm. Let us sing to the Lord, for he is gloriously magnified.[5]

Collect

Deus qui Portus Regii solitudinem, his novissimis diebus, hortum deliciarum plantasti tibi, et in eo	O God, who in these last times, hast changed the solitude of Port-Royal into a garden of delights, and hast

3. The translator would like to thank Fr. Benedict Andersen OSB and Dr. Luke Togni for consulting on this translation.

4. Translator's Note: Ezek 36:26–28 Douay-Rheims, with pronouns modified. Unless otherwise noted, all Scripture translations are from the Douay-Rheims.

5. Translator's Note: Exod 15:21.

solem veritatis lucere fecisti, ut germinarent virtutum omnium flores, ac fructus ferventissimae caritatis et ut simul esset portus poenitentibus; da nobis per intercessionem famulorum famularumque tuarum quos tibi illic reservasti in die irae ac furoris, cor sincere poenitans, gemitibus compunctionis mundatum, fletibus irrigatum, sole veritatis illustratum, igne tui amoris fructiferum, ut det tibi fructus quos missas in horreum tuum. Per Dominum nostrum Jesus-Christum.

caused to shine there the Sun of Thy Truth, so as to make bloom there the flowers of all the virtues, to produce there the fruits of the most perfect love, and to make of it a gate of salvation to every sort of penitent; grant us by the intercession of the servants whom Thou hast chosen for Thyself during the days of wrath and the fury of the wicked, a heart truly penitent, a heart penetrated with sorrow, bathed in tears, a heart illuminated by Thy divine lights, entirely aflame with Thy love, and capable of producing fruits worthy to be gathered into Thy eternal granaries. By Our Lord Jesus Christ.

Epistle

Lectio Epistolae Beati Pauli Apostoli, Ad Romanos

A Reading from the Letter of Saint Paul the Apostle to the Romans.

Fratres, scimus autem quoniam diligentibus Deum omnia cooperantur in bonum, iis qui secundum propositum vocati sunt sancti. Nam quos praescivit et praedestinavit conformes fieri imaginis Filii sui, ut sit ipse primogenitus in multis fratribus. Quos autem praedestinavit, hos et vocavit: et quos vocavit, hos et iustificavit quos autem iustificavit, illos et glorificavit. Quid ergo dicemus ad haec? Si Deus pro nobis, quis contra nos? Qui etiam proprio Filio suo non pepercit, sed pro nobis omnibus tradidit illum: quomodo non etiam cum illo omnia nobis donavit? Quis accusabit adversus electos Dei? Deus qui iustificat, quis est qui condemnet? Christus Iesus

Brethren, we know that to them that love God, all things work together unto good, to such as, according to his purpose, are called to be saints. For whom he foreknew, he also predestinated to be made conformable to the image of his Son; that he might be the firstborn amongst many brethren. And whom he predestinated, them he also called. And whom he called, them he also justified. And whom he justified, them he also glorified. What shall we then say to these things? If God be for us, who is against us? He that spared not even his own Son, but delivered him up for us all, how hath he not also, with him, given us all things? Who shall accuse against qui mortuus est, immo qui et resurrexit, qui est ad dexteram Dei, qui etiam interpellat pro nobis. Quis ergo nos separabit a caritate Christi? Tribulatio? An angustia? An fames? An nuditas? An periculum? An gladius? Sicut scriptum est. Quia propter te mortificamur tota die: aestimati sumus ut oves occisionis. Sed in his omnibus superamus, propter eum qui dilexit nos. Certus sum enim quia neque mors, neque vita, neque Angeli, neque Principatus, neque instantia, neque futura, neque fortitudo, neque altitudo, neque profundum, neque creatura alia poterit nos separare a caritate Dei, quae est in Christo Iesu, Domino nostro.

the elect of God? God that justifieth. Who is he that shall condemn? Christ Jesus that died, yea that is risen also again; who is at the right hand of God, who also maketh intercession for us. Who then shall separate us from the love of Christ? Shall tribulation? or distress? or famine? or nakedness? or danger? or persecution? or the sword? (As it is written: For Thy sake we are put to death all the day long. We are accounted as sheep for the slaughter). But in all these things we overcome, because of him that hath loved us. For I am sure that neither death, nor life, nor angels, nor principalities, nor powers, nor things present, nor things to come, nor might, nor height, nor depth, nor any other creature, shall be able to separate us from the love of God, which is in Christ Jesus our Lord.[6]

Gradual—Psalm 23[7]

Quis ascendet in montem Domini et quis stabit in loco sancto eius? Innocens manibus et mundo corde, qui non accepit in vano animam suam, nec iuravit in dolo proximo suo.

Who shall ascend into the mountain of the Lord: or who shall stand in his holy place? The innocent in hands, and clean of heart, who hath not taken his soul in vain, nor sworn deceitfully to his neighbor.

V. Hic accipiet benedictionem a Domino: et misericordiam a Deo salutari suo.

V. He shall receive a blessing from the Lord, and mercy[8] from God his Saviour.

6. Translator's Note: Rom 8:28–39. It is one of the key Scriptural passages on predestination.

7. Translator's Note: This is the Vulgate numbering; the more common enumeration in English is Psalm 24.

8. Translator's Note: The French rendition of the Latin here is the somewhat more inexact "recompense."

Alleluia, Alleluia	Alleluia, Alleluia
V. Descenderunt multi quaerentes judicium et justitiam in desertum et sederunt ibi. Alleluia.	V. Then many that sought after judgment, and justice, went down into the desert: and they abode there.[9] Alleluia.

Sequence[10]

Ad Portum currant Regium, Quibus amica Veritas: Hic mira Deus explicat. Antra florent, currunt rivi, Et erumpunt fontes vivi De profundis vallibus. Hic pro risu sunt lamenta. Cinis lectus & sarmenta, Molliori pro cubitu.	May those who love the Truth[11] Run to Port-Royal: The Almighty works miracles there. The hollows flourish, the streams flow, And from the depths of valleys gush forth Fountains of living water. Laughter is banned from this place, we weep there, We cry there; we hate softness there, and There is no other bed than cinders and branches.
Terrenorum abest cura. In tranquilo mens secura Conquiescit littore.	There, one does not know any of the cares that trouble the rest of mankind; And over this tranquil shore the spirit free of all cares Enjoys a perfect rest.
Quales hymnos! quem concentum Una promit vox canentum, Modulante pectore.	What hymns, what concert of voices! It is the heart that unites them And makes of them one accord.

9. Translator's Note: 1 Macc 2:29–30.

10. Translator's Note: Although no chant is noted, it's plausible that this could have been sung to the tune of either the *Dies Irae* or the *Stabat Mater*, both of which are mournful.

11. Translator's Note: I have translated directly from the French here, not the Latin. The differences between the two texts reflect the authentic interpretation of the Latin, which was certainly composed first.

Laus extensa, somnus brevis,
Gravis labor, cibus levis
Corpora conficiunt.

A long prayer, a short rest,
Hard work, light food
Slowly consume these innocent
victims.

Lex alumnos una regit
Amor ipse cunctos cogit,
Fortior imperiis.

One single law serves as their rule;
The love stronger than precept
Makes them act.

Altam domum expectantes
Ad te, Sion, suspirantes,
Habitant in casulis.
Ut columbae transvolantes,
Cuncta fide despectantes
Christo se reficiunt.
Labentis, heu! vix corporis
Pondus molestum sustinent;
Ardent Deo se jungere.

Awaiting the celestial homeland,
Always fixed toward Zion,
They live on earth as in tents.
Taking the rise of the dove,
Faith lifting them over everything,
They find no other consolation than
in Jesus Christ.
Burning with love and desire to
unite with God,
Alas! They support with the pain of
their staggering bodies
The painful burden.

Quam pura, qui te diligunt,
Qui se, suosque deserunt,
O Christe, libant gaudia.
Lux et via desertorum
Per abrupta vitiorum
Raptos, Christe, revoca.

What consolations do they not taste,
O Divine Savior,
Who love Thee, who renounce
themselves,
And who leave all for Thee?
Thou, Lord, art the light and the
guide of *solitaires*;
Deign to draw us back from the
abyss of vices
Where our passions have driven us.

Fac secessum nos amare,
Tibi soli da vacare,
Terris mentes evoca.
Amen.

Inspire us with the love of retreat,
And grant that our hearts, detached
from the goods of earth,
Would occupy themselves with the
sole desire of possessing Thee
eternally in Heaven.
Amen.

Gospel

Sequentia Sancti Evangelii Secundum Joannem

In illo tempore dixit Jesus Discipulis suis: haec locutus sum vobis ut non scandalysemini. Absque Sinagogis facient vos: sed venit hora ut omnis qui interficit vos, arbritetur obsequium se praestare Deo. Et haec facient vobis quia non noverunt patrem neque me. Sed haec locutus sum vobis ut cum venerit hora eorum reminiscamini quia ego dixi vobis.

The Continuation of the Gospel according to Saint John.

At that time, Jesus said to His Disciples: These things have I spoken to you, that you may not be scandalized. They will put you out of the synagogues: yea, the hour cometh, that whosoever killeth you, will think that he doth a service to God. And these things will they do to you; because they have not known the Father, nor me. But these things I have told you, that when the hour shall come, you may remember that I told you of them.[12]

Offertory

Deus tentavit eos, et invenit eos dignos se. Tamquam aurum in fornace probavit illos; et quasi holocausti hostiam accepit illos.

God hath tried them, and found them worthy of Himself. As gold in the furnace He hath proved them, and as a victim of a holocaust He hath received them.[13]

Secret

Omnipotens et misericors Deus, a quo cuncta impetrat unanimiter supplicantium vis grata Fidelium, suscipe hanc oblationem familiae tuae; et Sanctorum et Sanctarum Portus-Regii invictam in servanda Ecclesiae fide constantiam venerantibus, da veritatem caste quaerere, fortiter tueri, et in caritate facere. Per Dominum nostrum Jesum-Christum, etc.

O Almighty and Merciful God, who refusest nothing to the sacred violence[14] that the Faithful do unto Thee: deign to receive the offerings of Thy family, and as we honor the admirable zeal by which the Saints of Port-Royal have served Thy Church, grant us by their intercession the grace of searching purely for the truth, of defending it with power, and of practicing it in charity. By Jesus Christ our Lord, etc.

12. Translator's Note: John 16:1–4.

13. Translator's Note: Wis 3:5–6.

14. Translator's Note: Language also used by Nicole in his "Règles."

Preface

Per omnia secula seculorum.	Forever and ever, world without end.
R. Amen.	R. Amen.
Dominus vobiscum.	The Lord be with you.
R. Et cum spiritu tuo.	R. And with thy spirit.
Sursum corda.	Lift up your hearts.
R. Habemus ad Dominum.	R. We lift them up to the Lord.
Gratias agamus Domino Deo nostro.	Let us give thanks to the Lord our God.
R. Dignum et justum est.	R. It is right and just.
Vere dignum et justum est, aequum et salutare nos tibi semper et ubique gratias agere, Domine sancte Pater omnipotens aeterne Deus: et te laudare mirabilem in Sanctis tuis quos ante constitutionem mundi, in aeternam tibi gloriam praeparasti, ut per eos huic mundo Veritatis tuae lumen ostenderes; quos ita spiritu Veritatis armasti, ut nec blandimentis mundi demulcerentur, nec minarum metu flecterentur, nec sexus fragilitate deterrerentur. Cum ergo tui sit muneris quod vicerunt, quia nulla valet humana fragilitas, nisi tua hanc adjuvet pietas; his inspira, misericors Deus, intercedere tibi pro nobis, ut tibi soli adhaerentes mundum cum omnibus amoribus, terroribus et erroribus suis, virtute Spiritus sancti calcare possimus; et quos fecisti de sua felicitate securos, faciat pro nostra liberatione solicitos; per Christum Dominum nostrum,	Truly it is right and just, our bounden duty and our salvation, to offer Thee thanks in all times and places, Holy Lord, Father Almighty, eternal God, and to praise Thee, Thou who art admirable in Thy Saints, whom Thou hast chosen even before the creation of the world,[15] so that they might render eternal glory to Thy grace, and that they might illuminate the lights of Thy truth; whom Thou hast truly fortified with the spirit of Thy truth, so that neither the caresses of the world could soften them, nor its menaces intimidate them, and that they might be unshakable, despite the fragility of their sex.[16] Their victory being thus Thy work, man being capable of nothing by himself if Thy love comes not to help his weakness,[17] inspire them, Lord, to be our intercessors from Thy divine mercy; so that, attached to Thee alone, we might be able, by the virtue and power of the Holy Spirit, to vanquish

15. Translator's Note: A reference to the Augustinian doctrine of predestination.

16. Translator's Note: A phrase from the Common of Virgins, but here applied to the crisis of conscience the nuns endured during the Formulary Controversy and subsequent controversies.

17. Translator's Note: Another markedly Jansenist line; only the grace of Charity can efficaciously move humans to supernaturally good works.

per quem majestatem tuam laudant Angeli, adorant Dominationes, tremunt Potestates, coeli coelorumque Virtutes ac beata Seraphim socia exultatione concelebrant. Cum quibus et nostras voces ut admitti jubeat deprecamur, supplici confessione dicentes. Sanctus, etc.

the world with all its charms, terrors, and errors;[18] and interest in the work of our salvation those to whom Thou hast already assured beatitude; thus do we beseech Thee in Jesus Christ our Lord. It is by Him that the Angels praise Thy supreme majesty, that the Dominions adore it, that the Powers fear and revere it, and that the heavens, the Virtues of the heavens, and the blessed troop of the Seraphim celebrate Thy glory together in transports of holy joy: grant, Lord, that we might unite our voices to those of these blessed spirits, to chant without ceasing, Holy, holy, holy, etc.

Communion

Fortis est ut mors dilectio, aquae multae non potuerunt extinguere caritatem, nec fluminia obruent illam.

Love is as strong as death. Many waters cannot quench charity, neither can the floods drown it.[19]

Postcommunion

Deus qui spiritus es et eos qui te adorant, in spiritu et veritate jubes adorare: suffragantibus Sanctorum et Sanctarum Portus-Regii meritis purifica, quaesumus sancto amore corda nostra, ut te in omnibus et super omnia diligentes, sincera tibi pietate placeamus. Per Dominum nostrum, etc.

O God, who art spirit, and who commandest those who adore Thee to adore Thee in spirit and in truth, we beseech Thee, by the merits of Thy Saints of Port-Royal, to purify our hearts by Thy holy love, so that loving Thee in all things, and more than all things, we might be agreeable to Thy divine majesty by a sincere prayer. Thus do we beseech Thee by Our Lord, etc. Amen.

18. Translator's Note: Jansenist *mépris du monde* in a nutshell.

19. Translator's Note: Cant 8:6–7. In this context, the verse has a decidedly Jansenist flavor, hearkening back to the contritionism of Saint-Cyran and Arnauld; one must repent from charity, true love of God, and not simply servile fear of hell. One is also tempted to read "floods" here as the persecution that destroyed Port-Royal.

24. Philo-Jansenist Reform in Spain

Joseph Climent i Avinent

Translated by Andrea J. Smidt[1]

Joseph Climent i Avinent (1706–81) was a paragon of the reforming bishop: personally holy, dedicated to preaching and teaching his local church, and an energetic and conscientious pastor. Made Bishop of Barcelona in 1766, a year before the expulsion of the Jesuits from Spain, Climent's episcopal career illustrates important convergences between philo-Jansenism and Catholic Enlightenment.[2] Climent's most famous pastoral letter (26 March 1769), excerpts of which are translated below, was published in Castilian Spanish, Catalan, French, and Italian. It addresses the subject of local and universal church reform through the promotion of a book by the Gallican historian Claude Fleury (1640–1723). The Abbé Fleury was most famous for his twenty-volume *Ecclesiastical History* (published 1690–1720), but Climent wanted the more accessible *Manners of the Ancient Israelites and Christians* (1682) in the hands of every literate person in his diocese.[3]

1. The pastoral letter is printed in *Coleccion de las obras del il.mo Senor Don Joseph Climent, del consejo de S.M. y Obispo de Barcelona* (Madrid: Imprenta Real, 1788), 1:188–268. The excerpts below are on pages 189–90, 207–8, 211–12, 214–21, 256–57, 259–60, 267–68. The titles of the sections have been added by the editors of this volume.

2. Andrea J. Smidt, "Josep Climent i Avinent (1706–1781): Enlightened Catholic, Civic Humanist, Seditionist," in *Enlightenment and Catholicism in Europe: A Transnational History*, edited by Ulrich L. Lehner and Jeffrey D. Burson (Notre Dame, IN: University of Notre Dame Press, 2014), 327–49.

3. Published originally in French as *Moeurs des Israélites et des Chrétiens* (1682).

Climent made Fleury's *Manners* required reading for seminarians and urged everyone in his diocese, clergy and lay, to repeatedly read and study the work. The Bishop of Barcelona saw the book as "a catechism of practical morality" that would help clergy and laity alike to reform their *custombres* (that is, their behavior or way of life). True to the style of Catholic primitivism that philo-Jansenists and enlightened Catholics embraced, Climent saw historical learning as intrinsically connected with personal, societal, and ecclesial reform. Discerning the right path forward depended upon discovering the moral and spiritual life of the early church and imitating it as closely as one could. Echoing Fleury's careful moderation, Climent did not advocate a fanciful restorationism. Climent's pastoral letter includes a sophisticated discussion of change over time, arguing for disciplinary and pastoral accommodation that involves change, though "without altering dogma."

While Fleury's anti-ultramontane and Gallican credentials were sterling, he was no Jansenist. Climent's pastoral letter, however, bore all the marks of what is now described as Spanish philo-Jansenism: enlightened Catholicism in a Muratorian style, anti-Molinism, anti-laxism, anti-Jesuitism, and regalism. However, this final ingredient of Spanish philo-Jansenism is complicated in Climent's case. He was exceedingly cautious not to trade subjection to Rome for subjection to Madrid. For example, Climent advocated for synods and provincial councils, knowing very well that Spanish regalism was snuffing out these avenues for collegial episcopal action more completely than ultramontanists ever had.

The popular and provocative content of Climent's pastoral letter caused serious problems for him. Words of sympathy for the "Church of Holland" (Utrecht) coming from a prominent Spanish bishop incensed many in Rome, and Pope Clement XIV asked King Carlos III to investigate Climent. The regalist minister Manuel de Roda set up a mixed commission that exonerated the bishop but left him under a cloud of suspicion in the eyes of both conservative ultramontanists and authoritarian regalists. Ultimately, Climent was a victim of the advancing tide of regalism in Spain. He again fell afoul of the authorities and was forced to abdicate as Bishop of Barcelona in 1775.

Shaun Blanchard

Letter of the Illustrious Lord Don Joseph Climent, Bishop of Barcelona, to All of His Faithful

Fleury and the Appeal to Primitivism

The Abbé Claude Fleury was one of the most pious and wise men of France. Having been fortunate enough to have a naturally good soul, and to be adorned with excellent talents and a great desire to use them to obey God, he also had the joy of finding the best teachers who taught him religion and the sciences. . . .

On top of this, no one can ignore that the Israelite or Jewish church [*Iglesia*] is the same as the Christian; the one is united with the other through the cornerstone of our Lord Christ and built upon the foundation of the Prophets and Apostles. Consequently, we cannot form a complete idea of our religion without having some account of the Church and people of Israel. For such reasons St. Augustine, in order to teach a deacon who consulted him on the method of catechizing or instructing those who wanted to be Christians in the principles and elements of our religion, sent him as an example two discourses containing the important principal developments that we read about in the Old Testament. And with that knowledge, observing those discourses and following the example of that great Church Father, the Abbé Fleury composed his historical catechism.

In another way, the reading of this work [*Moeurs des Israélites et des Chrétiens*] could and should disabuse people of the notion that the comfortable and delectable life is more reasonable and natural than the arduous life of the Israelites. . . . In addition to such usefulness for all, the work on the customs of the Israelites is especially profitable for those who want to read and understand the sacred books. One can truly say that it is a prologue for Scripture. . . .

First, then, we counsel you not to content yourselves with reading this book once, twice, or three times; you should read it continually and study it until you have it memorized, as a catechism of practical morality. This is so that, by holding these examples ever present in your minds, you will try to imitate the early Christians. This is the most quick and effective means for everyone to reform their behavior [*custombres*]. Likewise, the reestablishment of the observance of the rules and laws that governed the universal Church for many centuries is the only way of reforming it. This is not the way that Luther and his followers attempted, but the way that St. Bernard desired; that is, [implementing] the very rules and canons the Church prescribed, without breaking unity nor lacking subordination. Because just as it is commonly said that empires preserved and restored themselves by the same maxims upon which they were founded, so too we should say that, in order to keep itself pure, the Christian Church has to govern itself by the same laws that were established at its beginning. . . .

Tradition is the safe passageway through which the doctrine of behavior [*costumbres*] is communicated to us purely. If you wish, my dear Christian brothers and sisters, to assure your salvation, do not what you see being done, but rather what you read in this book was done by the early Christians.

Neither do we deny that it was able to change, and that justly and prudently Ecclesiastical Discipline did adjust in some points according to what the changing times called for. In the first three centuries, when the Church was persecuted by pagan emperors, some rules were observed that were not as necessary in the following centuries in which the emperors were Christian. And in the later centuries, the changes were more or less useful so that the essence or spirit of the Christian religion remained intact. After the tenth century, changes were rarer, and finally public penances ceased, of which our author [Fleury] speaks in chapters 25 and 63. This was more due to the perversity of the sinners than the will of wise and zealous prelates, who knew how harmful the cessation would be for Christian behavior [*costumbres*]. But this removal [of public penance] was contained within the boundaries of Discipline, without altering Dogma. The Catholic Church always taught, and we all should believe, as we alerted in our Instruction to Moralists, that the Sacrament of Penance is a laborious Baptism, and that many tears and cries will be necessary in order to reach the grace of true repentance and forgiveness of sins. In spite of this, however, the authors of the book entitled *Imago Primi Saeculi Societatis Jesu* dared to publish that sins now are atoned for more quickly and happily than before, and that many barely contract stains of guilt as quickly as they are cleaned.[4] And the most astonishing thing is that those authors attribute the invention and source of this removal [of sin and stains of guilt] to the Society [of Jesus], as if it were a great glory to invent or feign a removal that has misled innumerable false penitents and [in reality] carried them to hell.

The change that we observe with the Abbé Fleury between the first three centuries and those following was very advantageous for the Church, for it serves as a sure guideline for Her ministers to govern in the various circumstances of time and place. Those called by God to preach the Gospel in countries of infidel princes had to imitate the Apostles and their disciples in the ministry of preaching; they also had to imitate them in their selflessness, patience, mercy, and zeal for the glory of God, and in the rest of the virtues. And using these means, and not what the political world dictated, it was certain, God blessing their work, that from the most arid land they would gather as much fruit as did the Apostles, and they would convert stones into the sons of Abraham and of God. Those of us who have the fortune to live under the gentle rule of princes as pious and Catholic as Constantine and Theodosius, for all accounting we find St. Ambrose and St. John Chrysostom the best examples of meekness and strength.[5] Despite the fact that they both conducted themselves in similar fashion, the notable difference is that the latter died exiled and persecuted because of the extravagant and pompous Empress Eudoxia, and the former was highly esteemed by the great Theodosius. St. Ambrose intervened with the Emperor [Theodosius] in order to exonerate the Thessalonians, who were true prisoners of *lèse-majesté*. Through St. Ambrose's requests, the pardon of the Emperor was extended. But after being provoked by some of his ministers, he commanded his soldiers to kill as many

4. Editor's Note: The *Imago* was a favorite target for Jansenist polemicists. On the *Imago*, see John O'Malley, *Art, Controversy and the Jesuits: The Imago Primi Saeculi (1640)* (Philadelphia: Saint Joseph's University Press, 2015).

5. Editor's Note: Climent is probably alluding to the "fortune" of those living under Bourbon princes who were anti-Jesuit and anti-ultramontane and generally favorable to philo-Jansenist reform. Constantine (r. 306–37) and Theodosius (r. 379–95) were often evoked as archetypal Christian Emperors. Ambrose was Bishop of Milan from 374 to 397 and John Chrysostom ("golden-tongued") began a troubled tenure as Archbishop of Constantinople in 397. Both are venerated as Doctors of the Church.

Thessalonians as they could find, up to a certain number, without concern for who was innocent or guilty. Informed of what occurred, the saint [Ambrose] separated the Emperor from the communion of the Church, and denied him entry into it, requiring the Emperor to do public penance for something that today many probabilist politicians would say is not a sin. And St. John Chrysostom, after many private and unfruitful admonitions, publicly rebuked the injustice of the Empress, in taking away a vineyard from a poor widow, and her vanity, in erecting a statue and making holidays in her own honor.

These memorable acts provide material for many reflections. While the Emperors were infidels, the bishops, considering them outside of the Church, neither rebuked them nor spoke out against their enormous crimes. They were their most loyal vassals and suffered patiently through their persecutions. But after the Emperors became Christians, the bishops of the cities in which the Emperors lived recognized them as their own sheep who must give an account before the Tribunal of God and seek to correct their vices. When the sins of Emperors were public and scandalous, the bishops, without denying them the obedience or respect that they owed them as their legitimate Sovereigns, excommunicated them and assigned them the corresponding penance. This, far from being rigor, was piety. Excommunication, corresponding to its very essence, is the strongest, most efficient, and even most necessary spiritual medicine for the sicknesses of the faithful when they reach a very grave condition. The circumstance of the Empress Eudoxia stands out before our eyes. She was irritated by St. John Chrysostom because of the vehemence with which this most saintly and eloquent Father rebuked her excesses. Not wanting to take vengeance into her own hands, she did not charge him with a crime against the state, but rather solicited the gathering of Councils of Bishops who were enemies of the Saint. They condemned him, without recognizing the merit of his sermons, and basing their unjust sentence on defects and faults that they falsely attributed to him. Such was the liberty that bishops had to preach the truth with zeal, with prudence, and without the least disturbance to the public peace. And such was the attention and respect that they merited from Christian princes, even the least pious.

No one can read this book with the attention it deserves and not admire the concord in those centuries between the priesthood and the Empire. My beloved brothers and sisters, in chapter 32 you will read that bishops were the only judges who arbitrated in all the complaints and differences that arose between good Christians; they were not allowed to quarrel before the courts of the unfaithful. And after the Christian Emperors knew the utility of these judgments of the bishops, they authorized them by law. Thus, for many centuries, the lay or secular power did not have the least resentment. But after the twelfth century, there were many and frequent discords between the clergy and royal courts about the limits and exercise of both jurisdictions. And today such discords are carried on in France with the greatest determination and fury. Abbé Fleury extensively treats this matter in discourse seven of his *Ecclesiastical History*. He wrote with such impartiality that both the Clergy and the Parlements of France are still attempting to support their positions with the testimonies and authority of our Author, universally venerated in his own country in a time in which it was pitifully divided, as much on the point of jurisdiction as doctrine. No Catholic that we know of took the pen in order to censure any of the numerous works that the Abbé published, an extremely rare thing in a country that was then, and is almost always now, inundated with critical and satirical papers in all genres of material and against all types of people.

A Friend of Utrecht in Spain

Not many days ago, we received a letter written to all bishops, in which the Church of Holland, in communicating to us their labors and afflictions, made present to us the unity of the Church and of the Episcopacy, from whence the necessary obligation to help her [the Church of Holland] is born. For how can it be that we are members, the principal members, of the same body, and not feel the evils that other members suffer, and try to alleviate them? This indifference and insensitivity were abominable in the eyes of St. Cyprian, St. Basil, and other Holy Fathers who have taught us the necessity of the mutual correspondence and assistance of the particular churches, no matter the distance, for the good of the Universal Church.[6] And in other times it is certain that

6. Editor's Note: St. Cyprian of Carthage (d. 258) and St. Basil the Great (330–79).

bishops in similar situations wrote to the Supreme Pontiff, Head of the Universal Church, in order to enlighten themselves on the reasons for his indignation against some particular church, and to beseech him to treat her with a mercy not lacking in justice. Abundant evidence of this truth is found in the famous letter that St. Irenaeus, Bishop of Lyon, wrote to Pope St. Victor, persuading him against the excommunication of the Churches of Asia that he was planning to fulminate.[7] But now, even though we sympathize with the unfortunate condition in which one finds that Church [of Holland]—very similar to that of the Early Church, poor in riches and rich in virtue—what can we do to console her, without the counsel and help of our brothers [the bishops]?

Anti-Jesuit Polemic against Casuistry and Laxism

We cannot deny that Christians are now much less liberal and merciful than they were in the early Church. The greater part we attribute to the fact that the license to opine reached such an extreme. Some Casuists have dared to say: "Eating and drinking only to satisfy oneself is only a vice and not a sin." And the reason they gave was more execrable: "Because the natural appetite can licitly enjoy its acts." Beyond this they teach: "That hardly among the laity, even among kings, is found a thing superfluous to one's state; and so hardly anyone is obligated to give alms, since one must give from what is superfluous to one's state [of being]." The abominable propositions slacken the reins of the appetite, extend luxury and profligacy, do away with moderation and mercy, and thus make men sensual and inhumane! Alas! If only the condemnation of these and other truly anti-Christian propositions by the Supreme Pontiffs would have prevented the teaching of them in schools, blocking them from the understanding of all the Casuists! But if we see that so many go to confession and receive Communion who are enemies

---

"Cyprianic" ecclesiology, which emphasized the authority of local bishops and the role of provincial councils, was particularly popular among philo-Jansenists. See Van Kley, *Reform Catholicism*, 17, 28–31, 41.

7. Editor's Note: St. Irenaeus (ca. 130–202) challenged Victor I (pope from 189 to 198 or 199) to deal amicably with Asian bishops during the "Quartodeciman" controversy concerning the celebration and dating of Easter.

of the Cross of Jesus Christ, that is, of the mortification of their senses [*sentidos*],[8] [we must conclude that] they do not have any other god except gluttony, vanity, and lust. What can one conclude, but that such people find confessors who are as blind as they are to lead them down the path to Hell?

Praise of the Enlightened Bourbon Reformer, Carlos III, King of Spain (r. 1759–88)

God has had mercy in giving us a king as religious as Josiah.[9] And just as this Prince [Josiah], moved by zeal for the honor of God, charged the priests with the duty to teach the law that the Lord promulgated by the mouth of Moses, which had been buried and forgotten by that people for a long time, so our Catholic Monarch, moved by the same zeal, has charged us priests to teach the law and doctrine that Jesus Christ gave us, according to the understanding and explanation of St. Augustine and St. Thomas, not according to the obscurations and disfigurements of some Casuists in these recent centuries. And just as Josiah was the most precise in observing the law and very severe in punishing those who broke it, so our Lord the King gives us the most admirable examples of modesty, piety, and religion. His Majesty is not content with just teaching correct doctrine, but also desires that it be practiced. . . .

Councils and Collegial Episcopal Action

Contemplating how old these bad behaviors [*costumbres*] are, we judge that [the Church] cannot be reformed with one fell swoop, but rather little by little, and with that gentleness with which it can endure being shaped and hardened without breaking. We do not presume to have enough authority to correct the disorders that have come to be universal in a province, for the reasons that St. Augustine explained in his letter to St. Aurelius, Primate of Africa,[10] beseeching him to convene a

8. Editor's Note: Climent is here contrasting fleshly appetites with reason, or sensual delight with spiritual things.

9. Editor's Note: The reign of Josiah (d. 609 BC), a righteous King of Judah, is recounted in 2 Kings 22–23 and 2 Chronicles 34–35.

10. S. Aug. Epist. XXII. alias 64. Ad Aurelium.

council in order to suppress the acts of irreverence that were committed in churches and during sacred festivities. Ecclesiastical authority principally consists in the teaching of its first pastors,[11] which is followed by the conviction of the faithful. But that authority will not be respected or obeyed unless we work together unanimously toward the same end.[12] But while this measure does not achieve universal reform, each one of you, my dear Christian brothers and sisters, are not free from the obligation of reforming your behaviors [*costumbres*]. Especially after reading this work, you will see the ways of the early Christians, which should be your ways. Happily, we say in conclusion with the pious and wise Author [Abbé Fleury], that in forming a just idea of a rational and Christian life, you will seriously put it into practice.

Barcelona, the 26th of March 1769.
Joseph, Bishop of Barcelona

11. Editor's Note: Climent here follows an ecclesiological vision dear to Gallican-conciliarists and philo-Jansenists: the ecclesiological norm is the co-governance of the church by "first pastors" (bishops) teaching their faithful and gathering in synods and councils when necessary. One is meant to deduce that direct papal or curial control is an aberration.

12. Editor's Note: Philo-Jansenists frequently made idealized appeals to the "unanimity" of the early Church, contrasted with the discord currently present in the Church. The culprits for modern discord were primarily Jesuits, guilty of innovations like Molinism and lax casuistry. Papal centralization since the eleventh century was also often blamed.

25. A Jansenist in Portugal: Pereira's Biblical Commentary

António Pereira de Figueiredo

Translated by Bradley T. Blankemeyer[1]

The career of the Oratorian António Pereira de Figueiredo (1725–97) epitomized a Portuguese fusion of philo-Jansenism, Muratorian strands of the Catholic Enlightenment, and regalism. Pereira emerges out of a moderate Catholic Enlightenment intellectual milieu in mid-century Portugal, authoring a defense of Lodovico Muratori (1748/49) and advocating for educational reform in his *Novo Methodo de Gramatica Latina* (1752). He became a key clerical supporter of the aggressive regalist reforms of King José I (r. 1750–77) and his minister Sebastião José de Carvalho e Melo (1699–1782), the Marquis de Pombal. Highly favored in part due to his support for Pombal's ferocious crusade against the Jesuits, Pereira became a consultor for the Royal Censors Office. In 1768, this governmental body centralized control over literary production and circulation throughout the Portuguese Empire. Pereira used his position to defend Jansenist authors and attack Jesuits and ideas associated with them, such as probabilism, Molinism, and

1. The excerpt below is a translation of *O Novo Testamento de Jesu Christo, traduzido em Portuguez segundo a Vulgata, com varias annotações, históricas, dogmáticas, e moraes, e apontadas as differenças mais notáveis do original greco. Por Antonio Pereira de Figueiredo, deputado ordinário da Real Meza Censoria*, vol. 3, *Que comprehende os Actos dos Apostolos, e a Epistola de S. Paulo aos Romanos* (Lisbon: Na Regia Offic. Typograf.: 1779), 285–95.

ultramontanism. In 1766, Pereira published *Tentativa Theologica*, a classic in regalist, anti-ultramontanist ecclesiology. This work received extra attention since it was published during a tense break in Portugal's diplomatic relations with the Holy See (the breach lasted from 1760 to 1769).

Perhaps of even greater fame than Pereira's ecclesiological works is his translation of the Bible into Portuguese. While by no means a concern only of Jansenists, the translation and dissemination of vernacular Scriptures had been a Jansenist preoccupation almost from the beginning. Based on the Latin Vulgate, Pereira's translation was completed and published from 1778 to 1790 and became the standard, approved Catholic Bible in Portuguese. It enjoyed wide popularity not just among Catholics; it was even reprinted by Protestant Bible Societies in the nineteenth century.

The excerpt below is from Pereira's commentary on St. Paul's Letter to the Romans, chapter 5.[2] While there is no doubt that much of what has been called Portuguese Jansenism is far removed from the prevailing concerns of Jansen and the nuns of Port-Royal, figures like Pereira were very much committed to defending Augustinian understandings of divine grace. In the commentary below, Pereira exalts Antoine Arnauld and seeks to distinguish the true (Augustinian) Catholic teaching on grace from Lutheranism and Calvinism. Pereira also demonstrates continuity with Port-Royal by reprinting commentary from the Jansenist translator of the French Bible, Le Maistre de Sacy (1613–84). The concern to be in line with the Council of Trent is genuine, as is Pereira's Muratorian moderation in respecting those who believe in undefined teachings such as the Immaculate Conception.

Sometimes, the late phase of Jansenism is misunderstood as essentially a political movement. Although certainly connected, theological concerns should not be seen as mere covers for political positions. While anti-Jesuit and regalist forces in eighteenth-century governments were certainly not above cynical exploitation, there were significant

2. Translator's Note: I have not followed the exact composition—including headers and page breaks—of the original text; rather, for clarity, I have provided the biblical verse upon which Pereira renders his commentary followed by the commentary in full.

Augustinian theological convictions among philo-Jansenist Catholics in Portugal, Spain, and their empires.

Shaun Blanchard

Romans Chapter Five

The righteousness acquired by faith makes us await the glory of the children of God. Jesus Christ, who died for the impious, will save us, being just. All are dead in Adam and all will live through Jesus Christ. His grace is more abundant than sin.

Verse 1: (a) Justified therefore by faith, we have peace with God by means of our Lord Jesus Christ.

(a) *Justified therefore by faith.* Those whom the Apostle [Paul] calls *justified by faith*, he calls when writing to the Ephesians (2:8) *saved by faith*. And then in verse 2 he adds, *that by faith God gives us access to grace*. Of all things the Protestants abuse, [this] is in order to establish another capital error also based on a very poor knowledge of the Apostle, which consists of reducing all the work of justification to faith. And what faith? The faith with which Man believes and is firmly persuaded that his sins are forgiven.

Luther was the first author of this error, as it is present in the Preface which appears at the beginning of his Works printed in Jena in 1564, and of his Acts with Cardinal Cajetan,[3] where they start. His loyal friend Melanchthon followed him in the *Loci Communes Theologici*, under the heading *De Vocabulo Fidei*. After them, Calvin embraced the same, just as much in his *Institutiones*, Book 1, chapter 2, numbers 7 and 16, as in the *Antidote* against the Council of Trent, printed in the same year in which the sixth session was held, which was in 1547.[4]

In his admirable treatise *Le Renversement de la Morale de J.C. par les erreurs des Calvinistes*, the great Arnauld impugned, leaving no room for contest, every perverse system of the Calvinists on the subject of

3. Editor's Note: Pereira is referencing the report Luther made of his debate with the Dominican Cardinal Cajetan (Tommaso De Vio) in Augsburg in 1518: *Acta Fratris Martini Lutheri Augustiniani apud D. Legatum Apostolicum Augustae*, often called the *Acta Augustana*.

4. Editor's Note: Session six of the Council of Trent produced the famous Decree on Justification. See Denzinger-Hünermann 1520–83.

justification.[5] He shows unequivocally in Book 9, chapter 5, that the present Article, which the Calvinists call *of justifying faith*, or *of faith in special mercy*, outside of being manifestly opposed to the principles of St. Paul, is increasingly repugnant and contradictory on its own terms. For if sins are forgiven to Man because Man believes that they are forgiven, we hold that the same justified faith (as they call it) is anterior and posterior to the remission of sins: anterior, as it is the cause of it; after, because it presupposes it.

As it is easy to have in hand the treatise of Arnauld, I only add that following the exposition in reference to the words of St. Paul that the Council of Trent had given in session six, chapter 8,[6] to be of the same mind which the Catholic Church has always been, our theologians respond that with [good] reason the Apostle assigns principally to faith the affair of justification and of salvation. Because even though faith is only one part of our justification, it is for all the beginning and foundation of it. It is the door through which we enter to grace: as it is by faith we confront the gravity of sin, the eternal punishment that it deserves, our incapacity to escape this state, and the necessity of divine succor to this effect. By faith we implore this succor; by faith we acknowledge the hope [we have] in the mercy of God; by faith we loath sins as offenses against an infinitely good God; finally, by faith we dispose ourselves so that He reconciles us to Himself. Following this theology of St. Paul, St. Augustine writes in the book *De natura et gratia*, chapter 44, that the same faith that redeems us redeemed the ancients.[7] In other words, faith in the Mediator, faith in His blood, faith in His Cross, faith in His Death and Resurrection: *Ea quippe fides justos salvavit antiquos, quae salvat & nos; id est, fides Mediatoris Dei & hominum hominis Jesu Christi, fides sanguinis ejus, fides Crucis ejus, fides Mortis, & Resurrectionis ejus.*[8] And in the book *De perfectione iustitia*

5. Editor's Note: Antoine Arnauld, *The Overturning of the Morality of Jesus Christ by the Errors of the Calvinists, Touching Justification* (Paris, 1672).

6. Editor's Note: Denzinger-Hünermann 1532 (Tridentine Decree on Justification).

7. Editor's Note: Augustine's *On Nature and Grace* was a response to Pelagius written in 415.

8. Editor's Note: "Indeed, that same faith which justified the ancient ones now saves us; that is, faith in the one Mediator between God and men, the man Christ Jesus, faith in His blood, faith in His cross, faith in His death and resurrection."

hominis, chapter 19, Saint Augustine professes this admirable proverb: that faith is the beginning of amending the heart: *Initium corrigendi cor fides est.*[9] PEREIRA.[10]

Verse 3: And not only in this hope, but also in tribulations; (b) knowing that the tribulation produces patience.

(b) *Knowing that the tribulation produces patience, etc.* Because in tribulation patience has its exercise: in this exercise of patience the soul experiences the protection and aid of God. With this protection and aid of God, the soul is encouraged to expect from Him the gift of His labors. PEREIRA

Verse 7: (c) Because for a just man, one rarely dies: yet for a good [man] perhaps one is found who has the courage to die.

(c) *Because for a just man, etc.* The Apostle shows the subtlety [*fineza*] of the Redemption of men by Jesus Christ, observing that while it is not easy to find anyone in the World who gives his life for a good man (in other words for a charitable man) then it is even rarer to find one who gives his life for a just man. However, so intense and so extreme was the love of God for men—though being poor, ungrateful sinners—He sought to die for men and with His death save them from eternal condemnation. PEREIRA.

Verse 12: For as by one man sin entered into this World, (d) and by sin death, therefore death also passed to all men by one man, (e) in whom all have sinned.

(d) *And by sin death.* From this divine faith is truly comprised, as the second Council of Milevis, canon one, defined against the Pelagians: if Adam had not sinned there would not have been death, neither for him nor his descendants. PEREIRA.

(e) *In whom all have sinned.* Here we have revealed the great Dogma of original sin, which is to say of the sin of Adam, transmitted through all his children, who therefore are all born sinners, enemies of God,

9. Editor's Note: "Faith is the beginning of the correction of the heart." In *On Man's Perfection in Righteousness*, another anti-Pelagian work of the year 415, Augustine rejects the idea that every sin can be avoided.

10. Editor's Note: The commentary by Pereira is signed as such, to distinguish it from the commentary he printed from others, like Sacy.

children of wrath, and guilty of eternal condemnation. Thus on this text the same Council of Milevis in canon two defined, declaring jointly that this was the sense in which the Catholic Church had always and everywhere understood it: *Quemadmodum Ecclesia Catholica ubique diffusa sempre intellexit.*[11] And by the same words the Council of Trent, session five, canon four,[12] defined this again, declaring however it was not of its intent to understand in this decree the most holy Virgin Mother of God. PEREIRA.

Verse 13: For even before the time of the Law there had been sin in the World, but as there had not been Law, (f) sin was not imputed.

(f) *Sin was not imputed.* The Law of which the Apostle speaks is the written Law, the Law of Moses. So this means that there had been sin in the World, but that this was not imputed because there was not yet Law. This ought to be understood in the sense in which he [Paul] said in chapter 4, verse 15, *That where there is no Law, there is no transgression of the Law.* Therefore sin was not imputed as a transgression of the written Law, even if it is certainly imputed as a transgression of the natural Law that existed thus with the first man. PEREIRA.

Verse 14: Meanwhile death reigned from Adam to Moses, even over them (g) who had not sinned by a transgression similar to that of Adam, (h) who was a figure of who was to come.

(g) *Who had not sinned by a transgression similar to that of Adam.* St. Jerome and St. Augustine understand this of children, who being born sinners did not sin by their own will (for before the use of reason they do not have it) but by that of Adam their father, with whom morally they form one same person. (*Quando omnes ille unus homo fuerunt,* the same St. Augustine says in his work *De peccatorum meritis et remissione*).[13] However, others identify this difference that St. Paul considers here in the fact that since Adam sinned against a Law expressed and

11. Editor's Note: "The manner in which the Catholic Church, spread out everywhere, has always understood it." The Council of Milevis, held in 402 in Numidia (North Africa), was attended by St. Augustine.

12. Editor's Note: See Denzinger-Hünermann 1514 (Tridentine Decree on Original Sin).

13. Editor's Note: "Since all were that one man" (book 1, chapter 11). Augustine wrote *On Merit and the Forgiveness of Sins, and on the Baptism of Infants* in 411–12.

spoken from God, men before the Law of Moses had sinned against a Law that was not expressed nor sensible, but was the natural Law that spoke only internally, by reason and by conscience. This understanding is that of the Greek Fathers, which Estius[14] says to be the more natural, and which St. Augustine also approved. PEREIRA.

(h) *Who was a figure of who was to come.* In other words, the figure of the future Messiah, or the figure of Jesus Christ, whom the aforementioned Apostle thus calls in another place *the second Adam.* The figure consists particularly, according to the sense of the Apostle, in that Adam is the natural head of all human sinners, just as Jesus Christ is the spiritual head of all Faithful. Furthermore, Adam, in the condition of a sinner, transmitted his sin to all his descendants by means of carnal procreation, just as Jesus Christ, supremely just, transmits His grace and His justice to all the Faithful by the regeneration of Baptism. SACY.

Verse 20: Now the Law with its entrance (i) allowed much sin to increase. But where sin abounds, grace superabounds.

(i) *Allowed much sin to increase.* Not because the Law makes sin or intent, but because, on the one hand, *where there is no Law, there is no transgression of Law*, as we hear above from the Apostle; and on the other hand, where grace is absent the Law gives occasion to many sins, since with the Law's prohibitions our concupiscence increases. *Ubi non est gratia liberatoris, auget peccandi desiderium prohibitio peccatorum*, says Saint Augustine in the book *De diversis quaestionibus octaginta tribus*, question 66, no. 1,[15] and in the Exposition on Psalm 83 discussed thus by the same Holy Doctor: *The Law was given to man, in order to convert Man, and to make him confess that he was ill, even when man believes that he is healthy. He was given* [*Law*] *to be made to see his sin, not to cure him. And what did the knowledge of his sin produce in him? The sin was further increased, it gained new strength, of a sort that while before man was a sinner, afterwards man became a transgressor* [*prevaricator*]. In chapter 7 [of Romans] this doctrine will be clarified even more by the same words of the Apostle. PEREIRA.

14. Translator's Note: The Dutch theologian Willem Hessels van Est (1542–1613), a student of Michel de Bay (Baius), wrote commentaries on the Pauline epistles.

15. Editor's Note: "Where the grace of the liberator is not present, the prohibition of sin increases the desire of the sinner."

26. Religious Toleration and Austrian Jansenism

Marx Anton Wittola

Translated by Andreas Oberdorf[1]

The Austrian priest Marx Anton Wittola (1736–97) was one of the most important figures in the world of German-speaking Jansenism. From 1774, Wittola was parish priest of Probstdorf, outside Vienna. Favored by Maria Theresa and some key ecclesiastical leaders, this *österreicher Pfarrer* (Austrian parish priest) was able to push a confrontational Jansenist agenda. We examine below the first of four influential tracts that Wittola wrote on the subject of religious toleration. That the Austrian State Council suggested Wittola write this tract shows the extent to which Joseph II's government was willing to promote reformist Catholicism, even through the pens of Jansenists.

While the issue at hand was of clear practical importance in the multiconfessional Holy Roman Empire, a genuinely theological openness to toleration and a polemic against coercive persecution was gaining steam in philo-Jansenist circles around Europe. In this first tract on toleration, Wittola argues that Christian unity cannot come about through violence and persecution—that has been tried and failed. Furthermore, such coercive tactics violate the duty of Christian love, which makes them inadmissible anyway. Given that "development of

1. The excerpt below is taken from *Schreiben eines österreichischen Pfarrers über die Toleranz nach den Grundsätzen der katholischen Kirche* (Vienna, 1781), 20–35.

doctrine" is usually evoked to justify contemporary Catholic teaching on the issue of religious liberty, it is noteworthy that Wittola does not appeal to development. In keeping with Jansenist methodology, he argues from a primitivist perspective, calling Catholicism back to its roots in "the time of the Apostles," when the church used only the means of patience, persuasion, prayer, and love. For late Jansenists, intolerance and coercion were the developments, and unhappy ones. As usual, the Roman Curia, the Jesuits, and the "monks" (e.g., Dominican Inquisitors) are blamed for a litany of crimes: ambition, violence, scandalizing Protestants, and inculcating superstition in the laity.

Published a month before a sweeping Edict of Toleration was promulgated by Joseph II, Wittola wanted to prepare the public for legal change with theological and moral arguments, rather than just pragmatic ones. He earned the ire of Alois Merz (1727–92) and authored a second tract against the fiery preaching of this Augsburg ex-Jesuit.

Note that Wittola uses the term *Religionsverwandte* (relatives in religious faith) as a friendly address for Protestants. This term, while irenic, is more cautious than using "brothers" or "brethren" (*Brüder*). He does use the language of *Brüder* to refer to Protestants, but prefaces it with *irrenden* or *irrige*. A literal translation of these terms is "erring," but they also have the connotation of "wandering." An avid reader of his Jansenist colleagues in France and Italy, Wittola was certainly aware that French Jansenists had come to support the civil toleration of Protestants, and that leading Italian Jansenists like Ricci and Vincenzo Palmieri were referring to Protestants as "brethren led astray" (*fratelli traviati*) and "separated brethren" (*fratelli separati*).

Shaun Blanchard

Letter of an Austrian Parish Priest Concerning Tolerance, According to the Principles of the Catholic Church (1781)

So, tell me, does the Catholic Church pray for the extermination of the heretics? No, is my answer, but rather for the extermination of the heresies that she cannot tolerate as a true mother of mankind. On Good

Friday, she prays for the conversion of all people, and in this way she still gives them solemn signs of her love.

Did she not at least approve the extermination of heretics by the Inquisition and other violent means? Oh, not at all! Voltaire and other shallow thinkers ascribe these horrendous incidents to the Church: we need not follow them, but, with *Bossuet, Noailles, Colbert, Soanen,* and other great bishops of recent times,[2] we should carefully separate, according to the rule of Saint Augustine and particularly his letters to *Januarius*, what the Church herself does from what the chaff and weeds in the Church do. Christ has never taught that His field would be without weeds and His barn without chaff. He also never promised that there would be fewer weeds and chaff. Only bad shepherds and priests seduced by monks became persecutors of heresy insofar as they have forgotten the spirit of the Church and the examples of their saintly predecessors.

If we consider the number of popes, bishops, and other shepherds of the last centuries who believed they were rendering a service to God when they slaughtered heretics, should we not conclude that the spirit of persecution is the spirit of the Catholic Church? Not at all; and we should ensure that nothing is exaggerated in the statement above. The many unclean animals that were led by God onto the Ark were not sunk. Where else should the chosen people seek refuge from the Great Flood? Even if the number of tolerant bishops, who are loving toward our relatives in religious faith [*Religionsverwandte*], is smaller today, they are not few. They refer with their doctrine and practice to the entirety of the Church's antiquity, and thousands of revered and saintly bishops of the Catholic Church are on their side: after all, the Catholic Church was not made today. We must not ascribe anything to Her that she did not recognize for herself in the time of the Apostles.

2. Editor's Note: It is notable that Wittola's "great bishops" here are all French and all anti-ultramontane. Jacques-Bénigne Bossuet (1627–1704), bishop of Meaux, was a champion of Gallicanism but not a Jansenist. The others were pillars of resistance to *Unigenitus*. Jean Soanen (1647–1740), bishop of Senez, and Charles-Joachim Colbert de Croissy (1667–1738), bishop of Montpellier, were two of the original four Appellants. Louis-Antoine de Noailles (1651–1729), Cardinal-Archbishop of Paris, refused to accept the Bull until finally succumbing under pressure in 1728.

Still inspired by the spirit of love and truth that she received from heaven on Pentecost, she groans because of her many bad shepherds; she has been groaning since nine hundred years before the Reformation. Three and a half hundred years ago, gathered in the general councils of Constance and Basel, she declared so loudly that all the world must have heard: Reformation is necessary in the head and members of the Church.[3] Since these groans were not heard over the centuries, is it not more convincing to conclude that the number of bad shepherds increased as a punishment for our sins? But the spirit of these sinners was not the spirit of the Church, which so wanted to improve, if only she only could. What has happened to her regarding these stranglers of heretics happened accordingly to the holy patriarch Jacob when his sons became the murderers of Shechem.[4] How could the Church of God approve the Inquisition? In Spain, for instance, it was the cause of numerous hidden Jews pretending to be Catholics because they did not want to get burned. They took Communion, and thus violated our most sacred sanctuary in the most dreadful manner of all. Was this for the glory of God and His Church? As little as probabilism and other heresies—of which many shepherds were infected for a few hundred years—could have decried the Church's pure doctrine; as little as the spirit of love and holiness could be displaced by robbers, murderers, and persecutors, even if they are numerous. Read, my friend, the translation printed by Trattner in 1772 of Fleury's *Ecclesiastical History*, along with its justification.[5] There you can find principles with which a Christian must strengthen himself against temptations and very common offenses.

Well, it is not difficult, my friend, to help you out of your grief, and to answer your third question: whether the toleration of false religions, founded upon the divine command to love one's neighbor, but

3. Editor's Note: Wittola cites here the monuments of the conciliarist tradition, the Council of Constance (1414–18) and the Council of Basel (convened in 1431). Reform in "head" refers to the papacy and, by extension, the Roman Curia.

4. Editor's Note: Genesis chapter 34 is noted in the margin of the text.

5. Editor's Note: Claude Fleury's twenty-volume *Histoire ecclésiastique* (1690–1720) was a Gallican and anti-ultramontane reading of church history. Wittola himself translated the 1772 German edition he references here.

not extending to the errors of heretics nor to harmful associations with them, is or could be detrimental to the Catholic Church?

The heretics, you say, will only become more brazen through this toleration. If they see that they can live unpunished under their false doctrines, they will never think of a return to the Church of their ancestors. Instead of being awakened by a salutary persecution, they would just make a virtue out of necessity, and thus be joined to us again.[6]

If the heretics become bolder through toleration, they will speak out about their doctrines much more freely. Thus they will become even easier to contest. In the true Church, there will be no lack of fundamental truths that refute their false doctrines. The children of the Church will rather be edified by these refutations, instead of the weak among us being tempted to [heretical] worship if we paint them [heretics] as martyrs through persecution. By the way, it seems to me that any necessary virtue imprinted through persecution is just hypocrisy, which is certainly contrary to God and therefore not beneficial to His Church either.

What else would a poor heretic do when we banish him from our country, than betake himself to a heretical country, where he will not hear any more Catholic doctrine in his life? However, when he lived among us, he easily could have encountered a pious priest who might eliminate his prejudices with patience and instruction in the teaching of the Apostles. Who is responsible for his soul and this detriment to the Church? I think his persecutor is.

However, some say that the heretic is too malicious to allow himself to be corrected through the mild ways of truth and love. I must confess that monks have given us this understanding of heretics. But I would rather consider them as sick people, who would rely more on our love the less that they feel their sickness themselves. Why should I hate my neighbor when he is fatally ill in his soul? Faith is a gift of God. When we see one of our fellow people without it, we must pray for the giver of good gifts to give him faith; but we cannot beat it into anyone with a cudgel. Religion is in the center of the heart, and this cannot be

6. Editor's Note: Wittola's argument here is that persecution would result only in false conversions: the "virtue" that the persecuted Protestants of the Empire would pursue would just be "necessity."

compelled. It is to be wished that all people had the true religion. For the same reasons, it is to be wished that they would speak the same language, maintain everlasting peace, and always stay healthy. However, because Adam's sons, due to their transgressions, must bear the marks of their outrage against God, these latter wishes are thwarted. The first wish will never come true, and the kingdom of God is only for people who welcome it like a child.

Should a zealous Catholic, particularly a priest, be eager to spread this kingdom? Yes, he should be, but only by the means that the Apostles used to spread the kingdom all over the world. My friend! The Dominican inquisitors—who made revenue, rather than the Lord, the judge of life and death—do you believe they were eager to spread the Kingdom of Christ? What about the Jesuits, who as court confessors shouted down all other ministers during the so-called religious conferences?[7] Those Jesuits told the Emperor that he would neither have fortune in the Ottoman Wars nor benefit his House if he did not exterminate the heretics, destroy their churches, take their children away, and burn their books. Do you really think that such people were eager to spread the kingdom of Christ? Oh, it is too clear that they only cared about spreading their own empire, which is entirely of this world! This is proved by the collegiate foundations established from numerous confiscated noble estates in Bohemia, Silesia, and Moravia. When a dying nobleman (for example, the Baron von Schoenaich) said to his sons, "Dear children, I would have bequeathed a good estate to you, if Catholic priests had not slandered me before my Emperor," it is no wonder that these children wished to separate from the Church. So, we may conclude that the Christian toleration of heretics is not only not detrimental to the Church, but rather advantageous.

All separations arise from the heat of bitterness, but through the reconciliation of the mind they can be settled again. But how can persecution be a means of reconciliation? Every judge of human nature will admit that the person I am supposed to convert must have firm confidence in me. This confidence can only be built through persuasion: that

7. Editor's Note: See, for example, Robert Bireley, *The Jesuits and the Thirty Years War: Kings, Courts, and Confessors* (New York: Cambridge University Press, 2003).

I am a good man who can and wants to serve him. What man can be persuaded of this by someone who openly persecutes him?

When I consider, on the one hand, the horrible malice of the Donatists, whose murderous hands were stained with the innocent blood of so many bishops and priests, and on the other hand, the noble requests made to them by the saintly bishops of Africa gathered in council in Carthage, I must conclude that the latter sought nothing but the kingdom of God and the salvation of their enemies. So, they made an offer to the Donatist: among other things, if they wished to come back into Christian unity, the Catholic bishops would resign in those cities in which a Donatist [bishop] was also present. God blessed their [the Catholic bishops'] loving indulgence so much that this old and vexing schism [*Trennung*] was finally overcome completely. Even with the most stringent and constant legislation from the Christian emperor, this could not have been achieved. And so, the toleration of even the worst heretics is beneficial for the Catholic Church.

Different times demand different counsels. That is what sophisticated priests say here. Yet their sagacity is based less on the Word of God than on their experiences. Is it not the case that since heretics have been persecuted, the Church has been severed more and more, down through the centuries? Have the separated communities not continuously grown under the pressure of persecution? Has the number of the Protestants in Poland and Hungary decreased in the two centuries of their persecution? Did not the most tolerant bishop of recent times, the gentle Saint Francis de Sales, convert the most heretics? Was he not Catholic enough when he tolerated the people of Geneva? They had been hardened opponents to St. Francis's predecessors, but in the last years of his life, they even started to consider moving the displaced episcopal see from Annecy back to their own city! Free from worry, let us try to speak in friendly ways with our erring brethren [*irrenden Brüdern*] about the things which belong to the peace of Jerusalem.[8] We will have so much to speak about together, that after fifty years of toleration the entire schism could come to an end. Particularly, if God wants

8. Editor's Note: By "the peace of Jerusalem," Wittola is metaphorically referring to the state of Christian communion. Psalm 121 (122 in the new numbering) is noted in the margin.

to be merciful to His people, He will allow a reformation led by a free church council, which has hitherto been prevented by the sycophants and flatterers at the Court of Rome. He will also strengthen the hand of the Catholic sovereigns against the appalling kingdom of the monks. We must beseech Him day and night for these things.

The monks, especially the more recent, have not only constantly breathed a spirit of persecution into us against the real heretics, but they have also seen heretics everywhere in the bosom of the Church. It is certainly true that the sin of heresy, like other sins, can also ensnare the children of the true Church. It only makes sense to persecute our fellow believers because they are not part of the Kingdom of God if we also persecute thieves, adulterers, drunkards, etc. These all have the same effect, according to the doctrine of St. Paul.[9] So would the Church of Jesus Christ become an eternal battleground, instead of being a kingdom of peace.

However, the evidence was often very lacking that the Christians persecuted by monks were actually heretics. They were often better Catholics than those criticizing them were. The religious orders committed themselves to the domination of the world, and to the intrigues of the court rather than to reading books. Especially since they invented game-playing with Bulls [*Bullenspiel*], they have known no end in hunting for heretics.[10] Anyone who disagrees with an Aristotelian Category of these theological Peripatetics (because he has read the Church Fathers) needs to be branded a heretic. But not only those: [the monks] also attack any who impair them in any sense, regardless of whether he is a bishop, a cardinal, or even the pope himself. We have exemplary

9. Editor's Note: 1 Corinthians 6:10 is noted in the margin of the text.

10. Editor's Note: The term *Bullenspiel*, a play on words with "ball games" [*Ballspiele*], probably has two allusions in mind. The first is game-playing with papal bulls, rather than balls. Wittola is accusing "monks" (primarily Jesuits in this case) with inventing a new "game," in which they hound good Catholics (Jansenists) with papal bulls they have solicited. *Bullenspiel* could also refer to the early modern practice of bull-baiting or bullfighting [*Bullenhatz*]. In this blood sport, various breeds of bulldogs and terriers were set on a captured bull, with spectators placing bets on which dog would kill the bull. If Wittola is also evoking this terrible practice, the nickname of the Dominicans, *domini canes*, "hounds of the Lord," would give the allusion added heft. I am grateful to Jürgen Overhoff for illuminating conversations on these points.

cases with the Cardinals Tournon, Noailles, and Passionei, and with the Popes Innocent XI [pope from 1676 to 1689], Benedict XIV [1740–58], and Clement XIV [1769–74].[11]

Once we shed all monkish prejudices, it becomes certain that Christian toleration is not only not detrimental to the Church of God, but is even beneficial to her, because she reconciles souls and gives hope for the return of her lost children.

It is a true detriment to the Church that so many priests stubbornly insist on abuses which have offended our erring brethren (*irrige Brüder*) from the beginning, and still offend them: such as the superstitious veneration of images, self-serving confraternities, fabulously ornate sanctuaries, and so on. If you value the souls of the Protestants, then you will groan with me at behavior which is so detrimental to the church: a bishop allows an insane priest to so many times name his lampoon—which is highly suspicious and brimming with false devotions—the *Katholischer Unterricht*.[12] Bossuet and Veronius,[13] along with many other learned men, have reminded us—and indeed, everything depends upon it—that we should neither encumber Protestants with errors that they do not really hold, nor declare something to be Catholic doctrine that the Catholic Church would not recognize as

11. Editor's Note: The "better Catholics" persecuted by "monks" refers primarily but not exclusively to the Jesuit "persecution" of Jansenists. The cardinals and popes mentioned were seen as either anti-Jesuit or philo-Jansenist by many, both friend and foe. Charles-Thomas Maillard de Tournon (1668–1710) was an inveterate opponent of the Jesuits in the Chinese Rites controversy. The enlightened Domenico Silvio Passionei (1682–1761) was a leader in Roman philo-Jansenist circles.

12. Editor's Note: *Catholic Teaching* (or *Instruction*). The "insane priest" is Patrizius Fast, a curate of St. Stephan's Cathedral in Vienna and author of the *Katholischer Unterricht und Erörterung aller Zweifel, welche in den Beyträgen zur Schilderung Wiens aufgeworfen werden* (Vienna, 1781). Fast opposed Jansenism and the Josephinist reforms, including religious toleration, and began a concentrated polemic against Wittola. Both Wittola and the anti-ultramontane canonist Joseph Valentin Van Eybel (1741–1805) wrote vociferously against Fast. The bishop in question can only be the Archbishop of Vienna, Cardinal Migazzi, who was once open to moderate Muratorian-style reform, but became a staunch opponent of the increasingly radical Jansenist and Josephinist reforms.

13. Editor's Note: Interestingly, the reference here is to a French Jesuit, François Véron (1575–1649).

such. The former would cause Protestants to avert their souls from the Church, and the latter would make us a laughingstock.

This is my opinion in its entirety: a good Catholic is not only allowed to tolerate our relatives who hold false religious faith [*falsche Religionsverwandte*], but, due to the strength of the great commandment to love, actually must gladly tolerate them. His toleration of them should extend as far as brotherly love reaches, and should have no qualms. Not only would this toleration by the true Church not be detrimental, it would be beneficial. Whoever persecutes people will disperse them; but whoever tolerates people will gather them.[14] Now the Church is an assembly. She asserts, among other things, this beautiful feature of her divine origin: just as God created human beings to be sociable, she also seeks to assemble all together in the bonds of brotherly love. She thus despises anything that harms unity or separates human society.

14. Editor's Note: Wittola echoes here Jesus' words in Matt 12:30.

27. Documents from the Synod of Pistoia: A Jansenist Vision for Liturgy and Devotion

Translated by Shaun Blanchard[1]

Convened in September 1786 by Bishop Scipione de' Ricci, the Synod of Pistoia was a diocesan gathering of about 250 clergy in a city near Florence, Italy. Under the protection of the Habsburg Grand Duke of Tuscany, Peter Leopold, the ten-day synod was the high-water mark of late Jansenism. The *Acts and Decrees* produced by Ricci's synod represent a synthesis of reformist strands, including the soteriological, ecclesiological, and political. The two texts excerpted below, concerning liturgy and devotions, illustrate one important plank in this multifaceted reform agenda.

The first text below, the Decree on the Eucharist, evinces a theological method common in Jansenist and Gallican circles, in which the patristic is privileged and the scholastic ignored or placed under suspicion. Priests are to "follow the style and teaching" of the Church Fathers when instructing the faithful and avoid "scholastic questions" (§2). Thus, while the real, bodily presence of Christ in the Eucharist is insisted upon, the term "transubstantiation" is not used. An anti-Baroque simplicity or even austerity in church ornamentation prevails. There is to be one altar in each church (§5), and no flowers or reliquaries are to be placed upon it. In keeping with earlier Jansenist tradition, devotion to "true" relics is to be retained.

1. The excerpts below is taken from the 1788 Bracali edition of the *Acts and Decrees*, printed in Pistoia: see Pietro Stella, ed., *Atti e decreti del concilio diocesano di Pistoia dell'anno 1786*, 2 vols. (Florence: Olschki, 1986), 1:123–33, 195–211.

Theologically, the Pistoians base their support of active lay participation on the position that the liturgy is "an action common to the priest and to the people" (§6) and that the faithful along with the priest offer the Sacrifice to God. Flowing from these theological commitments is the claim that worship in the vernacular is the ideal, though the synod acknowledges the need for patience in this regard. Thus, priests are exhorted to explain the Mass and to provide vernacular missals and other aids to worship. What is proposed here, then, is similar to Catholic worship in certain places in the decades leading up to Vatican II. The participation of the laity is seen as "essential" and the faithful in a state of grace have a "right" to receive Communion during Mass. Pastors who withhold this are in sin. In this and other ways, the Pistoian texts challenge entrenched polemical stereotypes about "Jansenism."

The second text is the Decree on Prayer of the sixth session. It begins with a radical Christocentrism, reminiscent of Pascal. The decree as a whole is indebted to François Philippe Mésenguy (1677–1763)[2] and Jacques-Joseph Duguet (1649–1733). Typical anti-Jesuit attacks on the Sacred Heart of Jesus devotion follow, as do cautions against superstitions related to devotions with "determined" numbers (such as the stations of the Cross). The decree's enlightened and Jansenist vision for devotion to Mary and the saints attempts to remove "every shadow of superstition" (§12–14). The document contains numerous prescriptions against what we would today call folk religion or popular Catholicism: relics and images are good but have no magical or innate "power" (*virtù*), and no image of a particular saint (e.g., Marian statues) should be appealed to above others (§15–17). While purgatory is real and praying for the dead is good, numerous superstitions have polluted Catholic practice (§20). In a stunning passage, the Pistoians argue that no one can be excluded from the liturgy "because no one can be excluded from love, which is the soul of every prayer" (§19). Finally, the synod calls for the reform of the Breviary and the Missal, since God "does not want to be honored with lies" (§23). While the document has sterling Jansenist

2. Editor's Note: Mésenguy, an opponent of *Unigenitus*, was well known for his works of biblical theology as well as his catechetical *Exposition de la doctrine chrétienne* (1744).

credentials, many of the concerns and even some of the language itself reflect a tradition stretching back to moderate enlightened Catholics like Muratori and humanists like Erasmus. The parallels with Vatican II and postconciliar reform, ranging from theological method (*ressourcement*) to numerous concrete prescriptions, are manifest. For these and many others reasons, the Synod of Pistoia's texts on liturgy and devotions are some of the most fascinating to emerge not just from the world of Jansenism, but from all of early modern Christianity.

Shaun Blanchard

Decree on the Eucharist, Session Four of the Synod of Pistoia (22 September 1786)

§1 Man cannot have devotion for his God, neither can he have life and salvation, except through the one who is established as the angel of the New Covenant. Jesus Christ is the eternal High Priest, the author and consummator of our salvation.[3] It was according to the counsels of His almighty Father, that He continued His dwelling among men, up to the consummation of the Saints.[4] In order that men could live His life by uniting themselves to it, He gave a sensible rite, as required by their nature.[5] . . .

§2 Concerning the power[6] of this rite, we believe that it belongs to the Catholic faith that after the consecration of the bread and the wine, Jesus Christ, true God and true man, is contained truly, really, and substantially under the species of those sensible things [bread and wine]. With the Church, we condemn those who say that [Christ] is contained only as a sign, as a figure, or in power.

3. Translator's Note: This language echoes Heb 12:2. Ironically, the Latin *Auctorem fidei* ("author of faith"), a phrase taken from the Latin Vulgate translation of Heb 12:2, was the title given to Pope Pius VI's condemnation of the Synod of Pistoia eight years later.

4. Translator's Note: The reference here is eschatological. Christ will be present sacramentally with His people until the eschaton.

5. Translator's Note: That is, Jesus gave a tangible religious ritual in view of the human nature of His flock.

6. Translator's Note: I translate the Italian word *virtù* as "power." In a religious context, however, the term connotates as innateness.

Furthermore, we believe that it is a truth belonging to the same Catholic faith, that when the substance of the bread and wine cease [after the consecration] and there remains only appearances, the whole Christ is contained in this Sacrament under each species [bread or wine] and under any part of each species that might be separated. And we condemn as contrary to the faith the sentiments of those who maintain that the substance of the elements remains, together with the Body and Blood of Jesus Christ.

And for those things that belong to scholastic questions on the mode in which Jesus Christ is under the species, or on the nature of the species themselves, and other similar things, it seems opportune to the Synod that the parish priests follow the style and the teaching of the Fathers. That is, not to be occupied by these questions, and not even to speak of them. May they consider and teach those mysteries with simplicity, endeavoring to animate and enkindle in the people a firm faith in the same [mysteries], by explaining the omnipotent love that God has for men.[7]

On the other hand, [the Synod] also commands the parish priests to employ the utmost care to remove from the minds of the faithful any base or material ideas concerning this mystery. They are to instruct them that the Body of Christ is not an animal body [*corpo animale*], but spiritual and life-giving. Christ is in the Eucharist not in the manner of other natural bodies, but in a supernatural and spiritual manner. Although we cannot express it with words, we nevertheless come to understand, when our thinking is illuminated by the faith, that this is possible for God.

The Articles up to this point have established, first, that the Eucharist is a Sacrament; it contains Jesus Christ, who is for us grace, life, and salvation. It contains Christ under an exterior sign, that is, under the species of bread and wine. These represent the food, the spiritual banquet of the soul. Secondly, it has been established that the Eucharist is singular; insofar as the other Sacraments have the power

7. Translator's Note: *Auctorem fidei* 29 condemned the "imprudent and suspicious omission" of the term "transubstantiation" as "pernicious, derogatory to the exposition of Catholic truth regarding the dogma of transubstantiation, [and] favorable to heretics." See Denzinger-Hünermann 2629.

[*virtù*] of sanctifying in the use of the same, it is in the Eucharist alone that the author of sanctity Himself is present, even outside of the use [eating or drinking].

Thus we believe with the Church that after the consecration Jesus Christ is present both before and after the use, and in the particles that are reserved, until the species are entirely altered or corrupted. And we renew the condemnation of the sentiments of the heterodox that are contrary to this truth. Regarding the conservation of the Eucharist, it pleases us to renew the ancient Canons which determined that only enough particles as are necessary for the use of the sick should be conserved, or for any [possible] cases of grave necessity. . . .

§4 Because the founder of our Religion has taught us that true worshippers worship God in spirit and in truth, we believe that the sacrifice of the Eucharist is one of a spiritual nature. Insofar as it is visible and external, we consider it, with St. Augustine, as the sign and the Sacrament of the true and invisible sacrifice. That is, we believe that in it is consumed a victim not carnal, but spiritual and incorruptible: the Body of Jesus Christ, from the fire of the charity of the Holy Spirit, through whom the Father sanctifies it. And we believe that Jesus Christ is the true Priest, who offers himself to the Father. From this perennial sacrifice an abundance of grace and heavenly blessings comes to us. . . .

§5 The Synod also desires that the priests observe with diligence all the prescribed ceremonies and rites, and that they pronounce the words distinctly and devoutly. May they not accelerate the action or excessively delay it in a manner inconvenient to those assisting.

Regarding the music of organs, it seems opportune to the Synod to establish that they remain silent during Masses from the Offertory to the Postcommunion and excluding the time of the Preface.

Regarding music and singing in the churches, the Synod considers, according to the mind of the Fathers, that these things were introduced to more greatly impress the sentiments of religion into the spirits of the faithful, and to enkindle the various affections of piety that are expressed by it. We reflect that in order to support this end, music should be simple, grave, modest, pious, and adapted to the sense of the words. We therefore forbid any music that is devoid of such qualities. . . .

With regard to the decoration [*ornamento*] of the churches themselves, it pleases the Synod that the rule of St. Augustine be retained. That is, that in matters of religion it is necessary to make use of human things, *ut inferioribus non offendamur, solis autem oblectemur superioribus.*[8] For this reason we determine it a duty to avoid the disorder of sordidness, and a rusticity that moves people to laughter and, by offending the senses, distracts the spirit from devotion.

And for the same reason, we determine that a decoration too varied or costly or affected be avoided, because it entices the senses and drags the soul down to delight in lower things. These abuses were condemned by the Fathers, the sentiments of which have been reported recently by the Archbishop of Salzburg in a religious instruction [pastoral letter]. On these matters we embrace it.[9]

We come then to deliberate on the altars of the churches. The holy Synod believes it opportune to establish the following decrees.

Because of the order of the Divine Offices and the ancient custom of the Church, we are persuaded that it is fitting that there is only one altar in each Temple.[10] It therefore pleases the Synod to reestablish this custom [*uso*].[11]

Neither reliquaries nor flowers are to be placed on the altars.[12] If any church possesses authentic relics, these are to be exposed to the veneration of the people under the altar, according to the custom of antiquity.

The Synod also wishes that the Sacrament be conserved in a place

8. Translator's Note: "So that the lower things might not offend, but we might delight only in the higher things."

9. See the Appendix to the Synod, §8. Translator's Note: Hieronymus Colloredo (1732–1812) was Prince-Archbishop of Salzburg from 1772 to 1803. A reforming enlightened Catholic, Colloredo sympathized with many elements of the Jansenist reform movement in Tuscany.

10. Translator's Note: *Tempio* here designates a house of Catholic worship (parish church, oratory, etc.).

11. Translator's Note: The Pistoian preference for only one altar was condemned in *Auctorem fidei* 31 as "rash, injurious to the very ancient pious custom flourishing and approved for these many centuries in the Church, especially in the Latin Church." See Denzinger-Hünermann 2631.

12. Translator's Note: This synodal decree was condemned in *Auctorem fidei* 32 as "rash, injurious to the pious and approved custom of the Church." See Denzinger-Hünermann 2632.

more apt to excite the attention and the reverence of the faithful. It desires that the ancient custom of raising the Ciboriums on high be renewed. Let the Sacrament be conserved in them.[13] In the place where the Sacrament will repose, may there not be any painting that is not appropriate [*analoga*] to the same.

§6 Since religion consists in Sacrifice, and since there is only one Sacrifice in the New Covenant, it is well to confess that the faithful have a part in it also.

Hence we embrace the custom and the Apostolic law of being present at the Sacrifice on Sundays and on feasts determined by the Church. And since the Canons that prescribe this to the faithful speak of the Parish Mass, we confirm the ancient laws on this point.

Consequently, we embrace the arrangement proposed by the Bishop in the instruction [pastoral letter] on the erection of the new parishes of Prato,[14] as well as those regulations concerning the public oratories of the countryside. We desire that these [oratories] be absolutely removed, if they are not found necessary for the benefit of the people. But if they are necessary, we desire that they be erected as parishes, and that in the meantime a chaplain might perform there the parochial functions of instruction and teaching Catechism. We leave, then, these determinations concerning the private oratories of the countryside to the prudence of the Bishop.

When we say that the faithful have a part in the sacrifice, we mean that they offer and immolate the victim together with the priest. They offer their very selves along with it.[15] The entire Liturgy contains only these parts of the Sacrifice, and the regulations of the actions with which the parts [of the Liturgy] themselves should be accompanied. For these reasons, it is according to the doctrine of the Fathers, the practice of antiquity, and the order and tenor itself of all liturgies, that [we proclaim] the Liturgy to be an action common to the priest and to the people.

13. Translator's Note: This is in keeping with longstanding Jansenist preferences, reflected in Saint-Cyran's writings on hanging pyxes.

14. See the Appendix to the Synod, §9.

15. Translator's Note: Grammatically, this sentence could mean that the faithful "offer their very selves" along with the priest, or along with the sacrifice. Either meaning would fit the liturgical theology of the Pistoians.

Convinced of these principles, the holy Synod desires to remove those reasons by which [these solid liturgical principles] have been in part forgotten: by recalling the Liturgy to a greater simplicity of rites, by expressing it in the vernacular, and by uttering it in an elevated voice.[16] However, because the present circumstances do not permit us to fulfill these desires, we halt at [*s'arresta*] renewing the law of the Council of Trent, in which it is prescribed that pastors, in every instruction they make during Mass on feast days, explain some part of the Liturgy.[17] They are exhorted to introduce books to the people in which the ordinary of the Mass is in the vernacular. Pastors should try to arouse interest in the people to read along and thus accompany the priest by this means.

Since the participation in the victim is an essential part of the sacrifice, the holy Synod desires that the faithful communicate[18] whenever they attend [Mass].

We do not however condemn as illicit Masses in which those present do not communicate sacramentally, because they do partake, although less perfectly, of the victim by receiving spiritually.[19] However, the Synod wills that anyone who is disposed to communicate, except in cases of grave necessity, might communicate during Mass, with particles consecrated in it [during that Mass]. Consequently, priests are enjoined to consecrate a suitable number of particles whenever they foresee that some are present at Mass that are disposed to receive. According to the Decree of the Roman Missal, the people communicate after the priest has communicated.[20] We warn the same [priests] that

16. Translator's Note: *Auctorem fidei* 33 condemned this proposition as "rash, offensive to pious ears, insulting to the Church, and favorable to the charges of heretics against her." See Denzinger-Hünermann 2633.

17. Translator's Note: See Trent, Session 22, Chapter 8 (September 17, 1562), Denzinger-Hünermann 1749.

18. Translator's Note: "Communicate" in this context means receiving the consecrated bread of the Eucharist (Holy Communion).

19. Translator's Note: The "insinuation" of this passage was condemned in *Auctorem fidei* 28 as "false, erroneous, suspect of heresy, and having the flavor of it." See Denzinger-Hünermann 2628.

20. Translator's Note: Eighteenth-centuries reformers like the Pistoians were trying to eliminate the custom that had arisen of the faithful receiving Communion outside of Mass. The insistence here is that the lay reception of Communion in Mass is

they are guilty of sin if one of the faithful wants to receive Communion during Mass and they do not comply with this right [of the faithful], depriving him of that particular fruit which comes from Liturgical Communion.

§7 It remains, finally, for us to determine the manner with which one must receive this Sacrament. Concerning this matter, we will begin by professing, with the Holy Fathers, that Eucharistic eating is not carnal eating, as the people of Capernaum believed.[21] If this food is spiritual, if it nourishes the life of the spirit, then the way of eating it should be spiritual too. Consequently, those who do not have a spirit disposed to receive it, although they might chew the Sacrament with their teeth, and thus receive the Body of Jesus Christ inside themselves, do not however feed on it fruitfully.

Coming then to the spiritual dispositions, we determine that each one [wishing to receive] should be instructed in the Faith thus: in addition to knowing how to discern the body of the Lord, they should be free [*immune*] from sin, because holy things should be treated as holy. As the Apostle warns us, *qui manducat & bibit indigne, judicium sibi manducat & bibit.*[22] In this matter, nobody who is conscious of mortal sin, even a Priest, should approach this table before having tried himself according to the rules which will be prescribed in the Treatise on Penance. . . .

§8 As well as this general oblation, we believe that we can make in the Liturgy a special commemoration of someone, living or dead, praying to God for them in a special way. Yet we do not believe that the priest can decide to apply the fruits of the Sacrifice to whomever he will. On the contrary, we condemn this error as greatly offensive to the rights of God, who alone distributes the fruits of the Sacrifice to whomsoever He wills, and according to the measure that pleases Him.[23]

---

the original custom and should be the norm. They are careful not to assert that a Mass is invalid if no one receives but the priest.

21. Translator's Note: A reference to the unbelieving crowd in Jesus' famous Bread of Life discourse in the Gospel of John 6:24–71.

22. Translator's Note: "Whoever eats and drinks unworthily, eats and drinks judgment upon himself" (1 Cor 11:27).

23. Translator's Note: *Auctorem fidei* 30 censures this passage as "false, rash, dangerous, injurious to the Church, leading to the error elsewhere condemned in Wycliffe."

This false opinion has been introduced to the people: those who give alms to a priest with the condition that he celebrate a Mass receive from the Sacrifice a special fruit. The Synod commands the parish priests [*Parochi*] to teach their flock that the Sacrifice of the Mass is of infinite value, but the application of the fruits of it depend on God. To participate more fully one should unite oneself to the priest who is offering it [the Mass] with firm faith and with a spirit of repentance, enkindled by charity. Those who gives alms will receive merit when they give in a spirit of charity, since God regards not the gift but the piety of the donor.

Decree on Prayer, Session Six of the Synod of Pistoia (27 September 1786)

§8 But the most essential of all the conditions of prayer is that it be done in the name of Jesus Christ. After the separation that sin has placed between God and man, we can no longer have access to the Throne of the divine Majesty on our own. We no longer have in us, or by ourselves, any reason that can oblige God to listen to us. Indeed, we merit nothing but rejection by Him; since all that we offer on our own is unworthy of Him, because we are infected with covetousness. There is therefore no other means by which we can approach God but by His only-begotten Son, who made Himself our propitiation, our High Priest [*Pontefice*], our Mediator. Since God loves us only through this unique object of His good pleasure, so He does not listen to us but by [Christ]. We declare, therefore, that for us it is an absolute necessity to pray in the name of Jesus Christ. This is so necessary that any prayer that is not made through Jesus Christ not only does not obtain the pardon of sins, but itself becomes a sin.

§9 Now, to pray in the name of Jesus Christ is, properly speaking, nothing other than relying solely on His love and on His merits, recognizing from Him the spirit that groans and prays in us, asking everything according to His will, and in line with the goods that He has

See Denzinger-Hünermann 2630. The reference to Wycliffe comes from a condemnation of the Council of Constance (1414–18). See Denzinger-Hünermann 1169.

merited for us, uniting oneself finally to the prayer and to the sacrifice of this our unique Mediator.

§10 Moreover, Jesus Christ not only prays for us as Priest, He prays in us as Head, while still being prayed to as God by us. For as He is, together with the Father and the Holy Spirit, true God and Author of every grace, so He must still be, with the Father and the Holy Spirit, the only object of our prayers, as He is of our adoration. And since it would be an error anathematized by the Church to adore Jesus Christ's humanity, his flesh, or a portion of this [flesh] separately from the Divinity, or with a sophistical precision, so it would be equally [an error] to direct to that humanity our prayers with such a division or abstraction.

Therefore, subscribing fully to the Pastoral Letter of our Bishop [Scipione de' Ricci] of 3 June 1781 concerning the new Devotion to the Heart of Jesus,[24] we reject this and other similar devotions as new and erroneous, or at least as dangerous.[25] And willing, therefore, that they be completely abolished in our Churches, it will be the duty of the pastors to exhort the faithful to adore, invoke, and pray to the undivided Jesus Christ.[26] And this should be done principally in His Mysteries, as the Church has always practiced.

§11 The Mystery of the Passion of Jesus Christ certainly must engage our piety and our continuous meditations in a particular way. It would also be desirable, and we inculcate with the outpouring of our whole heart, that this same piety and meditation might be free from all the useless and dangerous materiality to which superstitious devotees from recent centuries wanted to subject it. It would be too difficult to make them perfectly exempt.[27] The spirit of compunction and of fervor can certainly not be tied to a determined number of stations, or to arbitrary

24. See the Appendix to the Synod, §32.

25. Translator's Note: *Auctorem fidei* §62 censured this opposition to the Sacred Heart devotion as "false, rash, dangerous, offensive to pious ears and injurious to the Apostolic See." See Denzinger-Hünermann 2662.

26. Translator's Note: The insinuation that the Sacred Heart devotion "separates" or "divides" Christ was censured in *Auctorem fidei* §63 as "deceitful and offensive to the faithful who adore the Heart of Christ." See Denzinger-Hünermann 2663.

27. Translator's Note: The Pistoians refer here to the suspect, new devotions. Principally in view is the Sacred Heart devotion, but the next sentence shows they also

reflections [that are] often false, more often fickle, and always full of stumbling blocks.[28]

§12 Whenever we recommend a true and solid devotion to Jesus Christ, whenever we declare the necessity of His mediation, we do not intend to exclude the invocation of the Saints. All the members of the Church, in general, are united among themselves by the bonds of charity. This establishes among them a holy exchange [*commercio*], the end of which is the glory of God and the salvation of the Elect. As a consequence of this union, the Saints now reigning with Jesus Christ, secure in their immortality, have a desire for and interest in our salvation. This is what leads us to implore the intercession of the Saints, so that they might help us to obtain from God, through the mediation of Jesus Christ, our Savior and theirs, the grace which we need to reach the glorious eternity that they already enjoy.

§13 Therefore, although we hold as certain that the sole mediation of Jesus Christ is necessary simply and absolutely, and that the invocation of the Saints does not enter in an essential way into the plan of Redemption and of the salvation of men, we also confess with the holy Council of Trent that such invocation is good and useful. We also commend special devotion to the Blessed Virgin. She was chosen by God to be the Mother of Jesus Christ, and this election of love filled her with grace above all the other Saints. She is also now the common Mother of Christians, *quia*, says St. Augustine, *cooperata est charitate ut fideles in Ecclesia nascerentur, qui illius capitis membra sunt.*[29]

This special cult of the Blessed Virgin, however, just like that which is rendered to the other Saints, must be regulated according to the spirit of the Church, which knows how to place the appropriate distance between creatures and God, who is the only source of life and salvation. Trespassing these boundaries and giving to creatures, even the most holy, a cult that is due only to God would make us guilty of a very serious offense instead of meriting for us their [the saints'] assistance. And

---

take aim at other popular practices, including at least some elements of the Stations of the Cross devotion.

28. See the Appendix to the Synod, §33.

29. Translator's Note: "Because she cooperated in love so that the faithful might be born in the Church, who are all members of that Head [Christ]."

so the holy Synod wishes that the honor that we intend to give to the Saints might lead us to a greater commitment to imitate them, rather than to a sterile and vain admiration.

§14 For that which regards the external practices of devotion to the Blessed Virgin and the other Saints, we wish that every shadow of superstition be removed. This includes attaching a definite efficacy to a determined number of prayers and salutations.[30] For the most part, either the sense [of the prayers] is not perceived or the meaning is not understood, as is generally the case in other acts or objects that are external and material. It will therefore be the duty of the parish priests to exercise vigilance over the particular devotions of their people, too often inclined to superstition and materiality. In these matters we intend to conform ourselves to the vigilance of our Bishop, as demonstrated above, especially in his letter of 6 December 1784.[31]

§15 Pastors of souls should take no less care to inculcate in the faithful the true spirit of veneration [*culto*] that is to be given to relics and to images of the Saints. According to the most ancient custom and the spirit of the universal Church, relics of the saints must be regarded as the remains of bodies created by God to be instruments of His glory. Together with the soul, they were the living temple of the Holy Spirit and the members of Jesus Christ. The sight of these sacred remains, which must one day be reanimated and clothed with eternal glory, should arouse in us faith in the resurrection to come, and remind us of what we should do to await it with joy. Finally, the miracles that God is pleased to work in the presence of these sacred relics invite us to turn with confidence to the intercession of those blessed souls that are honored in these precious remains. Far from believing that there is any special power in them [the relics themselves], the faithful are reminded that all our hope should be founded on the power and goodness of He who honors His faithful servants as He pleases, and who fulfills our wishes [*voti*] in the manner that He judges is most appropriate for His own glory.

30. Translator's Note: *Auctorem fidei* §64 censured as "false, rash, scandalous, dangerous, injurious to the piety of the faithful, derogatory to the authority of the Church, and erroneous" an interpretation of these practices as "universally superstitious." See Denzinger-Hünermann 2664.

31. See the Appendix to the Synod §34.

§16 The sacred images should be honored and venerated with the same spirit. One should not believe that there is any divinity or special power in these things. This would lead to honoring them in a special way and fixing our confidence in them, in imitation of pagans who placed their trust in idols. When we honor images we must intend to refer this honor to the original of them; that is, to adore Jesus Christ in Himself and in His Saints.[32] Indeed, according to the Tradition of the Fathers, all of the usefulness of images consists primarily in being as a book for the illiterate [*ignoranti*], in which what they cannot learn by reading comes to be expressed to them. Furthermore, they [sacred images] serve generally, for all, as a most lively reminder of what Jesus Christ has done for us, the marvels that God has worked in His Saints, and the examples He has given us in them, in order that we might give Him thanks and remain encouraged [*eccitati*] to imitate them [the saints].

§17 Such are the principles upon which the holy Synod desires that the people be instructed, so that their devotion and prayers are regulated. All those images that are far from leading to the most holy ends that the Church has had in proposing images to us, but instead serve rather to distance us from these ends, should be entirely removed, as exceedingly dangerous stumbling blocks. This includes anything which (1) presents false dogmas, as those of the carnal Heart of Jesus; or give the occasion of error to the uneducated, as those of the incomprehensible Trinity;[33] or finally those which instead of edifying are a motive of scandal, like lascivious or ridiculous paintings, or [images that] give off an air of vanity and pomp. (2) Equally, let those images be removed in which it would seem that the people put special faith or recognize some special power contrary to the decrees and intentions of the Church. This can be deduced from observing that they render a special veneration to a given image, and resort to it more than to others, as if God and

32. Translator's Note: That is, veneration or adoration should be directed to the things the images represent.

33. Translator's Note: *Auctorem fidei* §69 censured this Pistoian decree "because of its generality" as "rash and contrary to the pious custom common throughout the Churches." That is, the Synod was faulted for not sufficiently distinguishing between approved and unapproved images of the Trinity. See Denzinger-Hünermann 2669.

the Saints listen in a special way to the prayers that are made before it, or that God has attached the promise of granting His graces to the veneration of it.[34] (3) To this same end, the holy Synod wishes that the pernicious custom of making distinctions between certain given images be completely removed. This is especially so in the case of the Virgin, who is distinguished by particular names and titles that are, for the most part, vain and puerile.[35] It would never be licit to give them [sacred images] denominations other than those analogous to the Mysteries which have been expressly mentioned in the divine Scripture.[36] To operate differently would be to multiply stumbling blocks for the people, who are accustomed to superstitiously put their trust in names that are pompous or are adapted to their particular interests. (4) The abuse of keeping certain particular images covered [veiled] should also be extirpated.[37] In addition to being an occasion for the people to suppose that there is a special power in them, and therefore to give them a particular veneration, it also destroys all the usefulness of images and their purpose. (5) Finally, the holy Synod wishes that the churches only keep images representing the Mysteries of the Redeemer, according to the custom and the forms prescribed by our Fathers. In addition to this, images of the Blessed Virgin and of the other saints should not be kept if they are doubles. But it is permitted, rather, to place for ornamentation paintings that represent some edifying historical event from the Old or the New Testament.

34. Translator's Note: A "rejection of special devotion" in a "general manner" is censured by *Auctorem fidei* §70 as "rash, dangerous, and offensive to the pious custom prevalent throughout the Church." See Denzinger-Hünermann 2670.

35. Translator's Note: This prescription sought to roll back the long and venerable devotional custom of having special titles attached to images of saints, especially Mary. This austerity proved exceedingly offensive to many of the people of the diocese. One cause of the riots that helped to hasten Ricci's downfall was the belief that the beloved *Madonna dell'Umiltà* (Our Lady of Humility) image in Pistoia was under threat.

36. Translator's Note: *Auctorem fidei* §71 censured this prescription as "rash, offensive to pious ears, and especially injurious to the due veneration of the Blessed Virgin." See Denzinger-Hünermann 2671.

37. Translator's Note: *Auctorem fidei* §72 censured this decree banning the veiling of images as "rash, contrary to the custom prevalent in the Church and [which was] introduced to foster the piety of the faithful." See Denzinger-Hünermann 2672.

Concerning Public Prayer

§19 To this [public prayer], especially, everyone has a right. There is no one who can be excluded from it, because no one can be excluded from love, which is the soul of every prayer. Enemies are included, as are heretics and infidels. Since, then, those that God has put in place to govern men as much in the spiritual order as in the civil order have a particular right to this [public prayer], we declare, according to the teaching of St. Paul and the constant practice of the Church, that it is a duty of religion and an act of justice to offer special prayers to God for the pastors both of the first and the second orders,[38] and for sovereigns, their royal families, and their ministers and magistrates. Therefore, founded on this incontrovertible truth, and adhering to the pastoral letter of our Bishop on the duties of subjects toward the Sovereign,[39] we wish that all priests always remember the Prince during the Sacrifice of the Mass, adding to the Canon after those words *Pro Antistite nostro & c.* this also: *& pro Magno Duce nostro & c.*[40] And in the other public prayers, may they not omit the prayers for the Bishop and for the Sovereign according to the order already established. It is, thus, the duty of pastors to instruct the people with zeal and care on the obligation that they have to unite themselves to this understanding.

§20 Likewise, by virtue of this intimate union of charity that establishes a holy exchange [*commercio*] among all the members of the Church, whether militant or suffering,[41] we recognize it to be holy and salutary to pray for those who died in grace. For these, who are retained in Purgatory, it remains to suffer some pains for the expiation of their sins, until divine justice is satisfied. Therefore, the holy Synod wishes that every first Sunday of the month each priest [*Pievano*] with his coadjutors [assistants] and other priests assigned to service in his Church, along with the brothers of the Company of Charity[42] and the other faithful, all join together in the Church of the respective parish

38. Translator's Note: That is, bishops and priests, respectively.

39. See the Appendix to the Synod §35.

40. Translator's Note: "For our Bishop, etc." and "for our Grand Duke, etc."

41. Translator's Note: The church "militant" refers to the church on earth, while the church "suffering" (*purgante*) refers to those redeemed souls suffering in Purgatory.

42. Translator's Note: Ricci created a *Compagnia della Carità* in each parish as an

to pray to God for the dead, singing or reading Vespers, the first Night Prayers [Compline], and Lauds from the Office which is called Of the Dead. On the following morning the Requiem Mass is to be celebrated by the same, according to the rubrics prescribed in the Calendar. Various errors of the most pernicious sort have snaked their way into the people on this subject. For example, that there are abandoned souls in Purgatory for whom no one prays and who therefore remain bereft of relief. Or, that the particular prayers of the faithful solely benefit those souls in purgatory for whom they are expressly made. Thus the holy Synod exhorts pastors to make every commitment to instruct the people prudently on these matters, showing them that such ideas are completely contrary to the Doctrine of the Church, according to which spiritual goods are common among the living members of Jesus Christ, through the love that unites them together. In this way, none of them [souls in purgatory] are excluded from the prayers of the Church, because love relates them to the good and the benefit of the whole body. And thus it is that special prayers made by the faithful for souls in purgatory benefit them especially, in proportion to the love and merit they acquired during their life, which have made them more capable of participating [in these benefits] in the next life. Also, the holy Synod intends to prohibit on this point all those practices that are not authorized by the Church, or that can engender any superstition in the people. . . .

§22 From these principles come an obligation for every Christian to take part in public prayer, to enter into the spirit and understanding [*intelligenza*] of the prayers and ceremonies of the Church. This includes the Divine Office, but especially the holy Sacrifice of the Mass. From hence also arises the duty of pastors to watch over the fulfillment of objects so important.

§23 First of all, however, we judge it our duty to cooperate with our Prelate [Bishop Ricci] in the reform of the Breviary and the Missal of our Church: changing, correcting, and putting the Divine Office in better order. Everyone knows that God, who is truth, does not want to be honored with lies. And on the other hand, the most learned and holy men, including, in more recent times, the popes themselves, have

---

amalgamation of all existing confraternities. This proved to be yet another controversial disruption of the status quo by the bishop.

recognized many falsehoods in our Breviary, especially as regards the lessons of the Saints.[43] They have confessed the need for a more exact reform. Regarding, then, the other parts of the Breviary, everyone understands that there are many things that either have little use or are less edifying, and that it is necessary to substitute for them other words, taken from the word of God or from the genuine works of the Fathers. Above all, the Breviary itself should be arranged so that in the course of a year, the entirety of the Sacred Scriptures are read. In the meantime, the holy Council adopts the corrective sample transmitted from the Bishop to the priests with the pastoral of January 1 of this year,[44] and remits to the Bishop himself to make some of our brother priests deputies to continue and conclude this holy work.

§24 Since, then, we know that it would be contrary to Apostolic practice and the designs of God not to procure for the common people [*semplice popoli*] the easiest means to unite their voice with that of the whole Church,[45] we believe it is good to give to the Bishop the charge to appoint some venerable fathers to attend to the compilation of a Ritual and of a Manual for the use of the City and Diocese of Pistoia. In addition to the necessary instructions and explanations, the prayers and rites of the Church for the administration of the sacraments, the Offices of the principal feasts of the year, the Ordinary of the Mass, and all that which will more easily lead to the instruction and edification of the people will be in Latin and the vernacular. The insertion of some more Psalms and Hymns will be procured for this Manual. These will be put into Italian verse, and substituted, as far as possible, for secular songs [*canzoni profane*]. This is so that we might have that same consolation that St. Jerome had in hearing the hard-working countrymen of Bethlehem accompany their labor with the singing of the Psalms.

43. Translator's Note: That is, in readings on saints' feast days.

44. See the Appendix to the Synod §36.

45. Translator's Note: *Auctorem fidei* 66 condemned this injunction "if understood [to mean] that the use of the common language should be introduced into the liturgical prayers," as "false, rash, disruptive of the order prescribed for the celebration of the mysteries, and easily productive of numerous evils." See Denzinger-Hünermann 2666. The Pistoians are here closely echoing a statement of Quesnel condemned in *Unigenitus* 86. The reading of Quesnel, recommended by §29 of the Decree on Prayer, is condemned in *Auctorem fidei* 68.

28. Jansenism and Eastern Catholicism: The Melkite Synod of Qarqafé

Translated by Kevin Blankinship and Mark Spinnenweber [1]

The Synod of Pistoia's reform agenda, institutionally speaking, was effectively crushed by the early 1790s, and the powerful bid for synodal reform around Europe was fatally compromised by the events surrounding the French Revolution. However, Pistoian principles found fertile soil as far afield as Lebanon, where Arabic-speaking Melkite Catholics jealously guarded the ecclesial heritage of their so-called "Uniate" (eastern rite) church from the interference of the "Court of Rome."

The Melkite Synod in Qarqafé in 1806 had striking similarities with Pistoia in both spirit and letter. Primarily responsible for this was a remarkable character, Archbishop Germanos Adam (1738–1809). Adam was primarily educated in Rome (1754–65) before being made bishop of Aleppo in 1777 (Aleppo became a metropolitan See in 1790). Adam spent some formative months with Scipione de' Ricci in Florence and was probably also influenced by other leading Italian Jansenists including Pietro Tamburini. The combination of a typical eastern Catholic resistance to Roman hegemony with the Jansenism and aggressive

1. The excerpt below is translated from the original Arabic text of the Acts of the Synod of Qarqafé, available at https://www.loc.gov/item/2021667206/. See pages 144–47 (or 164–67 starting from the cover and front matter). For an Italian translation of the Arabic synodal acts and other documentation (including Gregory XVI's brief) see *Mansi* 46:683–878, at 747–51.

anti-ultramontanism that Adam encountered in Italy was combustible. Adam adopted dangerous positions such as supporting religious toleration; he had a proto-ecumenical outlook, and he questioned "Roman" understandings of neuralgic issues like indulgences.

The excerpted text below comes from chapter six of the synodal acts of Qarqafé. The synod's views on indulgences draw from a common anti-Roman and anti-scholastic perspective that many Eastern Catholics shared with Jansenists, as well as a privileging of patristic texts and patterns of thought (*ressourcement avant la lettre*). Indulgences were not rejected, but the late medieval understanding of the "treasury of merit" was undercut in favor of an earlier Catholic understanding of indulgences as special remissions of canonical penances. Some other acts of this Melkite assembly, such as the Decrees on Sacraments and on Prayer, are directly reliant on the Synod of Pistoia.[2] In the Brief *Melchitarum catholicorum synodus* (1835), Pope Gregory XVI specifically condemned the Synod of Qarqafé as a Jansenist and Pistoian metastasis.

Shaun Blanchard

The Sixth Heading:
On the Definition of The Nature of Indulgences and Types of Their Canonical Usage
The Acts of Qarqafé (1806)

The western theologians who are most precise and knowledgeable concerning the primitive teachings of the Church [*tahḏīb al-kanīsah al-qadīm*], define indulgences in this way: they are the remission of a portion of the penance to be done, which remission occurs through the authority of legitimate superiors, by virtue of the keys of loosing and binding given to Saint Peter, head of the Apostles and the Catholic Church. This definition accords with the teaching of the eastern church and western church.

Thus, the faithful have always professed that Our Lord Jesus Christ

2. See Pietro Stella, *Atti e decreti* 2:140–45.

gave to the blessed Peter, then to all the Apostles, then through them to all the bishops succeeding them, power to loose and bind. He also gave them His word that He binds in Heaven whatever they have bound on earth, and that He the Most High looses in Heaven whatever they have loosed on earth. We know that the Apostles and their successors have used this power in all periods of history.

The power of absolution [loosing] is based on this: the penitent person is absolved of his sins by the bishops and priests from whom leave [for such absolution] is granted, after that person shows true repentance and returns to God Most High with a heartfelt conversion, detesting his old ways and resolving to keep His holy commandments and to be true to His divine justice by means of pious deeds. As for the power to bind, it is based on this: letting the sinner remain bound by his burdens [that come of sin] and be held back from partaking of the holy mysteries [sacraments], until he has prepared himself for them by carrying out works of penance as prescribed by the holy canons. These works would need to be carried out by sinners for a period of some years. Some penitents would need to continue in penance for seven, fifteen, twenty years, some for the rest of their lives, according to the different offenses [committed].

The bishops, as servants of the Church, witnessed on the one hand the ardor of penitents in committing acts of mortification. On the other hand, there was confirmed to [those bishops] the penitents' weakness and moral incapacity to fulfill all that had been set before them in those canons bestowed beneficently by the Lord. Therefore they [the bishops] exercised their absolving power to grant them, namely the penitents, fellowship in the Church and [access to] the holy mysteries[3] before the completion of their prescribed years of penance—this condescension was called "indulgence" [*ghufrān*] or "pardon" [*samāḥ*]

This discipline [*tahḏīb*] was continually preserved in the eastern church, with all precision, up until the year 383, or a little longer, during which time Nektarios, the successor of Saint Gregory of Nazianzus, was over the city of Constantinople. He was the Patriarch who abolished public penance in the church of Constantinople, [after which] the other

3. Translator's Note: The sacraments, especially Holy Communion.

eastern churches imitated his example, not immediately but gradually. As for the western church, public penance was observed therein up to the seventh generation [i.e., for seven generations].[4] Afterward, diverse customs were introduced which it is not necessary to expound upon herein. What we have said is proven by the twelfth canon of the First Council of Nicaea and in other canons of the ancient holy councils, and in the many witnesses of the holy fathers both east and west.

Based upon this, the fathers of the Council of Trent thus defined in session 25: "Authority to grant indulgences has been granted by the Lord Jesus Christ to the church and she made use of this authority granted by God in very ancient times as well. Indeed, the holy synod teaches and defines that using indulgences is truly beneficial to the Christian people and affirmed in the creeds[5] of the synods and must be preserved in the Church. It decrees anathema[6] upon those who either say indulgences are without purpose or deny the Church's authority to grant them. Rather, the synod desires to preserve moderation in granting them according to the ancient and accepted custom of the Church, lest prior ecclesiastical discipline be weakened by excessive mildness."

This definition teaches us two truths: the first truth is that the Church has the authority to grant indulgences according to the ancient discipline of the Church. The position of the Church in preceding generations was not to grant multiple indulgences, but one indulgence remitting a part of the canonical penance. It was granted to those who began to observe their penance ardently and energetically but were not able to fulfill all of its obligations for reasons of infirmity or because their life was cut short. Therefore, indulgences received in accordance with the spirit of the Church and its teachings are those which dispense with the need to fulfill the prescribed canons.

4. Editor's Note: The Italian translation reads "to the seventh century" (*al settimo secolo*) but the original Arabic refers to "the seventh generation" (*al-jīl al-sābiʿ*).

5. Translator's Note: "Shahādah," an Islamicate term, referring typically to the Islamic profession of faith. Here it is in the plural, while in Islamic contexts it would be singular.

6. Translator's Note: "Ḥarām," another Islamicate term, referring typically to what is forbidden by Islamic law.

The second truth is thus: the fathers of the council ruled that moderation in the granting of indulgences be observed according to ancient church custom, so that ecclesial discipline would not be weakened. From such statements [i.e., concerning "ecclesial discipline"], it is quite clear that the fathers are referring to public penitential discipline and the preservation of the canons that impose on all mortal sin.[7] Therefore, they warn and order that there not be too much leniency in granting this dispensation, but rather that it be granted according to the custom of the ancient church, which consisted in granting indulgences only to those who did not have time to fulfill the canonical obligations prescribed to them [because their lives were cut short], or those who did not have the ability to bear them because of bodily weakness, vocational obligations, or the tasks involved in maintaining a livelihood. Because the obligation of discharging [the duties of penance] comes from divine right, as decreed by the Lord of glory to all sinners, the Church is not able to dispense totally and without restriction from this divine ordinance.

Therefore, orthodox doctrine having been established, this holy synod, following the ancient discipline of our eastern church and in conformity with the decrees of the Supreme Pontiff Pope Benedict XIV,[8] holy be his memory, grants to all priests charged with administering the mysteries and ministering to human souls the power to grant plenary indulgences to all who make their confessions in their final illness, making use of the following prayer in granting them this indulgence. [This is the prayer] used by our Greek church, [and we do] not intend to add other prayers. Before granting them this indulgence, let them exhort the one lying on his deathbed to recite the acts of faith, hope, and charity, perfect contrition, and perfect submission to the divine will.

This is the formula of the prayer by which indulgences are granted at the hour of death:

Most Merciful Lord Jesus Christ, our God, who built thy Church upon Peter, the head of thine apostles and thy disciples, and granted the keys to the

7. Translator's Note: To ignore or disobey the canon was itself considered mortal sin.

8. Translator's Note: Prospero Lambertini, pope from 1740 to 1758, associated with the moderate "Catholic Enlightenment."

Kingdom of Heaven and by thy grace hath willed that he be granted all authority that what he sealeth on Earth be sealed in Heaven and what he looseth on Earth be loosened in Heaven, who hath made us, meritless and undeserving, worthy of thine indescribable charity unto man that we be successors of the authority which he hath granted in order that we thus loose and bind what gnaws upon thy people: Thou, O King of all goodness, loose this thy servant N. by means of me, thy lowly, unworthy servant, from every excommunication and suspension and interdict into which he may have fallen, for whatever reason, and forgive him in this indulgence all he has done wrong in this life, whether in word or deed or thought. Release him from every sanction and retaliation which was merited by his deeds and omissions, by the intercession of thy most pure mother and all thy saints, for thou dost not cease to be blessed and glorified for all eternity. Amen.

29. Le Paige on the Civil Constitution of the Clergy

Louis-Adrien Le Paige

Translated by Timothy Troutner[1]

We return to the now elderly Louis-Adrien Le Paige (1712–1802) for a Jansenist defense of the Civil Constitution of the Clergy. Passed on July 12, 1790, by France's revolutionary National Assembly, the radical reforms of the Civil Constitution included a reduction of dioceses in France from 135 to 82. This sweeping redrawing of diocesan boundaries is the pretext of Le Paige's tract below.

Many of the reforms of the Civil Constitution can be read as, if not the logical conclusion of Le Paige's judicial Jansenism, at least not incompatible with it. Le Paige correctly points out there is precedent for such acts: various Catholic sovereigns have, in times of need, redrawn parish and diocesan boundaries in their realms. Alienated not only from the papacy but from the French episcopacy—which he presents as a hodgepodge of ultramontane sycophants and time-serving Gallicans—Le Paige sees a strong temporal power as the best chance for reform in the image of the pristine early church.

What was so explosive about the revolutionary National Assembly, however, was that the will of the God-anointed sovereign of the

1. The excerpt below is letter three (20 March) from *Exposition des difficultés que présente la nouvelle constitution du clergé et réponses à ces difficultés* (Paris: Leclere, 1791), 15–19.

Ancien Régime had been transformed into the will of the nation, and in this case a nation rent with ecclesiastical division and wracked with anti-clericalism. Le Paige could not possibly have foreseen quite how radical such a transference in fact was. After a long career waging ecclesiastical and political battles in the Paris *Parlement*, Le Paige seemed to revel in the Civil Constitution's radicalism and to sincerely believe it opened the door to restoring the clergy of France to their former glory, before the catastrophe of the bulls *Vineam Domini* (1705) and *Unigenitus* (1713).

By no means all Jansenists, French or otherwise, supported the Civil Constitution and the extremes to which it subjected church to state. But the fact that a number of high-profile Jansenists did defend it, and on thoroughly Jansenist grounds, forever solidified their place in the counterrevolutionary and ultramontane "chain of errors" narrative. It would be simplistic to call the Civil Constitution a "Jansenist" document. Nevertheless, it was a piece of legislation imbued with a Gallicanism that was so radicalized by the twists and turns of the "century of *Unigenitus*" that it cannot be understood apart from the history of French Jansenism.

Shaun Blanchard

Exposition of the Difficulties Presented by the New Constitution of the Clergy, and Responses to These Difficulties

Offenses of the bishops of France, who have decidedly refused the new dispositions of territory that the Nation has believed necessary. The gravity of this offense. No authority can justify it. March 20 [1791].

To refuse for more than six months to accede to the wish of the Nation, and finally, by a definitive resolution, to refuse to at least exercise its right—allegedly exclusive—to dispose of the territories for the avowed need of the Realm, is the position which the bishops of France have taken in this circumstance. Such a refusal is always an offense as culpable as it is pernicious in proportion to the considerations of utility of which it deprives the Nation. The clergy have seen it and have defied it.

The clergy could not suppose that this refusal was without consequences, nor ignore those declared by the Decrees.[2] Its counselors have foreseen this abyss, while most of the bishops effectively saw only the interest or spirit of party. These counselors will have to search their hearts and judge whether they were not flattered by the vain idea of giving a great shock to public things, and above all by the reckless attempt to force the return to the preceding state and to ancient disorders. These too-confident (at the very least!) counselors have paraded before the clergy the merits of the martyrs and pretended duties. Where, [in reality,] the clergy have only the risk of a general subversion and of rushing into this abyss, without foreseeing how they would come out of it.

The Nation has seen no more than a spirit of rebellion, the necessity of repressing it, and the impossibility of retaining the confidence of the people in ministers who are so culpable. The pretension of the clergy has been beyond what is believable. For never have they been in possession of deliberating alone on the territories of their ministry. The princes, on the contrary, up until our time and before our eyes, have had no difficulty in taking it upon themselves. We saw in 1768 that the Duke of Modena, [when] brought the topographical map of his city, simply traced with his hand what he believed to be of the best service to the people; what he planned henceforth circumscribed the parishes. In 1771, under the ministry of Chancellor M. de Maupeou, what henceforth would contain the parish of St. Magdelaine de la Ville-l'Evêque was established, at the desire of the King, from portions that the council removed from St. Roch and from St. Eustache. He was given letters patent which were recorded. These letters were then served to M. de Beaumont, whose only too ordinary resistance was deemed vain and without effect.[3] On the part of the clergy, by claiming to have the exclusive right [in these affairs], they have only raised an equivocal quarrel of incompetence that increases troubles when they could avoid them.

2. Editors' Note: The "refusal" Le Paige references is the rejection by non-juring clergy of the National Assembly's decisions to reorganize ecclesiastical territories and drastically reduce the number of the dioceses of France.

3. Editor's Note: Le Paige references here his old enemy, the fiercely anti-Jansenist Archbishop of Paris, Christophe de Beaumont (1703–81), infamous for his leadership in the Refusal of Sacraments Controversy.

It is in the same spirit that we have referred to the bishops' quite dangerous convocation of a Council—a recourse that we have never judged necessary for a point which touches only on local needs *de commodo & incommodo*.[4] Or [to their appeal to] the authority of the Pope, which was even more foreign.

We are familiar, it is true, with this natural demand, in the course of such a distressing novelty: "What then, in this moment, has happened to the weight of the consideration due to the French clergy?" But no weight, no credit, no authority can cover the offense of its culpable resistance to the Sovereign in its civil police power. *He that resisteth the power, resisteth the ordinance of God*: Romans 13:2. *For there is no power but from God: and those that are, are ordained of God*. Ibid.[5]

It is necessary to respond more precisely to this demand: *What, then, is the French clergy?* One must say that the weight of this clergy is certainly no longer today what it was in the times of its glory. The French clergy was weightier in the Church, when in 1682 it established by healthy tradition—so ably defended by Bossuet—the Declaration of the sacred foundations that distinguish the two powers, which became the code of doctrine of all the Catholic nations in this matter. This clergy was weightier when, again under Bossuet's influence, it established in 1700 the whole moral doctrine on the obligation of loving God more than all things.[6] But the shadows began to spread over the French church at the death of this great prelate. Shameful equivocations began to prevail starting from 1705 with the Bull *Vineam*. [The shadows] especially [spread] through the influence seized by the too-celebrated Decree of 1713. From that moment on, the happy ascendency of the French clergy in the Church disappeared. When we saw the generation of those who had served as judges in Israel extinguished,[7] the bishops elevated by the new factions concerned themselves only with pushing

4. Editor's Note: To the advantage or disadvantage of local needs.

5. Editor's Note: Le Paige quotes directly from the Latin Vulgate. The second phrase is actually from Romans 13:1.

6. Editor's Note: This is a reference to the triumph of a penitential theology of "contrition" (sorrow for sin due to love of God) over "attrition" (sorrow for sin due to fear of punishment). The former was associated with Jansenism and Augustinianism, and the latter with Molinism and the Jesuits.

7. Editor's Note: This is an echo of Le Paige's lifelong dedication to figurism. The

for the triumph of these two famous decrees against the complaints of Christian sincerity and against the purest language of faith and morals. This great light disappeared by degrees; they only concerned themselves with condemning *en masse* pure truths confounded with equivocations intended by intrigue, guided by the principle of no longer risking oneself in positive teaching. Thus, these two decrees were the only means for achieving their ambition, and the episcopacy succeeded in subjugating in every part of France what yet remained of light and rectitude. Today this is, then, no longer that ancient clergy, so enlightened and so worthy of its reputation, which commanded public opinion. It is an informal coalition of men who are without common principles, driven into a single party by different and often opposed motives, some Ultramontane beyond measure, others still claiming Gallican maxims; some irritated by the loss of the revenues of their pomp, others moved by a piety without discernment; some express patriots, others decided enemies of the National Assembly; some acting by personal feeling, others by *esprit de corps* or by seduction. Where is to be found, in this chaos, the character of truly ecclesiastical acts, liberty, discussion, unanimity of principles? It is thus only an appearance of authority that one finds, and not the clergy of France, when one looks into its weight and authority today in the present controversy.

Jansenist or philo-Jansenist bishops are seen as prefigured by the righteous "judges of Israel."

30. A Convulsionary View of the Antichrist

Sister Angélique Babet

Translated by Richard T. Yoder[1]

The *convulsionnaire* movement may have subsided over time, but it did not die easily. Adherents of the *œuvre des convulsions*, or the "work of the convulsions," persisted for many decades. One of the most influential *convulsionnaire* leaders of this later phase was a married *petite bourgeoise* named Angélique Babet (d. 1786), also known as "the Peasant."[2] Active in Parisian convulsionary circles as early as the mid-1730s, she eventually rose through the ranks of a particular network of *convulsionnaires* known to historians as the Pinelistes, after the ex-Oratorian priest, Michel Pinel (1708–75). The Pinelistes advanced millenarian ideas that were common to many *convulsionnaire* groups: the imminent return of the Prophet Elijah, the conversion of the Jews to convulsionary Jansenism, and the end of the world. However, the Pinelistes crafted a complex hierarchy in which every member of the sect was endowed with new, apocalyptically significant titles and

1. Soeur Angélique [Babet], "Du 25 Août 1781," in *Receuil de prédictions intéressantes, faites depuis 1733, par diverses personnes, sur plusieurs Évènements importants*, ed. Claude Desfours de la Genetière (n.p., 1792), 55–63.

2. There seems to be some division in the literature as to the precise date of Angélique's death; this author follows the date given by Jean-Pierre Chantin, December 1786. See Chantin, *Les Amis de l'Œuvre de la Vérité: Jansénisme, miracles et fin du monde au XIXe siècle* (Lyon: Presses Universitaires de Lyon, 1998), 30.

responsibilities. At the top of this hierarchy with Pinel himself were two central prophetic figures: Sister Brigitte (d. 1781?), who left after Pinel's death, and Sister Angélique, who stayed. In her later years, Angélique did not usually receive violent *secours* like most other *convulsionnaire* sisters, nor did she tend to pronounce charismatic discourses. But she did have visions, and she wrote extensively. The *Journal* of her inspired correspondence was carefully collected and copied by her devotees, especially in Lyon and its environs.[3]

Some of these visions were published posthumously in the *Receuil de prédictions intéressantes* (1792). This volume appeared under the editorial supervision of Claude Desfours de la Genetière (1757–1819), a leader in one of the Lyonnais *convulsionnaire* circles that began as Pinelistes and ended as a far more radical and self-isolated sect. Many of the southern *convulsionnaires* were more politically conservative than their Parisian cousins. Desfours de la Genetière published his collection of prophetic discourses to attack the Revolution. He and his allies considered the Civil Constitution of the Clergy (1790) to be little more than a work of the Antichrist. Napoleon's 1801 Concordat with the Pope, an acceptable compromise for most Catholics, only deepened their crisis of conscience. To this day, latter-day remnants of these irreconcilable *convulsionnaires* exist in Lyon and Paris; they are known as the Petite Église and La Famille, respectively.[4]

Angélique's vision here anticipates this permanent rupture. It

3. See, *inter alia*, Chantin, *Les Amis de l'Œuvre de la Vérité*, 7–36; Daniel Vidal, *La Morte-Raison: Isaac la Juive, convulsionnaire janséniste de Lyon, 1791–1841* (Grenoble: Éditions Jérôme Millon, 1994), 26–27, 47–48; Catherine-Laurence Maire, *Les Convulsionnaires de Saint-Médard: Miracles, convlusions, et prophéties à Paris au XVIIIe siècle* (Paris: Éditions Gallimard/Julliard, 1985), 195–96, 205–6, 266n25, 266n32; Albert Mousset, *L'étrange histoire des convulsionnaires de Saint-Médard* (Paris: Les Éditions de Minuit, 1953), 170, 183; Père Crêpe, *Notion de l'œuvre des convulsions et des secours, sur-tout par rapport à ce qu'elle est dans nos provinces du Lyonnois, Forez, Mâconnois, etc.* (n.p., 1788), 322–61.

4. Véronique Alemany, *La dernière solitaire de Port-Royal: Survivances jansénistes jusqu'au XXe siècle* (Paris: Cerf, 2013); Serge Maury, *Une secte janséniste convulsionnaire sous la Révolution française: Les Fareinistes (1783–1805)* (Paris: L'Harmattan, 2019); Nicolas Jacquard, *Les Inspirés* (Paris: Éditions Robert Laffont, 2021); Jean-Pierre Chantin, *La Famille: Une dissidence Catholique au cœur de Paris, XVIIe–XXIe siècle* (Paris: Éditions Plein Jour, 2022).

turns the long-held Jansenist dream of a General Council on its head. Instead of a council which rectifies the abuses of *Unigenitus*, this one, headed by a papal Antichrist, ends by condemning the divine work of the *convulsionnaires*. Angélique is just as opposed to the Jansenist mainstream as to the pretensions of a papacy buried in the shadows of ultramontane error. What we are left with is a commentary on the very ecclesiological issues animating much of later Jansenist thought—but in a distinctively millenarian key, and from below.

Richard T. Yoder

Extract from the Discourses of Sister Angélique

25 August, 1781

I was at High Mass at Saint Victor,[5] and I had there this vision; I saw a great assembly seated on two sides of the nave. On one side there was a multitude of prelates and ministers, and on the other, there were only ministers. At the head of the nave, and in the midst of this assembly, was an altar, upon which was seated a man vested in pontifical robes. He had around him a multitude of candles, which produced a surprising light. I remarked that there was, upon each of these candles, a written paper, as big as two fingers. . . . I asked, *Why are there strips of paper on each candle?* A voice said to me, *They are the wonders that have been done, and they name the miracles wrought by his intercession. . . .* Everything was in a great silence. I steadily watched the side where there were only ministers, and I perceived that they were our Fathers (the Appellants). They all had their gaze fixed upon these lights, with a satisfied air.

I watched as a great armchair was brought in, elevated and magnificent. Next there appeared a great man vested in pontifical robes.[6] When this pontiff had been seated, everyone saluted him, and all the

5. Translator's Note: The Abbaye de Saint-Victor de Paris, a twelfth-century foundation of Canons Regular on the left bank of the Seine.

6. Translator's Note: A second, earthly Pope in tandem with the first, spiritual Pope. These are, respectively, the False Prophet and the Beast of Revelation 13. For an earlier precedent on the theme of twinned beasts in Angélique's thought, see her discourse of 18 June 1744, Bibliothèque Nationale de France, NAF Ms. 11006, f° 59v.

cardinals sat down. A priest came with a painting, and handed it to a cardinal. They chanted a *Veni Creator*,[7] but with a beautiful chant. After the *Veni Creator*, the one who was on a beautiful chair said an *Oremus*;[8] and when he was finished, one could hear a voice which spoke with a terrible strength: *Ah! This is beautiful! Pope of Heaven! Pope of the Earth!*

Next, the one who had said the prayer stood up and said, "Brothers and friends, today we can say that the Most High has helped us in the day of evil. The heavy shadows depriving us of light made us like unto someone limping on both sides, and who could only walk in trembling. Let us remove ourselves from these spirits of darkness and falsehood, and let us follow the star which leads us to all truth."

He took the painting, which he showed to all, even unto our Fathers, and said to them: "Look, examine, and see what has never been before, and what the Almighty has never done." He caused them to examine this painting, as well as the man who was upon the altar.

And all applauded, and said, "You are right. Amen!"

Each took again his place, and the one who had made the prayer, standing up still, continued his discourse. "Brothers and friends, that which you see with your eyes and which you touch with your hands, by the marvelous power of the Most High, commands us by that same power, to annul the Formulary and the Constitution *Unigenitus*, because these two objects, execrable in the sight of God, were invented by Hell's prince of darkness alone."

All said aloud, "That is what we want. We flattered these two beasts, but we desired their end."[9]

There was in the midst of this assembly a table on which were several golden books, an inkstand, and a ring of gold, but as heavy as those

7. Translator's Note: *Veni Creator Spiritus*, the hymn to the Holy Spirit used especially on Pentecost, but also at other major events, such as papal conclaves. It was central to most *convulsionnaire* worship services.

8. Translator's Note: That is, a collect, a short prayer toward the beginning of the Mass. The whole proceeding has a liturgical character, perhaps inspired by the Mass that Angélique was witnessing.

9. Translator's Note: The "two beasts" of the Formulary and the Bull mirror the two Papal beasts of the Apocalypse in the room.

which one sees by the river.[10] They removed a book from below this table, and two cardinals presented it open to the man on the chair, who took this book, ripped out what was within, threw it to the ground, stomped upon it with his feet, and next ordered that all of it should be annihilated in the fire. Everyone with a common voice pronounced the *Anathema*[11] against that which had been enclosed in the book, and remained in silence. All these pontiffs and ministers were prostrate, and after some time, I said to the divine wisdom,[12] *I am truly at pains to know what this means.*

She replied to me, *It is the mystery of iniquity! You see by the spirit what will arrive in a time of times; and happy the one who will be judged worthy of death by that beast!*

I said, *But look, they are all prostrate and praying to God, and by the order of this man seated on the altar, they have crushed falsehood, and thrown it into the fire, so as to reestablish the truth. As this pontiff makes truth sit upon the throne, how can he make me see the mystery of iniquity?*

Wisdom said to me, *They are wolves who wear the skins of sheep to devour the sheep. All appearance of truth is not truth. The serpent is subtle, and under the appearance of truth, he condemns lies, so as to cause the triumph of the Father of Iniquity, who is the Antichrist—who, beneath false appearances of miracles, will seduce this unhappy nation,*[13] *which has not stopped desiring that God, who is the Truth, would stop talking to them.*

As she was still speaking to me, all these men who were prostrate arose and sat down. Only the one upon the armchair still stood, and he said, "My friends, we are all brothers; let us be one in heart, spirit, and sentiments. May God keep us from sowing again the tares of error and of falsehood." And, turning to the side of our Fathers, he said to them,

10. Translator's Note: Meaning, probably, a heavy ring for a chain on the docks.

11. Translator's Note: A solemn condemnation by the Church.

12. Translator's Note: *La Divine Sagesse* is a common figure in Angélique's writings. See "Suite du Journal de l'Angélique de Bb. pour l'année 1777," Bibliothèque Municipale de Lyon, Ms. 2007–2008 (2 vols.).

13. Translator's Note: Probably France, but possibly the whole of the apostate Catholic Church—or "gentility," as it was frequently referred to in the figurist language of the *convulsionnaires*.

"And you, children of the Fathers of Truth, teach us the way that leads to it. May your lights efface our shadows; may your wisdom instruct us. Let us make together an act of union, that by the profession of the same faith, we might all live in peace."

And all said, "So be it."

One of our Fathers arose and said, "We are nothing, and it is only by Jesus Christ and in Jesus Christ that we have received some lights. We have learned from our Fathers the manner of conducting ourselves in these times of shadows . . . and without ceasing we give thanks to the Most High, for having given us Fathers whom we could call cedars of Lebanon, who resisted the tempest of the Formulary and the Bull, who withstood the fury of these beasts. . . . But the same grace which sustained them and fortified them, illuminated them against that legion of Hell (the instruments of the *œuvre*),[14] who rose up amidst the truth. . . . They did what was prescribed for them to do by Jesus Christ, in declaring their feelings; and by a *Consultation* (against the *œuvre*),[15] they made it known that the *œuvre des convulsions* was not from God, but from the spirit of darkness, who leads to lies and error. And that which was predicted by our Fathers has presently appeared by a pretended reign of a false Christ. . . . Thus we can only condemn this spirit of error, and by the Holy Spirit, we can and must reject that Antichrist spoken of by the Apostle, Saint Paul, who begets only lies, and sows only division."

At the same instant, all said, "We will be of one heart and one spirit with you. We see that you are men of the Most High, and we will follow your desires, seeing that they come from God."

At these words, the one seated upon the armchair took up the large ring of gold, and said, "Let us make an alliance!"

And all of them passed their arm beneath; and the one who held the ring, who was the Pope of the Earth, said, "Let us live in the peace and union of the Father, Son, and Holy Spirit."

14. Translator's Note: That is, the *convulsionnaires*.

15. Translator's Note: This is the so-called *Consultation des Trente Docteurs*, a 1735 attack upon the *convulsionnaires* signed by thirty leading Jansenist theologians and clerics. It represented a definitive, irrevocable point of rupture within the Jansenist fold over the question of the convulsions.

Next the Pope of the Earth asked the one who was surrounded by candles if it was necessary to make a profession of faith against the reign of this Antichrist, and if he must insert there the *Consultation*. He replied, "Eh! That is why I appear today in the midst of you."

At the same moment, he made two men come in, who wrote under the dictation of the one surrounded by candles; and when all was written, one of the cardinals read it aloud. And all, after their applause, signed this formula.[16]

16. Translator's Note: Bitter irony—they have done away with one formulary only to replace it with another, this time dictated by the Antichrist himself, to attack the *convulsionnaires*.

31. The Abbé Grégoire Eulogizes Port-Royal

Henri Jean-Baptiste Grégoire

Translated by Glauco Schettini[1]

Henri Jean-Baptiste Grégoire (1750–1831) is one of the most fascinating figures of the age of Enlightenment and revolutions. A leader of the French clergy who took the oath accepting the Civil Constitution of the Clergy (1790), Grégoire was elected Bishop of Blois. After these "Constitutional" Catholic clergy were excommunicated by Pope Pius VI as schismatics, Grégoire remained a zealous pastor who resisted the dechristianization campaign and managed to survive the Reign of Terror. He held a variety of political offices from 1789 to 1820. In addition to his career as a political and ecclesiastical leader, Grégoire was an ardent abolitionist and promoter of the rights and dignity of Africans. A celebrated literary, cultural, and religious figure in French history, his body was reinterred in the Panthéon in Paris in 1989.

We present here a selection from Grégoire's *The Ruins of Port-Royal* (1809), a nostalgic eulogy for the center of Jansenism on the one-hundredth anniversary of its destruction. In passages of great tenderness, Grégoire celebrates the virtue and learning of the women of Port-Royal, the great male thinkers associated with it, and the *solitaires*.

1. Henri Jean-Baptiste Grégoire, *Les ruines de Port-Royal des Champs, en 1809, année séculaire de la destruction de ce monastère*, 2nd ed. (Paris: Levacher, 1809), 162–75. The first edition was published in 1801, with a different subtitle; the second edition was an expanded version meant to address the centennial of the 1709 destruction.

Grégoire's eulogy is evidence of a historicization of the Jansenist tradition. This historicization allowed future generations to approach Jansenist authors apart from bitter and sometimes archaic religious polemic, which consequently broadened their appeal. From works like Grégoire's, one can see how nineteenth-century French liberals could grow to admire Jansenism not as a set of theological doctrines but as a political, moral, and intellectual tradition. Leading "Jansenists" could be read and admired not for their views on penance or divine grace, but as inspirational archetypes of integrity, learning, and conscience.

Grégoire's personal affinity for Jansenism, however, was certainly also theological. His interest in the signs of the times and especially the conversion of the Jews drew deeply from Jansenist figurism. As evidenced by his ecclesiastical career, especially his leadership at the National Assembly and in the "National Councils" of 1797 and 1801, Grégoire's views of liturgy, devotions, and most of all ecclesiology had strong affinities with the radical conciliarist agenda of late Jansenism, and of the Synod of Pistoia in particular.

Though physically destroyed by a tyrant, "Port-Royal still exists, through the writings that it published and the examples it gave." Grégoire has been proven right in his prediction that Port-Royal, representing an ideal and a religious and intellectual tradition, "will again edify future generations, who will say with the Psalmist, 'These are things that we have heard and known, things our ancestors have told us'" (Psalm 77).

Shaun Blanchard

The Ruins of Port-Royal des Champs (1809)

Port-Royal is destroyed, and like the temple of Solomon, not a stone upon another is left of it. But it is a blessed land. Crowds of zealous visitors flock to it every spring.

Not far stood the court of the haughtiest of despots.[2] Virtuous men,

2. Translator's Note: The Court of Versailles, which was the residence of the kings of France until the French revolutionaries brought Louis XVI back to Paris in October 1789, and then abolished the Bourbon monarchy in 1792.

fleeing that refuge of scandal, came to this lonely place to seek sanctuary; and so did some famous penitents, who retreated from the world under the burden of remorse. That court and the Jesuits have disappeared.[3] One no longer hears of brilliant conversations, but there are still obdurate sinners.

For the sake of letters, for the honor of the human race, Port-Royal, this shelter for virtue and talent, should have survived every revolution. However, if Port-Royal had escaped destruction at the beginning of the eighteenth century, it would have still met its end at the close of the century; its religious, political, and literary merits would have been one more crime in the eyes of atheists.[4] Stormed by persecutors and vandals, Port-Royal would have seen the ax of destruction or the torch of arson fall upon its walls.

Now, every day the hand of time consumes some more of the ruins of this monastery; and the century that is just over leaves only a few traces of it to the century that follows. But the centuries that will pile up, one after the other, will honor the writings and the memory of the virtues that blessed this Thebaid of France.[5]

One day, perhaps, like-minded people will build a new edifice on these ancient foundations. But today, would anyone prevent some friends of religion, of sciences and arts, celibate by choice, from organizing, there or anywhere else, a free congregation, one without vows and with the consent of public authorities, more or less similar to those of Bérulle's sons?[6] That is, the famous congregation of which Bossuet

3. Translator's Note: The Society of Jesus was suppressed by Pope Clement XIV in 1773, at the end of a European anti-Jesuit campaign that had seen the Jesuits expelled from Portugal (1759), France (1764), and Spain, Parma, and Naples (1767). The Society was only restored in 1814.

4. Translator's Note: In 1793–94, during the time conventionally known as the Terror, the French revolutionaries targeted religious buildings and personnel and promoted a process of violent dechristianization of the country.

5. Translator's Note: In the centuries of early Christianity, the Thebaid, a province in southern Egypt, was home to the monks and hermits known as the Desert Fathers, who had an oversized influence on the development of Christian spirituality and monasticism.

6. Translator's Note: Pierre de Bérulle (1575–1629) was the founder, in 1611, of the French Oratory, a priestly congregation.

said, "There, one obeys without being subject, and governs without commanding."[7] Does anyone prevent the friends of religion from creating, as happens in England, free establishments that, acting under the government's auspices and invoking its surveillance, cultivate amidst Christian virtues every knowledge apt to hasten the progress of the human spirit?

One can easily misrepresent this project and bring disfavor upon it; this is the fate this project will meet among that crowd of people, always below or above the limits set by reason, who distort every opinion in order to refute what no one has ever claimed. In this project, they will certainly see the rebirth of cloisters, and of all the abuses that made the suppression of cloisters necessary;[8] I can already hear the taunts and the vulgarities they will utter. But why go so low as to respond to these claims and refute such people? For their ignorance or malevolence, they are incapable of justification. Why show them the difference that exists between the associations I propose and the abuses of which they will pretend to fear the rebirth?

After all, if my desire is fantastical, let me revel in this delusion. If it were to come true, there would never have been a dream more legitimate, a vow more sincere than this.

The travelers who can frequently be seen at Port-Royal are moved by the sight of these ruins as the descendants of Israel by the ruins of Jerusalem; they sing canticles in the place known as *the desert*; they pray and dine where once stood the church. Accusers will not miss the chance to cry "fanaticism" and "superstition." These are the arguments in fashion today against religion.

Arriving at the ruins of the monastery, it is impossible to find anyone who could answer the questions that piety and curiosity ask with such alacrity. Farmers in the area used to have a certain openness of mind and knowledge they had acquired by frequenting the scholars we have mentioned, who never refused to talk to the common people to

7. Translator's Note: Jacques-Bénigne Bossuet (1627–1704), the bishop of Meaux, was the court preacher to Louis XIV and the most prominent defender of Gallicanism in the seventeenth century.

8. Translator's Note: Religious orders had been suppressed during the French Revolution.

educate them; all the parish priests were once enamored with the same principles and the same love for the good, and they used to enlighten and edify this region.

All of that is over. One makes up for this inconvenience by means of an octavo book, published in 1763 and titled *Handbook for the Pilgrims to Port-Royal des Champs*.[9] The anonymous author is the Abbé Gazaignes, from the diocese of Albi, better known under the name of Philibert. He has published the four quarto volumes of the *Annals of the Society of Jesus*.[10] The work contains historical information and takes travelers by the hand, as it were, and leads them to the spots that are connected to some remarkable events. The book successfully employs scriptural passages to allude to Port-Royal's adversaries, as in the following example: "We are not like the many who corrupt God's word. We preach it with complete sincerity, etc. As God has chosen us and entrusted his gospel to us, we do not speak to please men, but God, who sees the bottom of our hearts. When people curse us, we respond with blessings, etc."[11]

In the *Handbook*, historical notices are followed by moving prayers.[12] In the book titled *Lamentations over the Destruction of Port-Royal* there is one for the Jesuits.[13] Religion confesses this memory, which it alone has inspired.

During one of these pious trips, someone asked whether it is possible to honor a saint who is not canonized. Cardinal Bellarmine[14] already had an answer:

9. Translator's Note: Jean-Antoine Gazaignes, *Manuel des pèlerins de Port-Royal des Champs* (Au Désert, 1767); see the excerpt in this volume.

10. Translator's Note: Jean-Antoine Gazaignes, *Annales de la Société des soi-disans Jésuites*, 5 vols. (Paris, 1764–71).

11. Editor's Note: The first reference is to 2 Cor 2:17, and the second to 1 Thess 2:4. The final sentence paraphrases multiple New Testament passages.

12. There exists the manuscript of a work titled *Office and Pilgrimage to the Saints of Port-Royal*. It contains hymns, prose, and other pieces that could be used if the *Handbook* were ever to be reprinted.

13. Translator's Note: Pierre Boyer and Jean-Baptiste Le Sesne d'Étemare, *Gemissements d'une âme vivement touchée de la destruction du saint monastère de Port-Royal des Champs en 1710* (n.p., n.d.).

14. Translator's Note: Cardinal Robert Bellarmine (1542–1621), a Jesuit, was among

It is permitted to honor him with a particular cult, but not with a public service performed in the name of the church. 1. It is permitted to believe and call *saint* or *blessed* someone who has not been canonized, but not to talk of him as if he had been added by the church to the register of saints. 2. It is permitted to invoke him even if other people can hear, but not in the course of public supplications. 3. It is not permitted to have a public celebration in his honor, but it is permitted to give testimony to a special joy on the day of his birth to heaven, and to pay special attention to the things of God by commemorating this saint. 4. It is permitted to have his image and venerate it, but not to put it in churches; nor is it permitted to display his relics [in the church], but it is permitted to preserve and honor them. Such is the practice of the Catholic Church. Upon a martyr's death, the faithful would hasten to get his relics; in the same way, upon the death of a man who was celebrated for the sanctity of his conduct, many faithful show their devotion by kissing his hands or his feet, and by preserving a strip of his garments as a relic; this has never been forbidden.[15]

These principles, clearly established by one of the most famous writers who ever honored the Society of Jesus, justify the tender devotion that will rise upon the tombs and upon the debris of this monastery, on which is engraved, so to speak, the memory of the virtues that made this place immortal. Everything here speaks of God, of those who loved Him, and of the sorrow of loving anything else but Him—and he does not love God who is attached to anything the world can deprive him of.[16]

Meditation seems to inhabit this land where long ago resounded the melodious voices and the heavenly chants of the virgins. Silence reigns here today, barely interrupted, every now and then, by the slat of a mill or the wails of a solitary pigeon that dwells in the forest. How could anyone walk through this land without feeling the most piercing emotion?

On this terrace of the house of the *Granges*, where so many scholars devoted to work and study meditated upon the days of eternity, how

---

the most prominent figures of the counter-reformation church and a skilled defender of Roman orthodoxy.

15. See the work of Bellarmine, *Sur la beatification et la canonisation des saints*, Paris, 1613, vol. 2, ch. 10, p. 703.

16. Duguet, *Explication de la passion.*

many times have I visited the ancient trees, planted by d'Andilly in person, which used to welcome the *solitaires* under their shade![17] How many times, as the sun descended, have I sat on top of the boulders that overlook the road from Chevreuse and reflected on the sunset of life! How many times have I surrendered myself to the feelings inspired by the sight of these places, and thought that I was perhaps contemplating this lonely land for the last time! Whether my eyes dive from the hills all around into the valley, or from the valley look to the horizon, which is circumscribed by the hills and isolates me from the universe, there is no place where I do not encounter my memories. The eloquence of these ruins pierces my soul with a religious feeling, and past and future, in a state of tumult, flood it. One forgets about death in the places that it ravages most frequently, cities; here I can still find its image; hope robs it of its gloomy appearance; and death becomes nothing more than the passage from darkness to light, from fear to certitude, from desire to reality, from exile to the promised land.

In that grotto, Sacy, always valetudinary, used to repeat to God the prayer he had borrowed from Saint Fulgentius:[18] *Da mihi modo patientiam et postea indulgentiam*; give me patience, and then have mercy on me.

On these paths, I encounter Hamon, who is bringing the succor of his art and his purse, and the consolations of charity, to the ailing.[19]

Here, fatigued by countless disputations, Nicole, with his usual kindness, invites Arnaud to lay down his quill, and Arnaud replies with vivacity, "Don't we have eternity to rest?"[20]

Here, on a path out of the way, I glimpse Pascal.[21] Perhaps he is

17. Translator's Note: The Solitaires of Port-Royal were ascetics who lived on the monastery's premises. Robert Arnauld d'Andilly (1589–1674) was one of them, a statesman and a writer.

18. Translator's Note: Louis-Isaac Lemaistre de Sacy (1613–84), who translated the Bible into French.

19. Translator's Note: Jean Hamon (1618–87), a doctor of Jansenist convictions.

20. Translator's Note: Pierre Nicole (1625–95) and Antoine Arnauld (1612–94), among Port-Royal's leading theologians.

21. Translator's Note: Blaise Pascal (1623–62), one of the most prominent thinkers of seventeenth-century France. He wrote on philosophy, theology, science, and mathematics.

solving a problem that brought many a scholar of geometry to despair, or developing a new demonstration of the divinity of Christianity.

And a bit further away, with Tillemont and Lancelot, wander Racine, La Bruyère, Despréaux, and Dodart, who have come to visit their friends.[22] Erudition, genius, good taste, and piety preside over their meeting. In those days, men of letters also endeavored to become better men; today, they just crave to shine. In those days, they yearned less for celebrity than for a reputation of integrity; one could seldom tell the philosophers of their time, "Preceptor of humankind, you preach virtue to me; I will read your works. But please hide your actions from my sight."

Echoes of this desert, ancient trees, you could not retain the memory of these famous men! If you could, how respectfully would I come ask you questions, and collect the tales you would have kept!

Man has divided into discrete periods that succession of beings that is known as *time*. By returning to the same epoch again and again, he cannot add anything or change the nature of things past; but he likes fixing his imagination upon times gone by, to which he attaches memories his soul holds dear, and moral and religious ideas. The course of seasons, of years, of centuries reminds him that fleeting are his days on this earth, which he only gently touches until the earth receives his mortal remains; it reminds him that soon enough he will fall for good.

This is the reason why almost all peoples have established periodic celebrations, such as the feasts that were celebrated with great pomp in Rome every century. A public crier announced them this way: "Come to a feast the likes of which you have never seen and will never see again." In the corner of Asia, the only people that adored the real God [the Jews] observed a jubilee year every fifty years; this institution took a new form in the Catholic tradition, which celebrated its first jubilee in 1300. In 1640, the Jesuits celebrated the centennial of their establishment, even in the Philippines.[23]

22. Translator's Note: Louis-Sébastien Le Nain de Tillemont (1637–98), a historian; Claude Lancelot (1615–95), who wrote on grammar and ancient languages; Jean Racine (1639–99), a famous playwright; Jean-Louis Barbeau de la Bruyère (1710–81), a historian and hagiographer; Nicolas Boileau-Despréaux (1636–1711), a writer; and Denis Dodart (1634–1707), a doctor.

23. *Histoira de Philipinas de la compañia de Jesus: Segunda parte*, by father Murello Velarde, book 2, ch. 13, pp. 123 f.

. . . At the extraordinary assembly of the clergy of France of 1782, occupying a pulpit that still seemed to resound with Bossuet's majestic accents, the bishop of Senez, Beauvais, orator of the clergy, explained the reasons why citizens must be attached to their country, and the specific reasons why we must be even more attached to ours.[24] He recalled the doctrine that the clergy of France sanctioned in their famous declaration of 1682, and consecrated its centennial by solemnly professing the same doctrine.[25]

Although the centennial of Port-Royal's destruction brings us to tears, there is also reason for consolation, and for tempering bitterness. Port-Royal was a beacon that shed its light everywhere; but this light offended envy, which combined with hatred to annihilate it; and they were successful. In the eyes of faith, this all makes sense.

But Port-Royal still exists, through the writings that it published and the examples it gave. In the writings of Port-Royal, the truths we should believe and the virtues we should practice as Christians and citizens shine bright; these writings will survive across the centuries and continue to educate our most remote descendants. And the examples of Port-Royal, collected by historians, will again edify future generations, who will say with the Psalmist, "These are things that we have heard and known, things our ancestors have told us."[26] They told us of these learned men, of these warriors, of these Christian virgins, who used to retreat from the world and ready themselves for eternity. "Since we are overwhelmed by so great a cloud of witnesses, let us free ourselves from our burdens . . . and let us run with patience on the path that lies ahead of us, keeping our eyes fixed upon Jesus, the author and finisher of faith."[27]

How sweet is the thought that those who have left this life to begin a better one make up with us a single family, are tied to us by ties of

24. Translator's Note: Jean-Baptiste-Charles-Marie de Beauvais (1731–90), bishop of Senez. The extraordinary assembly of the clergy of France of 1682 had adopted the Gallican *Declaration of the Clergy of France*, drafted by Bossuet. Grégoire begins this sentence with "let me immediately repeat" but we delete this since he is referring to a conversation mentioned before this selection begins.

25. See the *Procès verbal de l'assemblée extraordinaire de 1782*, p. 17.

26. Psalm 77.

27. Hebrews 12:1.

charity, and take interest in our needs; they will be our protectors, if we are their imitators. As St. Jerome said of pilgrimages to the Holy Land, what is praiseworthy is not having been to Jerusalem, but having lived well there. What is the point of visiting this famous desert if you do not work indefatigably to accumulate good works for heaven and forget that the ground flees under your feet and devours its inhabitants? And perhaps some people are already planning to speak ill of these pilgrimages, from which, they say, it would be wise to abstain.

The feelings that will always make us remember Port-Royal grow stronger now, as the first centennial of its destruction approaches, and gain new energy from our present circumstances. Our august religion commands us to respond to evil with good. The sacrificers of Port-Royal bequeathed their fury to the ensuing century; their victims, falling under the sword of iniquity, bequeathed their unwavering sweetness. The men who continue to offend truth and its defenders must especially be the object of your kindness and your prayers.

Addressing your vows to the Everlasting, do not forget the disasters of a church that was once the very model of Christianity.[28] Did the pastors who are deaf to the voice of piety and of their country, and who perpetuate internal divisions, contribute to the church's ruin? Are they, in the decrees of heaven, the culpable instruments of vengeance? A great man warns us that religion, like a traveler on earth, only asks for the freedom to pass through. Lands where religion once flourished are now enshrouded in the darkness of error and infidelity. Whatever destiny divine justice or mercy assigns to us, let us remain inviolably united to this Catholic Church, which, across the ages, raises her radiant head amidst the sects that rise one after the other and collapse around her. Confident in the promises of her divine founder, this Church will march on until the end of time.

28. Editor's Note: Grégoire here references the misfortunes that have befallen the Gallican Church, that is, the church of France.

APPENDIX: IMAGES

FIGURE 1. Philippe de Champaigne. *Portrait of Mère Angélique Arnauld* (1654). Courtesy of the Musée du Louvre, via *Wikimedia Commons.* Public Domain.

The Abbess of Port-Royal is shown here seated, albeit possessed of the unmistakable vigor that characterized her reforms.

FIGURE 2. Magdeleine Horthemels. *View of Port-Royal des Champs* (early eighteenth century). *Wikimedia Commons.* Public Domain.

A commemorative depiction of Port-Royal des Champs that became popular after its destruction in 1709–11.

FIGURE 3. Anonymous. *Expulsion of the Nuns of Port-Royal and the Destruction of the Abbey* (early eighteenth century). Courtesy of the Bibliothèque Nationale de France via *Gallica.BNF.fr.*

This dire scene combines the dispersal of the nuns of Port-Royal (1709) and the convent's eventual destruction (1711). Jesuits burn Jansenist books and encourage the soldiers to manhandle the nuns, who share an intimate farewell.

FIGURE 4. Anonymous. *The Custom of the Jesuits* (mid-eighteenth century). Courtesy of the Bibliothèque Nationale de France via *Gallica.BNF.fr.*

A dragon spews forth regicidal Jesuits, knives in hand, who are described here as "eternal enemies of the supreme powers"—that is, both God and king.

FIGURE 5. Anonymous. A Representation of the Appeal in Holland (1750s–1790s). Courtesy of the Rijksmuseum via *Wikimedia Commons*. Public Domain.

Pasquier Quesnel appears at the center of an imagined procession of appellant clergy, including representatives of the Church of Utrecht, on their way to the long-hoped-for ecumenical council that would overturn Unigenitus.

FIGURE 6. Jakob Folkema. Frontispiece for the *Nouvelles ecclésiastiques*, 1728, 1729, 1730 (printed 1730). Courtesy of the Bibliothèque Nationale de France via *Gallica.BNF.fr.*

In the first of many annual frontispieces, the Nouvelles ecclésiastiques *presents scenes of persecution endured by Jansenists.*

FIGURE 7. Anonymous. Portrait of François de Pâris. (c. 1727–1740). © The Trustees of the British Museum.

The Deacon François de Pâris is shown here as a penitent and, implicitly, an intercessor praying for his devotees.

FIGURE 8. Jean Frédéric Bernard and Bernard Picart. *The Cemetery of Saint-Médard and Different Agitations of the Convulsionnaires.* In Antoine Banier and Jean-Baptiste Le Mascrier, *Histoire générale des cérémonies, moeurs, et coutumes religieuses de tous les peuples du monde*, Vol. IV (Paris: Rollin Fils, 1741). Courtesy of the Pitt Theological Library, Emory University. Public Domain.

Above, a representation of the convulsionary miracles taking place at the Cemetery of Saint-Médard; below, a scene of convulsionnaires *worshiping together in private after the cemetery's closure.*

FIGURE 9. Anonymous. *Ecclesiastical Pride Confounded by the Parlement* (mid-eighteenth century). Courtesy of the Bibliothèque Nationale de France via *Gallica.BNF.fr.*

During the Refusal of Sacraments Controversy (1749–56) and the expulsion of the Society of Jesus (1761–64), the Parlement took a leading role in advancing Jansenist agendas. Here, they are inspired by the Holy Spirit—just like an ecumenical council.

FIGURE 10. Carlo Lasinio. The Synod of Pistoia (1786). *Wikimedia Commons.* Public Domain.

A view of the Synod of Pistoia, presided over by Bishop Scipione de' Ricci.

FIGURE 11. Anonymous. *Allegory of Emperor Joseph II's Toleranzpatent* (1786). *Wikimedia Commons.* Public Domain.

Jansenist-influenced reformers in the Holy Roman Empire supported religious toleration, granted by Joseph II in 1781. This watercolor, in which the Emperor points to a crucifix in front of a crowd of many different kinds of believers, expresses the evangelistic hopes behind that policy. The narrow-armed crucifix here is a type sometimes dubiously referred to as the "Jansenist crucifix."

FIGURE 12. Charles Motte. *The Abbé Grégoire Swears His Oath* (1819). Courtesy of the Bibliothèque Nationale de France via *Gallica.BNF.fr.*

The Abbé Grégoire, having been elected in 1819 as a Deputy for Isère, is depicted here swearing his oath of loyalty to Louis XVIII as one part Jansenist bishop, one part Napoleonic senator, and one part Republican regicide.

BIBLIOGRAPHY

Archival Sources

Bibliothèque de l'Arsenal, Ms. 1145. "Sur les Cérémonies Chinoises Épître."

Bibliothèque Municipale de Lyon, Ms. 2007–2008 (2 vols.). "Suite du Journal de l'Angélique de Bb. pour l'année 1777."

Bibliothèque nationale de France, BNF f. fr. 17791. Letter of Mère Angélique Arnauld to Louis Macquet, 4 January 1635.

Bibliothèque nationale de France, BNF Ms.fr. 23500. *Nouvelles ecclésiastiques*, January 1690, f°34 et sq.

Bibliothèque nationale de France, BNF Ms.fr. 23503. *Nouvelles ecclésiastiques*, 1693, f°89–90.

Bibliothèque nationale de France, BNF NAF Ms. 11006, f° 59v. Soeur Angélique, discourse of 18 June 1744.

Primary Sources

Actes et décrets du ii. concile provincial d'Utrecht tenu le 13 septembre M.DCC. LXIII. dans la Chapelle de l'Eglise Paroissiale de Sainte Gertrude, à Utrecht. Utrecht: Aux dépens de la Compagnie, 1764.

Appeal of March 5, 1717, in Jacques Parguez, *La bulle Unigenitus et le jansénisme politique: Avant-coureur de la Révolution français*. Paris: Maurice Glomeau, 1936, 203–10.

Arnauld, Agnès. *L'Esprit du monastère de Port-Royal*. In *Les constitutions du monastère de Port-Royal du Saint Sacrement*, 297–420. Mons: Gaspard Migeot, 1665.

Arnauld, Agnès. *L'image d'une religieuse parfaite et d'une imparfaite, avec les occupations intérieures pour toute la journée*. Paris: Charles Savreux, 1665.

Arnauld, Angélique. *Lettres de la révérende mère Marie Angélique Arnauld, abbesse et réformatrice de Port-Royal*. Vol. 1. Utrecht, 1742.

Arnauld, Angélique. *Œuvres completes*. Vol. 1, *Lettres*. Edited by Jean Lesaulnier, Françoise Pouge-Bellais, and Anne-Claire Volongo. Paris: Classiques Garnier, 2020.

Arnauld, Antoine. *De la fréquente communion, ou les sentimens des Pères, des Papes, et des Conciles, touchant l'usage des Sacrements de Pénitence et d'Eucharistie, sont fidèlement exposez: pour servir d'adresse aux personnes qui pensent sérieusement à se convertir à Dieu, et aux Pasteurs et Confesseurs *zelez pour le bien des âmes*. 7th ed. Paris: Pierre le Petit, 1683. First edition 1643.

Arnauld, Antoine. *Seconde lettre de M. Arnauld, Docteur de Sorbonne, à un Duc et Pair de France. Pour servir de réponse à plusieurs Écrits, qui ont été publiés contre sa première Lettre; sur ce qui est arrivé à un Seigneur de la Cour, dans un Paroisse de Paris*. 2nd ed. Paris, 1655.

Arnauld, Antoine, and Pierre Nicole. *Réponse au P. Annat, Provincial des Jésuites. Touchant les cinq propositions attribuées à M. l'Évesque d'Ipre*. N.p., 1654.

Arnauld d'Andilly, Angélique de Saint-Jean. *Relation de captivité d'Angélique de Saint-Jean Arnauld D'Andilly*. Edited by Louis Cognet. Paris: Gallimard, 1954. First edition 1711.

Arnauld d'Andilly, Angélique de Saint-Jean. *Writings of Resistance*. Edited and translated by John J. Conley. Chicago: University of Chicago Press, 2015.

Arnauld d'Andilly, Robert. *Les Vies des saints Pères des deserts et de quelques saintes écrites par des Pères de l'Église et autres anciens auteurs ecclésiastiques*. 2 Vols. Paris: J. Camusat et P. Le Petit, 1647–53.

Augustine of Hippo. *De Genesi ad litteram libri duodecim. Sant'Agostino: S. Aurelii Augustini Opera Omnia*. Augustinus.it/latino.

Augustine of Hippo. *Les Confessions de S. Augustin, Traduites en François, Par Monsieur Arnauld d'Andilly*. Translated by Robert Arnauld d'Andilly. Paris: La Veuve Jean Camusat and Pierre le Petit, 1649.

Augustine of Hippo. *Letters. Sant'Agostino: S. Aurelii Augustini Opera Omnia*. Augustinus.it/latino.

Augustine of Hippo. *On the Profit of Believing*. Translated by C. L. Cornish. In *Nicene and Post-Nicene Fathers, First Series*. Vol. 3. Edited by Philip Schaff. Buffalo, NY: Christian Literature, 1887. New Advent.org. Revised and edited for *New Advent* by Kevin Knight.

Augustine of Hippo. *On the Sermon on the Mount*. Book 2. Translated by William Findlay. In *Nicene and Post-Nicene Fathers, First Series*. Vol. 6. Edited by Philip Schaff. Buffalo, NY: Christian Literature, 1888. NewAdvent.org. Revised and edited for *New Advent* by Kevin Knight.

Augustine of Hippo. *Sermons. Sant'Agostino: S. Aurelii Augustini Opera Omnia*. Augustinus.it/latino.

Augustine of Hippo. *Tractates on John* 96. Translated by John Gibb. In *Nicene and Post-Nicene Fathers, First Series*. Vol. 7. Edited by Philip Schaff. Buffalo, NY: Christian Literature, 1888. New Advent.org. Revised and edited for *New Advent* by Kevin Knight.

[Babet], Sœur Angélique. "Du 25 Août 1781." In *Receuil de prédictions intéressantes, faites depuis 1733, par diverses personnes, sur plusieurs Évènements importants*. Edited by Claude Desfours de la Genetière. N.p., 1792, 55–63.

Buñuel, Luis, dir. *La Voie lactée*. Fraia Film, 1969. 1 hour, 41 minutes, 31 seconds. https://tubitv.com.

Cambout de Pontchâteau, Sébastien-Joseph du. *La Morale pratique des Jésuites, second volume, divisé en sept parties, où l'on représente leur conduite dans la Chine, dans le Japon, dans l'Amérique, et dans l'Éthiopie, le tout tiré de Livres très-autorisez, ou de pièces très-authentiques*. Cologne: Gervinus Quentel, 1683.

Carré de Montgeron, Louis-Basile. *La vérité des miracles opérés par l'intercession de M. de Pâris et des autres appellans, démontrée avec des observations sur le phénomène des convulsions*. Vol. 3. Cologne: Librairies de la Compagnie, 1747.

Clément, Augustin-Jean-Charles. *Journal de correspondances et voyages d'Italie et d'Espagne, pour la paix de l'Eglise, en 1758, 1768 et 1769*. Paris: 1802.

Climent i Avinent, Joseph. *Coleccion de las obras del il.mo Senor Don Joseph Climent, del consejo de S.M. y Obispo de Barcelona*. Vol. 1. Madrid: Imprenta Real, 1788.

Crêpe, Père. *Notion de l'œuvre des convulsions et des secours, sur-tout par rapport à ce qu'elle est dans nos provinces du Lyonnois, Forez, Mâconnois, etc*. N.p., 1788.

de Colonia, Dominique, and Louis Patouillet. *Dictionnaire des livres jansénistes, ou qui favorisent le Jansénisme*. Vol. 2. Antwerp: Jean-Baptiste Verdussen, 1752.

"De Paris." *Les Nouvelles ecclésiastiques*. 7 August 1749. 125–28. https://*gallica.bnf.fr*.

Denzinger, Heinrich, ed. *Compendium of Creeds, Definitions, and Declarations on Matters of Faith and Morals*. 43rd ed. Revised, enlarged, and, in collaboration with Helmut Hoping, edited by Peter Hünermann for the original bilingual edition. Edited by Robert Fastiggi and Anne Englund Nash for the English edition. San Francisco: Ignatius Press, 2012.

D'Étemare, Jean-Baptiste Le Sesne des Ménilles. *Explications de quelques prophéties touchant la conversion future des juifs, et spécialemente de celle du ch. 11. de l'épître aux romains, avec une Réponse à des difficultez qui ont été proposées sur cette Explication*. N.p., 1724.

Duguet, Jacques-Joseph. *Institution d'un prince, ou Traité des qualités, des vertus & des devoirs d'un souverain. Par la M. l'Abbe Duguet. Nouvelle edition. Avec la Vie de l'Auteur*. London: Jean Nourse, 1750. First edition 1739.

Duvergier de Hauranne, Jean-Ambroise. *Théologie familière, avec divers autres petits traitez de dévotion*. Paris: François Muguet, 1669. First edition 1644.

Duvergier de Hauranne, Jean-Ambroise. *Lettres chrestiennes et spirituelles de Messire Jean Duverger de Hauranne, Abbé de St-Cyran*. Rouen: Jean Viret, Jacques Besongne, and Clément Malassis, 1645.

Gazaignes, Jean-Antoine. *Manuel des Pèlerins de Port-Royal*. Au Désert, 1767.

Grange, Ursule de la [pseud.]. *Lettre d'une dame de Paris au Pape sur Constitution de 8. Septembre 1713 contre* Le Nouveau Testament, avec des Réflexions morales. *Nouvelle edition*. N.p., 1714.

Grégoire, Henri Jean-Baptiste. *Les ruines de Port-Royal des Champs, en 1809, année séculaire de la destruction de ce monastère*. Paris: Levacher, 1809.

Gudvert, Jacques. *Jesus-Christ sous l'anatheme et sous l'excommunication*. Amsterdam: Nicolas Potier, 1731.

Hamon, Jean. *Entretiens d'une âme avec Dieu; qui comprennent un grand nombre de prières pleines de l'esprit des divines Écritures et des Saints Pères, et exprimées pour la plûpart dans leurs propres paroles, nouvelle edition*. Avignon, 1740.

Huysmans, Joris-Karl. *Là-bas*. Paris: P.V. Stock. 1891.

Jacquemont, François. *Instruction sur la vérité et les avantages de la religion Chrétienne; suivie d'une Instruction historique sur les maux qui affligent l'Église, et sur les remèdes que Dieu promet de ces maux, par la Tradition et par l'Écriture*. N.p., 1795.

Jacquemont, François. *Avis aux fidèles sur la conduit qu'ils doivent tenir dans les disputes qui affligent l'Église*. France, 1796.

Jansen, Cornelius. *Augustinus seu doctrina S. Augustini de humanae naturae sanitate, ægritudine, medicinâ adversus Pelagianos & Massilienses*. Vol. 2. Leuven: Jacobus Zeger, 1640.

Jansen, Cornelius. *The Predestination of Humans and Angels* (Augustinus, *Tome III, Book IX)*. Translated by Guido Stucco. Washington, DC: The Catholic University of America Press, 2022.

Lambert, Bernard. *Avis aux fidèles, ou principes propres à diriger leurs sentimens et leur conduit dans les circonstances présentes*. Paris: Dufresne, 1791.

Lambert, Bernard. *Avertissement aux fidèles, sur les signes qui annoncent que tout se dispose pour le retour d'Israël, et l'exécution des menaces faites aux Gentils apostats*. Paris: Le Clère, 1793.

Lefranc, Anne. "Relation de la maladie et de la guérison d'Anne le Franc." In *Recueil des Miracles opérés au tombeau de M. de Pâris, Diacre, avec les Requêtes présentées à Monsieur de Vintimille Archevêque de Paris, par Messieurs les Curés de cette Ville, et un Discours Préliminaire sur les Miracles*. Vol. 1. Utrecht, 1733, 301–9

Le Paige, Louis-Adrien. *Paradoxes, sophismes, déguisemens, faux principes, principes dangereux pour la tranquillité de l'État, calomnies, fausses citations, qui sont contenues dans une Instruction Pastorale que M. l'Archev. de Paris a signée & adoptée, qu'il a lûe publiquement dans l'Église de Conflans, lieu de son exil, qu'il a fait imprimer à Chartres, et qu'il a distribuée dans Paris et au dehors*. N.p., 1756.

Le Paige, Louis-Adrien. *Exposition des difficultés que présente la nouvelle constitution du clergé et réponses à ces difficultés*. Paris: Leclere, 1791.

Mansi, Giovanni Domenico, et al., eds. *Sacrorum conciliorum nova et amplissima collectio*. 54 vols. Paris: H. Welter, 1901–27.

Montherlant, Henri de. *Port-Royal*. Paris: Gallimard, 1954.

Nicole, Pierre. "Règles pour les tems d'épreuve et de persécution." In Jean Hamon and Pierre Nicole, *Principes de conduite dans la défense de la vérité par Monsieur Hamon, avec des règles pour les tems d'épreuve et de persécution par M. Nicole*. N.p., 1734, 161–77.

Pascal, Blaise. *The Thoughts of Blaise Pascal, Translated from the Text of M. Auguste Molinier*. Translated by C. Kegan Paul. London: Kegan Paul, Trench, and Co., 1885

Pascal, Jacqueline. *A Rule for Children and Other Writings*. Edited and translated by John J. Conley. Chicago: University of Chicago Press, 2003.

Pereira de Figueiredo, António. *O Novo Testamento de Jesu Christo, traduzido em Portuguez segundo a Vulgata, com varias annotações, históricas, dogmáticas, e moraes, e apontadas as differenças mais notáveis do original greco. Por*

Antonio Pereira de Figueiredo, deputado ordinário da Real Meza Censoria. Vol. 3, *Que comprehende os Actos dos Apostolos, e a Epistola de S. Paulo aos Romanos.* Lisbon: Na Regia Offic. Typograf., 1779.

Quesnel, Pasquier. *Le Nouveau Testament en français avec des réflexions morales sur chaque verset.* [Suite du] Vol. II. Amsterdam: Joseph Nicolai, 1727.

Restif de la Bretonne, Nicolas. *Monsieur Nicolas, ou le cœur humain dévoilé.* Vol. 2. Paris: Isidore Liseux, 1883. First edition 1796–97.

Stella, Pietro, ed. *Atti e decreti del concilio diocesano di Pistoia dell'anno 1786.* Vol. 1. Florence: Olschki, 1986.

Wittola, Marx Anton. *Schreiben eines österreichischen Pfarrers über die Toleranz nach den Grundsätzen der katholischen Kirche.* Vienna: Sonnleithnerischen, 1781.

Secondary Sources

Abercrombie, Nigel. *The Origins of Jansenism.* New York: Oxford University Press, 1936.

Agten, Els. *The Catholic Church and the Dutch Bible: From the Council of Trent to the Jansenist Controversy (1564–1733).* Leiden: Brill, 2020.

Aiardi, Alessandro, ed. *Scipione de' Ricci e la realtà pistoiese della fine del Settecento: Immagini e documenti.* Pistoia: Edizioni del Comune di Pistoia, 1986.

Alberigo, Giuseppe. *Lo sviluppo della dottrina sui poteri nella Chiesa universale: Momenti essenziali tra il XVI e il XIX secolo.* Rome: Herder, 1964.

Alemany, Véronique. *La dernière Solitaire de Port-Royal: Survivances jansénistes jusqu'au XXe siècle.* Paris: Cerf, 2013.

Alimento, Antonella. "Il 'secolo dell'*Unigenitus*'? Politica e religione in Francia nel Secolo dei Lumi." *Rivista di Storia e Letteratura Religiosa* 2 (2001): 323–46.

Allen, Rupert M. A. F. "The Last Sentinels of Gallicanism: The Evolution of La Petite Église from Episcopal Protest to Lay Church." Master's thesis, University of Bristol, 2020.

Amadieu, Jean-Baptiste and Simon Icard, eds. *Du jansénisme au modernisme. La bulle* Auctorem fidei, *1794, pivot du magistère romain.* Paris: Beauchesne, 2020.

Andurand, Olivier. *La grande affaire: Les évêques de France face à l'Unigenitus.* Rennes: Presses universitaires de Rennes, 2017.

Appolis, Émile. *Le 'tiers parti' catholique au XXVIIIe siècle: Entre jansénistes et zelanti.* Paris: Picard, 1960.

Appolis, Émile. *Les jansénistes espagnols.* Bordeaux: Sobodi, 1966.

Aretin, Karl Otmar F. von. "Cattolicesimo riformatore, illuminismo cattolico e assolutismo illuminato." In *Il sinodo di Pistoia del 1786*, edited by Claudio Lamioni, 1–9. Rome: Herder Editrice e Libreria, 1991.

Armogathe, Jean-Robert. *Études sur Antoine Arnauld (1612–1694).* Paris: Classiques Garnier, 2018.

Barnett, S. J. *The Enlightenment and Religion: The Myths of Modernity.* Manchester: Manchester University Press, 2003.

Baudin, Tessel M. *Surrealism and the Occult: Occultism and Western Esotericism in the Work and Movement of André Breton*. Amsterdam: Amsterdam University Press, 2014.

Beales, Derek. *Joseph II*. 2 vols. Cambridge: Cambridge University Press, 1987, 2009.

Beales, Derek. "Joseph II and Josephism." In *Enlightenment and Reform in Eighteenth-Century Europe*, edited by Derek Beales, 287–308. London: I.B. Tauris, 2005.

Belvederi, Raffaele. "Il giansenismo negli anni di Benedetto XIV." In *Benedetto XIV (Prospero Lambertini): Convegno internazionale di studi storici, sotto il patrocinio dell'Archidiocesi di Bologna: Cento, 6-9 dicembre 1979*, 1:379–443. Cento, Italy: Centro Studi Girolamo Baruffaldi, 1981.

Bergin, Joseph. *The Politics of Religion in Early Modern France*. New Haven: Yale University Press, 2014.

Berlis, Angela, and Dirk Schoon. "Jansenism across the Border: The Interaction in the 17th and 18th Century between Catholic Theologians in France and in the Dutch Republic." *Internationale kirchliche Zeitschrift* 99 (2009): 145–69.

Bini, Enrico. "*Mysteria mystice*: La pronuncia del canone della messa. Dibattiti teologici ed esperimenti liturgici nel settecento Italiano." *Memorie Teologiche* 8 (2015): 57–153.

Bireley, Robert. *The Jesuits and the Thirty Years War: Kings, Courts, and Confessors*. New York: Cambridge University Press, 2003.

Blanchard, Jean-Vincent. *Éminence: Cardinal Richelieu and the Rise of France*. New York: Bloomsbury, 2011.

Blanchard. Shaun. "John Lingard's Dislike of Newman: An Enlightened Cisalpine Confronts the Second Spring." In *Scholar, Sage, Saint: The Legacy of John Henry Newman*, edited by Kenneth L. Parker, Christopher Cimorelli, and Elizabeth Huddleston. Washington, DC: The Catholic University of America Press and the National Institute for Newman Studies, anticipated 2025.

Blanchard, Shaun. "Settling Old Scores: *Pastor Aeternus* as the Final Defeat of Early Modern Opponents of Papalism." *Newman Studies Journal* 17, no. 1 (2020): 24–51.

Blanchard, Shaun. "The Popes and the Enlightenment." In *The Cambridge History of the Papacy*, vol. 1, edited by Joëlle Rollo-Koster and Iben Forresberg-Schmidt. Cambridge: Cambridge University Press, forthcoming 2025.

Blanchard, Shaun. *The Synod of Pistoia and Vatican II: Jansenism and the Struggle for Catholic Reform*. Oxford: Oxford University Press, 2020.

Blanning, T. C. W. *Reform and Revolution in Mainz*. Cambridge: Cambridge University Press, 1974.

Bloch, Marc. *The Royal Touch: Sacred Monarchy and Scrofula in England and France*. Translated by J. E. Anderson. Abingdon: Routledge, 2015. First English edition 1973. French 1961.

Boutry, Phillippe. "Autour d'un bicentenaire: La bulle *Auctorem fidei* (28 août 1794) et sa traduction française (1850) par le futur cardinal Clément

Villecourt." *Mélanges de l'École française de Rome: Italie-Méditerranée* 106, no. 1 (1994): 203–51.

Boutry, Phillippe. "Tradition et autorité dans la théologie catholique au tournant des xviiie et xixe siècles: La bulle *Auctorem fidei* (28 août 1794)." In *Histoire et théologie: Actes de la Journée d'études de l'Association française d'histoire religieuse contemporaine*, edited by Jean-Dominique Durand, 59–82. Paris: Beauchesne, 1994.

Bouwsma, William J. *The Waning of the Renaissance, 1550–1640*. New Haven: Yale University Press, 2000.

Brading, David A. "El jansenismo español y la caída de la monarquía católico en México." In *Interpretaciones del siglo xviii mexicano: El impacto de las reformas borbónicas*, edited by Josefina Zoraida Vásquez, 187–215. Mexico City: Nueva Imagen, 1992.

Brandl, Manfred. *Marx Anton Wittola: Seine Bedeutung für den Jansenismus in deutschen Landen*. Steyr: Ennsthaler, 1974.

Bremond, Henri. *Histoire littéraire du sentiment religieux en France depuis la fin des guerres de religion jusqu'à nos jours*. 11 vols. Paris: Bloud et Gay, 1916–26.

Broglio, Francesco Margiotto. "Estremisti e moderati nelle lotte dottrinali e politiche del Seicento e del Settecento." *Rivista di storia della chiesa in Italia* 16 (1962): 275–310.

Broglio, Francesco Margiotto. "L'origine giansenista della formula cavouriana 'libera chiesa in libero stato.'" *Rivista di Storia e Letteratura Religiosa* 50, no. 3 (2014): 509–14.

Brown, Howard G. *Mass Violence and the Self: From the French Wars of Religion to the Paris Commune*. Ithaca: Cornell University Press, 2019.

Bruun, Mette Birkedal. "Prayer, Meditation, and Retreat." In *The Oxford Handbook of the Baroque*, edited by John D. Lyons, 667–87. Oxford: Oxford University Press, 2019.

Bruun, Mette Birkedal. "A Private Mystery: Looking at Philippe de Champaigne's *Annunciation* for the Hôtel de Chavigny." In *Quid est sacramentum? Visual Representation of Sacred Mysteries in Early Modern Europe, 1400–1700*, edited by Walter S. Melion, Elizabeth Carson Pastan, and Lee Palmer Wandel, 606–55. Leiden: Brill, 2020.

Bugnion-Secrétan, Perle. *La Mère Angélique Arnauld, 1591–1661, après ses écrits*. Paris: Cerf, 1991.

Burkhard, Dominic, and Tanja Thanner, eds. *Der Jansenismus—eine "katholische Häresie"? Das Ringen um Gnade, Rechtfertigung und die Autorität Augustins in der frühen Neuzeit*. Münster: Aschendorff, 2014.

Burson, Jeffrey D. "The Papal Bull *Unigenitus* and the Forging of Enlightened Catholicism, 1713–1764." *History Compass* 12, no. 8 (2014): 672–84.

Burson, Jeffrey D., and Jonathan D. Wright, eds. *The Jesuit Suppression in Global Context: Causes, Events, and Consequences*. Cambridge: Cambridge University Press, 2015.

Caffiero, Marina. "'La verità crocifissa': Dal sinodo di Pistoia al millenarismo giansenistico nell'eta rivoluzionaria." In *Il sinodo di Pistoia del 1786*, edited by Claudio Lamioni, 313–25. Rome: Herder Editrice e Libreria, 1991.

Caiani, Ambrogio A. "The Cesena Popes, Pius VI and Pius VII: The Papacy in Revolution, 1775–1823." In *The Cambridge History of the Papacy*, vol. 1: *The Popes and the Papacy*, edited by Joëlle Rollo-Koster and Iben Forresberg-Schmidt. Cambridge: Cambridge University Press, forthcoming 2025.

Caiani, Ambrogio A. "The Concile National of 1811: Napoleon, Gallicanism and the Failure of Neo-Conciliarism." *Journal of Ecclesiastical History* 70, no. 3 (2019): 546–64.

Caiani, Ambrogio A. *To Kidnap a Pope: Napoleon and Pius VII, 1800–1815*. London: Yale University Press, 2021.

Calasso, Roberto. *The Ruin of Kasch*. Translated by William Weaver and Stephen Sartarelli. Cambridge: Harvard University Press, 1994. Italian 1983.

Callahan, William James. *Church, Politics, and Society in Spain, 1750–1874*. Cambridge, MA: Harvard University Press, 1984.

Camaiani, Bruna Bocchini, and Marcello Verga, eds. *Lettere di Scipione de' Ricci a Pietro Leopoldo, 1780–1791*. 3 vols. Florence: Olschki, 1990–1992.

Campa, Pedro F. "*The Imago Primi Saeculi Societatis Jesu* (1640): Devotion, Politics, and the Emblem." *Imago: Revista de Emblemática y Cultura Visual* 9 (2017): 55–71.

Campbell, Ted A. *The Religion of the Heart: A Study of European Religious Life in the Seventeenth and Eighteenth Centuries*. Eugene, OR: Wipf and Stock Publishers, 1991. First Edition, University of South Carolina Press, 1991.

Carreyre, Jean. *Le jansénisme durant la régence*. Louvain: Bibliothèque de RHE, 1932.

Ceyssens, Lucien. "Les cinq propositions de Jansenius à Rome." *Revue d'histoire ecclésiastique* 66 (1971): 449–501, 821–86.

Ceyssens, Lucien. "Les papiers de Quesnel saisis à Bruxelles et transportés à Paris en 1703 et 1704." *Revue d'histoire ecclésiastique* 44 (1949): 508–51.

Ceyssens, Lucien, and Joseph A. G. Tans. *Autour de l'Unigenitus*. Louvain, 1987.

Chadwick, Owen. *The Popes and European Revolution*. Oxford: Clarendon Press, 1981.

Chantin, Jean-Pierre. *La Famille: Une dissidence catholique au cœur de Paris, XVIIe–XXIe siècle*. Paris: Éditions Plein Jour, 2022.

Chantin, Jean-Pierre. *Les Amis de l'Œuvre de la Vérité: Jansénisme, miracles et fin du monde au XIXe siècle*. Lyon: Presses Universitaires de Lyon, 1998.

Charles-Daubert, Françoise. *Les Libertins érudits en France au XVIIe siècle*. Paris: Presses Universitaires de France, 1998.

Chédozeau, Bernard. "Idéal intellectuel et vie monastique à Port-Royal." *Chroniques de Port-Royal* 37 (1997): 57–74.

Chopelin Blanc, Caroline. "L'*Institution d'un Prince* de Duguet, un traité d'éducation à la charnière des XVIIe et XVIIIe siècles. Entre programme de formation et idéal de cité chrétienne." *Chrétiens et société XVIe–XXIe siècles* 19 (2011): 19–38.

Choudhury, Mita. *Convents and Nuns in Eighteenth-Century French Politics and Culture*. Ithaca: Cornell University Press, 2004.

Choudhury, Mita. *The Wanton Jesuit and the Wayward Saint: A Tale of Sex,*

Religion, and Politics in Eighteenth-Century France. University Park: Pennsylvania State University Press, 2015.

Clark, Ruth. *Strangers and Sojourners at Port Royal: Being an Account of the Connections between the British Isles and the Jansenists of France and Holland*. Cambridge: Cambridge University Press, 1932.

Clémencet, Charles. *Histoire littéraire de Port-Royal*. Vol. 1. Paris: Librairie de l'Union Chrétienne, 1868.

Clossey, Luke. *Salvation and Globalization in the Early Jesuit Missions*. Cambridge: Cambridge University Press, 2008.

Cognet, Louis. "Jansenism in Eighteenth-Century France." In *History of the Church*, vol. 6: *The Church in the Age of Absolutism and Enlightenment*, edited by Hubert Jedin and John Patrick Dolan, translated by Gunther J. Holst, 395–405. New York: Crossroad, 1991.

Cognet, Louis. *La Mère Angélique et Saint François de Sales, 1618–1626*. Paris: Flammarion, 1951.

Cognet, Louis. "Le jansénisme, drame gallican." *L'année canonique* 10 (1966): 75–83.

Cognet, Louis. "The Jansenist Conflict to 1713." In *History of the Church*, vol. 6: *The Church in the Age of Absolutism and Enlightenment*, edited by Hubert Jedin and John Patrick Dolan, translated by Gunther J. Holst, 48–53. New York: Crossroad, 1991.

Cojannot-Le Blanc, Marianne, ed. *Philippe de Champaigne, ou, La figure du peintre janséniste*. Paris: Nolin, 2011.

Coleman, Charly. *The Virtues of Abandon: An Anti-Individualist History of the French Enlightenment*. Stanford: Stanford University Press, 2014.

Congar, Yves. "L'ecclésiologie, de la Révolution française au Concile du Vatican, sous le signe de l'affirmation de l'autorité." *Revue des Sciences Religieuses* 34 (1960): 77–114.

Conley, John J. *Adoration and Annihilation: The Convent Philosophy of Port-Royal*. Notre Dame: Notre Dame University Press, 2009.

Conley, John J. "Agnès Arnauld (1593–1671)." *Internet Encyclopedia of Philosophy*. *IEP.utm.edu*. Accessed 2 June 2022.

Conley, John J. "Jacqueline Pascal (1625–1661)." *Internet Encyclopedia of Philosophy*. *IEP.utm.edu*. Accessed 5 August 2022.

Conley, John J. *The Other Pascals: The Philosophy of Jacqueline Pascal, Gilbert Pascal Périer, and Marguerite Périer*. Notre Dame: University of Notre Dame Press, 2019.

Cottret, Monique. "Aux origines du républicanisme janséniste: le mythe de l'Église primitive et le primitivisme des Lumières." *Revue d'histoire moderne et contemporaine* 31 (1984): 99–105.

Cottret, Monique. *Histoire du Jansénisme*. Paris: Perrin, 2016.

Cottret, Monique. *Jansénismes et lumières: Pour un autre XVIII*e *siècle*. Paris: Éditions Albin Michel, 1998.

Cottret, Monique. "*Les Nouvelles ecclésiastiques* et l'histoire religieuse du XVIIIe siècle: un chantier en mouvement." In *Les Nouvelles ecclésiastiques: Une aventure de presse clandestine au siècle des Lumières (1713–1803)*, edited by

Monique Cottret and Valérie Guittienne-Mürger, 11–48. Paris: Beauchesne, 2016.

Cousin, Victor. *Jacqueline Pascal: Premières études sur les femmes illustres et la société du XVIIe siècle*. Paris: Didiere et Cie, 1878. First edition 1845.

Crichton, J. D. *Saints or Sinners? Jansenism and Jansenisers in Seventeenth Century France*. Dublin: Veritas, 1996.

Cutter, Elissa. "Monastic Reform in Seventeenth-Century France: The Cistercian and Tridentine Influences on Angélique Arnauld's Reform of the Convent of Port-Royal." *Cistercian Studies Quarterly* 52, no. 4 (2017): 425–51.

da Langasco, Caissiano. "Un esperimento di politica giansenista? La Repubblica Ligure, 1797–1800." *Analecta Gregoriana* 71, no. 4 (1954): 195–210.

Dammig, Enrico. *Il movimento Giansenista a Roma nella seconda metà del secolo XVIII*. Vatican City: Biblioteca Apostolica Vaticana, 1945.

Darnton, Robert. "The Forbidden Best-Sellers of Pre-Revolutionary France." In *The French Revolution: The Essential Readings*, edited by Ronald Schechter, 110–37. Malden, MA: Blackwell, 2001.

Darnton, Robert. *The Literary Underground of the Old Regime*. Cambridge, MA: Harvard University Press, 1982.

Davanzati, Domenico Forges. *Giovanni Andrea Serrao: Vescovo di Potenza e la lotta dello Stato contro la Chiesa in Napoli nella seconda metà del Settecento*. Manduria: Lacaita, 1999.

De Franceschi, Sylvio Hermann. "Le spectre turinois d'un renouveau du gallicanisme et du fébronianisme. La condamnation romaine des thèses juridictionalistes du canoniste Giovanni Nepomuceno Nuytz." In *États de Savoie, Églises et institutions religieuses des réformes au Risorgimento. Actes du colloque international de Lyon, 17–19 octobre 2013*, edited by M. Ortolani, Ch. Sorrel, and O. Vernier, 139–57. Nice: Serre, 2017.

De Franceschi, Sylvio Hermann. "Les problématiques ecclésiologiques françaises au prisme des lectures italiennes. Gallicanisme et antiromanisme janséniste au temps de la papauté intransigeante (de la mi-XVIIIe siècle à la mi-XIXe siècle)." In *Les échanges religieux entre l'Italie et la France, 1760–1850. Regards croisés—Scambi religiosi tra Francia e Italia, 1760–1850, Sguardi incrociati*, edited by F. Meyer and S. Milbach, 59–78. Chambéry, France: Presses universitaires de Savoir, 2010.

Deinhardt, Wilhelm. *Der Jansenismus in deutschen Landen: Ein Beitrag zur Kirchengeschichte des 18. Jahrhunderts*. Munich: Kösel/Pustet, 1929. Reprint, Hildesheim, Germany: Gerstenberg, 1976.

Delforge, Frédéric. "Barcos, Martin de." In *Dictionnaire de Port-Royal*, edited by Jean Lesaulnier and Antony McKenna, 143–45. Paris: Honoré Champion, 2004.

Delforge, Frédéric. *Jacqueline Pascal (1625–1661): Biographie*. Paris: Classiques Garnier, 2017.

Delforge, Frédéric, and Antony McKenna. "Appendice IV: Les solitaires de Port-Royal." In *Dictionnaire de Port-Royal*, edited by Jean Lesaulnier and Antony McKenna, 1057. Paris: Honoré Champion, 2004.

De Lubac, Henri. *Surnaturel: Études historiques*. Paris: Aubier, 1946.

Delumeau, Jean. *Catholicism between Luther and Voltaire: A New View of the Counter-Reformation*. London: Burns and Oates, 1977. French 1971.

DeMeuse, Eric J. "'The World Is Content with Words': Jansenism between Thomism and Calvinism." In *Beyond Dordt and De Auxiliis: The Dynamics of Protestant and Catholic Soteriology in the Sixteenth and Seventeenth Centuries*, edited by Jordan J. Ballor, Matthew T. Gaetano, and David S. Sytsma, 245–76. Leiden: Brill, 2019.

Denis, Philippe. *Edmond Richer et le renouveau du conciliarisme au XVIIe siècle*. Paris: Cerf, 2014.

Diefendorf, Barbara. *Beneath the Cross: Catholics and Huguenots in Sixteenth-Century Paris*. New York: Oxford University Press, 1991.

Diefendorf, Barbara. *From Penitence to Charity: Pious Women and the Catholic Reformation in Paris*. Oxford: Oxford University Press, 2004.

Dieudonné, Philippe. "Fragilité de la Paix de l'église." *Chroniques de Port-Royal* 29 (1980): 17–33.

Doyle, William. *Jansenism: Catholic Resistance to Authority from Reformation to the French Revolution*. London: Palgrave Macmillan, 2000.

Duffy, Eamon. "'A Rubb-Up for Old Soares': Jesuits, Jansenists, and the English Secular Clergy, 1705–1715." *Journal of Ecclesiastical History* 28, no. 3 (1977): 291–317.

Durand, Jean-François, ed. *Pascal-Mauriac: L'œuvre en dialogue. Actes du colloque du Sénat, 4-6 Octobre 1999*. Paris: L'Harmattan, 2000.

Fantappiè, Carlo. "L'eredità del giansenismo e le radici del 'cattolicesimo liberale' in Italia: Il dibattito storiografico e le nuove prospettiva." In *Libéralisme chrétien et catholicisme libéral en Espagne, France et Italie dans la première moitié du XIXe siècle: Colloque international, 12-13-14 novembre 1987*, 21–37. Aix-en-Provence: Université de Provence, 1989.

Fantappiè, Carlo. *Riforme ecclesiastiche e resistenze sociali: La sperimentazione istituzionale nella diocesi di Prato alla fine del'antico regime*. Bologna: Mulino, 1986.

Farge, Arlette. *Subversive Words: Public Opinion in Eighteenth-Century France*. Translated by Rosemary Morris. Cambridge, UK: Polity Press, 1994. French 1992.

Fauchois, Yann. "Les jansénistes et la constitution civile du clergé: Aux marges du débat, débats dans le débat." In *Jansénisme et Révolution*, edited by Catherine Maire, 195–209. Paris: Chroniques de Port-Royal, 1990.

Fillafer, Franz. "Habsburg Liberalisms and the Enlightenment Past, 1790–1848." In *In Search of European Liberalisms: Concepts, Languages, Ideologies*, edited by Michael Freeden, Javier Fernández-Sebastián, and Jörn Leonhard, 37–71. New York: Berghahn, 2019.

Fillafer, Franz. "Il crepuscolo del giansenismo: La chiesa come repubblica durante l'età delle rivoluzioni—una prospettiva globale." In *Penitenza e Penitenzieria al tempo del giansenismo (secc. XVII–XVIII): Culture–Teologie–Prassi,* edited by Ugo Taraborrelli, 129–45. Rome: Libreria Editrice Vaticana, 2019.

Fleming, Julia. *Defending Probabilism: The Moral Theology of Juan Caramuel.* Washington, DC: Georgetown University Press, 2006.

Ford, Caroline. *Divided Houses: Religion and Gender in Modern France*. Ithaca: Cornell University Press, 2005.

Forrestal, Alison. *Fathers, Pastors, and Kings: Visions of Episcopacy in Seventeenth-Century France*. Manchester: Manchester University Press, 2004.

Forrestal, Alison. *Vincent de Paul, the Lazarist Mission, and French Catholic Reform*. Oxford: Oxford University Press, 2017.

Franklin, James. *The Science of Conjecture: Evidence and Probability before Pascal.* Baltimore: Johns Hopkins University Press, 2015. First edition 2001.

Gandelman, Claude. "La De-Iconisation janséniste de l'art: Pascal, Philippe de Champaigne." *Hebrew University Studies in Literature* 5 (1977): 213–47.

Gastellier, Fabian. *Angélique Arnauld.* Paris: Fayard, 1998.

Gay, Jean-Pascal. *Morales en conflit: Théologie et polémique au Grand Siècle (1640–1700)*. Paris: Les Éditions du Cerf, 2011.

Gay, Peter. *The Enlightenment: An Interpretation.* 2 vols. New York: Knopf, 1966–1969.

Gazier, Augustin. *Histoire générale du mouvement janséniste depuis ses origins jusqu'à nos jours*. Sixth ed. 2 vols. Paris: Honoré Champion, 1924.

Gazier, Augustin. *Jeanne de Chantal et Angélique Arnauld, d'après leur correspondence (1620–1641)*. Paris: Honoré Champion, 1915.

Girard, Aurélien. "Le jansénisme et le gallicanisme sont-ils des 'articles d'exportation'? Jalons pour une recherche sur le parcours et la doctrine de Ğirmānūs Ādam, archevêque grec-catholique d'Alep au tournant des XVIIIe et XIXe siècles." In *Église, Mémoire(s), Éducation, Mélanges offerts à Jean-François Boulanger*, edited by Véronique Beaulande-Barraud and Benoît Roux, 135–54. Reims: Éditions et presses universitaires de Reims, 2014.

Giraud, Marie Sophie. "Convulsionary Miracles and Women in Print Culture in France, 1737–1747." Master's thesis, University of Birmingham, 2014.

Golden, Richard M. *The Godly Rebellion: Parisian Curés and the Religious Fronde, 1652–1662*. Chapel Hill: University of North Carolina Press, 1981.

Goldmann, Lucien. *The Hidden God: A Study of Tragic Vision in the Pensées of Pascal and the Tragedies of Racine*. Translated by Philip Thody. London: Verso, 2016. French 1956.

Gouhier, Henri. *Blaise Pascal: Commentaires*. Paris: J. Vrin, 2005. First edition 1984.

Grasso, Grazia. "La plus forte réaction italienne à la bulle *Auctorem Fidei*: Les Riflessioni in difesa di M.r Scipione de Ricci e del suo Sinodo di Pistoja sopra la costituzione *Auctorem fidei*." In *Du jansénisme au modernisme: La bulle* Auctorem fidei, *1794, pivot du magistère romain*, edited by Jean-Baptiste Amadieu and Simon Icard, 135–52. Paris: Beauchesne, 2020.

Greco, Gaetano. *Benedetto XIV*. Rome: Salerno, 2011.

Gres-Gayer, Jacques. *Le Jansénisme en Sorbonne, 1643–1656*. Paris: Klincksieck, 1996.

Gres-Gayer, Jacques. "The Magisterium of the Faculty of Theology of Paris in the Seventeenth Century." *Theological Studies* 53 (1992): 424–50.

Gres-Gayer, Jacques. "The *Unigenitus* of Clement XI: A Fresh Look at the Issues." *Theological Studies* 49 (1988): 259–82.

Gres-Gayer, Jacques. *Théologie et pouvoir en Sorbonne: La Faculté de théologie de Paris et la bulle* Unigenitus. Paris: Klincksieck, 1991.

Griffiths, Paul J. *Why Read Pascal?* Washington, DC: The Catholic University of America Press, 2021.

Gross, Hanns. *Rome in the Age of Enlightenment: The Post-Tridentine Syndrome and the Ancien Régime*. Cambridge: Cambridge University Press, 2002.

Gubernatis, Angelo de. *Eustachio Degola, il clero costituzionale e la conversione della famiglia Manzoni: Spogli da un carteggio inedito*. Florence: Barbèra, 1882.

Guerra, Alessandro. *"Contro lo spirito del secolo": Giovanni Marchetti e la biblioteca della Controrivoluzione*. Rome: Edizioni Nuova Cultura, 2012.

Guilbaud, Juliette. "Die Rezeption der Constitutio *Unigenitus* (1713) im Alten Reich: Eine unterschätzte Diskussion?" In *Central European Pasts: Old and New in the Intellectual Culture of Habsburg Europe, 1700–1750*, edited by Ines Peper and Thomas Wallnig, 141–69. Berlin: De Gruyter, 2022.

Guilbaud, Juliette. "Die Wiener Kirchenzeitung im Spiegel der *Nouvelles Ecclésiastiques* (1784–1789)." In *Der Jansenismus im deutschsprachigen Raum, 1670–1789: Bücher, Bilder, Bibliotheken*, edited by Christoph Schmitt-Maaß, 185–201. Berlin: De Gruyter, 2023.

Guittienne-Mürger, Valérie. *Jansénisme et libéralisme: Regards de Jean-Louis Rondeau sur l'Empire et la Restauration*. Rennes: Presses Universitaires de Rennes, 2022.

Hamscher, Albert N. "The Parlement of Paris and the Social Interpretation of Early French Jansenism." *Catholic Historical Review* 63 (1977): 392–410.

Harrison, Carol E. *Romantic Catholics: France's Postrevolutionary Generation in Search of a Modern Faith*. Ithaca: Cornell University Press, 2014.

Hazard, Paul. *The Crisis of the European Mind, 1680–1715*. Translated by J. Lewis May. New York: New York Review of Books, 2013. French edition 1935.

Hera, Alberto de la. "El movimento conciliar regalistica en America en la epoca del sínodo di Pistoya." In *Il sinodo di Pistoia del 1786*, edited by Claudio Lamioni, 441–75. Rome: Herder Editrice e Libreria, 1991.

Hersche, Peter. *Der aufgeklärte Reformkatholizismus in Österreich: Hirtenbriefe 1752–1782*. Bern: Peter Lang, 1976.

Hersche, Peter. *Der Spätjansenismus in Österreich*. Vienna: Österreichischen Akademie der Wissenschaften, 1977.

Hersche, Peter. "Die Auswirkungen der Synode von Pistoia (1786) auf Deutschland, insbesondere auf das Erzbistum Mainz." *Archiv fur Mittelrheinische Kirchengeschichte* 41 (1989): 275–94.

Hersche, Peter. "Erzbischof Hieronymus Colloredo und der Jansenismus in Salzburg." *Mitt(h)eilungen der Gesellschaft für Salzburger Landeskunde* 117, no. 2 (1977): 231–68.

Hersche, Peter. "Jansenistiche Sympathien in der deutschen Reichskirche im letzten Drittel des 18. Jahrhunderts." In *Deutschland und Europa in der Neuzeit: Festschrift für Karl Otmar Freiherr von Aretin*, 2 vols., edited by

Ralph Melville and Klaus Scharf et al., 1:395–418. Stuttgart: Franz Steiner, 1988.

Hildesheimer, Françoise. *Le Jansénisme en France aux XVIIe et XVIIIe siècles.* Paris: Publisud, 1991.

Hollerweger, Hans. *Die Reform des Gottesdienstes zur Zeit des Josephinismus in Österreich.* Regensburg, Germany: Pustet, 1976.

Hsia, Ronnie Po-chia. *A Jesuit in the Forbidden City: Matteo Ricci, 1552–1610.* Oxford: Oxford University Press, 2010.

Hsia, Ronnie Po-chia. *The World of Catholic Renewal, 1540–1770.* New York: Cambridge University Press, 2005.

Hudson, David. "The *Nouvelles Ecclésiastiques*, Jansenism, and Conciliarism, 1717–1735." *Catholic Historical Review* 70, no. 3 (1984): 389–406.

Icard, Simon. *L'Apocalypse janséniste: Port-Royal et la défense de la vérité.* Paris: Cerf, 2023.

Icard, Simon. *Port-Royal et saint Bernard de Clairvaux (1608–1709): Saint-Cyran, Jansénius, Arnaud, Pascal, Nicole, Angélique de Saint-Jean.* Paris, Honoré Champion, 2010.

Jacob, Margaret C. *The Secular Enlightenment.* Princeton: Princeton University Press, 2019.

Jacquard, Nicolas. *Les Inspirés.* Paris: Éditions Robert Laffont, 2021.

Jacques, Émile. "Les petits foyers du Jansénisme à Bruxelles au confluent des XVIIe et XVIIIe siècles." In *Jansénius et le jansénisme dans les Pays-Bas: Mélanges Lucien Ceyssens*, edited by M. Schrama and J. van Bavel, 161–97. Leuven: Peeters Publishers, 1982.

James, E. D. *Pierre Nicole, Jansenist and Humanist: A Study of His Thought.* The Hague: Martinus Nijhoff, 1972.

Janssen, Guy. *La Petite Église en trente questions.* La Crèche, France: Geste Édition, 1999.

Johns, Christopher. *The Visual Culture of Catholic Enlightenment.* University Park: Penn State University Press, 2014.

Jones, Frederick M. *Alphonsus de Liguori: The Saint of Bourbon Naples, 1696–1787.* Dublin: Gill and MacMillan, 1992.

Kantorowicz, Ernst. *The King's Two Bodies: A Study in Medieval Political Theology.* Princeton: Princeton University Press, 1957.

Keen, Ralph. "The Critique of Calvin in Jansenius's *Augustinus*." In *Crossing Traditions: Essays on the Reformation and Intellectual History in Honour of Irena Backus*, edited by Maria-Cristina Pitassi and Daniela Solfarolil Camillocci, 405–15. Leiden: Brill, 2017. https://doi.org/10.1163/9789004356795_026.

King, Charles W. *The Ancient Roman Afterlife: Di Manes, Belief, and the Cult of the Dead.* Austin: University of Texas Press, 2020.

Klueting, Harm. "Der bekannte Unbekannte: Der Jansenismus in der deutschsprachigen Forschung." In *Der Jansenismus im deutschsprachigen Raum, 1670–1789: Bücher, Bilder, Bibliotheken*, edited by Christoph Schmitt-Maaß, 11–40. Berlin: De Gruyter, 2023.

Klueting, Harm. "The Catholic Enlightenment in Austria or the Habsburg

Lands." In *A Companion to the Catholic Enlightenment in Europe*, edited by Ulrich L. Lehner and Michael Printy, 127–64. Leiden: Brill, 2010.

Kołakowski, Leszek. *God Owes Us Nothing: A Brief Remark on Pascal's Religion and the Spirit of Jansenism*. Chicago: University of Chicago Press, 1995.

Kostroun, Daniella. "A Formula for Disobedience: Jansenism, Gender, and the Feminist Paradox." *Journal of Modern History* 75 (2003): 483–522.

Kostroun, Daniella. *Feminism, Absolutism, and Jansenism: Louis XIV and the Port-Royal Nuns*. Cambridge: Cambridge University Press, 2011.

Kovács, Elisabeth. *Ultramontanismus und Staatskirchentum im Theresianisch-Josephinischen Staat. Der Kampf der Kardinäle Migazzi und Franckenberg gegen den Wiener Professor der Kirchengeschichte Ferdinand Stöger*. Vienna: Wiener Dom-Verlag, 1975.

Kreiser, B. Robert. *Miracles, Convulsions, and Ecclesiastical Politics in Early Eighteenth-Century Paris*. Princeton: Princeton University Press, 1978.

Kremer, Elmer J., ed. *Interpreting Arnauld*. Toronto: University of Toronto Press, 1996.

Kremer, Elmer J., ed. *The Great Arnauld and Some of His Philosophical Correspondents*. Toronto: Toronto University Press, 1994.

Krumenacker, Yves. *Du Jansénisme à la secte: Vie de monsieur Claude Germain, curé de Lacenas (1750–1831)*. Paris: Publisud, 1999.

Krumenacker, Yves. "Henri Bremond et l'École française de spiritualité." *Chrétiens et sociétés* 9 (2002): 115–38.

Lacotte, Rémy Hême de. "De la polémique anti-gallicane à l'affirmation d'un catholicisme intransigeant: Les usages d'*Auctorem fidei* dans les controverses religieuses en France dans la première moitié du XIXe siècle." In *Du jansénisme au modernisme: La bulle* Auctorem fidei, *1794, pivot du magistère romain*, edited by Jean-Baptiste Amadieu and Simon Icard, 177–200. Paris: Beauchesne, 2020.

Lamb, Christopher. "Church for the 'Pure' Is Heresy, Francis Warns Curia." *The Tablet*. 22 December 2022.

La Mère Agnès Arnauld (1593–1672). Chroniques de Port-Royal 43 (1994).

Lamioni, Claudio, ed. *Il sinodo di Pistoia del 1786: Atti del convegno internazionale per il secondo centenario Pistoia-Prato, 25–27 settembre 1986*. Rome: Herder Editrice e Libreria, 1991.

Légier-Desgranges, Henry. *Du jansénisme à la Révolution: Mme de Moysan et l'extravagante affaire de l'Hôpital général, 1749–1758*. Paris: Hachette, 1954.

Lehner, Ulrich L., and Jeffrey D. Burson, eds. *Enlightenment and Catholicism in Europe: A Transnational History*. Notre Dame, IN: University of Notre Dame Press, 2014.

Lehner, Ulrich L., and Michael Printy, eds. *A Companion to the Catholic Enlightenment in Europe*. Leiden: Brill, 2010.

Lehner, Ulrich L. "Johann Nikolaus von Hontheim and His Febronius: A Bishop and His Censored Ecclesiology." *Church History and Religious Culture* 88 (2008): 93–121.

Lehner, Ulrich L. *On the Road to Vatican II: German Catholic Enlightenment and Reform of the Church*. Minneapolis: Fortress Press, 2016.

Lehner, Ulrich L. *The Catholic Enlightenment*. New York: Oxford University Press, 2016.

Lehner, Ulrich L. "The Many Faces of the Catholic Enlightenment." In *A Companion to the Catholic Enlightenment in Europe*, edited by Ulrich L. Lehner and Michael Printy, 1–61. Leiden: Brill, 2010.

Lennon, Thomas M. *Sacrifice and Self-Interest in Seventeenth-Century France: Quietism, Jansenism, and Cartesianism*. Leiden: Brill, 2019.

Lesaulnier, Jean. *Images de Port-Royal*. 2 vols. Paris: Nolin, 2002.

Lesaulnier, Jean. "Hamon, Jean." In *Dictionnaire de Port-Royal*, edited by Jean Lesaulnier and Antony McKenna, 504–9. Paris: Honoré Champion, 2004.

Luez, Philippe. *Port-Royal et le Jansénisme: Des religieuses face à l'absolutisme*. Paris: Éditions Belin/Humensis, 2017.

Lyon-Caen, Nicolas. *La boîte à Perrette: Le jansénisme parisien au XVIIIe siècle*. Paris: Éditions Albin Michel, 2010.

Lyon-Caen, Nicolas, ed. *Les Jansénistes*. Paris: Société éditrice du Monde, 2013.

Maire, Catherine. "Aux sources politiques et religieuses de la Révolution française: Deux modèles en discussion." *Le Débat* 130 (2004): 133–53.

Maire, Catherine. *De la cause de Dieu à la cause de la Nation: Le jansénisme au XVIIIe siècle*. Paris: Éditions Gallimard, 1998.

Maire, Catherine-Laurence. *Les Convulsionnaires de Saint-Médard: Miracles, convulsions, et prophéties à Paris au XVIIIe siècle*. Paris: Éditions Gallimard/Julliard, 1985.

Maire, Catherine. "Les jansénistes et le millénarisme. Du refus à la conversion." *Annales. Histoire, Sciences Sociales* 63, no. 1 (2008): 7–36.

Maire, Catherine. "Port-Royal: The Jansenist Schism." In *Realms of Memory: Rethinking the French Past*, edited by Pierre Nora, translated by Arthur Goldhammer, 1:301–52. New York: Columbia University, 1996. French 1992.

Marichal, Juan. "From Pistoia to Cádiz: A Generation's Itinerary, 1786–1812." In *The Ibero-American Enlightenment*, edited by A. Owen Aldridge, 97–111. Urbana: University of Illinois Press, 1971.

Marin, Louis. *Philippe de Champaigne, ou, La présence cachée*. Paris: Hazan, 1995.

Marin, Louis. "Signe et Représentation: Philippe de Champaigne et Port-Royal." *Annales. Histoire, Sciences Sociales* 25, no. 1 (1970): 1–29.

Martimort, A. G. *Le gallicanisme de Bossuet*. Paris: Cerf, 1953.

Martin, Henri-Jean. *The French Book: Religion, Absolutism, and Readership, 1585–1715*. Translated by Paul and Nadine Saenger. Baltimore: Johns Hopkins University Press, 1996.

Masselli, Domenico. Introduction to *Memorie di Scipione de' Ricci, vescovo di Prato e Pistoia*, edited by Agenore Gelli, 1:9–53. 2 vols. Pistoia: Tellini, 1980 [Florence: Le Monnier, 1865].

Matava, R. J. "A Sketch of the Controversy *de auxiliis*." *Journal of Jesuit Studies* 7, no. 3 (2020): 417–46. https://doi.org/10.1163/22141332-00703004.

Matteucci, Benvenuto. *Scipione de' Ricci: Saggio storico-theologico sul giansenismo italiano*. Brescia: Morcelliana, 1941.

Maury, Serge. “Histoire d’un groupe convulsionnaire tardif à la fin du XVIIIe siècle: ‘les Fareinistes.’” PhD diss., Université Jean Moulin Lyon 3, 2014.

Maury, Serge. *Une secte janséniste convulsionnaire sous la Révolution française: Les Fareinistes (1783–1805)*. Paris: Éditions l’Harmattan, 2019.

McCullough, Lissa. *The Religious Philosophy of Simone Weil: An Introduction*. London: I.B. Taurus, 2014.

McGinn, Bernard. *The Persistence of Mysticism in Catholic Europe: France, Italy, and Germany, 1500–1675*. New York: Crossroad, 2020.

McMahon, Darrin M. *Enemies of the Enlightenment: The French Counter-Enlightenment and the Making of Modernity*. Oxford: Oxford University Press, 2001.

McManners, John. *Church and Society in Eighteenth-Century France*. 2 vols. Oxford: Oxford University Press, 1998.

McMillan, James F. “Jansenists and Anti-Jansenists in Eighteenth Century Scotland: The *Unigenitus* Quarrels on the Scottish Catholic Mission, 1732–1746.” *Innes Review* 39, no. 1 (1988): 12–45.

Menozzi, Daniele. “La società religiosa di fronte alla Rivoluzione.” *Ricerche per la storia religiosa di Roma* 9 (1992): 31–48.

Mestre, Antonio. “La repercusión del sínodo di Pistoya en España.” In *Il sinodo di Pistoia del 1786*, edited by Claudio Lamioni, 425–40. Rome: Herder Editrice e Libreria, 1991.

Miller, Samuel J. “Dom Frei Joaquim de Santa Clara (1740–1818) and later Portuguese Jansenism.” *Catholic Historical Review* 69, no. 1 (1983): 20–40.

Miller, Samuel J. *Portugal and Rome, c. 1748–1830: An Aspect of the Catholic Enlightenment*. Rome: Università Gregoriana Editrice, 1978.

Miller, Samuel J. “Portugal and Utrecht: A Phase of the Catholic Enlightenment.” *Catholic Historical Review* 63, no. 2 (1977): 225–48.

Miller, Samuel J. “The Limits of Political Jansenism in Tuscany: Scipione de’ Ricci to Peter Leopold, 1780–1791.” *Catholic Historical Review* 80, no. 4 (1994): 762–67.

Moreau, Denis. “Antoine Arnauld: Cartesian Philosopher?” In *The Oxford Handbook of Descartes and Cartesianism*, edited by Steven Nadler, Tad M. Schmaltz, and Delphine Antoine-Mahut, 344–57. Oxford: Oxford University Press, 2019.

Moriarty, Michael. *Disguised Vices: Theories of Virtue in Early Modern French Thought*. Oxford: Oxford University Press, 2011.

Moriarty, Michael. *Pascal: Reasoning and Belief*. Oxford: Oxford University Press, 2020.

Mousset, Albert. *L’étrange histoire des convulsionnaires de Saint-Médard*. Paris: Les Éditions de Minuit, 1953.

Mungello, D. E., ed. *The Chinese Rites Controversy: Its History and Meaning*. Abingdon: Routledge, 2018. First edition Steyler Verlag, 1994.

Murdoch, Jessica M. “The New Jansenism.” *First Things*. 21 February 2017.

Nadler, Steven. *Arnauld and the Cartesian Philosophy of Ideas*. Princeton: Princeton University Press, 1989.

Neveu, Bruno. "Juge suprême et docteur infaillible: Le pontificat romain de la bulle *In eminenti* (1643) à la bulle *Auctorem fidei* (1794)." *Mélanges de l'École française de Rome, Moyen Âge-Temps modernes* 93, no. 1 (1981): 215–75.

Neveu, Bruno. *L'erreur et son juge: Remarques sur les censures doctrinales a l'epoque moderne*. Naples: Bibliopolis, 1993.

Neveu, Bruno. *Sébastien Joseph du Cambout du Pontchâteau (1634–1690) et ses missions à Rome, d'après sa correspondance et des documents inédits*. Rome: Publications de l'École Française de Rome, 1968.

Noel, Charles C. "Clerics and Crown in Bourbon Spain, 1700–1808: Jesuits, Jansenists, and Enlightened Reformers." In *Religion and Politics in Enlightenment Europe*, edited by James E. Bradley and Dale Van Kley, 119–53. Notre Dame, IN: University of Notre Dame Press, 2001.

Oakley, Francis. *The Conciliarist Tradition: Constitutionalism in the Catholic Church, 1300–1870*. Oxford: Oxford University Press, 2003.

O'Brien, Charles H. *Ideas of Religious Toleration at the Time of Joseph II: A Study of the Enlightenment among Catholics in Austria*. Philadelphia: American Philosophical Society, 1969.

O'Brien, Charles H. "Jansenists and Josephinism: *Nouvelles ecclésiastiques* and Reform of the Church in Late Eighteenth-Century Austria." *Mitteilungen des österreichischen Staatsarchivs* 32 (1979): 143–64.

O'Connor, Thomas. *Irish Jansenists, 1600–1670: Religion and Politics in Flanders, France, Ireland, and Rome*. Dublin: Four Courts Press, 2008.

O'Connor, Thomas. "Jansenism." In *The Oxford Handbook of the Ancien Régime*, edited by William Doyle, 318–36. Oxford: Oxford University Press, 2012.

O'Malley, John. *Art, Controversy, and the Jesuits: The Imago Primi Saeculi (1640)*. Philadelphia: Saint Joseph's University Press, 2015.

O'Malley, John. *Vatican I: The Council and the Making of the Ultramontane Church*. Cambridge, MA: Harvard University Press, 2018.

Orain, Arnauld. "The Second Jansenism and the Rise of French Eighteenth-Century Political Economy." *History of Political Economy* 46, no. 3 (2014): 463–90.

Orcibal, Jean. *Cornelius Jansenius*. Paris: Études Augustiniennes, 1991.

Orcibal, Jean. *Jansénius d'Ypres (1584–1638)*. Paris: Études Augustiniennes, 1989.

Orcibal, Jean. "Jansénius et Rome." In *Études d'histoire et de littérature réligieuses: XVIe–XVIIIe siècles*, edited by Jean Orcibal, Jacques Le Brun, and Jean Lesaulnier, 869–86. Paris: Klincksieck, 1996.

Orcibal, Jean. *Jean Duvergier de Hauranne: Abbé de Saint-Cyran et son temps*. Paris-Louvain: J. Duculot, 1947.

Orcibal, Jean. *La spiritualité de Saint-Cyran avec ses écrits de piété inédits*. Paris: J. Vrin, 1962.

Orcibal, Jean. *Saint-Cyran et le Jansénisme*. Paris: Éditions du Seuil, 1961.

Palmer, Douglas. "The Republic of Grace: International Jansenism in the Age of Enlightenment and Revolutions." PhD diss., Ohio State University, 2004.

Palmer, Thomas. *Jansenism and England: Moral Rigorism across the Confessions*. Oxford: Oxford University Press, 2018.

Parguez, Jacques. *La bulle Unigenitus et le jansénisme politique: Avant-coureur de la Révolution française*. Paris: Maurice Glomeau, 1936.

Parker, Charles H. *Faith on the Margins: Catholics and Catholicism in the Dutch Golden Age*. Cambridge: Harvard University Press, 2008.

Parrot, David. *1652: The Cardinal, the Prince, and the Crisis of the Fronde*. Oxford: Oxford University Press, 2020.

Passerin d'Entrèves, Ettore, and Francesco Traniello. "Ricerche sul tardo giansenismo." *Rivista di storia e letteratura religiosa* 3 (1967): 279–313.

Passerin d'Entrèves, Ettore. "La politica dei giansenisti in Italia nell'ultimo Settecento." *Quaderni di cultura e storia sociale* 1 (1952): 150–56, 230–36, 321–26; 2 (1953): 359–67; 3 (1954): 269–88, 309–29.

Passerin d'Entrèves, Ettore. "La riforma 'giansenista' della Chiesa e la lotta anticuriale in Italia nella seconda metà del Settecento." *Rivista storica italiana* 71 (1959): 209–34.

Pasztor, Lajos. "La curia romana e il giansenismo: La preparazione della bolla *Auctorem fidei*." In *Actes du Colloque sur le jansénisme organisé par l'Academia belgica. Roma, 2 et 3 Novembre 1973, Bibliothèque de la Revue d'histoire ecclésiastique* 64: 89–104. Louvain: Publications Universitaires de Louvain, 1977.

Pecklers, Keith F. "The Jansenist Critique and the Liturgical Reforms of the Seventeenth and Eighteenth Centuries." *Ecclesia Orans* 20 (2003): 325–38.

Pelletier, Gérard. *Rome et la Révolution française: La théologie et la politique du Saint-Siège devant la Révolution française (1789–1799)*. Rome: École française de Rome, 2004.

Pépino, Éric. *Julien Green au miroir du Grand Siècle: Pascal et Port-Royal dans l'œuvre de Julien Green*. Paris: Les Éditions du Cerf, 2020.

Pierre Nicole (1625–1695). Chroniques de Port-Royal 45. 1996.

Plazenet, Laurence, ed. *Port-Royal*. Paris: Flammarion, 2012.

Plongeron, Bernard. "Benoît-Joseph Labre au miroir de l'hagiographie janséniste en France (1783–1789)." In *Benoît Labre: Errance et sainteté. Histoire d'un culte 1783–1983*, edited by Yves-Marie Hilaire, 25–54. Paris: Cerf, 1984.

Plongeron, Bernard. "Nacimiento de una cristiandad republicana (1789–1801): El abate Grégoire." *Concilium* 221 (1989): 39–53.

Plongeron, Bernard. *Théologie et politique au siècle des lumières (1770–1820)*. Geneva: Droz, 1973.

Plongeron, Bernard. "Unità tridentina e diversità francese: Filoromani, giansenisti, gallicani e costituzionali." In *I tempi del Concilio: Religione, cultura e società nell'Europa tridentina*, edited by Cesare Mozzarelli and Danilo Zardin, 145–70. Rome: Bulzoni, 1997.

Pomplun, R. Trent. *Jesuit on the Roof of the World: Ippolito Desideri's Mission to Tibet*. Oxford: Oxford University Press, 2010.

Pomplun, R. Trent. "The *Alphabetum Tibetanum* of Agostino Antonio Giorgi (1711–1797): Between Augustinianism and the History of Religions." *History of Religions* 59 (2020): 193–221.

Popkin, Jeremy. *A New World Begins: The History of the French Revolution.* New York: Basic Books, 2019.
Popkin, Richard H. *The History of Skepticism from Erasmus to Spinoza.* Berkeley: University of California Press, 1979.
Préclin, Edmond. *Les jansénistes du XVIIIe siècle et la Constitution civile du clergé: Le développement du richérisme, sa propagation dans le bas-clergé 1713–1791.* Paris: Gamber, 1929.
Printy, Michael. "Catholic Enlightenment and Reform Catholicism in the Holy Roman Empire." In *A Companion to the Catholic Enlightenment in Europe,* edited by Ulrich L. Lehner and Michael Printy, 165–214. Leiden: Brill, 2010.
Printy, Michael. *Enlightenment and the Creation of German Catholicism.* Cambridge: Cambridge University Press, 2009.
Pugivert, Joaquin, and Joan Bada, eds. *Bisbes, Illustració, i Jansenisme a la Catalunya del S.XVIII.* Girona, Spain: Eumo, 2000.
Quaghebeur, Toon. "The Reception of *Unigenitus* in the Faculty of Theology at Louvain, 1713–1719." *Catholic Historical Review* 93, no. 2 (2007): 265–99.
Quantin, Jean-Louis. *Le catholicisme classique et les Pères de l'Église: Un retour aux sources (1669–1713).* Turnhout, Belgium: Brepols, 1999.
Raab, Heribert. "Zur Geschichte und Bedeutung des Schlagwortes 'Ultramontan' im 18. und frühen 19. Jahrhundert." *Historisches Jahrbuch der Görres-Gesellschaft* 81 (1962): 159–73.
Radner, Ephraim. *Spirit and Nature: The Saint-Médard Miracles in 18th-Century Jansenism.* New York: Crossroad, 2002.
Ranum, Orest. *The Fronde: A French Revolution, 1648–1652.* New York: W.W. Norton, 1993.
Rapley, Elizabeth. *The Dévotes: Women & Church in Seventeenth-Century France.* Montreal: McGill-Queen's University Press, 1990.
Rea, Lilian. *The Enthusiasts of Port-Royal.* London: Methuen, 1912.
Rosa, Mario. *Il giansenismo nell'Italia del Settecento: Dalla riforma della Chiesa alla democrazia rivoluzionaria.* Rome: Carocci, 2014.
Rosa, Mario. "Pope Benedict XIV (1740–1758): The Ambivalent Enlightener." In *Enlightenment and Catholicism in Europe,* edited by Ulrich L. Lehner and Jeffrey D. Burson, 43–60.
Rosa, Mario. *Riformatori e rebelli nel'700 religioso italiano.* Bari: Dedalo, 1969.
Rosa, Mario. "The Catholic Aufklärung in Italy." In *A Companion to the Catholic Enlightenment in Europe,* edited by Ulrich L. Lehner and Michael Printy, 215–50. Leiden: Brill, 2010.
Rota, Ettore. "Il giansenismo in Lombardia e i prodromi del Risorgimento italiano." In *Raccolta di scritti storici in onore del prof. Giacinto Romano,* Ettore Rota et al., 363–626. Pavia: Fusi, 1907.
Ruffini, Francesco. *I giansenisti piemontesi e la conversione della madre di Cavour.* Turin: Bocca, 1929.
Sainte-Beuve, Charles-Augustin. *Port-Royal.* 5 vols. Paris: L. Hachette, 1837–59.
Sales Souza, Evergton. *Jansénisme et réforme de l'Église dans l'Empire portugais (1640–1790).* Paris and Lisbon: Centre culturel Calouste Gulbenkian and Fundação Calouste Gulbenkian, 2004.

Sales Souza, Evergton. "Jansénisme et réforme de l'Eglise dans l'Amérique portugaise au xviiie siècle." *Revue de l'histoire de religions* 2 (2009): 201–26.

Sales Souza, Evergton. "L'incontournable jansénisme: L'Église d'Utrecht et la réforme ecclésiastique portugaise." *Histoire, Economie et Société* 4. (2005): 555–72.

Santos, Cândido dos. "António Pereira de Figueiredo, Pombal e a Aufklärung: Ensaio sobre o regalismo e o jansenismo em Portugal na 2a metade do século XVIII." *Revista de História das Idéias* 4, no. 1 (1982–1983): 167–203.

Santos, Cândido dos. *Jansenismo e antijansenismo em Portugal: Estudos e documentos*. Porto, Portugal: Universidade Católica Editora, 2014.

Santos, Cândido dos. "Os jansenistas franceses e os estudos eclesiásticos na época de Pombal." *Máthesis* 13 (2004): 67–104.

Santos, Cândido dos. *Padre António Pereira de Figueiredo. Erudição e polémica na segunda metade do século XVIII*. Lisbon: Roma Editora, 2005.

Sarrailh, Jean. *L'Espagne éclairée de la seconde moitié du XVIIIe siècle*. Paris: Imprimerie Nationale, 1954.

Saugnieux, Joël, ed. *Foi et Lumières dans l'Espagne du XVIIIe siècle*. Lyon, France: Presses Universitaires de Lyon, 1985.

Saugnieux, Joël. *Le Jansénisme Espagnol du XVIIIe Siècle, ses Composantes et ses Sources*. Oviedo, Spain: Universidad de Oviedo, 1976.

Saugnieux, Joël. *Les jansénistes et le renouveau de la prédication dans l'espagne de la seconde moitié du XVIIIe siècle*. Lyon: Presses Universitaires de Lyon, 1976.

Schettini, Glauco. "The Catholic Counter-Revolution: A Global Intellectual History, 1780s-1840s." PhD diss., Fordham University, 2022.

Schmitt-Maaß, Christoph, ed. *Der Jansenismus im deutschsprachigen Raum, 1670–1789: Bücher, Bilder, Bibliotheken*. Berlin: De Gruyter, 2023.

Schrama, M., and J. van Bavel, eds. *Jansénius et le jansénisme dans les Pays-Bas: Mélanges Lucien Ceyssens*. Leuven: Peeters Publishers, 1982.

Sedgwick, Alexander. *Jansenism in Seventeenth-Century France: Voice from the Wilderness*. Charlottesville: University Press of Virginia, 1977.

Sedgwick, Alexander. *The Travails of Conscience: The Arnauld Family and the Ancien Régime*. Cambridge: Harvard University Press, 1998.

Shagan, Ethan. *The Birth of Modern Belief: Faith and Judgment from the Middle Ages to the Enlightenment*. Princeton: Princeton University Press, 2018.

Simmonds, Gemma. "Jansenism: An Early *Ressourcement* Movement." In *Ressourcement: A Movement for Renewal in Twentieth-Century Catholic Theology*, edited by Gabriel Flynn and Paul D. Murray, 23–36. Oxford: Oxford University Press, 2012.

Smidt, Andrea J. "*Luces por la fe*: The Cause of Catholic Enlightenment in 18th-Century Spain." In *A Companion to the Catholic Enlightenment in Europe*, edited by Ulrich L. Lehner and Michael Printy, 403–52. Leiden: Brill, 2010.

Smidt, Andrea J. "Josep Climent i Avinent (1706–1781): Enlightened Catholic, Civic Humanist, Seditionist." In *Enlightenment and Catholicism in Europe: A Transnational History*, edited by Ulrich L. Lehner and Jeffrey D. Burson), 327–49. Notre Dame, IN: University of Notre Dame Press, 2014.

Smit, Peter-Ben. *Old Catholic Theology: An Introduction*. Leiden: Brill, 2019.

Sorkin, David. *The Religious Enlightenment: Protestants, Jews, and Catholics from London to Vienna*. Princeton: Princeton University Press, 2008.

Stehlin, Stewart A. "The French Constitutional Church and Christian Renewal, 1795–1801." *Journal of Church and State* 13, no. 3 (1971): 493–515.

Steinruck, Josef. "Bemühungen um die Reform der Reichskirche auf dem Emser Kongreß (1786)." In *Reformatio ecclesiae: Festgabe für Erwin Iserloh*, edited by Remigius Bäumer, 863–82. Paderborn: Schöningh, 1980.

Stella, Pietro, ed. *Atti e decreti del concilio diocesano di Pistoia dell'anno 1786*. 2 vols. Florence: Olschki, 1986.

Stella, Pietro. "Il dissidio con la Chiesa di Utrecht e la vertenza giansenista: Due questioni irrisolte negli anni di Clemente XIV." In *L'età di papa Clemente XIV: Religione, politica, cultura*, edited by Mario Rosa and Marina Colonna, 125–68. Rome: Bulzoni, 2010.

Stella, Pietro. *Il giansenismo in Italia*. 3 vols. Rome: Edizioni di Storia e Letteratura, 2006.

Stella, Pietro, ed. *Il Giansenismo in Italia II/I: La bolla 'Auctorem Fidei' (1794) nella storia dell'Ultramontanismo; Saggio introduttivo e documenti*. Rome: Libreria Ateneo Salesiano, 1995.

Stella, Pietro. "La '*duplex delectatio*': Agostinismo e giansenismo dal sinodo di Pistoia alla bolla *Auctorem fidei*." *Salesianum* 45 (1983): 25–48.

Stella, Pietro. "L'oscuramento delle verità nella Chiesa dal sinodo di Pistoia alla bolla 'Auctorem fidei' (1786–1794)." *Salesianum* 43 (1981): 731–56.

Stella, Pietro. "Pietro Tamburini nel quadro del giansenismo italiano." In *Pietro Tamburini e il giansenismo lombardo: Atti del Convegno internazionale in occasione del 250 della nascita (Brescia, 25–26 maggio 1989)*, edited by Paolo Corsini and Daniele Montanari, 151–204. Brescia: Morcelliana, 1989.

Strayer, Brian. *Suffering Saints: Jansenists and Convulsionnaires in France, 1640–1799*. Eastbourne: Sussex Academic Press, 2008.

Stucco, Guido. Introduction to Cornelius Jansen, *The Predestination of Humans and Angels: Augustinus, Tome III, Book IX*, 1–48. Translated by Guido Stucco. Washington, DC: The Catholic University of America Press, 2022.

Tanzini, Reginaldo. *Istoria dell'assemblea degli arcivescovi e vescovi della Toscana tenuta in Firenze l'anno 1787*. 3 vols. Florence: Gaetano Cambiagi, 1788.

Taveneaux, René. *Jansénisme et politique*. Paris: Librairie Armand Colin, 1965.

Taveneaux, René. *Le jansénisme en Lorraine*. Paris: Vrin, 1960.

Tomsich, Maria Giovanna, *El Jansenismo en España. Estudio sobre Ideas Religiosas en la Segunda Mitad del Siglo XVIII*. Madrid: Siglo Veintiuno Editores, 1972.

Van Damme, Stéphane. "La mappemonde sceptique: une géographie des 'libertins érudits.'" *Littératures classiques* 92 (2017/1): 77–112.

Van Kleef, Bastiaan Abraham, "Das Utrechter Provinzialkonzil vom Jahre 1763." *Internationale kirchliche Zeitschrift* 49 (1959): 197–228.

Van Kley, Dale K. "Catholic Conciliar Reform in an Age of Anti-Catholic Revolution: France, Italy, and the Netherlands, 1758–1801." In *Religion and*

Politics in Enlightenment Europe, edited by James E. Bradley and Dale Van Kley, 46–118. Notre Dame, IN: University of Notre Dame Press, 2001.

Van Kley, Dale K. "Civic Humanism in Clerical Garb: Gallican Memories of the Early Church and the Project of Primitivist Reform, 1719–1791," *Past and Present* 200 (2008): 77–120.

Van Kley, Dale K. "From the Catholic Enlightenment to the *Risorgimento*: The Exchange between Nicola Spedalieri and Pietro Tamburini, 1791–1797." *Past and Present* 224, no. 1 (2014): 109–62.

Van Kley, Dale K. "Jansenism and the International Suppression of the Jesuits." In *The Cambridge History of Christianity*, edited by Stewart J. Brown and Timothy Tackett, 7:302–28. Cambridge: Cambridge University Press, 2006.

Van Kley, Dale K. "Piety and Politics in the Century of Lights." In *The Cambridge History of Eighteenth-Century Political Thought*, edited by Mark Goldie and Robert Wokler, 119–45. Cambridge: Cambridge University Press, 2006.

Van Kley, Dale K. *Reform Catholicism and the International Suppression of the Jesuits in Enlightenment Europe*. New Haven: Yale University Press, 2018.

Van Kley, Dale K. "Religion and the Age of 'Patriot' Reform." *Journal of Modern History* 80, no. 2 (2008): 252–95.

Van Kley, Dale K. "Setting the Scene: The Roman *Archetto* and Its French Connection in the Making of the International Campaign against the Jesuits." In *Memoria de la Expulsión de los Jesuitas por Carlos III*, edited by Immaculata Fernández Arillaga, Verónica Mateo Ripoll, Manuel Pacheco Albalate, and Rosa Tribaldos, 29–39. Madrid: Anaya, 2018.

Van Kley, Dale K. *The Damiens Affair and the Unraveling of the Ancien Régime, 1750–1770*. Princeton: Princeton University Press, 1984.

Van Kley, Dale K. "The Estates General as Ecumenical Council: The Constitutionalism of Corporate Consensus and the *Parlement*'s Ruling of September 25, 1788." *Journal of Modern History* 61, no. 1 (1989): 1–52.

Van Kley, Dale K. *The Jansenists and the Expulsion of the Jesuits from France, 1757–1765*. New Haven: Yale University Press, 1975.

Van Kley, Dale K. *The Religious Origins of the French Revolution: From Calvin to the Civil Constitution, 1560–1791*. New Haven: Yale University Press, 1996.

Vaussard, Maurice. *Jansénisme et Gallicanisme aux origines religieuses du Risorgimento*. Paris: Letouzey et Ané, 1959.

Vaussard, Maurice. "Les jansénistes italiens et la Constitution civile du clergé." *Revue historique* 75 (1951): 243–59.

Vidal, Daniel. *La Morte-Raison: Isaac la Juive, convulsionnaire janséniste de Lyon, 1791–1841*. Grenoble: Éditions Jérôme Millon, 1994.

Vidal, Daniel. *Miracles et convulsions jansénistes au XVIIIe siècle. La mal et sa connaissance*. Paris: Presses Universitaires de France, 1987.

Vila, Anne C. "Shaking Up the Enlightenment: Jansenist *Convulsionnaires* and Their Witnesses in Mid-Eighteenth-Century Paris." *Alif: Journal of Comparative Poetics* 41 (2021): 9–37.

Vismara, Paola. "L'influence de la France, du synode de Pistoia à *Auctorem fidei*." In *Les échanges religieux entre l'Italie et la France, 1760–1850*, edited by

Frédéric Meyer and Sylvain Milbach, 43–58. Chambéry: University of Savoy, 2010.

Visser, Jan. "The Old Catholic Churches of the Union of Utrecht." *International Journal for the Study of the Christian Church* 3, no. 1 (2003): 68–84.

Voekel, Pamela. *For God and Liberty: Catholicism and Revolution in the Atlantic World, 1790–1861*. Oxford: Oxford University Press, 2022.

von Collani, Claudia. "The Jesuit Rites Controversy." In *The Oxford Handbook of the Jesuits*, edited by Ines G. Županov, 891–917. Oxford: Oxford University Press, 2019.

Wandruszka, Adam. "Ems und Pistoia." In *Spiegel der Geschichte: Festgabe für Max Braubach*, edited by Konrad Repgen and Stephan Skalweit, 627–634. Münster: Aschendorff, 1964.

Wandruszka, Adam. *Leopold II: Erzherzog von Österreich, Grossherzog von Toskana, König von Ungarn und Böhmen, Römischer Kaiser*. 2 vols. Vienna: Herold, 1963–1965.

Ward, W. R. "Late Jansenism and the Hapsburgs." In *Religion and Politics in Enlightenment Europe*, edited by James E. Bradley and Dale Van Kley, 154–86. Notre Dame, IN: University of Notre Dame Press, 2001.

Watkins, Daniel J. *Berruyer's Bible: Public Opinion and the Politics of Enlightenment Catholicism in France*. Montréal: McGill-Queen's University Press, 2021.

Weaver, F. Ellen. "Erudition, Spirituality and Women: The Jansenist Contribution." In *Women in Reformation and Counter-Reformation Europe: Public and Private Worlds*, edited by Sherrin Marshall, 189–206. Bloomington: Indiana University Press, 1989.

Weaver, F. Ellen. "Scripture and Liturgy for the Laity: The Jansenist Case for Translation." *Worship* 59, no. 6 (1985): 510–21.

Weaver, F. Ellen. *The Evolution of the Reform of Port-Royal: From the Rule of Cîteaux to Jansenism*. Paris: Beauchesne, 1978.

Weaver, F. Ellen. *The Inner History of a Reformation That Failed: The Monastery of Port-Royal (1647–1684)*. Princeton: Princeton University Press, 1973.

Wilson, Lindsay. *Women and Medicine in the French Enlightenment: The Debate over* Maladies des Femmes. Baltimore: Johns Hopkins University Press, 1993.

Winters, Michael Sean. "The Four Cardinals and Their Five Doubts." *National Catholic Reporter*, 23 November 2016.

Wright, Anthony D. *The Divisions of French Catholicism, 1629–1645: "The Parting of the Ways."* Abingdon: Routledge, 2016.

Yoder, Richard T. "From the Dove to the Eagle: Jansenist Visual Culture between Piety and Polemic." *Catholic Historical Review* 107, no. 4 (2021): 528–60.

Županov, Ines G., and Pierre Antoine Fabre, eds. *The Rites Controversies in the Early Modern World*. Leiden: Brill, 2018.

CONTRIBUTORS

SHAUN BLANCHARD is lecturer in theology at the University of Notre Dame Australia. He is the author of two books and, with Ulrich Lehner, coedited *The Catholic Enlightenment: A Global Anthology* (The Catholic University of America Press, 2021).

University of Notre Dame Australia

RICHARD T. YODER is a doctoral candidate in history at Penn State University. His research examines the history of the supernatural and gender, and he is writing a dissertation on the Jansenist *convulsionnaires*.

The Pennsylvania State University

• • •

BRADLEY BLANKEMEYER is a historian of early modern Europe and South Asia, specializing in religious and cultural history of the Portuguese Empire and the Society of Jesus during the sixteenth and seventeenth centuries. He earned his DPhil in history at the University of Oxford in 2021 and currently works in academic publishing.

Independent Scholar

KEVIN BLANKINSHIP is assistant professor of Arabic at Brigham Young University, where he teaches courses on Arabic language and literature, Islamic civilization, and the Qur'an. His research centers around the poetry of the Islamic Mediterranean, with a special focus on the blind poet and alleged heretic al-Ma'arri (d. 1058 AD).

Brigham Young University

ELISSA CUTTER is a feminist historical theologian whose research contributes to efforts to recover the voices of women, like Mère Angélique Arnauld, as theological sources. She is currently assistant professor of religious studies and theology at Georgian Court University in New Jersey.

Georgian Court University

JEAN-PASCAL GAY is a former student of the École Normale Supérieure (Paris) and former fellow of the École Française de Rome. He holds his PhD from the University of Strasbourg and is currently professor of history of Christianity (early modern and modern times) at UCLouvain. His research deals with the history of the Society of Jesus and the social and cultural history of theology.

Université catholique de Louvain

MARIE GIRAUD is a doctoral candidate in history at Queen Mary University of London. Her doctoral research on Jansenism, women, and print culture in eighteenth-century France is funded by the London Arts and Humanities Partnership.

Queen Mary University of London

KEANU HEYDARI is an advanced doctoral candidate in history at the University of Michigan, Ann Arbor. Heydari's research examines the Union of Iranian Students in France—Union des étudiants iraniens en France (UEIF)—in the postwar period up to and including the Iranian Revolution of 1979.

University of Michigan

ELIZABETH A. HUDDLESTON is head of research and publications at the National Institute for Newman Studies and associate editor of the *Newman Studies Journal*. She also teaches in the Department of Catholic Studies at Duquesne University. She completed her PhD in Theology from the University of Dayton in 2019.

National Institute for Newman Studies

JOHN MEINERT is an associate professor of theology at Benedictine College. He is the author of the recent *Peace in the Thought of Thomas Aquinas: Philosophy, Theology, and Ethics*, also with The Catholic University of America Press.

Benedictine College

ANDREAS OBERDORF is lecturer for theory and history of education at the University of Münster, Germany. His dissertation about the educational reformer and enlightened Catholic priest Demetrius A. Gallitzin (1770–1840) was published by F. Schöningh, Paderborn, in 2019. He is currently working on the history of the American College at St. Maurice in Münster, a seminary for the training of young priests for the United States in the 1860s/1870s.

University of Münster

MAXWELL PINGEON is a doctoral candidate at the University of Virginia specializing in American Catholic history. His research explores the themes of language, religion, and nationalism in the context of French-Canadian migration to New England, 1880–1930.

University of Virginia

PHILIP PORTER is an assistant professor of theology at Saint Louis University–Madrid. His research interests include dogmatic theology, Latin patristics, Medieval philosophy and theology, and the theology of death.

Saint Louis University–Madrid

GLAUCO SCHETTINI is postdoctoral associate and lecturer in the humanities at Yale University. He works on the intellectual and religious history of early modern and modern Europe. His first book, *The Invention of Catholicism: A Global Intellectual History of the Catholic Counterrevolution, 1780–1849*, is forthcoming with Oxford University Press in 2025.

Yale University

ANDREA J. SMIDT retired from Geneva College, where she served as professor of European history and humanities for seventeen years, and continues to study the intersection of religion and politics in eighteenth-century Spain as well as enlightened programs of Catholic reform, particularly those of Josep Clement i Avinent, Bishop of Barcelona, 1766–75.

Independent Scholar

MARK SPINNENWEBER is a PhD student in Comparative Theology at Boston College. He holds a Master of Theological Studies in World Religions World Church from the University of Notre Dame, where he studied Islam, Christian-Muslim relations, and Eastern Christianity.

Boston College

GUIDO STUCCO earned a PhD in historical theology from Saint Louis University in 2003. He has authored four books about the history of the Catholic doctrine of predestination and several translations from French, Italian, and Latin texts.

Independent Scholar

LUKE TOGNI is a research fellow of the Franciscan Institute at St. Bonaventure University. His work has focused on the works of St. Bonaventure, including his integration of Franciscanism and the inheritance of Pseudo-Dionysius, and he is currently working with other scholars to examine Bonaventure as a reader of Albert the Great. He lives in Dartmouth, Nova Scotia, where he teaches courses in classics and religious studies at Dalhousie University and St. Mary's University.

St. Bonaventure University

TIMOTHY TROUTNER is completing his PhD in systematic theology at the University of Notre Dame and is currently a visiting instructor of theology at Assumption University in central Massachusetts. His research focuses on the contemporary reception of apophaticism and conciliar Christology.

Assumption University

DANIEL J. WATKINS is an associate professor of history at Baylor University. He is the author of *Berruyer's Bible: Public Opinion and the Politics of Enlightenment Catholicism in France* (McGill-Queen's University Press, 2021) and specializes in the history of the eighteenth-century Catholic Church.

Baylor University

INDEX